THE BOOK *of* WAR LETTERS

ALSO BY THE EDITORS

The Book of Letters (2002)
The Book of Love Letters (2005)

THE BOOK *of* WAR LETTERS

100 Years of
Private Canadian
Correspondence

COMPILED *and* EDITED *by*

AUDREY *and* PAUL GRESCOE

M&S

Library and Archives Canada Cataloguing in Publication

The book of war letters : 100 years of private Canadian
correspondence / compiled and edited by Paul and Audrey Grescoe.

Includes bibliographical references and index.
ISBN 1-55199-105-5 (bound).–ISBN 0-7710-3557-8 (pbk.)

1. Canada–History, Military–Sources. 2. Soldiers–Canada–
Correspondence. I. Grescoe, Paul, 1939- II. Grescoe, Audrey

FC25.B65 2003   355'.0092'271   C2003-902292-7
FI005.B65 2003

We acknowledge the financial support of the Government of Canada through the
Book Publishing Industry Development Program and that of the Government of
Ontario through the Ontario Media Development Corporation's Ontario Book
Initiative. We further acknowledge the support of the Canada Council for the
Arts and the Ontario Arts Council for our publishing program.

Typeset in Sabon by M&S, Toronto
Printed and bound in Canada

Front cover image: Company Sergeant-Major D.D. Perkins,
writing home aboard an LST (Landing Ship Tank) en route to France on D-Day.
(Ken Bell/National Archives of Canada/PA-132881)

Back cover image: Letters to and from Gordon Winning, a private with the
Seaforth Highlanders in the Second World War. One, dated May 24, 1940,
from Winning's parents in Vancouver, is stamped "salved from the sea";
the other, dated March 1944, from Winning, is stamped "salvaged from air crash."
The remnant inside begins: "Just a short note to let you know all is well,
and I am getting your mail fine." (Photo by Rebecca Salmon)

This book is printed on acid-free paper that is 100% recycled,
ancient-forest friendly (40% post-consumer recycled).

McClelland & Stewart Ltd.
The Canadian Publishers
481 University Avenue
Toronto, Ontario
M5G 2E9
www.mcclelland.com

1 2 3 4 5   09 08 07 06 05

For those who kept the letters

❖

And while we stun with cheers our homing braves,
O God, in Thy great mercy, let us nevermore forget
The graves they left behind, the bitter graves.

– Robert Service
from "The March of the Dead"

Contents

INTRODUCTION

"It's letters that do the most good"

The tears of a fallen Canadian soldier's widow stain a letter of condolence
written by Major Charles W. Gordon, a First World War chaplain
who had become famous under his pen name Ralph Connor.

In early 2002, Canadian soldiers went overseas as warriors – not peacekeepers – for the first time in nearly fifty years. They served alongside the U.S. 101st Airborne Division in Afghanistan as the Americans tracked al-Qaeda terrorists and their Taliban protectors in the wake of the previous September's attacks on the World Trade Center and the Pentagon. That April our troops suffered their first active-combat losses in half a century when U.S. warplanes mistakenly bombed members of the Princess Patricia's Canadian Light Infantry during a night training exercise. The deaths of the four men and the wounding of eight others shook Canadians. That they were victims of "friendly fire" – as so many Canadians were in the two world wars – made it all the more tragic. Once again we were reminded of the sacrifice we routinely ask our troops to make: scores of soldiers have been killed and hundreds more wounded as peacekeepers since the Korean War ended in 1953.

In the outpouring of national grief (and anger) that followed the deaths in Afghanistan, Canadians heard from politicians and military officials and, most affectingly, from the victims' loved ones. We could also hear, in certain newspaper articles, the voices of the men themselves. A few reports included excerpts from letters soldiers had written from the front to girlfriends and family members. There was the typical bitching about the heat, the dust, the lack of sleep. But these soldiers were writing mostly to reassure the folks back home that everything was fine, they were safe, not to worry. And, of course, to maintain relationships, often romantic, over distance and time. Another Afghanistan-related letter that received some prominence, on Web sites if not in print, came from the Canadian Armed Forces' chief of the land staff as he tried to console the victims' families and fellow soldiers.

During the past century – when Canadians have gone abroad to defend the nation, the Empire, western allies, and the United Nations – correspondence sent from the battlefront has always served those four purposes: venting, heartening those left behind, sustaining ties, and comforting the bereaved. Letters from home have done similar duty, bucking up the fighting men and women without dwelling unduly on domestic problems that would add to their burden.

Among the millions, if not billions, of letters that have been exchanged – and the thousands that were read in compiling this book – are many remarkable exceptions to run-of-the-mill, censor-conscious correspondence. These are letters that truly illuminate, that explore the deepest feelings and frankest opinions, that describe the bitter reality of battle, the often-appalling conditions of combat zones, the sheer boredom of waiting. Duress – the extreme experience war sometimes produces – brings out the most remarkable human qualities.

The Book of War Letters offers correspondence both typical and extraordinary, though this selection emphasizes the latter. The earliest letters date from the South African (or Boer) War, which began in 1899, when Canada sent its first expeditionary force overseas. The most recent are from Afghanistan in 2002. Between are letters from the First and Second World Wars, the Korean War, and a number of peacekeeping missions. All these were external, not domestic, conflicts in which Canada officially deployed its troops (which was not the case in the volunteer-only Spanish Civil War and Vietnam War).

In Afghanistan some of our troops took advantage of the new communications technology. Those with easy access to the Internet sometimes corresponded via e-mail; a couple of examples appear in these pages. These electronic missives bookend a century of war correspondence that began with letters laboriously inscribed with metal-nibbed pens dipped in precious bottles of ink.

Even in the era of quick e-mails and cheap long-distance calls, people in combat and their correspondents at home usually set down their thoughts and feelings in letters. Peacekeeper Kurt Grant wrote his wife from Croatia in 1994: "My platoon commander has given me carte blanche to call you whenever I feel the need. It is truly a generous offer as we have been limited in our time on the phones as you well know. I am reluctant to make use of this offer . . . while I love you very much, talking to you every day would take away from the pleasure I derive from writing to you. It is quite selfish I realize, but by spacing out our communiques the anticipation of contact with you is heightened." For the person who's been under fire, having time to reflect upon the circumstances of battle within the safe zone of a letter can help make sense of what otherwise may be senseless. And often a letter-writer can, on paper and to people far away, unveil fears not easily confessed to comrades-in-arms, as poet John McCrae does in suggesting to his mother some of the terror of "our sojourn in this Hades."

Of course, letters from the front are also useful vehicles for allaying the fears of the folks back home. In his classic work on the literary implications of the First World War, *The Great War and Modern Memory*, Paul Fussell speaks of the phlegm, the affected unflappability, that infected the correspondence of British officers and infantrymen – to the point of denying that war was heck, much less hell. "The main motive determining these conventions," he explains, "was a decent solicitude for the feelings of the recipient."

That stoicism, born of a regard for the sensitivities of family and friends, sometimes shows up in letters written by Canadians. Pierre Berton, in *Marching As to War*, writes: "In their letters home, the men at the front also did their best to relieve their mothers' anxieties by playing down the horrors and discomforts of the front." Canadian Arthur Stratford was a master of British dispassion when he wrote on December 5, 1914, to his brother in Brantford, Ontario: "All day and night firing goes on, and one gets so used to it that it doesn't worry one at all. Every day there are funny things happening. The Germans have a gramaphone in their trench, and they give us a concert." In his letters home from the Second World War, Sergeant Donald Law refrained from describing the action he saw while in Sicily and Italy. In training he was bombed and strafed by German planes; he was later shelled, and barely eluded death from an enemy howitzer that deafened him for days and left him with lifelong tinnitus. Yet nothing of this is revealed in his correspondence. Early on, his father had sent him a photograph of Don's mother sitting forlornly on the porch at home. "My mother thought I was never coming back," he explained, "so there's really nothing in the letters about war. And we weren't allowed to put anything in – they were all censored."

Military censorship prevailed in both world wars. Soldiers in the Great War were encouraged to use Whizz Bangs, postcards that listed convenient – and non-inflammatory – statements to be checked off, such as "I am quite well" or "I have received no letter from you . . . lately/for a long time." Canadian soldiers who wrote letters had to leave them unsealed, to be read either by officers in the field or by censors back at the company base. After a time, field officers came to trust the discretion of some of their men, such as Fred Albright, a Calgary lawyer, who told his wife that his lieutenant was willing to pass any of his letters to her without reading them. Albright also explained that battalions were issued green envelopes to bypass censorship in the field: "They can be used when one writes about some private matters which he doesn't want read by officers known to him. Then they can be posted anywhere – and at times when no battalion mail is censored. As for example when it is in the line or on the march. At such times the officers are not allowed to censor letters, but if they are put in green envelopes they may be dropped in a civil post office box and they will be forwarded to the base censor." Jeffrey

A. Keshen, writing in *Canadian Historical Review*, says: "Soldier correspondence was checked by military authorities, but its sheer volume meant that some material painting a less than glorious view of war got through." Canadian officers, who had little of the reserve displayed by their British counterparts, were free to send their own mail uncensored.

Getting around the censors was a game for some. In the Great War, Noel Farrow of Calgary gave his mother a clue: the first letter of the surname of an acquaintance was the first letter of the country where he was stationed. From a Second World War prison camp, Jack Rose – evading his Japanese captors' warning not to mention any prisoner who died – signalled the death of two friends to his parents: "Deepest sympathies to Mrs. Thomas and Mrs. White . . ."

Many men caved in to the power of the censor and made no effort to write about what was happening around them. But observant men and women with imagination, ideas, and ideals were able to avoid the touchy topics that twigged the censor's obliterations and to write graphically about the chaos and carnage of war. As war progressed from initial *Boy's Own Annual* anticipation to combat-weary disillusionment, the troops in the field tended to write with increasing frankness, perhaps believing they were entitled to say what they had learned.

As a result, much of the correspondence in this book is raw and unreserved. To understand the sheer madness of combat, you have only to read the well-educated Barlow Whiteside on the horrors of the Great War, or the less-schooled Private Ernest Ludkin's riveting summary of Dieppe, 1942, or Captain Edis Flewwelling's account of comrades killed by their own officers during commando training in the Second World War.

Letter-writers are often curiously circumspect about battle-induced psychoneuroses. Dinky Morrison, a newspaper correspondent during the South African War, derides "funk" and "pom-pom fever, Mauseritis and sky-line fever" (leaving his readers to guess that the men are suffering the strain of being shot at by new fast-firing guns). In another letter, however, he states unequivocally: "It is remarkable the number of officers and men who have been afflicted with brain troubles . . ." Great War soldiers got "shell shock," a term coined in 1915 because it was thought that there must be some physical explanation (the concussion of exploding shells) for the thousands stricken with inexplicable physical symptoms, such as hysterical blindness or paralysis. During the Second World War, the military favoured "battle exhaustion," perhaps because it suggested that a good rest would put the man right. During the Korean War, Gordon Croucher wrote home that one of his fellow engineers "was taken to the hospital with something called battle fatigue." Later conflicts have left us with "traumatic and post-traumatic stress disorder." If soldiers mention psychological collapse in letters home, they do so obliquely ("my nerves are holding up"), implying that it was (as it remains) more dreaded than physical injury and certainly more disgraceful. Few are as honest as Robert Duncan, who wrote about the aftermath of a horrific night in January 1915, "The cooks had a hot breakfast for us . . . but all the time we ate the lot of us cried like babies."

Letters written in the Great War, Paul Fussell points out, tended to be highly literate. Serge Durflinger, a historian with the Canadian War Museum in Ottawa, has observed the differences in correspondence emerging from the First and Second World Wars. "The letters from the Second World War didn't have the elegance of those from the First," he says. "The boom period in the decade preceding World War I would have facilitated the family economies to sustain education. Canada was one of the countries hardest hit by the Depression and among the slowest to recover. Large numbers of people were on some form of social assistance. So in their formative years, the young men fighting in the Second World War were disadvantaged: by 1939 there were numbers of them with only Grade 6 or 7 education. The level of literacy among the soldiery was much lower." Yet much of the correspondence from that war is, if not grammatically correct, expressive and compelling.

Morale among the troops rises and falls with the mail. Even in the South African War, the Canadian Post Office Department sent out a postal corps of five men with the First Contingent to make sure the soldiers remained in touch with distant Canada. Soldiers in the field could get downright grouchy when they didn't hear from home. As Private Earl Bolton scolded one of his sisters, "It is a wonder you wouldn't write a little oftener don't tell me you haven't got time how do you think we get time I write under shell fire. There is always time for everything." In 1944 Dr. Joseph Greenblatt wrote his fiancée from Normandy: "It so happened that last night quite by accident we got some mail in & it certainly was a very welcome present. It served to boost up morale no end because after some of the terrific shellacking we took we felt lost & out of touch with the world. The mail served to regain contact & really was a lifesaver."

That same year Mary Buch, serving in England with the Women's Division of the Royal Canadian Air Force, wrote a friend in Canada: "Of all the things anyone could possibly need, it's letters that do the most good. Things go wrong, one's temper gets shorter and shorter. We become intolerant of the food, the weather, the place, the people. It is, in fact, a Blue World. And then, when we have just about disproved the theory of the will to survive, and tried the patience of everyone around us, mail arrives. No one remarks on the sudden change of attitude and outlook. We all know. Word has come from halfway across the world and, figuratively, the sun is shining again."

The importance of letters in the lives of soldiers, sailors, and air crew is heartbreakingly evident in two tattered envelopes sent to and from Gordon Winning, a private with the Seaforth Highlanders in the Second World War. On one, dated May 24, 1940, which his parents sent him from Vancouver, are the words SALVED FROM THE SEA – the letter was rescued after an Allied ship was attacked. The other, dated March 1944, had been mailed home. The remnant inside begins: "Just a short note to let you know all is well, and I am getting your mail fine." But it's the words stamped on the envelope that reverberate: SALVAGED FROM AIR CRASH. Correspondence was considered so vital to the morale of the troops that it was retrieved from disaster scenes and sent on, whatever its condition, to keep the communication going.

Halfway across the world, families watched anxiously for letters, hoping for yet another envelope addressed in a loved one's hand-writing and dreading the official and unofficial ones written by strangers. Letters of condolence were the terrible obligation of officers and chaplains. They tremble in our hands even today, but few touch us as deeply as the letter held by Ann Ramsay, widow of William Ramsay of Winnipeg (see page 1). As she read the compas-sionate words of Major Charles W. Gordon (a popular Canadian author who wrote under the pen name Ralph Connor), her tears fell on the page and blurred the ink.

The letters Canadians have written while fighting wars, keeping the peace, supporting the troops, and holding down the home front are proud and self-deprecating, stoic and complaining, brave and fearful, tender and violent, funny and poignant. They tell us some-thing about what it means to be Canadian, and what it means to be alive.

Editors' Note

For practical reasons, we have not tried to reproduce actual letters. Often we had to work with less-than-clear copies of original corre-spondence. In some cases the letter-writers' handwriting was nearly illegible. Occasionally, we failed to figure out a word; in that case, we either take an educated guess, enclosing the likely word in [brackets] or indicate a missing word with a question mark in brackets [?]. To maintain each letter's integrity, we have not corrected the writer's spelling and grammatical errors unless we thought these might confuse the reader. In those cases, we have made corrections or pro-vided short explanatory notes [in brackets]. We've preserved personal eccentricities as well as peculiarities of punctuation – the habit of avoiding commas, for example, or using dashes rather than full stops, or starting a sentence with a lower-case letter. We sometimes omit sentences, or paragraphs, that seem less relevant or interesting than the rest of the letter. We signal such omissions with ellipses (. . .).

We've done our best to obtain permission to reproduce each letter in this book. Errors or omissions brought to our attention will be corrected in future printings.

The next in the Book of Letters series – *The Book of Love Letters* – is scheduled for 2004. We invite readers to tell us about letters of love or friendship written by or to Canadians, or to submit copies (not originals), along with background material and contact information, including address, e-mail address, and/or daytime phone number.

Audrey and Paul Grescoe
Box I-33
Bowen Island, B.C.
V0N 1G0
agrescoe@shaw.ca
pgrescoe@shaw.ca

SOUTH AFRICA, 1899–1902

"The sand came down like hail stones"

*In a letter during the Boer War, Lieutenant J. Harry Kaye of
New Brunswick drew this illustration about the Battle of Majuba, which had
been a humiliating defeat for British forces nearly a decade earlier.*

The Canada of 1899 was a callow country of seven provinces, thinly populated by five million people of mostly Anglo-Saxon stock. A mere thirty-two years old as a nation, it was a colonial outpost firmly clasped to the bosom of Britain. Yet Canada's character was changing. The Klondike gold rush was bringing fortune-seekers from around the world, and peasant immigrants were flooding in from central and eastern Europe – 7,500 Doukhobors from Russia that year alone – to settle the prairies.

Elsewhere, two world powers were flexing their imperialist muscles. The United States, fresh from winning Puerto Rico, Guam, and the Philippines in the jingoistic Spanish-American War of 1898, began a bloody 3½-year conflict to quash Filipino insurgents. And Britain, a year after machine-gunning thousands of tribespeople to dominate the North African territory of Sudan, was about to embark on another war, this time in South Africa.

The Boers (Dutch for "farmers") declared war on Britain on October 11, 1899, and Britain called on its overseas colonies to gird for battle. There were intriguing parallels to the global state of affairs a century later: public opinion in Germany and France (along with the Netherlands, ancestral home of many Boers) was strongly opposed to an invasion based on questionable motives – in this case, Britain's expansionist ambitions in South Africa. As Canadian historian Robert Page points out, "Unlike the world wars of 1914 or 1939, Mother Britain was not in danger, for the Boer Republics' total available manpower was not much more than that of the city of Toronto."

And Canada, then as in 2003, was led by a Québécois Liberal who was reluctant to commit his countrymen to fight on foreign soil. The only major external conflict Canadians had engaged in was the British-led, North American War of 1812, which ended in a draw – although the Canadas had ultimately repelled the invaders.

Yet, in a land where less than a third of the population was French-speaking, loyalty to the British crown was still intense in 1899, only two years after Queen Victoria's Diamond Jubilee. The Canadian Constitution rested in London, not Ottawa, and couldn't be amended without British consent. Although Prime Minister Wilfrid Laurier had been knighted during the Jubilee celebrations, he tried to keep Canada out of the war – reflecting the anti-British feeling of French Canadians. He was soon swayed by the hope that aiding the Imperial forces might boost the young nation's political status and leave it stronger and more independent of the Mother Country. Paradoxically, he also hoped that sending troops overseas would cement ties with Britain at a time when American protectionism was increasingly closing the U.S. border to Canadian goods.

Three days after war broke out, the Dominion of Canada, urged on by British colonial secretary Joseph Chamberlain, issued a recruiting order to organize the First Canadian Contingent for South African service – Canada's first expeditionary force. Among English Canadians, this decision was popular, supported by the press and politicians across the country, except in Quebec (which in 2003 registered the most opposition of any province to an invasion of Iraq).

The government at first decided to dispatch only a thousand troops, half Australia's contribution and even smaller than New

Zealand's. Sending them off on October 31, Laurier parroted English-speaking sentiment: ". . . the cause for which you men are going to fight is the cause of justice, of humanity, of civil rights and religious liberty. This is not a war of conquest or subjugation, but it is to put an end to the oppression by a tyrannical people."

Fine words, but false. The war was about gold and land. Britain had been jousting with the Netherlands over the territory since 1795, more than a century after the Dutch East Indies Company established the first white colony around the Cape of Good Hope. Now, on the cusp of the 20th century, the resident Boers were of Dutch, German, and Huguenot ancestry. A decade after British settlers began muscling into the Cape Colony in 1820, the Boers had trekked northeast to establish three republics, killing and displacing the Bantu natives. But Britain eventually annexed Natal and then the Orange Free State, when diamonds were found there, and briefly took over the Transvaal Republic (renaming it the South African Republic). It regained its independence and its former name in 1881. Five years later British prospectors rushed into the Transvaal after newly discovered gold, the largest deposits in the world. The Boers, fearful of losing their last territory to the Uitlanders (outsiders), enacted laws to restrict the vote to long-term residents.

Imperialist-minded British politicians and mining interests conspired to force a regime change on South Africa, led at the time by Paul Kruger, a passionate, patriarchal figure. Among his foes was the Cape Colony's prime minister and the owner of the Kimberley diamond mines, Cecil Rhodes, who wanted to paint the map of South Africa in Empire red. In 1895 he financed a raid on the Transvaal city of Johannesburg, an attack that failed and fomented even more hostility. Four years later Kruger offered to reform the voting restrictions, but the British refused the olive branch and dispatched military reinforcements to South Africa.

In October 1899 the high commissioner of the Cape Colony disregarded a forty-eight-hour ultimatum to remove all British troops from the Orange Free State and the Transvaal. Britain had been on the verge of declaring war itself.

The confrontation that young Canadians went to marked a turning point for the world's generals and their soldiers. As the new century loomed, belief in science and technology was ascendant. Although the British inventor Lord Kelvin had just announced that heavier-than-air flying machines were impossible, the German Karl Jatho built a gasoline-powered biplane that year and the American brothers Wilbur and Orville Wright were building their first box kite, a precursor of their manned aircraft of 1903. The South African, or Boer, War would still make good use of the horse for transport and battle (see page 29), but it would also rely on new marvels such as the heliograph, which used reflected sunlight to flash coded messages (see page 41). The British introduced armoured trains with naval guns mounted on railway wagons (in a railway system overseen by a French-Canadian officer) and manned observation balloons to direct artillery fire. The Boers carried the latest German Mauser rifles, with their smokeless powder, and the British relied on the Lee-Metfords. Both of these rifles were loaded with multiple-bullet magazine clips. Each side used the ruthlessly effective Maxim machine guns, invented fifteen years earlier, which the Boers converted to a water-cooled, belt-fed piece of light artillery called the "pom-pom." This war was also the first to employ the widespread use of concentration camps, the British herding African and Boer civilians into disease-ridden encampments, where nearly 28,000 people died. They were a creation of Lord Horatio Kitchener, a hero of the British war in the Sudan, now chief of staff to Lord Frederick Roberts, the British commander in chief during the Boer campaign.

Players in this first major war of the century would later have starring roles in other scenarios. Winston Churchill was a special correspondent for a London newspaper, Mahatma Gandhi a British stretcher-bearer, Robert Baden-Powell a commander and a spy for the British (before founding the Boy Scouts), Arthur Conan Doyle a field-hospital supervisor, Rudyard Kipling an army newspaperman who advised the Canadians to "look out for the water." John McCrae of Guelph, Ontario, was a gunner; during the First World War, he would compose the poem "In Flanders Fields."

Two Canadian officers who wet their feet in their country's first fighting overseas went on to play controversial parts in the Great War to follow. The Royal Canadian Regiment went off to battle under Lieutenant Colonel William Otter. A well-bred, aloof career soldier, he'd had his baptism of fire in 1866 as an adjutant in a militia unit that fled from Fenians invading Canada during their fight for Ireland's independence from Britain. As a commander, he saw another major defeat during the Metis-led Riel Rebellion in 1885 when the Cree chief Poundmaker routed his force at Cut Knife Hill. In fact, Otter – whom his men nicknamed "the Old Woman" – never did win a battle during his entire career.

Sam Steele, son of a British naval captain, had also fought Fenians as a militiaman in 1866 and natives as a Mountie during the Metis uprising. He'd been the third enlistee in the North-West Mounted Police and ridden two thousand kilometres on horseback during the force's Great March to the West. The florid, moustached Steele, who had policed the building of the Canadian Pacific Railway and ably controlled crime during the Klondike gold rush, was commander of Strathcona's Horse, a new mounted regiment (renamed Lord Strathcona's Horse in 1911).

The Boers were commanded in the beginning by General Piet Cronje, a sixty-four-year-old veteran of campaigns against native tribes. A good friend of President Kruger, he had led his commandos to victory against the Rhodes-financed raiders of Johannesburg. Conan Doyle called him "a hard, swarthy man, quiet of manner, fierce of soul." As in all wars, each side demonized the other, with the British describing the Boers as brigands, barbarians, and perfidious savages. As the conflict raged, the British had to admit that the enemy (outnumbered 500,000 to 70,000) was cool in combat, in both senses – the South Africans often carried parasols, even on horseback, to shade them from the awful sun.

At first the British condescended to their Canadian cousins, who did, however, acquit themselves well. As Pierre Berton writes, the British looked upon the first batch of Canadians as "a token force of colonials whose presence on the battlefield would go far to cement the

Empire and fulfill Joseph Chamberlain's dream of imperial union. The British were quite prepared to wrap up the war by themselves without the need for any more colonials." How self-deceived they were.

HEAD OVER HEELS

Mabel Cawthra, daughter of a comfortably off Toronto family, was among the new breed of Edwardian women in Ontario: well read, well travelled, an accomplished horsewoman, headstrong, agnostic, a feminist of her time. In the autumn of 1899 the auburn-haired, attractive twenty-eight-year-old was about to marry Agar Adamson. He was a good-looking, charming fellow of little means, a clerk of the Canadian Senate in Ottawa, and a militia captain in the Governor General's Foot Guards. Knowing his wish to fight in South Africa, where war had erupted two weeks earlier, she wrote to him.

October 26th, 1899

My darling Agar
. . . Yesterday was a red-letter day for Toronto. I spent from 1.30 to 6 o'clock seeing troops off and I have never seen such enthusiasm before. First of all the mater and I went to the Armouries where we got seats in a gallery. The proceedings there lasted for an hour and a half and mostly consisted in cheering, though at intervals people made speeches which nobody could hear, and the South Africa contingent were presented with all sorts of things from flowers to silver match-boxes and writing material. The cheering made one feel positively choky, every man was cheered individually and colectively, again and again "Our Bark" [R.K. Barker, captain of C Company of Toronto] quite shared the honours with Col. Otter and the Queen, and eventually he had to make a speech. At the Armouries I met all the Hendrie family. They were so excited over Murray enlisting that they did not know whether they were standing on their heads or their heels. After the contingent left the Armouries accompanied by the four city regiments, we raced down Simcoe Street to see them pass there and then

we went to the station where there was a howling, seething, perspiring mob. We pushed and fought our way up the train to where Murray Hendrie was hanging out of a window looking the veriest "tommy" of the lot . . . The train with the troops on board could hardly get out of the station owing to the people on the track . . .

Ever yours

Mabel

On the day Mabel Cawthra wrote this letter, the Boers invaded Natal and the Cape Colony. Agar Adamson went to fight in South Africa. Although Mabel had expressed her willingness to go there with her new husband, she never did.

TROOPSHIP TALES

*Scottish-born **J. Frederick Ramsay** was raised near Toronto and educated at Upper Canada College. Although the Ramsay family returned to Scotland, Frederick came back to Canada as a young man and became a travelling tea salesman. Now twenty-nine, he was eager to see action. He sailed with the first contingent of troops on the* Sardinian, *a converted cattle boat forty-six-feet wide in which, a reporter said, the men slept "side by side like eggs that come crated in pasteboard casings." On the voyage the punctilious Colonel William Otter caused serious cases of sunburn by insisting his men get used to the blazing heat by removing their shoes, baring their chests, and rolling up their trousers and sleeves.*

On board Troopship "Sardinian"

en route to S. Africa.

November 22nd, 1899

My dearest Sisters,

. . . While there [in Salt Lake City, Utah] I learnt of the proposed regiment for Transvaal from Canada. I at once returned to Chicago, reaching there after 2 days travel on the 18th. Leaving there on the 20th I reached Toronto on 21st and enlisted in the Royal Canadian Regiment on the 23rd as a Private. The regiment is made up of 8 companies, having 125 in each, making 1,000 in all. The Toronto contingent is No. 38 C Company and is the crack company of the regiment . . .

We left Toronto on the afternoon of the 25th October amidst terrific enthusiasm, the streets being packed, women, children and in many cases even men crying. It was the greatest demonstration I ever experienced.

We had a special colonist train and reached Montreal 6 a.m. of the 26th and Quebec City the same afternoon when 8 companies (which came from all parts from the Atlantic to the Pacific) formed into a regiment under the command of Colonel Otter.

We slept in the emigrant sheds, on the floor, while at Quebec and had regular Barrack duties to perform.

We sailed from Quebec on S.S. Sardinian on 30th, when another great send-off was given us, firing of guns etc., and a number of excursion steamers followed us down the river for two hours playing national and popular airs.

Since leaving Quebec, we have had most wonderful weather with the exception of the first two days after leaving the St. Lawrence. The ocean has been as calm as Lake Ontario. It is most fortunate as we are packed like sardines in our bunks and hammocks.

Only one serious casualty has taken place on board. A private in D Coy. died in the Guard Room while a prisoner and was buried at sea [Pte. Edward Deslaurier died on November 3, officially of heart failure.] We had some minor casualties such as broken limbs, bruises, burns etc. and one case of typhoid fever. All on board have been vaccinated. Since coming on board I have been promoted to Corporal and hope to become a Sergeant before returning.

We have all the duties of a British troopship. Reveille sounds at 5 a.m., when every man must be out of his bunk and fold his mattress and blankets then parade on deck, and get under the hose for a bath. Breakfast consists of coffee without milk, bread, butter and cheese.

Dinner – Soup, meat, principally canned beef, and potatoes – and since coming into warm weather – lime juice and water.

Tea – Tea, bread and butter.

The men wash their own dishes and forks and knives etc. I don't do this being a non-com. officer and am in charge of my mess.

On account of room being limited, each Company has one hour drill per day and of course men from the companies are detailed daily for respective duties such as orderlies, fatigues, watch, guardroom and water guard. I am to-day Corporal of the Water Guard and will not be relieved until 9 a.m. tomorrow. I post and receive letters every 2 hours.

Every afternoon the fire alarm sounds when every officer and man takes a post, remains steady and silent. When not on duty our fatigue dress is trousers and flannel shirt only – trousers turned up to the knees and shirt sleeves rolled above the elbow, unbuttoned down the front and tucked in leaving the chest bare. On our heads we wear a knitted cap, so we make a good looking gang of pirates especially since we have become so browned by the sun . . .

We are looking forward to reaching Capetown on the 28th where we will go into barracks for a couple of weeks, and then for the front and the Boers.

About 100 men will be left at Capetown to forward on supplies, etc. I forgot to mention Last Post sounds at 8.45 p.m. when every man is expected to prepare for bed and 15 minutes later "lights out" sounds when every man except those on watch or guard must be in bed. So you will see we have to practise the strictest discipline. No liquor is issued on board, so we have all been teetotalers since leaving Quebec and I think it agrees with the men, as all are looking well and gaining weight. I have gained eight pounds and am now over 12 stone and never felt or looked better . . .

Well! goodbye dearest of sisters.

Your loving Brother,

Fred

The free-spending soldiers, sporting maple leaf badges, had a fine time on their one-night leave in Cape Town. They had a month's salary in gold to lavish on drinking, dining, and watching brief-

skirted dancers in a "bowery concert hall" – impressing the South Africans with the supposed wealth of Canada.

INTO THE FRAY

The Boers seized the advantage in the early months of the war. The ailing General Petrus Joubert beleaguered the northern Natal town of Ladysmith, while General Piet Cronje's forces were laying siege to Robert Baden-Powell's British garrison at Mafeking and the De Beers diamond centre of Kimberley. British troops, attempting to recover Kimberley, had to fight off Boer commandos near the Belmont train station. Meanwhile the Canadians had seen no action. Travelling by train into the highland veldts, they'd stopped a few days at the quickly despised village of De Aar and a sand-strafed camp at Orange River, where the nighttime temperatures neared 38 degrees Celsius. Finally they arrived at Belmont, where they put up tents next to henhouses. **Private Claude (Tod) Snider** *wrote his insurance-man father in Portage la Prairie, Manitoba (misspelling the railway stop's name).*

Belmonte, Dec. 14/99

Dear Father,

. . . We left Cape Town for the front on the 1st. Dec. but had to stay off at De Aar for a few days. The country from Cape Town to De Aar is beautiful, lovely trees and hills. We left De Aar on the 7th. and arrived at Orange River the same day. We had a good sand storm, I would rather have snow. At Orange River we camped on the battle ground. It is a small but very important place to the British. On the 9th. we left Orange River and arrived at Belmonte on the same day. This is where a terrible battle was fought. The British had a hard position to carry and they won a brilliant victory here. The Boers left a lot of dead on the Kopje [small hill] and when we have to go out there to do out-post duty, which occurs every three days and we are on for twenty-four hours, the stench is something horrible, it nearly makes a fellow sick. We are kept busy every day doing fatigue duty, etc.

We are within twenty-five miles of Modder River where there is a terrible battle now going on and every few hours there is a train-load of wounded pass through here. The poor fellows try to be jolly. War is a terrible thing when a person sees the results with their own eyes.

We would have been into it a few days ago but were not relieved so we are left here to guard this very important place, for if the Boers should get possession of this point they would cut off the British supplies. However we are all ready for the fray as soon as we are ordered right to the front.

We had a funeral yesterday, a young fellow who died from some disease. We never keep Sunday, it passes before we know we are at it.

An armored train went up last night. I expect the British will soon have the Boers in their hands now. We take prisoners every day here . . .

I am very well. The weather is very hot. Good-bye. I am your Son,

Tod.

During Black Week, December 10–16, the British charged well-protected enemy battlefield positions and were defeated at Stormberg, Magersfontein, and Colenso, sustaining many more casualties than did the Boers. Snider would come home with the Queen's South Africa Medal with bars for service in the Cape Colony and the Battle of Paardeberg; he lived until 1935.

HARD-ROCK CHRISTMAS

*At Orange River two hundred Canadians soldiers and five officers, including **Lieutenant John Henry Kaye**, were detailed to construct a railway siding and platform. With no railway construction expertise, men and officers fell to work with picks and shovels and ingeniously*

*devised methods for laying sleepers and rails for a half mile of track.
When they had completed a large landing platform, a train arrived
carrying Lieutenant Colonel Percy Girouard, a military engineer
from Montreal, appointed by the British as their director of railways
in South Africa. After a few nights at Orange River, the battalion
travelled in open train cars to Belmont, where Lieutenant Kaye wrote
to his mother.*

[December 1899]

. . . Oh!! these flies are horrible I can hardly write they bother me so.
= See the men lying in their tents trying to keep cool and I suppose
wondering what kind of a Christmas they will have = I invested in
some butter scotch and lemonade and other flavoured crystals which
we put in water to make a drink also a canvas bag to put water in a
flask . . . I am getting used to sleeping with my head on a rock you
would be astonished how well you can sleep that way = I am sitting
on a blanket on the ground with this on my knee a little hard = we
have another fatigue at 4.30 earth works. I am tired of them. the
weather is too warm for that sort of thing = I hear they are going to
send out another Canadian Contingent = do not know if it is true yet.
they seem to be pushing the men in now from all over and I believe
"Roberts" [Lord Roberts, commander in chief of the British forces] is
coming out to take command and see what he can do for us . . .

Christmas morning [1899]

This seems a funny Christmas some of the men have been trying to
sing hymns also last evening = Everyone seems to be thinking of
home and good Christmas dinners = Will tell you later what our bill
of fare is . . .

December 26 [1899]

. . . We had dinner together last evening rather poor every man had
to bring his own cup knife fork spoon. I could not get any salt, at

least only a little and the grub was rather poor = everything poorly cooked . . . I inclose [for] you [the] top of the Belmont Hotel bill of fare. The Hotel is something like a very poor class of house at home. The men tried to make a Christmas by singing and dressing up they are a cheerful lot under the circumstances.

I understand the Canadians got some praise for work they did on the railroad at Orange River. We laid some track and made a platform = of course working here is doubly hard to what it would be at home. The heat is so terrible = Have not seen any of the Queens candy [a Christmas gift from Queen Victoria]. Perhaps she did not send any = I see the cart just coming back with water we have to cart all water to camp & some is brought up from Orange River . . . the man who owned this place DE KOCK skipped out at the commencement of the war but his wife and family are here still. Saw another Boer woman yesterday her husband had left her & the children she was crying = there must be a good deal of misery over this thing = think they all want to be on the winning side & try to play cards both ways = The Boers have very peculiar modes of throwing up fortifications on the hills sometimes behind a large rock and sometimes a pile of rocks . . . with a man behind and scattered all over the places they want to defend. We find piles of empty cartridges behind these stone places called I believe "Sand Gors". do you wonder they make such good shooting when they are so entirely protected and our men rush up against them = They say we are soon to go on to Modder River but we can never tell until the actual time to move comes . . .

Your loving Son

J. Harry Kaye

The hotelier, De Kock, was a prisoner of the British in Cape Town and awaiting trial as a Boer inciter. Kaye's "Sand Gors" were fortified stonework lookouts called sangars. He was wrong about the rumoured move; the Canadians remained at the Belmont Garrison for sixty-five days.

BRAINS AND HORSEPOWER

*All that Lord Strathcona's Horse knows of **Herbert Samson** is this information, noted in handwriting on the final page of his letter: "age about 37 educated at Rugby and Oriel College Oxford. Has been farming in the NWT ever since he left Oxford about 15 years ago . . ." And in yet another hand: "Calgary Weekly Herald of 1 March reported that he had gone to South Africa privately to go to fight Boers." His name does not appear on the nominal roll of the regiment or on the official list of those killed in action.*

Calgary
December 27th/99.

My dear Ada

I expect you know the Canadian Government is sending out another contingent. Part of it is 250 Mounted rifles from the North West Territories. About 200 of the Mounted Police are going and the other 50 is made up of picked horsemen and rifleshots from the ranges. There are hundreds of applicants; I volunteered but have been cast as not coming up to the standard height. The Commissioner has tried to get the government to make an exception in my case, as he wants me to go, but up to now they have refused. There is still an off chance that they may take me, but am afraid it is a very slight one. It is most disappointing as I am very keen to go and I feel that I should be a good man for the job. If Father could work it with Balfour or Lord Lansdowne to get me a job as a trooper in one of the Volunteer Regiments you might cable me. They ought to take me as I am a good horseman, a good shot and have spent most of my life out on the plains and in the mountains. I would furnish my own horse and outfit and pay my own way. I could be in England in about 2 weeks after getting a cable. It is easy to criticize but it seems to me that the Government made a big mistake. If they had taken the Colonists in Natal & Cape Colony with their native horses and got about 5000 of the same sort from here and Australia, they would only have had to send out artillery and a few battalions of infantry. Such a force could have fought the Boers and employed the same tactics that they employ. They could move rapidly over the Country and would not have to wait for transport. I can take a horse here and carry food enough for myself for two weeks and picket the horse out at nights to rustle grass for himself. Every man in such a force could do the same and consequently could get all over the country in a short time. The Authorities are prejudiced in favour of regulars, particularly infantry, and most of our Generals have come to the front through conspicuous personal bravery. We want strategists and men with brains. Nearly every man is brave enough if he happens to get the chance. Please get Father to hurry up and try to do something for me.

Best love to all

Ever your loving brother

Herbert

CANADA'S CENTURY

On the first day of the 20th century, one hundred Canadians (a century in Roman military terminology) fought in Canada's first overseas battle. Captain R.K. Barker (see Mabel Cawthra's letter on page 17) led the men of C Company from Toronto against a Boer camp at Sunnyside, northwest of Belmont. In a letter to his family, Private J. Frederick Ramsay (see pages 18 and 40) described that national baptism of fire.

Camp Belmont.

January 8th, 1900.

Since last writing I have had a great experience – that of being for the first time under fire.

When writing to you on 30th December from here I think I mentioned that we had orders to hold ourselves in readiness to move at a moment's notice. Well! about noon of the 31st the order came that 100 men were to be picked from the Canadians to form a flying column – these were picked from the Toronto Company exclusively and I was amongst the number. We also took our maxim [machine gun] section of two guns and 21 men. We joined the Queenslander Mounted Infantry (150 men) – The Royal Munster Mounted Infantry (about 50 men) – The Remington Scouts (25 men) and two guns of the Royal Horse Artillery and 60 men – all told about 400 officers and men. We also had 14 transport wagons drawn by 10 mules, each for carrying supplies, ammunition etc., and for carrying our blankets, kits etc. and occasionally give us a ride when the roads were good.

We left Belmont at 2 p.m. on Sunday, the 31st December and after marching 19 miles bivouacked at Cook's Farm for the night. At 5 a.m. next morning we again started and about 11.30 a.m., after making a forced march, we came upon the Boers encampment. We were looking for a place called Sunnyside . . .

The enemy's encampment was immediately at the foot of a large rocky kopje to which they took for cover when we opened fire and then from behind rocks they gave us a pretty warm reception.

Our rifle fire was delivered from 1200 to 1500 yards and our artillery fire from 1600 to 1750 yards. The Boers had no artillery. After firing had gone on for half an hour my section (about 25 men) got orders to retire, and support the artillery. To do this we had to cross an open space of about 300 yards and we did it successfully, although bullets were singing about our ears and we had many narrow escapes. Our men were so tired after our forced march, we couldn't double as we were ordered so quietly marched across and took up our position with the guns. The Australians nobly exposed themselves to all kinds of danger, in fact everybody behaved splendidly. Firing lasted until 3 o'clock in the afternoon when our fellows and the Australians charged the Boers kopje from the left, and the latter put up the white flag. We captured 43 prisoners, 14 tents, 7 wagons, and mules, any amount of fodder and nearly 200,000 rounds of ammunition. We lost two killed and four wounded – all Australians. One officer amongst the wounded was shot four times, but is doing well I am glad to say. We don't know the exact casualties on the Boer side as they carried away a number of their dead and wounded, but we think they lost about 10 killed and 30 or more wounded. Their strength was 390 and all were supposed to be loyal British subjects – prisoners are to be treated as rebels . . .

We reached Douglas about 3 p.m. on Tuesday the 2nd January after another forced march. Although in time to relieve the town we were too late to engage the enemy; they had shipped out of the town about one hour before our arrival and were too far away to be followed and our horses were completely done up. We captured 70,000 rounds of ammunition and a lot of other stuff.

Both the British and black inhabitants fairly wept with joy when we marched down the hill into the pretty little town – they even broke into our ranks and grasped us by the arms and hands, bringing us water and milk to drink, and they turned the houses into kitchens to get food ready for us. I shall never forget our entrance into Douglas although we were so tired we could scarcely drag one leg after the other, and our lips were all cracked with the heat and thirst.

On receiving the cheers of the few inhabitants (especially of the white women, as we hadn't seen any for weeks) we braced up and quickened our step and, although we should like to have returned the cheering, we marched on to the centre of the town without looking to the right or left and without an answering cheer.

The heat was terrific. After being dismissed we removed our accoutrements and lay down where we could find shade. In the evening we all had a swim in the Vaal River which was most refreshing. A number of our fellows were completely knocked out and before reaching Douglas had to be lifted into the wagons, however we made no stop although our horses and mules were almost useless, many of the Australians having to walk.

We bivouacked at Douglas for the night and at 6 a.m. on the 3rd started back for Weber's Farm with 74 refugees, women and children. We left Weber's Farm about 3 p.m. and reached Cook's Farm the same evening at 8.0 . . .

About 9.0 that evening the alarm was given that 1200 Boers were advancing to cut us off from Belmont. We packed up all our stuff in the dark and started on a flying march for Belmont (19 miles) reaching here before 8 a.m. on Friday the 5th, a very tired, weary, sleepy lot, but proud of our success.

We received a warm reception back at camp and have got telegrams of congratulation from [British] General [Redvers] Buller and others. Our prisoners and refugees have been sent on to Capetown. So my New Year 1900 is one to be remembered. I did not experience any fear while under fire, but expected every moment to be struck with a bullet. While we were in support of the guns a number of us lit our pipes and were chatting away with the bullets whistling round us when an Artillery officer came up and remarked "Well you are the coolest lot of beggars I have seen. One would think you were just at target practice"!

We suffered terribly with thirst and ran completely out of water while in action; if the firing had kept up much longer we could not have stood it. The Boers used our ambulance wagons as targets being large covered wagons and white on the top – they were struck frequently . . .

[J. Frederick Ramsay]

BIRTH OF A REGIMENT

Baron Strathcona and Mount Royal made his fortune as Donald A. Smith, a Scottish emigrant employed by the Hudson's Bay Company as a fur trader in Labrador for thirty years. He invested his and others' money wisely and bought stock in the company that employed him, becoming its chief shareholder. In the 1870s he sat in both the legislative assembly of Manitoba and the House of Commons and was behind the Canadian Pacific Railway syndicate. It was he who drove the last spike at Craigellachie, British Columbia. Smith had been elevated to the peerage in 1897 and was the Canadian high commissioner in London when he made this offer to the colonial secretary, Joseph Chamberlain.

January 10, 1900

Dear Mr. Chamberlain,

I beg to refer to our conversation of yesterday and to state that if the proposal should meet with the approval of H.M. Government I should like to provide and send to South Africa at my own expense two squadrons of mounted men and officers, say, 400 men and horses.

My idea is that both men and horses should be largely drawn from the Canadian North West, the men to be unmarried, expert marksmen, at home in the saddle, and efficient as experienced rough riders or rangers.

I propose to pay the cost of the equipment, similar to that of the Canadian Contingent, and the transport of both men and horses to South Africa, where they would be taken over by the Imperial Government, I presume on the same terms as the other Colonial contingents. After the close of the campaign the men to have the option of returning to Canada the same way as those serving with the contingents sent by the Government of Canada, the horses and arms being taken over by H.M. Government.

The suggestion has I may say, commended itself to the Dominion Government, and they are prepared to allow the use of their organization for recruiting and equipping purposes.

I shall be glad to hear at your early convenience if it is the opinion of yourself and your colleagues that the force proposed to be raised would be of substantial benefit in South Africa. If the proposal is in every way favorably regarded from that specific point of view, I will arrange to put the matter in train without delay.

Incidentally, I had just a word with the Marquis of Lansdowne a few days ago in regard to the project; and I need only add that for the present at any rate, I do not wish my name to be publicly mentioned in connection with it.

Believe me,

Yours sincerely,

Strathcona

P.S. Since the above was written I have received a further cable message from Sir Wilfred [sic] Laurier in the matter, and if you can quite conveniently let me have your answer today, I shall feel greatly obliged.

Chamberlain sent a telegram the next day: "Offer most gratefully accepted in principle. Details to be arranged later. No difficulty expected." Three squadrons of horsemen were recruited in western Canada for Strathcona's Horse. Lieutenant Alec Strange was typical, recommended in a letter to Lord Strathcona by his father, a retired officer, as "a single man, 32 years of age, near 6 feet and tough as they are made on the Prairie. He can of course ride everything and been a cowboy since he was 17 . . . He is a first rate shot with rifle and revolver and can follow a trail almost like an Indian." Dr. Duncan McEachran, dean of the Faculty of Comparative Medicine and Veterinary Science at McGill University, purchased the horses and wrote to Lord Strathcona, "I have secured 536 horses . . . 95 percent of them are thoroughly broken to cow-boy work. Taught to rein by the neck, stop suddenly, turn on the hind feet as a pivot, stand with the reins over their head on the prairie, ford and swim rivers, and go at a rapid pace up or down steep hills. They are stout animals with good short legs and strong quarters; good bone and as active as cats – horses which know nothing of stables or grooms; accustomed to be ridden half a day or more, and at night are simply stripped of saddle and bridle and turned loose to find their feed." Strathcona's stout horses and men arrived in Cape Town on April 10, 1900, dealt with an outbreak of disease among the horses, and saw action with General Redvers Buller's force in Natal in June.

BORROWED COMFORTS

After the Sunnyside affair, the Canadian battalion at Belmont settled into garrison life, building fortifications and marching out into the country to launch mock attacks. The soldiers endured sandstorms and enervating heat, and grumbled about being held back while other regiments passed by on their way to the front. **Lieutenant John**

Henry Kaye (see page 22), who would serve with the Headquarters Staff of the 7th Canadian Infantry Reserve Brigade during the First World War, wrote to his mother.

Richmond Farm
G. W. South Africa
24th January 1900

Dear Mother

The G. W. at the head of my letter means Griqualand West in fact Belmont is in Griqualand . . . Our Company was sent out here Monday as a sort of base for another column further out. this place is about twelve or fifteen miles from "Belmont" & as different as chalk from cheese. the place is not so much cut up & we don't have all the sand there seems plenty of small trees about (we would call these bushes.) but to have trees of any kind is a blessing after Belmont and best of all we are eating our meals off a table with a <u>table cloth</u> – and can sit in a house, lie on a sofa. write letters on a table & find books to read. To explain = we are stationed at this farm belonging to an Englishman named "Wayland" he left on account of the Boers and went in nearer Belmont taking his children and family with him, he is at his brothers. The day we marched in he rode over here, said we could use the house. – we have Kaffir [black African] girls to cook and use his sitting & living rooms all the luxuries of the season, and the tubs to Bath in = there is only one objection we have to sleep outside instead of the bedrooms. the Kaffirs are very funny = can only speak a little english = but we are making use of Waylands pantry and today had pancakes. tonight the darky girl made a cake. last night we had pig. we have just finished one bottle of honey and best of all the darkies have made us some good bread. the first we have had since leaving the Steamer & even on the steamer it was not too good – I am sitting in the front room by the piano writing and the photos on the wall the rocking chairs all look homelike = I see an English parsons photo stuck up on a rack = the people that lived here evidently came from "Brighton" England = we have lots of Kaffir huts scattered about and little naked kids running all over = In the

middle of last night I was going around the sentries with two men
one ahead of me. I saw him stop & look down as he did so there
was a dreadful scream and a jump it appears some Kaffirs were sleeping outside there hut and when they saw him stoop over them thought
they were done for. They are in Mortal dread of us. dont know which
they are most afraid of ourselves or the Boers. I am trying to draw a
picture of the house here to send you. also Kaffir girl carrying pail
on her head = it is very delightful to sit at a table again I actually
found myself looking for a Napkin. we have to work pretty hard
every third day. and then have two easy ones. I am afraid they will
only have us here a few days. this will do our men all the good in the
world and fit them for hard work . . .

Your loving Son
Harry

PAARDEBERG'S BLOODY SUNDAY

*Finally the Royal Canadians learned that they and three British reg-
iments were to form the 19th Brigade under Major General Horace
Smith-Dorrien (see page 83). They oiled their rifles and polished
their buttons for inspection before setting off for the most costly
battle of the war. A five-day trek of 120 kilometres brought them,
near dawn on Sunday, February 18, to the turbid but swift Modder
River, which they crossed with the help of ropes stretched shore to
shore. The battlefield was an open plain where the Boers were concealed in deep dongas – steeply eroded watercourses – shaded by
trees and cut branches. The Canadian and British forces had to fight
in the open, inching on their bellies and sheltering behind every rock
and anthill while the Boers maintained a withering fire. The attack-
ers suffered alternately under the broiling sun and chilling rains. As
day ended, Lord Kitchener ordered the colonel in charge of the
Cornwall regiment to make a desperate fixed-bayonet charge, in
which the Canadians joined. Private Douglas McPherson, of Dutton,
Ontario, described the attack.*

Paardberg Drift,
March 3, 1900

Dear Mamie, –

You have heard all about our wanderings long before this no doubt. We have had plenty of fighting to suit everybody, and we all hope it requires no more. We have also found out that campaigning is no fun but hard work and very bad for one's health without the hard fighting we have had.

We started from Belmont on Sunday night, and while we were marching to the train not a sound was made, for we all felt that we were going to a dangerous part of the country. We bivouacked at Gras Pan that night and at three a.m. we started our march along with three other regiments which formed our brigade (the nineteenth). We had to carry two days' rations, emergency rations, overcoats and ammunition and when the heat of the day came we felt like dropping, and before we reached Ram's Dam [Ramdam] about 80 had fallen out overdone with thirst. Here we got some very dirty water to drink, and some weak coffee with biscuits for supper.

Again at five we were off for the Riet River 14 miles away and it became terribly hot about 9.30. Still we plugged along, until about one o'clock, when we were halted and our company and D Company were sent about two miles away to reconn[o]itre a kopje where we remained until the rear guard of the column had passed. The sun was terrible, not a cloud, not a speck of shade and among burning stones with no water. But even that ended and we stumbled, almost fainting, up to the banks of the river, where we stayed, eating nothing until after six o'clock at night except our hard tack biscuits. During the afternoon we dragged the naval guns across the river and at night we had soup. Next morning we had only nine miles to go, so we did that by 8.30 but had to furnish outposts on arriving, so we had no rest that night, and next morning we pressed on to Jacobsdal, where we had a good feed of meat and hoped for rest but had to go on twelve miles that night to the Modder River, all the time hoping to come up with Cronje and the Boers, but he was a veritable Will'o the Wisp to us. The next night we went twenty three miles to this place, arriving at 6 a.m. After a hasty drink of coffee and some rum to revive us we forded the Modder River and advanced on the enemy's position. At eight we were firing at the place where we saw smoke, for no Boers were visible, although only 500 yards from their trenches. Here we lay all day with the bullets whistling and cracking all around us and no cover except the ant hills which were far too scarce. Well, at about 5.30 p.m. we got the order to fix bayonets which was received with satisfaction, for we were being cut up very badly and were unable to move from our scanty cover all day. Well, we charged but we lay down where we were and when darkness came retired, but all night we were bringing in wounded. Next day, when the Boers left the position I went all through their trenches and the place seemed to me to be impregnable to anything but artillery, and my only wonder was that more of us were not killed.

[Douglas McPherson]

Despite their overwhelming numerical superiority – 30,000 to 4,000 – the British failed to dislodge the Boers. About 800 Royal Canadians (of 1,039 originally on strength) fought on that Sunday. Twenty died and sixty were wounded. Two days later the Canadians hugged the earth for shelter while the Boers introduced them to their pom-pom gun, the automatic Vickers-Maxim, which rapidly fired one-pound shells, twelve to a belt. For several more days they manned trenches, did outpost duty, and endured icy night rainstorms, until word came that they were to attack.

CRONJE SURRENDERS

The final assault of the Paardeberg battle began in the dark early morning of February 27. The Canadian companies were ordered to advance in silence towards the Boer trenches and to enter them if possible. If they were fired on, they were to lie down and return fire so that the engineers behind them, carrying spades and picks, could dig trenches from which the British could more effectively fire on

*the Boers. **Frederick S. Lee**, in E' Company of the Royal Canadians,*
wrote his parents from a laager (an encampment or a defensive posi-
tion) captured from the Boers.

Kloopf Laager, 28 Feb. 1900

My dear Mother & Father

Since writing you the last few lines we have been in two more engagements through which I have come out safely, the first one was during
the day it was not as fatal as the one I have already told you about,
the second one was a night attack on the Boer trenches it was simply
awful we advanced on to about 25 yards from the trenches without
being fired on but as soon as we got within that distance the Boers
sent volley after volley right in amongst us, we immediately lay down
& then the firing was not so dangerous although quite as heavy, the
Boers numbered 5000 & the Canadians about 800 so you will not
be surprised when you hear we had to retire under the same fire, it
was all a scheme to let the Royal Engineers get in some work which
had to be done so the Canadians were sent out to make the attack so
as to draw the fire away from the Engineers we all thought we were
going to have a chance to get our bayonets into work but we were
disappointed although perhaps lucky for some of us our casu[a]lties
are about 60 counting dead & wounded it was sad to hear some of
the poor fellows moaning & crying after they were hit. In the
morning we were just having our coffee when an officer came in on
horse back & said Cronje has surrendered unconditionally you may
imagine the excitement that was all over the camp the Boers came
out of their trenches without arms & were immediately taken prisoner & sent to the Cape, we then entered their laager & trenches
which was a sight to see, today we have been on fatigue collecting all
their arms & ammunitions & burning all their clothes wagons & all
sorts of rubbish . . .

I am your
loving son
Fred

HORSE POWER

Following the defeats of December 1899, the British had asked Canada to raise a second contingent, which was quickly assembled and launched from Halifax. Two ships left in late January 1900, and the final one, the SS Milwaukee, left on February 21. Unlike the first contingent of infantry, this one had almost as many horses as men. W.H. Snyder wrote to his school principal, L.D. Robinson.

On board Str. Milwaukee,
Feb. 28th, 1900

My Dear Mr. Robinson,
I have a little leisure now, and will try to get a letter ready to send to you at the first opportunity. I have just come off a twenty-four hour continuous watch, so if my letter appears disconnected, please pardon on this account, as I naturally feel a little sleepy.

We are now eight days out on our long voyage and have come about 1,900 miles. It is rumored that we will be at the Cape Verde Islands by Saturday, and that we will be convoyed by a British Man O'War from there.

The first three days out was very rough but since then the water has been as calm as a lake. I was quite sick for two days but am all right now.

We are fairly comfortable but our sleeping quarters are pretty cramped. We sleep in hammocks, wedged in like sardines. We get up at a quarter to six and go at once to stables. The horses, poor creatures! Have the hardest time. Already some eight have died and been thrown overboard.

The weather to-day is simply perfect, the sea is like a mill pond. A breeze, like one is accustomed to meet on a balmy day in June, is sweeping over the decks. I am writing this stretched out on the deck. All over the ship is hustle and bustle. Some are drilling, others at fatigue work, others at target practice, while many are reading or writing. We seem to be altogether out of the track of sailing craft.

Occasionally a steamer can be discerned away off on the horizon but never near.

We have a sort of impromptu concert on board every night, consisting of Songs, Instrumental Music, Stump Speeches, &c. Occasionally a sportive whale, shark or porpoise pays us a close call.

One of the prettiest, or at least one of the most impressive sights I ever saw, was the Parade Service last Sunday at 10 a.m. Imagine a large steamer steaming rapidly over a trackless sea. On her decks some 600 men assembled in a Service of Parade[.] One of the old, familiar tunes is given out by Rev. Mr. Lane and as the organ strikes the first note the time is taken up by hundreds of voices. The strain of praise echoes and re-echoes far out over the waters and I feel as if it must reach even the little town in the dear home land where are all I hold dear. God bless and keep all! I hope once again in the future to meet you all, but if it is my lot to offer my unworthy life for my Queen and country, I promise, God helping me, to die like "a soldier and a man."

The strange feature of our voyage seems to be the fact of being away from all news. I dare say stirring events are taking place. The general health of the men is good. Yesterday, and for two days before, we were being vaccinated. I was rather amused at the antics of some of the men when they bared their arms for the surgeon's lancet. It took quite a while for some of them to get the proper courage. One fellow remarked to me that he always fainted at sight of blood. I wonder what he will do on the battlefield!

Today is wash day on board. Our troop have their turn this afternoon . . .

Green Point Camp,
Cape Town, S. A.,
April 1st, 1900

My Dear Mr. Robinson:
. . . You doubtless know long ago that we arrived in Cape Town on March 21st, just exactly four weeks from the time we left Halifax.

We met hardly any sailing craft while coming over, but once we entered Table Bay we found a perfect hive of steamers of all sizes – men of war transports. We heard of the capture of Cronje [at Paardeberg] and of the relief of Ladysmith, shortly after our arrival, and cheer after cheer rent the air from six hundred of Canada's sons. We did not know for a few hours about the gallant part our first Canadian Contingent had played in it, but when we did hear, cheer after cheer was given for our gallant comrades from the Land of the Maple Leaf.

I am wondering if you will be able to read this, for I am writing on the ground by the flickering candle. The camp where we are located along with the Regulars is about twenty minutes walk from the main part of the city. There are about 5000 men in camp.

Last week we had our first experience of an African sand storm. The sand came down like hail stones, cutting one's face and hands till it brought the blood. Our tent blew down and our horses got frightened and stampeded. Altogether it was quite an experience.

It seemed a great change to find when we arrived here that the trees were all leaved out and the weather like our summer. The winter or rainy season is about commencing. The houses are very pretty, with beautiful lawns and gardens attached. You will meet nearly all kinds of people in Cape Town.

I was detailed, with about 150 more, to act escort to Boer prisoners yesterday. They were taken to St. Helena by the same boat that we came out in. There were about 400 of them. They took matters very philosophically and laughed and chatted. I was talking to one. He said the Boers didn't blame Englishmen for fighting but thought that Canada had no business to get mixed up in it and that the Boers were laying for the Canadians particularly . . .

The cars in Cape Town, both steam and electric, are different from ours. The electrics are double deckers; the upper passengers go by a winding staircase. The steam cars are lower than ours, with three compartments and the door opens on the side.

Every day pedlars bring apples, grapes, tomatoes, eggs, pomegranate and other fruits to sell. Grapes are sixpence a pound, apples one penny apiece, tomatoes sixpence a dozen. The apples are small and insignificant.

Most of the vehicles are two wheeled and the mule is chiefly used. The natives get themselves up in very fantastic dresses . . .

April 3rd. [1900]

We go to the front to-morrow at 2 p.m. – to take part, if things turn out as anticipated, in what may be the deciding battle of the campaign.

I am well and in the best of spirits, and will give a good account of my self.

In haste,
Your old School Boy,
W.H. Snyder

Some squadrons of the second contingent had left Cape Town early in March, thinking they too were going to the front. Instead they marched eight hundred kilometres out into the Karroo Desert and back, scouting for rebel forces and protecting lines of communication, but not fighting until late July. Weakened by heat and shortages of food and clean water, men and horses fell ill and died.

BESIEGED

After fighting at Sunnyside on New Year's Day, **J. Frederick Ramsay** *(see page 26) transferred in March to the 1st Brabant's Horse and was commissioned a lieutenant. He was one of 160 men of the regiment sent to garrison the town of Wepener in early April. In this letter, he described the siege of the town and its 1,898 men by General Christiaan de Wet, leading a much larger Boer force. When British reinforcements arrived, the Boers retired. Lord Frederick Roberts, known as "Bobs" by the men, was commander in chief of the British forces.*

Near Thabanchu,
Orange Free State
1st Brabant's Horse.
May 8th, 1900.

. . . We reached Wepener, Orange Free State, on the 4th April about 1600 strong with 7 guns. On the 8th we had just taken up a position and were putting up trenches etc. when 7000 Boers sailed down upon us with ten guns and completely surrounded us, and there we were totally isolated.

Lord Roberts heliographed us to hold our position at any cost, and we should be relieved in a few days. We were a small but determined body, so we set to work. The first week passed and no relief. News came we would be relieved tomorrow. Tomorrow came and no sign of reinforcements, and so it went on for nearly three weeks, provisions running short, horses and cattle starving, raining torrents, the trenches at times flooded, the casualty list increasing daily, then the startling orders, "Reserve ammunition, it is running short", and the Boers pouring shot and shell into us at a terrific rate. One day we counted their shells and they amounted to 473. Our casualty list reached 33 killed and about 180 wounded not counting camp followers of which there were a large number killed and wounded – horses and cattle we lost by hundreds. The din and noise was terrific – the screams of dying horses and the screeching of shells etc.

We could only bury our dead and remove the wounded at night for the d . . . d Boers fired on our stretcher bearers and funeral parties – they also fired continually on our hospital and killed several of the inmates. A hospital assistant was dressing the wounds of a poor fellow on the verandah of the hospital, when both were riddled with bullets and killed. Another case – a man had been in hospital for some days badly wounded, but was so keen to get back to the trenches it was decided to let him go. He was at the door of the hospital and turning round, remarked to one of the attendants "I will avenge poor Jack or die" – at that moment an explosive bullet hit him on his head killing him on the spot. Such is the Boers idea of fair warfare, and they use their ambulance wagons to carry ammunition to their guns and still we respect their ambulance flag.

I had charge of one of the most important positions and out of 17 men lost one killed and five wounded. I was struck with a piece of shell on the back of my left hand which is still bandaged and a bullet wound in the right leg near the ankle – both slight and which I asked the doctor not to report to save you all worry.

One of my non-coms. was shot dead – he was sitting beside me and we were talking together – the bullet went in at his right breast and came out under the left arm then passed through two of my blankets on which I was lying at the time.

The Boers three times tried to rush our trenches but failed. Once at 2.0 in the morning it was very dark and we could only see the flash of their rifles, still they came on thinking by their over-whelming numbers they could make us give in, but Colonials know what Boers are and would rather die than be taken prisoners. They sent in word advising us to lay down our arms and if not they would "blow us to hell". Our Commanding Officer politely replied "We prefer hell"!

That morning we fought until daylight, but we held our position and the Boers left several hundred on the field, their total casualty list, so we heard afterwards, amounted to nearly 700 – ours a little over 200. There were many cases of reckless bravery too numerous to mention. I and my men were twice driven from our trenches by shell fire, but we took them again. My orders were to hold the position and I did it. When the relief column did arrive the Boers fled Northward and we are now on their tracks.

Lord Roberts telegraphed his congratulations to us and hopes to meet all the officers personally. I have been recommended with one other officer in our regiment for a commission in the regular army; but I am afraid I cannot accept it – pay is too small so I shall endeavour to get an appointment in one of the irregular forces, which will be raised in this country after the war is over in which pay is sufficient to live upon. We hope soon to run down the balance of these Free Staters and to lick them, then we will go to Bloemfontein to be refitted.

When we do meet the Boers again, they will be shown very little, if any, mercy. All we want is to meet the brutes hand to hand with the bayonet, then God help the Boers! My wounds amount to nothing and have not incapacitated me in any way and still I shall have a couple of scars to show and feel proud that I have received them for "Queen and Country" . . .

[J. Frederick Ramsay]

A few days later, Canadians took part in the lifting of a more famous siege. C Battery of the Royal Canadian Field Artillery travelled a roundabout route by sea, rail, and foot to approach from the north Mafeking, a hamlet in the northeastern corner of the Cape Colony, where a small force commanded by Lord Robert Baden-Powell had been besieged since October 1899. On May 15, after a vigorous artillery duel, the Boers were driven away and the 215-day siege ended, leading to joyful celebrating in the cities of the Empire and introducing a neologism for street celebrations – mafficking.

OTTER'S TALE

After Paardeberg, the 19th Brigade continued its march to Bloemfontein, engaging the Boers from time to time before reaching the capital of the Orange Free State in mid-March. In their camp just outside town, the Canadians attempted to recover from the effects of short rations and bad water. While they repaired their tattered clothing and observed Easter, preparations were made for a month-long, 480-kilometre march to Pretoria, capital of the Transvaal. The regiment set out on April 21; four days later they fought at Israel's Poort, where their commanding officer, **Colonel William Otter,** *was wounded. After recovering at Bloemfontein, Otter was back in command when the regiment fought a bloody* *engagement at Doornkop on May 29. The authoritarian Otter and his likeable second-in-command, Lieutenant Colonel Lawrence Buchan, had once had a good relationship but their later disdain for one another reached a peak during the Israel's Poort battle, as Otter's letters to his wife and Buchan's letter to his daughter revealed.*

Bloemfontein
28 April/oo

My Dear Molly,

. . . We moved forward and as Major Pelletier was in charge of the first line and I knew his excitable temper[a]ment I kept close up to him. After moving for about a mile we came to a wire fence with white stone posts about 700 yards from the foot of one of the kopjes and the Boers opened on us pretty hotly – of course we all dropped to the ground but as we had but little cover some of the men began to run back for better shelter and fearing that such might be taken by the enemy for cowardice and by our own men in rear for a retirement I stood up and [stayed] them. I had hardly sat down, half lying on my left side and looking to the front when something hit me on the right side of my chin and I thought my jaw was broken – I began to bleed like fun but my faithful Ogilvy who was near ran over and bound me up with his red bandana and I was able to continue to direct until the forces on the left began to take them in the flank, when we advanced and took their position which ended the thing. Our good little French doctor Fiset came up and dressed me [and] found that the bullet had entered my chin and came out on the right side of my neck narrowly missing the jugular . . . I am none the worse, my pulse never quickened. They made a great fuss and insisted on my lying down on a stretcher with an awning . . . I forgot to say that the bullet that struck me . . . spoiled the badge on my right shoulder . . . on analyzing my own wound I am much satisfied that there were two bullets, the one hitting me the other going thru' my shoulder badge and that my escape was rather a marvellous one . . .

Johannesburg
31 May/oo

My Dear Molly,

. . . I had a very hearty reception from the regiment . . . I was just in time in rejoining the Battn as . . . I led it across the Vaal River, the first infantry corps of the army to cross into the Transvaal and then I came in for the fight on the 29th inst which was a very important one and though we got out of it with only seven wounded our neighbours the Gordons who were attacking the same heights as ourselves got fearfully cut up. Personally I was very careful of myself . . .

Springs 20 miles east of Johannesburg
14 June 1900

My Dear Molly,

. . . I am afraid that friend! B. was at his old tricks when I was away – of course it is only from odd hints that I gather this and consequently cannot take any action . . . but if ever I learn positively that it has been so – well! Was ever a man so handicapped as I have been – the one who should be my greatest assistance I dare not trust . . .

With Love to all,
yours
Willie

Lieutenant Colonel Lawrence Buchan took issue with Otter's account.

Springs, S.A.
July 2, 1900

My dear little Dotter,

. . . I think this may catch the mail so I just enclose clippings from the "Mail" and "Globe" of 30 April about Otter's action at Israels Poort – or Yster Nek as we call it – with some comments thereon by myself. The facts are these. According to O's system of things it was the left half-Battalion's turn to lead that day so he could not very well direct me to take Pelletiers ½ Battn and go ahead leaving my own ½ Battn. Pelletier was sent ahead in the attack and O followed in the <u>second</u> line <u>for his first time</u>. I following in the third line <u>also for the first time behind the first line for me</u>. When fire opened from the kopjes at about 1500 yds my 3rd line was up with O's and P's 1st and 2nd lines, which were both in a small donga with an ordinary wire fence crossing it. There were no "entanglements" or anything of the sort. I and my men were on their left and up somewhat in advance of them. I saw them retiring and rushed my men up further to counteract this going back on their part and got hold of a good position to hang on to whilst my men got breath and kept up a steady fire on the kops. Whilst doing so, O's pet-puppy Ogilvie came over to me in an awful state of excitement and fright telling me the Col. was hit and all was lost if I did not go over and stop the panic in their part of the line. After making a few further inquiries from him and finding out that the Col was practically none the worse beyond loss of blood and excess of funk, I told him to go back and tell the Col I would stay where I was until I deemed it time to advance when I would take the whole Battn on and rush the kops. Also, that everything was allright and I had the men well in hand. When the flanking movement by the rest of our Brigade had sufficiently developed . . . I went over to see the Col and found him excited and bandaged as to his chin but otherwise quite as fit as I was, <u>physically</u>, and sitting in the cover of some long grass in a little donga and <u>quite safe</u> . . . afterwards the Col <u>was carried into our bivouac on a stretcher</u>. He could have walked as well as I did. That is the true history of how he was "twice wounded whilst leading a charge". The bullet that struck his chin glanced onto his shoulder strap. That accounts for the <u>twice wounded</u>. The <u>subsidised reporters</u> and the pet-puppy Ogilvie, who is of the same kidney, account for the newspaper glorifications of this "gallant and brave officer". I am waiting to see the account of Dornkop [*sic*] where both O and his pet-puppy were too scared to come forward with the Battn at all and only found us that night, long after dark, by accident. Thank goodness all in the Battn noticed

their conduct on that occasion and can vouch for it if necessary . . .
The newspaper accounts are so palpably absurd I write this in self
defence . . . The diary of my command from 26 April to 26 May will
I suppose be published in due course, like O's, if he has not sup-
pressed it: which I hardly think he would dare to do.

> Good bye dear little girl with much love
> from your aged
> father

*Most accounts of this and other battles involving Canadians depended
on Otter's self-serving descriptions. Recent research by Serge
Durflinger, a historian at the Canadian War Museum, has uncovered
Buchan's contradictory letters, which Durflinger says "will undoubt-
edly cause students of Canada's participation in the South African
War to reinterpret Otter's oft-repeated version of these events."*

RIDING TO PRETORIA

*In May, as the Imperial forces marched north to the capital of the
Transvaal, Canadian units shared in heavy fighting at the Zand River
and Faber's Put, as well as at Doornkop, before Johannesburg fell to
the British on May 31. Lord Roberts entered Pretoria on June 5
without opposition. When the news reached Toronto, thousands of
citizens indulged in a night of mafficking. The war now moved into
a chase-and-evade phase: the British pursued an enemy they could
rarely find while the Boers avoided open battle in favour of guerrilla
sorties.* **Lieutenant E.W.B. (Dinky) Morrison** *commanded the left
section of D Battery of the Royal Canadian Artillery and reported
its activities in letters to* The Ottawa Citizen *and* The Hamilton
Spectator. *The battery had spent five months trekking and scouting
without seeing action before Morrison received orders to entrain his
detachment for Pretoria. He described his battle initiation.*

Fort Wonderboom,
north of Pretoria
July 15 [1900]

... for two days and two nights we rushed northward at an average speed of nearly ten miles an hour, past Roodival [Rooiwal], with its wrecked station, burned cars and little lines of graves beside the track, where sleep the dead of the Railway Pioneer regiment amid the debris; past Honing Spruit, with its bullet-spattered buildings and little shelter trenches, where the released prisoners from Pretoria stood off the Boers so well a fortnight ago (more graves); past the fire-blackened rocky kopje beside which the Derbyshire militia were cut up, and so on to Kroonstadt, over deviations, past blown-up bridges and culverts, between vistas of torn up track, the rails lying in squirming lines beside the right-of-way, bent into all sorts of shapes, the graves becoming thicker and the asvogels circling in sluggish flocks over the carcasses of horses and oxen that dotted the blackened veldt ...

At noon we pulled into Pretoria ... as we approached we heard the boom of big guns and the rattle of rifles just over the kopje, but night was closing down and we were not engaged ...

Dewegendrift, July 21 [1900]

D battery, R.C.A., has been in its first action, and has come off well ... We were marching slowly along with the cavalry out in front and the lines of infantry closer in, when there was a "boom!" from the kopje over two miles to the left, and then we heard an eerie whistle like the wind in the chimney of a haunted house (and it gave you about the same chill down your spine), then a shell plunked into the ground a couple of hundred yards from the battery and threw up a cloud of dust like a dynamite blast on a sewer. Major Hurdman wheeled the battery into line and we got "action left." Before our horses were clear with the limbers [the detachable front shafts of the gun carriage] there was another boom and doleful whistle, this time over our heads, and a shell plunged into the ground about 150 yards right in rear of the battery. Says I to myself, says I, they've got us bracketed – one short and one long – the next will land right on us. Now any man who did not listen for the next shell with extreme anxiety must have more nerve than most people. All this time we were working away with the usual "fire discipline" routine prior to opening fire ourselves, but every second seemed a minute, and while I mechanically gave my orders and looked after things as we have had it drilled into us, my senses were keenly alive to the fact that there was another shell coming that would probably divide the bracket and do other things. At last she came – "boom!" – I heard the crooning whistle in the air coming right for us, and I thought for three seconds that I was the only man on earth and that shell was bound to land in the pit of my stomach. Whoo-oo-oo, it swooped down over the heads of my section, and threw a shower of dirt and gravel over the men on the limbers as they moved to their proper position in the rear. Then we opened fire, and I got very busy looking after the working of my own guns. After that I think I can honestly say that the shells didn't bother me much . . . Our casualties, except the drivers [native] and mules, were nil, but we had had our baptism of fire all right and were correspondingly happy.

[Lieutenant E.W.B. Morrison]

NEARLY A WIDOW

*In April 1900, with the main force of Strathcona's Horse already in South Africa, **Lieutenant Agar Adamson** (see pages 53, 79 and 154) left Canada in command of fifty reinforcements and travelled by sea to England and on to Natal. Unable to join the regiment immediately, the horsemen were attached to the South African Light Horse. On July 5 at Wolve Spruit, twenty-four kilometres north of Standerton, Adamson was one of thirty-nine men who took on eighty Boers at close quarters. After several Strathconas were shot and the remainder ordered to retire, Sergeant Arthur Richardson rode back on a wounded horse to within 275 metres of the enemy and picked*

*up Corporal Alex McArthur, who had been wounded. In a strangely
punctuated account, Adamson told his wife about the encounter but
did not mention Richardson's Victoria Cross–winning feat.*

Standerton
Sunday 8th July [1900]

My own darling Mabel,
The enemy did their best to make you my sweetheart a widow on
the 5th but only succeeded in wounding my horse, taking two prisoners unwounded with their horses, short Sergt. Stringer, The MFH
[Master Farrier Horse?] late groom. and Isbester of Ottawa. A boy
with red hair. McDougall of Ottawa shot through knee. McArthur of
N.W.T. through thigh and arms. and poor old Sparkes clean through
the neck. a most wonderful escape all doing well. left three horses on
the field wounded. I will try and give a fuller account later on.

Wed. 4 July . . . Took the two troops out scouring the country to the
east, found nothing. Commandeered one horse. Bitterly cold. thick
frost every morning. horses doing well owing to my insisting upon
their being blanketed at night and not watered till about 10. I found
they would not drink the cold water. I also have them when lean
herded and allowed to graise. I mix salt with their oats and find they
eat well which they would not do before. Your sleeping cap is a great
comfort. But oh for an Egyptian cigarette. The South African Light
Horse 600 strong to whom we are attached as a distinct unit are a
very fine lot mostly men living in the country, the four senior officers
are Imperial chaps . . . my men are learning many tips from them.
There is no wood in the country. We cook with dried cow manure,
which the kaffirs bring us. All the fence poles for miles have been
burnt long ago. We are in tents, which I brought although told not
to. I have 22 old Strathconas attached to me, poor devils. have our
thin thin karki no blankets and very few saddles . . . I am in tele-
graphic communication with Steel[e] who is at Valkfontein with one
squadron at Greylingstad. Try and follow our movements on a map

. . . it will make it more interesting to you dear. I have had all my horses branded S.D. and the commandered ones A.A. I hear [Lieutenant Colonel Samuel] Steel[e] says many of his younger officers are no good. his men excellent . . .

Ever thine

Agar

SAM'S GOOD SCOUTS

Lieutenant Colonel Samuel Benfield Steele was Lord Strathcona's choice to command his cavalry regiment. Fifty years old when he went to South Africa, he had spent his life in military and policing adventures – with the militia during the Fenian raids of 1866, with the expedition to put down the Riel uprising in 1870, and with the North-West Mounted Police during the North-West Rebellion and the Klondike gold rush. In July and August 1900 Steele reported to Lord Strathcona about the regiment's activities in the southernmost Transvaal, near the Vaal River. Greylingstad was a British fort on the railway line to Johannesburg. Paardekop, meaning horse head, is a common place name in South Africa.

Paardekop

4th August, 1900

Dear Lord Strathcona,

. . . We arrived here, yesterday on our march from the North. The troops are concentrating here for an important move. Gen. Rundle's division and another, all under Sir Redvers Buller will make a long march North some day through Swaziland. Lord Dundonald's brigade consists now of the South African Light Horse, the Strathcona's, "A" Battery, [of] R.H.A. [Royal Horse Artillery] and three other corps, now en route from the South. We guarded the train all the way from Graylingstadt [sic], a very considerable responsibility, the supply column being at least three miles in length. From Standerton to here it was increased by the addition of one hundred mule teams. I put out a very strong rear guard and it was fortunate I did so for the right rear was threatened by a couple of hundred of the enemy who seeing the rear guard did not venture to attack but satisfied themselves with firing (without effect) upon our flankers. Poor Sergt. Parker who wrote you re his commission was killed on the 29th. He was with 18 men under Lt. White-Fraser sent by the Commandant at Watervaal bridge to get the arms of some Boers who sent in word by two others that they wished to surrender, but preferred the others to think that they were taken prisoners. This was a "ruse de guerre". The men went out with two black scouts and at the house named the two blacks and Parker, who were sent on in advance were shot dead, and Pte. Arnold dangerously wounded from the fire of about seventy Boers behind a breastwork near the house, which by the way, had a white flag flying. The Boers are a very treacherous people, and unfortunately are trusted too much. They are allowed into the camps to sell stuff on any excuse as long as they have passes to show that they have given up their arms and taken the oath. These are their spies and so are the women. One of the latter near here is reported to have employed her black servant to cut the telegraph line. I quite believe it. Pte. Arnold was brought in and his wound is a severe one. He may lose his leg. Sgt. Parker was a dead shot, but rash. He had killed two of the enemy a few days ago at a very long range when he and one of the men were surrounded. He forced the enemy to retire. Both of the men killed on this sort of duty in "C" Squadron were ex officers of the army. The regiment continues to work well. Their scouting is excellent. The papers have, in Canada, said things against the horses of the Corps. purchased by Dr. McEachran. All of it is untrue, very few of the horses have died; they are the best in this army – everyone wants them. They are a good advertisement. I have already used up and received at least four hundred Argentines [horses] and others since I left the Cape, while only three or four Canadians have succumbed. They are really very fine and much more intelligent than many others . . .

Hoping that you are enjoying good health, I am,
Respectfully yours
S.B. STEELE

PILLAGE AND RAPE

*In the third week of July **Agar Adamson** and his men linked with Strathcona's Horse. Early in August the entire regiment travelled north in the Transvaal attempting to drive the enemy towards Belfast and a showdown. En route, Adamson wrote to his wife.*

on Komatie River
15th August 1900

My dear Mabel.

. . . We have entered and taken 3 towns, the first was Amersfoort. I had the advance guard and 2 small galloping guns under me with orders to enter if possible, if not hold for main columns (Flying) to come up. We were not fired upon until within about 1000 yards of the town. When we charged in open order from three sides, we rode very hard, the bullets simply rained in upon us, some of the escapes were marvelous, saddle, horses and water bottles suffered but not one man actually killed. I was the first to reach the actual Town being in the centre of the semi circle. the advance guard formed in charging [?] dismounted and drove the brutes out of town. Our orders were not to follow them. We held the town until the Flying Column came up. I commandeered the Parsons house put men on guard with 12 guns remained there for two nights. the joy of a bed and many other things were thoroughly appreciated. the Parson was out fighting and his house full of ammunition. The town was given over to loot, which was most thorough and perhaps a mistake. two big shops were sacked of everything, bicycles, baby carriages, pianos, organs, smashed to pieces, silk stockings and womens under clothes by the hundreds found happy [?] homes on tommy's legs. A Jeweller's shop gave many valuables to the soldiers of the Queen. a general Inspection would reveal many a valuable toy. houses were pulled to pieces simply to build huge fires. Our Parson's wife we protected inside her home as she did her best for us but all her sheep, chickens, geese, pigs, wagons, carts, wood, and fodder were either stolen or smashed. I had always been under the impression that we did not loot, but in this case it was general and no attempt made to prevent it . . . I had a troop on the flank the next day, and owing to the advance guard mixing up the orders got into Ermilo [Ermelo] ahead of them with very little attempt at resistance . . . We rushed to the Town Hall, pulled down the Transvaal flag, posted guards over Post office and several buildings and awaited rest of our column who surrounded the Town . . . I commandeered the largest house in town, put a guard over it, and sent 3 men to cook dinner for us and make arrangements for 10 officers to sleep there. It turned out to be owned by a very rich Hungarian Merchant, who I found to be a Mason. he had been out with the Commandos but wished to surrender. I promised him to do my best for him. he got his pass and is now living with his most charming wife and sister in law (German). he did us very well. 12 dined with him and he produced Sauterne, most excellent Claret (Chateau Margaux) and Sweet champagne, a most Comfortable bed, cigars and cigarettes a most superior and interesting person. We remained 2 nights 3 of my men sleeping in his stable to look after a £200 Victoria. I also gave him six men to look after his shop and thus the brother lost nothing to being a Mason[.] And we gained much. the second night owing to camp orders I only slept in his house under an [e]iderdown quilt that would have done a Royal Princess proud. About 3 in the morning I heard a great racket at the front door and in a short blue shirt went around the Veranda to see the cause, and was mét by a fair maiden whose only language was German. My brother Mason appeared in night robe and translated the young woman's fast and furious flow of language, while my legs grew stiff with cold, which was that 3 soldiers had entered her house which was close by and were in bed with her two sisters trying to rape them . . . After I had my breeches on, for to be caught without ones breeches on any occasion is not the most Comfortable, and in that case circumstantial evidence might implicate me . . . I did what I could and the brutes made their escape in double short order, but I greatly fear they were our own men . . . I am afraid when the truth gets out in Canada there will be a great deal of dirty linen washing about the S.H. [Strathcona's Horse] the men are heartly sick of most of the officers who with few exceptions are a most incompetent lot, very selfish and most ignorant and not particularly anxious to learn. Col. Steel[e] most thoroughly hated. it is a great pity and hard on old Lord Strathcona . . . Steel[e]'s language and general handling of his men is Billingsgate [foul and abusive] personified and although I said in my last letter a good fighter, I have my doubts if he is not too excitable . . . I personally have not spoken a word to him except officially. his only confidants are his batmen with whom he is on most friendly terms, dines with them, and I hear when able gets beastly drunk with them. I rather fancy there must have been some good reason for keeping them 6 weeks in Capetown doing nothing . . . It is too cold to write more . . .

Good night Mabel

Your husband

Agar

A MONEY-MAKING COUNTRY

Private Robert S. Robinson arrived in Cape Town on March 21, 1900, on the SS Milwaukee, *as a member of A Squadron of the Canadian Mounted Infantry of the second contingent. His squadron was chosen to escort prisoners to the island of St. Helena and then travelled by train to Bloemfontein in April. On July 16, the squadron fought at Witpoort. He wrote to his friend Art Galoska.*

Bankfontein

August 3, 1900

Dear Art,

. . . I have some Boer arms and Kruger coins and pennies, which I may be able to bring back to Canada at some future time when the CMRifles go home. This seems very indefinite just now, as we are in much the same position as Moses when the light went out, as regards to the finish of the war . . .

Our battalion doesn't muster anything like one half of our original strength. Our squadron A only muster 50 men out of the 150 that left Halifax; the balance are sick, wounded, and a few dead. And there were about 20 who joined the mounted police and the railway, which was voluntary to all colonials. The pay rate is at seventy shillings per week including rations and clothing – in fact, everything under the army system. You may think the pay large, but it is the regular wage in this country, which appears to be the finest money-making country in the world. The mines are nearly all working, and I believe the average wage is one pound per day.

The towns are small and have the appearance of having sprung up quickly. As regards to the country, it is a great pastureland with a few acres cultivated in the vicinity of the house. The land doesn't require manuring and is easily worked. But the Dutch don't cultivate the one one-hundredth part of their farm, being content with the fruit of the Kaffirs' labour. These niggers don't hurt themselves working. I expect they don't do more than 3 months labour in a year. Their work is mostly driving the herds to the pasture and back. Most every Dutch farm has its Kaffir kraal [fenced groups of huts] or family of niggers on the farm who grow their own mealies.

Each Kaffir male is allowed two or three wives, and I don't think the black population will run out for a year or two. They are not a fierce or wild race by any means; in fact, they appear to be the natural servant or slave of the whites who they look upon as a very superior being. And they seem to take pleasure in serving him. They haven't adapted the custom of wearing clothing yet, with the exception of a blanket when the weather is cold. And when 'old sol' comes out strong, the family's clothing could be put into a matchbox. Here and there, throughout the veldt, are villages of Kaffir kraals. These niggers live independently and own their own herds, etc. . . .

You have read of our fight on the 16th of last month . . .

The Boers used explosive bullets mostly, and they were whistling and cracking like firecrackers in all directions. In a little while, Brown fell wounded through the chest. He may recover. Soon after, Lieut. Borden fell exclaiming, "I'm done for boys", and expired. They were both behind me, a little higher up the kopje. The bullets must have gone over our heads (of third troop). Some Boers had advanced and were among the rocks at the foot of the kopje and were killed or taken prisoners. But not before Lieut. Birch of our troop was killed, and Mulloy fearfully wounded – the bullet entering the temple, tearing out one eye and part of his nose, and damaging the other eye. He may retain the sight of one eye, the doctor says, but is very doubtful. . . .

. . . between you and me, there is a lot of shell fever or mauseritus especially among the non-coms from the RCD's [Royal Canadian Dragoons] from Stanley barracks. In the fight on the kopje on the 16th, there was only one sergeant from the RCD's, Sergeant Fuller. The other ten officers and Sergeants were either with the ammunition wagon, water cart, or with led horses . . .

. . . Every man of the six that left Toronto for Montreal with me to make up the third troop of A, are still at the front. They have not missed a day. Out of 13 men from Ottawa in our troop, 6 have gone back sick; also 4 men from Montreal out of 5 went back sick. There is 1 man left to represent Peterborough district out of 8. All those men cut quite a figure with their braid and brass buttons and swords and spurs, while we 6 from Toronto were pure civilians, unattached. They were a nice lot of fellows alright, but they don't cut any ice up here. I guess it's too hot . . .

> So good bye
> Robert Ray
> Reg'l number 188
> 3rd troop A squad
> CMR

FAREWELLS

Privates Robert (Bert) Rooke and Charles Rooke, two of the eight sons of Hannah and William Henry Rooke, served in South Africa with Strathcona's Horse in 1900. In the autumn the British advanced north through the Transvaal, attacked and ambushed by the "bitter enders" – Boers who would not give up. Bert wrote to his mother in

Saltcoats, Saskatchewan, mentioning the farewell address of General Redvers Buller, who had been demoted as British commander in chief after the black week of defeats in December 1899.

11 October 1900
Mach[a]dodorp, Trans.

Dear Mother,

. . . We have just got back from a long march through the Lydenburg Mountains, by Lydenburg, Spitz Kop & Pilgrim's Rest. I tell you, it was a terrible rough road, but we kept the enemy on the move all the time. They are so badly broken up now that you might say the war is over.

When we got here the day before yesterday, Gen. Buller left for home. Before leaving, he addressed a few words to each of the regiments under his command. He told us that he had orders to break up the Natal Field Force & return home. He then said he had spent some of the happiest months in the Can Northwest & that, when he heard at the beginning of the war, that there were men coming from there to the front, he did his best to get some of them under his command. He thought for a long time that he was not going to succeed, but, at last had his wish fulfilled when we joined him. Since then, he said, we had proved as brave, willing & useful a body of men as he could have wished to have. He then wished us goodbye and goodluck & you may depend we gave him three hearty cheers. We have a splendid brigade general also, viz, Lord Dundonald. He is a soldier & a gentleman in every sense of the words.

Trains are going through here by the dozen taking troops down country. We expect to go down soon, but it is no use trying to say when or how, whether by march or by rail, as everything is so uncertain. Volunteers were called for from the irregular corps for the policeforce. Our fellows who joined left for Pretoria yesterday. We did not join as I think it will be a very unsatisfactory job while the country is unsettled. Besides, I am pretty sure I could not stand the heat which is just coming on. The pay in the police is not bad, being 10 s per diem, free rations & free quarters on a 3 month probation.

Yesterday a list came around, they are asking us whether we wanted our discharge in Cape Town, remain in England, take leave in England or return to Canada. Charlie & I put down for leave in England & if the cash box is heavy enough, we will run up to the north . . .

Your affec.son,

Bert

Bert and Charles sailed for England and remained there on furlough for several months before returning to Canada. In December 1901 Bert, Charles, and a younger brother, George, enlisted in the 2nd Canadian Mounted Rifles, which went to South Africa in 1902. At the end of the war George came home while Bert and Charles stayed to work for the South African railway. Charles spent the rest of his life in South Africa.

SAVE THE GUNS

The men of the first and second contingents had signed on for a year's service. Although some chose to stay (as British scouts, receiving an extra ten shillings a day), most were ready to go home. The first six companies left Cape Town on October 1, 1900, and sailed to Canada. Another lot went to England first, where they were royally feted. In November the second-contingent units had a month's service remaining when a detachment of the Royal Canadian Dragoons and D Battery of the Royal Canadian Field Artillery faced the Canadians' most desperate situation in the war, at a farm named Leliefontein south of Belfast. Two horse-drawn field guns and ninety-five dragoons, under Colonel François-Louis Lessard, were guarding the rear of a long, slow-moving column of transport and infantry when two hundred mounted Boers attacked. **Lieutenant E.W.B. (Dinky) Morrison** *(see page 47) described the struggle in a letter home.*

[November 7, 1900]

. . . As our shells drifted into the Boers they dismounted and took cover, but still continued coming on – rushing from cover to cover and firing . . . We had not fired a dozen rounds when Colonel Lessard came galloping across from the other flank, and as he got up he shouted: "For God's sake, Morrison, save your guns!" . . . And he pointed towards our left rear. One glance was enough. For over half a mile back on our left flank the Boers were swarming over the hills from the west. Good old Cockburn looked too, and without a word he turned and shoved in the rest of his two troops against the enemy . . . No. 5 limbered up smartly and we started at a gallop for the ridge, which was our next position. We had not gone fifty yards before the Mausers began to sing Hark from the tomb! . . . I turned in my saddle and saw a sight the like of which had not been seen before in this war. Square across our rear a line of Boers a mile long was coming on at a gallop over the plain, firing from their horses. It looked like the spectacular finale in a wild west show. They were about 1,500 yards away, but coming on rapidly and shooting at our gun . . . On we went, hell-for-leather, the drivers' whips going and the Mausers cracking. Every moment I expected a horse to go down, but still our luck held with us and they were not gaining. They were firing from their horses and their aim was wild. Then my poor old horses began to fag. They slowed from a gallop to a trot and gradually from a trot to a walk . . . We halted and went into action . . . I gave them shrapnel . . . It smashed through the line and burst a hundred yards behind them. I gave them another . . . It burst nicely about 50 yards in front of them and the shrapnel bullets made a wide gap. But the line still came on . . . I realized that it was no good trying to stand them off . . . So we limbered up and started again to make one more effort to reach the ridge and our infantry supports . . .

[Lieutenant E.W.B. Morrison]

The gunners reached the ridge and kept shelling the enemy. The day-long fighting ended when the Boers retired after their commanders had been killed. Three Canadian Victoria Cross winners were named after Leliefontein: "Good old" Lieutenant (later Major) Hampden Zane Churchill Cockburn, Lieutenant (later Lieutenant General and Sir) Richard Ernest William Turner (see page 83), and Sergeant (later Major) Edward James Gibson Holland. Later in the month, Morrison observed British and Canadian troops executing orders to remove women and children from their homes and burn or blast the houses. He wrote: "It was the first touch of Kitchener's iron hand. And we were the knuckles . . . we could not help approving the policy, though it rather revolted most of us to be the instruments." In December Morrison, with about nine hundred men of the second contingent forces, sailed from Cape Town, reaching Halifax early in January. Morrison received the Distinguished Service Order for his work in South Africa, commanded the 1st Artillery Brigade in the First World War, rose to the rank of major general, and was knighted in 1919.

IN HARM'S WAY

In 1901 Canada sent a fourth contingent of about 1,200 men who were assigned to the South African Constabulary. Sam Steele commanded a division of this police force. The British military divided the veldt into sections fenced with barbed wire, rounded up the Boers (mostly women and children), and transported them to the world's first concentration camps. Of the 116,000 Boers confined in the camps, 28,000 died. **Corporal W.H. Snyder** *(see page 37) was sent to England in July 1900 with enteric fever and dysentery. When he had recovered, he saw "Her Gracious Majesty, Queen Victoria, at Buckingham Palace" before returning to South Africa. He wrote to Rev. D.H. Simpson of Berwick, Nova Scotia, where after the war Snyder ran a real estate and insurance business.*

Zondogskraal, Transvaal,
Dec 12th, 1901

My Dear Mr. Simpson.

. . . We are "out on the veldt" in genuine earnest. I am on outpost duty with a squad all by myself . . . The last few days we have had plenty of excitement as numbers of Boers come very close to our squad. One of my men and myself had a very narrow squeak day before yesterday. I had just come back to my post from No. 14 Troop, when away off in the Valley below I saw a stray horse making straight for the skyline, and a horseman in pursuit.

When I got down to my outpost one of the men told me that McDonald was after a stray horse. Handing my rifle over, I immediately started out to help him. As I got to the foot of the Kopje, McDonald and horse disappeared over the skyline. When I got up to the top I saw the pair disappearing over the next skyline. I followed on, but got no sight of them, so I concluded to await developments. Time passed and I began to feel uneasy. (I may say that 400 Boers under Botha and others were not more than two miles away and are still out there and we are looking for an attack everyday.) I mounted and went on. Soon I espied two horses coming towards me. I felt relieved and was congratulating McDonald on his success, when over the skyline next me I saw McDonald coming waving his hat. At once I knew they were Boers. My first impulse was to fly, for remember we were both unarmed, but I saw that McDonald's horse was completely played and I could not desert a comrade, so I waited. Pretty soon he was up to me, and his first exclamation was that he was almost into the Boer lines. Now our race, perhaps for our lives, commenced. The Boers got near enough to fire, and soon those little bursts of dirt around showed us that they had the range, and on we went, my horse leading the way. His tired one plucked up heart and before long we were out of harm's way, for my outpost had seen us coming. Now we might have been all right but it was one of the narrowest escapes from death or capture I have yet had in the S.A.C. . . .

(Corporal) W.H. Snyder,
17 Troop S.A.C.
C. (Eastern Division), Transvaal.

A FINAL SHOT

*Born in 1880 on a farm near Jarvis, Ontario, **Chester Rodgers** was in the 2nd Canadian Mounted Rifles, which went to South Africa in February 1902 as part of the fifth Canadian contingent. Chester wrote to Sadie McCarter of Jarvis, mentioning the March 31 battle of Boschbult (or Hart's River), the last and bloodiest action of this war in which Canadians died – thirteen were killed and forty wounded.*

Klerksdorf, Transvaal, May 23/02

Dear Sadie

. . . You wonder how I can write when in so much danger my why thats easy. I wrote Stace Boyd a part of a letter the first time I was under fire wrote it while the guns were firing as he wanted a letter off the battle field. Am awfully tickled to hear you say I write a nice letter I never knew before that I could do anything nice.

. . . this coming out here is nothing of course I suppose we risk our lives but thats nothing we have only got to turn up our toes once.

Our fruit has played out pretty well now still day before yesterday we camped near a fine orange orchard and was over and got my horses nose bag full it is nice to pick oranges and eat them still apples would be much nicer now . . .

We have been on the go nearly all the time just came to town and got provisions and then out again. The boers have been steering pretty clear of us since the Boschbolt fight just snipe at us as we march along. We had a man severely wounded a couple of days ago by the boers sniping at us. The last trip we made was a big drive from here to Vayburg Cape Colony 125 miles. We were 7 days steady marching and covered 125 miles each man was 30 yds apart and then had behind them supports of artillery and troops and then marched across the country driving the boers ahead of us. About the third day out about 20 of us were sent out on outpost after we had camped and some boers about 50 took a fancy that they would like to give us the lead fever so started popping at us and we had a fine time shooting at each other till dusk when we went back to camp. None of us were hit but they come close enough to hear them zip along.

Well on drive we captured 361 boers some 150 wagons some 3000 cattle 13000 sheep and goats some 300 horses and small arms and ammunition. I used to go at night on the march after dark and throw a goat on my back (didn't steal it you know just took it and walk off and then we would kill it and have a fry for breakfast. One day I got a Spring Buck [springbok] that is a S[ou]th African deer and it was immence [sic] in taste but very small in size. In Vayburg I went to town one day as we never camp within a mile of town and I thought a nice meal would go good so we went to an hotel waited until all the officers and civies were through and then paid 3s 6d = 84 cents for a dish of soup a little meat no potatoes no tea or coffee no desert [sic] a little bread though . . .

To day makes just 5 months I have put in 7 months more now to serve and then for dear old Canada so if I go back I get there about Feb just in time for the dances . . .

Your sincere friend

Ches

Reg. No 765

2nd Troop C Squadron

2nd <u>Can</u> Mt'd Rifles

South Africa

Am going to send a few S.A. flowers.

The day Rodgers wrote this letter, the Sixth Contingent sailed from Canada, but on May 31, 1902, the Boers signed a surrender in Pretoria. Enthusiastically, loyally, naively, Canada had sent a force of 7,368 to abet England's imperialist ambitions; another 1,004 served as garrison troops in Halifax, freeing a British battalion to fight. Because the casualty toll was low – 89 killed in action, 135 dead of disease, 252 wounded – the experience in South Africa, as Pierre Berton wrote, "convinced a generation of young Canadians that war was not terribly dangerous." For Chester Rodgers, who was killed in action on March 1, 1917, and for thousands like him, the Great War would destroy that illusion.

THE GREAT WAR, 1914–1918

"As terrible as hell can possibly be"

A Canadian soldier improvises, using logs for a chair and a writing table, to write a letter from a First World War battlefield in Europe, where nearly 620,000 troops from Canada served.

In the ten years after the South African War, Canada and the other Dominions were not consulted as Britain manoeuvred diplomatically among the tetchy nations of Europe and finally decided to go to war with Germany. By the end of the Great War, however, the Dominions had earned and demanded the right to sit with the most powerful nations as new world policy was made.

Canada's prime minister, Robert Borden, played a key role in winning a voice for Canada in Britain's inner circles. Borden, a Conservative, had been elected in October 1911, ousting Sir Wilfrid Laurier, who had presided for a dozen years while the country prospered and grew in population and size (with the addition of Alberta and Saskatchewan). Borden stepped in at the tail end of this boom; in 1913 foreign investment dried up, prices for exports dropped, and the cost of money rose. A year later, in the walk-up to the war, Canada stood on guard, but powerless while Britain weighed its continental commitments.

The assassination of Archduke Franz Ferdinand, heir to the Austro-Hungarian throne, sparked the First World War. What is obscure is how, as a result of a Serbian nationalist's act of defiance, more than twenty nations could have been drawn into a war that would for more than four years be fought in Europe, East Africa, Macedonia, Mesopotamia (now Iraq), and the Dardanelles. The answers lie in old wars and new jealousies, and in the complex web of defensive treaties that linked European nations.

Among the underlying factors were France's hatred of Germany for having annexed its coal-rich provinces, Alsace and Lorraine, in 1871; Germany's desire to subjugate its two bordering enemies, France and Russia; the German kaiser's determination to build an empire and a navy equal to that of Britain; the Russian czar's need to stave off a looming domestic revolution by warring with Serbia; and, in the crunch, Britain's failure to make it immediately clear that it would come to the defence of Belgium.

In June 1914, when Franz Ferdinand was killed, the nations of Europe had chosen their sides and formalized them in defensive pacts. Germany, Austria-Hungary, and Italy had formed the Triple Alliance in 1882 (though Italy later secretly negotiated a treaty with France to remain neutral if Germany attacked France). In 1907 Russia joined the British–French *entente cordiale* to form the Triple Entente, in which each member agreed to co-operate politically. Other bilateral treaties also came into play in the summer of 1914, bringing the tower of accords tumbling down.

When Austria-Hungary declared war on Serbia on July 28, Russia met the obligations of a treaty with Serbia by mobilizing its army. On August 1, Germany, having agreed to come to Austria-Hungary's aid, declared war on Russia. When France also ordered mobilization, Germany declared war on her. Italy, arguing that Germany was fighting an offensive (not defensive) war against France, opted for neutrality – until 1916, when it joined the Entente powers. Britain's proposals to prevent war failed; it was drawn into the fight by a moral obligation to France and Russia and by a seventy-five-year-old pact to protect Belgium.

On August 2, Germany issued an ultimatum to Belgium: let us pass through your country to reach France or we'll go to war with you. The Belgians refused. On August 4, Britain gave its own ultimatum to Germany: get out of Belgium or else. When the midnight deadline expired with no reply from Germany, Britain was at war. Her self-governing colonies – Australia, India, New Zealand, the Union of South Africa, and Canada – were also thus at war. Historian Donald Creighton wrote that "Canada's mind was made up at once. She was not merely legally at war; she was morally at war as well; and the great majority of Canadians felt an urgent need of participation in the approaching struggle and a deep sense of responsibility in its outcome."

Canada had little of practical value to offer. The country had no navy, an army of only three thousand men (the Permanent Force), and a militia of about sixty thousand trained citizen soldiers. It also had a mixed asset in Colonel Sam Hughes, whom the governor general, Lord Connaught, called "a conceited lunatic." The minister of militia and defence had been warning for years about a coming war with Germany and had got the federal government to increase spending for defence (to $11 million in 1914). That summer he had organized training manoeuvres for ten thousand militiamen at Petawawa, Ontario.

A day after the war began, Hughes announced that Canada would send a force of 25,000. He directed 226 militia units to prepare lists of men willing to serve, but the enthusiasm of volunteers outran his planning. Masses of men leapt onto trains and headed to Valcartier, north of Quebec City, where Hughes had ordered a camp constructed on undeveloped land. For six weeks, some 35,000 men were put on oath, sheltered, fed, clothed, medically tested, and minimally trained while Hughes issued orders and counterorders about how the 1st Canadian Division was to be organized. In the matter of outfitting the troops, Hughes's decisions were essentially bad: he ordered 48,000 made-in-Canada boots (some of which would last only ten days in wet conditions in England). He bought 25,000 useless entrenching shovels, at a cost of $33,750. And he insisted that the troops carry the Canadian Ross rifle which, with only five rounds in its magazine and a tendency to jam, was responsible for many deaths in battle until it was scrapped in 1916. (Ever practical, Canadian soldiers tossed the Ross away when a Lee-Enfield rifle could be snatched from the hands of a dead tommy. One Canadian officer, however, ordered punishment for those found with Lee-Enfields.)

Despite Hughes's constant rejigging, a division was organized. It had four brigades, each with four battalions of one thousand men (there was also a seventeenth provisional infantry battalion). As well, there were companies of engineers and signallers, a medical corps, a small postal service, a company of cyclists, and two cavalry regiments. In this first Canadian Contingent, which was ready to sail two months after war began, two thirds of the 32,000 men had been born in Britain, though two thirds of the officers were Canadians.

The overall command of the Canadian troops was held in turn by three generals. Sir Edwin Alderson, a British officer with the Canadians during the Boer War, commanded the 1st Division and the Canadian Corps, formed in September 1915 when the 2nd Division arrived in France. Likely because he challenged Sam Hughes over the Ross rifle (he issued a questionnaire to his officers, one of whom replied that it was murder to send men into war with that gun), Alderson was replaced in May 1916 by the aristocratic Lieutenant General Julian Byng, whom King Edward VII had nicknamed "Bungo." Finally, in June 1917, the corps acquired a Canadian-born leader – Lieutenant General Arthur Currie, a rotund real-estate agent from Victoria, British Columbia, and a painstaking, unflappable master tactician. Unlike Field Marshall Douglas Haig, commander in chief of the British armies, who sacrificed thousands of lives for inconsequential gains on the ground, Currie hated unnecessary casualties. Despite his planning and precautions, Canadians died in numbers we can barely comprehend.

The Canadian Corps made itself into one of the war's most successful fighting units. Its policy of promoting officers from the ranks created a military meritocracy in which the most able (rather than the bluest-bloods, as in the British army) were in command. Led by men who respected their intelligence and ingenuity, Canadian soldiers – initially thought incompetent and unruly – earned a reputation for achieving the impossible on the battlefield.

MEN, HORSES, BICYCLES

A lieutenant in the 36th (Peel) Regiment before the war began, **Alexander T. Thomson** *of Port Credit, Ontario, was among the eager volunteers who reported for training at Valcartier in Quebec. Late in September 1914, Thomson observed the First Canadian Contingent assemble on the St. Lawrence River near Quebec City: five cruisers and four battleships escorted thirty-two merchant transports carrying 1,547 officers, 29,070 men, 100 nurses, 7,679 horses, 70 guns, 110 motor vehicles, 705 horsed vehicles, and 82 bicycles. The contingent sailed on October 3 and the following day passed near St. John's, Newfoundland, where it was joined by the SS Florizel with the first five hundred volunteers of the Newfoundland Regiment aboard. Thomson wrote to his brother.*

Sept 30th/ 1914

Dear Doug

I'm on the steamer "Scandinavian" belonging to the "Allan Line", we are anchored in the middle of the St Lawrence River about a half mile up the river from Quebec, there are two lines of steamers up the river and as each boat gets loaded they at once pull out from shore in a line. I was just up on the bridge and I can see fifteen anchored all loaded and the ones waiting to be loaded are below Quebec altogether there will be about twenty or twenty-five, there may be some more loaded around the bend in the river then when they all get loaded, they will pull out together.

About ten miles down the river the cruisers and gunboats are waiting to convoy us over. There are six cruisers and two gunboats so I'm told. A sailor was telling me there are two tramp steamers up river waiting to get under the protection of the convoy, to get across the ocean. I think it will be a great sight when we get started.

I can read the names of some of the steamers there is the Allan lines "Scotion" [sic] and the "Corinthian" and the Cunard liners "Alaunia" and "Adania" and I understand there are the "Royal George" the "Megantic" and the "Zealand" and the "King George" [there was no transport so named], I can't remember the rest, the scenery is great from here.

I have been wondering whether they are preparing a second contingent or not. I'm with G. Co. 10th Battalion until I get into England anyway. I have taken stock of the men in our company through Attestation papers and I find the youngest man in G.Co. is 21 years past and then the next youngest is 22 years past but the majority are over 30 years old, and in selecting their companies the old war dogs passed over the young boys, they said they wouldn't stand the hardship.

We haven't any idea where we are going.

We have the 10th Battalion number about 1140 men and what is called "One General Hospital" consisting of about 150 sergeants and privates and 40 doctors, they act as a base hospital.

That totals about 1400 all told, we are not crowded because the Col of the 103rd Col Rattray got the job of ass. director of transport and he gave us a boat that was decent and would just accommodate our one battalion so we wouldn't get mixed up.

We may be anchored here a few days yet and then perhaps two weeks to cross because we have to go just as fast as the slowest steamer and then more delay for disembarking, but that doesn't matter we are fed like kings and have good cabins.

You know it is about 600 miles from here down the mouth of the river, take a map and look it up.

I will write you when I land if I ever do the time seems to go so that I'll be away from home six months before long.

Alex

AND A SPY

The First Contingent crossed the Atlantic without mishap, but not without incident, as 26-year-old **Chattan Stephens,** *a lieutenant in the Royal Highlanders of Canada who sailed on the* Alaunia, *reported to his wife, Hazel, in Montreal.*

Salisbury Plain, Wilts.
Saturday Oct 17th/14

Dearest Hazel

. . . We arrived near the Coast of England late on the 13th Oct and were heading for Southampton. We received orders from British scout cruisers to immediately proceed to Plymouth, which was nearer to us than Southampton, and where we arrived the morning of the 14th. The reason for this change, which we found out later, was that German submarines were said to have been seen in the Channel. We were the first to enter the Harbour where we were joined all through the day and night by the remainder of our fleet . . .

Oct 27th/14
Salisbury Plain

. . . By the way, we caught a German Spy in my company and had him in irons for a week on board ship. On our arrival at Plymouth Ry[,] Kent and myself had the pleasure of turning him over to the Military Authorities. The whole episode was quite thrilling as we left him at liberty on the ship for some time after our discovery having him shadowed all the time. He had a cipher message on him which, when translated (it took some work) showed an appointment in London with a German and some details which I can't tell you . . .

your own
Chat

After Hazel travelled to England in 1914 with their daughter, Chattan Stephens's mother and the young couple's twenty-month-old son set out to join them. They were among those who died on the torpedoed Lusitania (see page 90). After only a few weeks at the front line in 1915, Chattan Stephens caught trench fever – an infection transmitted by body lice – which damaged his heart. He died in Canada in the influenza epidemic in 1918.

PASTURES GREEN

When the First Contingent ships dropped anchor, Winston Churchill, first lord of the admiralty, cabled Ottawa: "Canada sends her aid at a timely moment." The people of Plymouth were more effusive. As the soldiers marched to the railway station, young women marched alongside, men shook their hands, and the mob cheered. **Barlow Whiteside**, *eldest son of a clergyman, left his medical studies at McGill University in Montreal to sign up with Canada's No. 5 Field Ambulance Corps. He wrote to* The Toronto Standard *from the Salisbury Plain training ground.*

> Salisbury No. 1. General Hospital,
> 1st. Can. Contingent
> Dec. 13, 1914

Sir:

I thought it might be interesting to some of the fellows to know something about the life we are living, the experiences we are having and the contingencies we are meeting here on Salisbury Plains. As this is my birthday [his twenty-third] and I have an hour off from duty (the two facts have no connection); also as I received today the first dailies I have seen this year, reading them from first column to last, I thought there would be no fitter time or better opportunity to do it.

As you know, we left Canada, October first, I have seen the picture of our departure in the 'Standard' and it was a very wonderful and creditable one indeed – especially so, as the ships sailed out from Quebec three and four at a time, collected in Gaspe Bay and sailed out late in the evening . . . we did not sight land till the fifteenth. Then the grand old hills of England slowly crept within our ken . . .

We remained on board ship off Devonport for five days, when we disembarked and marched through the town listening to the rolling cheers and peons [paeans] of praise, grasping the hands of innumerable young ladies, exchanging addresses and handing over quarters, dimes and nickels, button badges and maple leafs till our pockets and uniforms were empty and stripped. Arrived at the station, we awaited the train, some young ladies in the meantime very kindly distributing cigarettes and chocolates – at 3d. per. Bye and bye a little, one-horse engine hove in sight, drawing in its train a system of most amazingly got-up coaches or "kerridges", as they are called here . . .

We got out at a station of which I forget and never knew the name [it was Patney], and marched eight miles to our camp on Salisbury Plain. It was our first march in England and was interesting and inspiring in the extreme. We passed churches built ages ago, when England was young and thought and recked nothing of Kaisers and militarism, their walls covered with ivy, green, thick and beautiful, slowly but surely crumbling their granite masonry into dust; houses as old as the churches and covered with the same historic ivy, under trees that have seen the coming of that other Kaiser, William the Conqueror, green, fresh and ivy-covered, past hedges as old as the trees, thick and impenetrable as a stone wall; lawns as fine and soft as Brussels carpet, that have been mown and rolled and rolled and mown for centuries; up hills as old and unchangeable as England; down vales, beautiful and rich with everlasting verdure, peaceful and bespeaking only of calmness and joy and rest – not the faintest sign anywhere of the titanic life and death struggle going on at this very moment two hundred miles away. At least that must have been the kind of country we passed through. Travelers, writers, historians, all who have passed through England in the daytime, say it is everywhere like that; everywhere the churches and houses and trees and hedges are old and ivy-grown and historic; everywhere the hills and vales are beautiful and everlasting and everywhere everything is peaceful and bespeaks only of calmness and joy and rest. But we boarded the train at ten p.m. and we saw nothing of the route we traversed and were too tired to take notice had we been able to . . .

We are all very busy – called at six in the morning, to go to sleep again at six-thirty; called again at six thirty nine, to be once more called again just as we are dozing off again. This keeps up til seven and the covers are pulled off and we go down to breakfast of bread, bacon, cheese, jam. At seven-thirty we go on continuous duty till seven-thirty at night. Dinner consists of stew, bread, tea, potatoes, cheese and jam, while for supper, we have tea, bread, cheese and jam. There are four McGill fellows in the corps, Sgt. F.W. Saunders from dentistry, W. Thistle, G.G. Miller, and myself. At the next mock parliament we intend to bring in a bill for the abolition of the cheese and jam industries in all countries, doubtless seconded by the McGill Regiment of the second contingent. We are probably going to the front sometime, but have given up guessing when.

Barlow Whiteside

IMPROMPTU ACCORD

The Canadians were spared the first mass slaughters of the war; there were more than 1.6 million casualties on both sides before Christmas 1914. **Lieutenant Arthur Stratford**, *one of five Brantford, Ontario, brothers who served with the 1st Bedfords of the British Expeditionary Force, wrote to his sister, Mayden, about the Christmas Day truce.*

December 26th. 1914

My darling Mayd,

. . . Well Mayd I spent Christmas eve and Christmas day in the trenches. We were relieved last night. It was very funny in the trenches yesterday, there was hardly a shot fired. About noon one of the Germans, they can nearly all speak English, shouted over "Merry Christmas" of course we shouted back "Merry Christmas". "Come over here" one of them called. "You come over here" we answered. "We'll come half way if you come the other half" replied the German. So a couple of our men stood up in the trench and the Germans did the same. Pretty soon we were scrambling over our trenches towards one another, without rifles of course, and we met half way. Both sides were a little shy at first but we soon warmed up and shook hands and laughed and joked. Soon one of them said "you sing us a song and we'll sing you one". So we gave them "Tipperary" which they enjoyed very much. They sang us a couple of songs, I don't know what they were but they sounded all right. The Germans told our men frankly that they didn't mind charging the French, but they charged our lines with much less gusto. The men had a huge time with the Germans and all were mighty sorry when dusk began to fall and we thought it time to get back to our lines . . .

We had great fires in the trenches and we spent the remainder of the evening singing until we were relieved. The Germans told us they were very fed up with the war and would be mighty glad when it was over . . .

Write, my love, my rose of the world.
Your loving brother,
Arthur Stratford.

Later, such fraternizing was prohibited. In a letter to his children, **Lance Corporal George D'All** *described Christmas Day 1915 in a trench thirty metres from the Germans: "We had strict orders to hold no parley with the enemy should he make any advances, but in spite of this warning, when Fritz called over 'Merry Christmas Canadians' our sentries bobbed up their heads and returned the compliment. In a few minutes there was a whole bunch looking over the parapets from both sides, and one old fellow with a big whisker waved a box of cigars at us and invited us over. A sargeant [sic], however, put a stop to it by opening fire and hitting two of their men, and when they returned it, one of our lads was shot through the head." Arthur Stratford went with the Bedfords to Egypt and transferred to the King's African Rifles. He was serving in Nyasaland when the war ended.*

FIERY BAPTISM

The Princess Patricia's Canadian Light Infantry (PPCLI) was financed by Montreal millionaire Hamilton Gault and named for the daughter of the Duke of Connaught, Canada's governor general. The regiment arrived in France on December 21, 1914, as part of the British 27th Division. In February, from the front line near St. Eloi, south of Ypres, the PPCLI introduced the practice of raiding German trenches and were the first Canadian regiment to engage the enemy. **Captain Agar Adamson** *was a forty-eight-year-old veteran of the Boer War when he joined the PPCLI in 1914. His wealthy wife, Mabel, came to live in England, where she could be with him when he was on leave. From there, she organized a relief project for Belgian civilians and met her husband's requests for replacement eyeglasses, canned oysters, and rubber gloves to wear in the wet trenches. She was unable, however, to obtain machine guns from the United States, as he once asked. Adamson wrote her from regiment headquarters, the Belgian town of Dickebusch (location B), southwest of Ypres.*

B

3-3-15

My dear Mabel,

It is beyond my powers to describe what has happened in the last 4 days, but I know if I read what I am going to write, I doubt if I would be able to believe it was not written by a liar or the ravings of a maniac.

In my trench I lost 6 killed, 21 wounded, the regiment lost 17 killed, 46 wounded. Poor Colquhoun who went out alone in the dark to place his snipers, never came back. The K.R.R. [King's Royal Regiment] report having found him in the German sap in front of trenches with 6 bullets in his head. Crabb another officer who led the charge had 3 fingers shot off. Major Ward shot through the head is still alive but paralized down one side. Major Gault who tried to rescue a wounded man after the stretcher bearers had had to desert, went out with another man to rescue him in broad daylight, which they succeeded in doing, but Gault was badly hit in the wrist, he still carried on for 24 hours until the C.O. insisted upon his going back to England for treatment. As Keenan said, complications were sure to set in if he did not get absolute rest and quiet, it almost took force to get him to go. He has played the game magnificently, night and day, crawling from trench to trench and cheering up the men . . .

At the present moment, the Germans have all the best of it, their bomb and mortar throwing is perfect, also their flares and we are infants at it. Their trenches are beautifully made, they have men that do nothing else, and they are drained and all communicate with each other. Their sniping is organized, the snipers having fixed rifles with telescopic sights firing from about 300 yards. Their particular game is to infalaide [enfilade: to shoot along a line from one end to the other] trenches. They fire all day picking up certain points where they know the men will be working at night, mending old or making new entrenchments and at night keep up a steady fire about every 30 seconds, generally from both sides of the advance trenches and from the front of the back trenches . . .

The suffering of the men is very great after they came out of the trenches; their feet and hands all swelled and a stiffening of their joints set in. They rub each other to get the circulation and then a curious tickling sensation sets in and lasts about 24 hours. During this time the men are unfit for any kind of duty. That is why we can only stand a 48 hour go and I doubt if 24 would not be wiser . . .

Goodbye old girl. I wont let them take you away from me if I can help it, unless I feel it has to be.

Ever and always your
Agar

B
4-3-15

My dear Mabel,

. . . I have six most difficult letters to write to relatives of men shot the day we were bombarded in the trenches. Cameron and I have written a report on Gault's action in bringing the wounded man which I hope will get him the V.C. [Victoria Cross] as he certainly deserves it. He thoroughly realized what certain 1000 to 1 chance he was taking of certain death and did it. I thought of doing it myself, but was not man or mad enough to attempt it, so sure did I feel that it was certain death, that I almost decided to shoot Gault in the leg to prevent his attempting it, even this I had not the decision to do, although I am certain a man like Buller or Ward would have done without a moment's hesitation. I suppose it is a case of training, but I think it is really more than that, it is something very hard to fathom. What really makes a real man. The best men I have known always openly say they are cowards and hate the situation they find themselves in and really are afraid, perhaps it is partly their education which helps them to realize the danger, but there is a great deal in being one of a long line of soldiers in a family, although this only partly accounts for it, for men who never saw a soldier and for generations have led useless lives, have behaved, in a similar manner when put against it out here, including some French Canadians I had with me during my last 24 hours. It must be a matter as difficult as the definition and reason for the production of a real genius.

The whole regiment was out all last night under subalterns working under the instructions of the R.E. building new trenches . . .

They are trying to build trenches like the Germans and have German prisoners to coach them. When they are completed we are going to retire the whole line back 500 yds or more as the present trenches are only death traps and might have been built by first year boy scouts. They will have pumps, drainage, proper loop holes, observing posts, out of which you can see without being seen and also shoot. They are to be connected with each other and connecting trenches built to connect with support trenches. All this should have been done long ago . . .

I found the other day that opium was of great effect in relieving wounded men and putting them to sleep until night comes. Send me a few capsules. One poor chap never woke, but I think he would have died anyway and it made it easier. The ones they use are very similar to the iodine capsules you gave me which by the bye, Hance [Agar's servant] has thrown away as they were so wet and he feared the cotton wool top might be infected by the awful graveyard water they had been soaked in. Keenan is giving me another lot, even

smaller. It is very difficult in dressing a wounded man in a bombarded trench, his clothes are very tight owing to being soaked. For
instance, a man shot only with one bullet in the shoulder. You cannot
take off his fur coat, his serge, his shirt and vest to get at him. It is
too painful and really quite impossible, so you cut if off with a knife
and this is most difficult and few men have really sharp razor blades
or knives which are required. The only thing to do is to give him
opium and then try and pour two iodine capsules over the place
which is often impossible to see as you cannot use a light; the moon
helped. You then use safety pins (which all men carry) to fashion
together part of his cut clothing . . . I think every trench should have
a medical student and many lives might be saved . . .

Goodnight dear old girl,

Agar

GASSED AT YPRES

*In February 1915 the three brigades of the 1st Canadian Division
went to France and entered the front line trenches at Armentières. In
April the division moved north in preparation for the Second Battle
of Ypres. The ancient, moated Belgian city was still in Allied hands
but sat in an area fourteen kilometres wide and six kilometres deep,
surrounded on three sides by the Germans. This was the infamous
salient, "the world's worst wound," in the words of poet Siegfried
Sassoon. Although the salient had no strategic value, the British and
French were determined to hang on to it. They had fought there in
late 1914, the First Battle of Ypres, and then hunkered down in
trenches over the winter, enduring the enemy's pinpoint sniping and
artillery fire. The 1915 battle began on April 22 with the usual bombardment but took a wicked twist at 5 p.m., when for the first time
in the war the Germans released poison gas. More than 5,700 cylin-
ders of chlorine were opened into a light wind that carried a cloud of
green vapour towards French colonial troops positioned north of the
Canadians. Half-suffocated, eyes streaming, the surviving French fled,*

*opening a gap in their line through which German infantry poured. The Canadians were sent in to plug the gap. **Brigadier General Sir Richard Ernest William Turner,** a Victoria Cross veteran of the South African War, commanded the 3rd Canadian Brigade. He wrote to his wife, quoting the British general, Horace Smith-Dorrien, and giving his opinion of General Sir Edwin Alderson, the British officer who had just taken over the command of the Canadian Division.*

3 May 1915

My Darling Hetty

I have not had any letters for sometime, and I fear letters were lost, as part of our mail in Ypres was blown up.

The troops have all had a heavy strain put upon them, and our losses have been large. It will be a long time before brigades will be found to equal our former Canadian Brigades. My highlanders died at their posts, and I knew before the end came that they could not withdraw, as it was absolutely necessary to delay the enemy as long as possible. My men have been continously [*sic*] under fire now since the 18th April, but if everything goes well they are to be withdrawn at 2.15 tomorrow morning . . .

It is hard to explain all that happened. When the French fell back on my left it uncovered my flank for 5000 yards, and with a front of 2300 yards, made my Bde [brigade] responsible for 7300 yards frontage. At 6.30 pm on the 22nd, I really thought all was lost. The enemy came sweeping down round our rear, and all that I had left were our servants, the Engineer Company, and about 50 of my grenade co. All the rest had been sent forward to fill the gap.

The engagement was mine until the 26th morning, when General Hull relieved me with his brigade.

8 May 1915

We have had a heavy toll to pay, but I think Canada during those days absolutely saved the situation. Things happened to make matters worse that I dare not write about . . .

We left Ypres on the night of 4th May; it was an eventful time. The following <u>must</u> <u>be</u> <u>kept</u> <u>to</u> <u>the</u> <u>family</u> <u>only</u>. General Alderson may get all the credit but during those hard days 22, 23, 24 April, we never saw him or his Staff. I fancy it was too hot for them. General S-D [Smith-Dorrien] called the day before yesterday, almost as soon as we had arrived here, and he said to me "I thank you for what you and your gallant men have done. You have saved Ypres and all our Army from a terrible disaster."

When part of my troops asked when they would be permitted to fall back, owing to the enemy's heavy fire, I had to answer to them that there was no falling back. Later Canada will know what a debt of honour is due to the brave souls that laid down their lives in the Ypres Salient. I have gathered accounts from different sources, the thinking of them brings tears to my eyes for my gallant lads, officers and men . . .

Goodbye my darling for a day, love to my bairns, and dearest love to You my dearie.

from your hubby Ernest

Briefly in command of the Canadian Corps in 1916, Brigadier General Turner was embroiled in controversy over the Canadians' failure at St.-Eloi in the spring of 1916 and was removed from command. He oversaw Canadian troop training in England and later became chief of the general staff at Canadian Military Headquarters in London.

NERVE-RACKED RANKS

Just before midnight on April 22, 1915, following the first gas attack, the 10th and 16th Canadian Battalions were ordered to retake a large copse of trees, Kitcheners Wood, which had fallen to the enemy. (The wood – not named for Lord Kitchener – had been a safe place for French unit cooks, who called it Bois des Cuisiniers.) **Captain John Campbell Matheson,** *an accountant in the Medicine Hat branch of* *the Canadian Bank of Commerce when he enlisted in August 1914, described the attack.*

[May 10, 1915]

To begin with I might say that I have experienced, in no small measure either, that war is 'hell.' You have no doubt read many detailed accounts of the recent fierce fighting in which the Contingent has played a very prominent part. I am proud to say that the trusty old 10th Battalion delivered the goods, too, in true historical fashion. I am not permitted to say much on account of the severe censorship. However, the following is a brief account of the most desperate action we took the initiative in. On the afternoon of 22nd April we were hurriedly called out. We were told that the enemy through the use of poisonous gases, etc., had broken through the line held by the French and that we were to go out as supports only. However, after marching out about four miles we halted and lay down awaiting further orders. About 10.30 word came along that the 10th Battalion were commanded to take a line of trenches, also a wood [Kitcheners Wood] in rear, at all costs. The whole thing was to be done in silence at the point of the bayonet. About 11.30 p.m. the Battalion was formed up in two lines, one in rear of the other, and the 16th Battalion was formed up in the same way about thirty yards in rear of us. Then came the order to advance. Believe me there was some excitement in the ranks. We didn't seem to realize what we were up against. However, we kept on going. When we got within a hundred yards of the trench the 'Huns' opened fire on us. The wood seemed to be literally lined with machine guns, and they played these guns on us with terrible effect. Our men were dropping thick and fast. However, those remaining sailed right ahead and cleared the wood with a vengeance. A few 'Huns' were taken prisoners, but damned few. We had enough to do to take care of ourselves and our own wounded to bother about prisoners. Our Battalion was sadly cut up by the time we got to the far side of the wood, so badly in fact that on account of day breaking and the small muster we were ordered back to hold a trench alongside of the wood. The consequence was that the wounded and dying and killed were left in the wood. All day long we had to stick to our posts in case of a counter attack, and believe me it was more nerve-racking than the bayonet charge itself, as all around us were the dead and wounded. All day we stood and all through the night, and at daybreak on Saturday the 10th Battalion were ordered out of the trench to reinforce the 8th Battalion, who were about four miles away on our left and were being terribly pressed by the enemy. 190 men represented our Battalion as reinforcements. Of course there were a few more men scattered elsewhere that we couldn't get in touch with. From then on we were continually under fire day and night until the Wednesday morning at daybreak when we were relieved, but we still had to hold ourselves in readiness in reserve trenches. We lost a lot of men right there too.

It is impossible for me to adequately describe the scene or the fierce fire, both of rifle and heavy shells and bombs. Out of twenty-three days our Battalion was twenty days in the trenches, and for the five days of the fiercest fighting we were without sleep altogether and had practically no food or water. How I have ever come through is a mystery to me. With the exception of being hit by a rifle bullet on the cheek and a piece of shrapnel in the side, I am still fit. I got hit on the cheek in the charge and the other I received on Saturday, but I never left the field. I eventually got fixed up when I got back to Battalion headquarters by our own doctor, who, poor devil, was hit five days ago and has since died of wounds. I have bullet holes in my hat, equipment and clothes, but evidently I am slated to do some more evil in this world yet. I have seen two or three accounts in the papers, and in each case it says that the 16th Battalion led the charge. This is wrong, all honour to the 16th Battalion, but the 10th Battalion led and drove home the charge with the gallant support of the 16th Battalion.

I was a proud boy when the Brigadier-General in addressing the remaining few of the Battalion said that the 10th Battalion were the very first of all the Canadian forces to actually encounter the ruthless foe, and he was glad to say with terrifying effect.

J. C. Matheson

On April 24 the Germans again released gas, immobilizing the 8th and 15th Canadian Battalions and breaking their defensive line. Fifteen hundred Canadians were captured, the largest number taken at one time during the war. Tear gas, chlorine, the more lethal phosgene, and, worst of all, the persistent mustard gas would be wielded by both sides for the rest of the war, killing and maiming more than a million men (and incidentally the rats that infested the trenches). Wearing filter respirators, the troops managed to deal with these attacks most of the time. Captain Matheson was awarded the Military Cross and demobilized in September 1919.

PRELUDE: FLANDERS FIELDS

Dr. John McCrae, a 1900 graduate of McGill University's School of Medicine, had served in the South African War and was a surgeon with the 1st Field Artillery Brigade in the Great War. During the Second Battle of Ypres, on May 2, 1915, he said the committal service for a friend and former student, Lieutenant Alexis Helmer of Ottawa. The following day, he took a break from operating on the wounded and, sitting on the back of an ambulance near the dressing station, composed "In Flanders Fields." Punch magazine published the poem, anonymously, that December. McCrae's journal described the bombardments, intermittent shellings, and a German attack preceded by gas clouds, but a letter to his mother was less graphic.

Belgium, 1 May, 1915

My dearest Mater:
When things quiet down I hope to give you an extended account of our sojourn in this Hades – now the ninth day in which we have stuck to this ridge. And I assure you it has been a "stick" and the batteries have fought with a steadiness that is beyond all praise. If I could say what our casualties in men, guns and horses had been you would see at a glance that it has been a hot corner, but there can be no doubt that we have given better than we got for the German casualties

from this front have been largely from artillery, except for the Fr. attacks of yesterday and the day before, when they advanced appreciably to our left. The front, however, just here remains as it was, and the artillery fire is very heavy, I think as heavy here as on any part of the line with the exception of certain cross roads which are, of course, the particular object of the artillery fire. The first four days the anxiety was terribly wearing for we did not know at what minute the reputed so many army corps of the Germans would come for us. We lie out in support of the French troops entirely and as a matter of fact [are] working with them. Since that time evidently great reinforcements have come in and now we have a most formidable force of artillery to bear on them. We came in at daylight on Friday morning a week ago, and are here yet. Personally I shall be very glad when we can get cleared out of this, but duty says "sit right there!" Fortunately, the weather has been good, and the days are hot and summerlike. Yesterday in the pass of bad shells I got a whiff of a hedgerow in bloom and it was a relief, I assure you. The blackbirds perch in the trees above our heads, many of the trees are cut off by shells, and twitter away as if there was nothing to worry about. Bonfire is still well. The morning we came in a horse was killed by a shell about 5 yards from him. I do hope the poor old chap gets through all right.

The story will be interesting to tell if I get a chance to write it, but really life is too unsettled to sit down to details. So my best love to the whole family.

Yours,

"Jack".

Lieutenant Colonel McCrae died of pneumonia on January 28, 1918, at the age of forty-five, still on active service.

CLOSE SHAVE

The Second Battle of Ypres lasted until May 25, 1915. **Corporal Gordon Patrick**, *from Edmonton, father of two young sons, wrote to his sister.*

France May 29th 1915

Dear Sister:

A few lines to say that I am well and hope you are the same I am sitting in the trench while I am writing this we have been in them for over a week now that is we are in the third line trenches act as reserves for the rest of our Battn which is in the firing line or front trench in any trench we are under shell fire most of the time but dont get much rifle fire but the snipers are trying for us all the time I am not allowed to tell you what part of the Battle line we are at but there has been some hard fighting done here this last week and the Canadian boys are going fine their fighting is magnificent the papers in England can not praise them enough and they certainly saved the situation at Ypres one night our artilary started to bombard the German trenches and done so for half an hour then our side made a charge and took two line of trenches they started at 6h Pm and were in the first German trench in 15 minutes we were watching them do it as we were about half a mile back and it was some sight the earth was trembling with the shock of the shells bursting and the roar of the cannon and the shells going screeching through the air is like rockets it is like a 4th of July celebration but you dont enjoy it in the same spirit for here every shell means death to some one or a few of them does so and at night it is just a continuous spurt of flame from bursting shells and the cannons you can't hear yourself think sometimes but I think that it will soon be over this has been a pretty country but nothing except a mass of ruins as the Huns shell every town and farm in reach of their guns and dont leave a building standing and it will take many years to repair the damage done as the fields are full of trenches and holes dug by the shells bursting some are deep enough to put a good sized house in I had rather a close shave with one the other night when I had charge of a sentry post I was standing at about 3h am with two of the sentrys talking when a shell drop[p]ed and burst 15 feet from us we were not hit but it threw a lot of dirt over us one of the men has the jumps ever since when he hears a shell then another night we were taking rations into the firing line when the Germans seen us and opened fire with shrapnel shells at short range and wounded 7 men out of 25 it is a wonder that they did not get us all of course every[thing] is not serious here we have a little pleasure once in a while if you ever came into our trench you would think we were [miles?] from the Battle line we will be sitting around talking and there will be a whise bang and every one dives for the [dugout?] . . . if we did not laugh and joke it would drive us crazy but why worry . . .

well I must close so by by

with love to all
Corpl G Patrick No 18675
No 2 [Company]
lst Batt 1st Brigade
Canadians on active service France

A year later, when Patrick died after the botched fighting at St.-Eloi craters, Lieutenant William Cooke wrote to Patrick's young sons, "Masters W.A. & H.S. Patrick," to commiserate with them over "the irreparable loss of your very brave father" – "a man honoured and beloved by his comrades." In the Second Battle of Ypres the 1st Canadian Division – fighting with the badly flawed Ross rifle – suffered 6,036 casualties (2,000 dead). But the Canadians had begun to build their reputation as the Allied forces' most impressive shock troops.

PARENTS' BRAVERY

Ernest C. Cowper was aboard the Lusitania *when the British ship sailed from New York on May 1, 1915.* Jack Canuck, *for which Cowper was on assignment, was a weekly review for Canadian soldiers published in Toronto by Percy Rogers, who was also a passenger. When the* Lusitania *was hit on May 7, she was south of Queenstown, Ireland. Back in Canada, Cowper wrote to the son of Elbert Hubbard II, an American writer of philosophical texts.*

"The Province" Office
Vancouver, B.C.
March 12, 1916

Dear Mr. Hubbard:

I should have written what I have written to you a long while ago –
but I don't know, it seems as if the Lusitania left its seal on every one
who was in it, and even now, almost a year later, I am afraid all the
survivors are thinking more seriously of May 7, than they are of their
business or the other things they should attend to. I know that is the
case with me.

If you have been informed that there was a man on board who
was in the company of your father and Mrs. Hubbard on many occasions, I guess they have me in mind, for we really did spend a lot of
time together – so much so that he took to calling me "Jack." I don't
know why, unless it was that I was then going on an assignment for
the paper called Jack Canuck . . .

I did not see [Mr. Hubbard] again until the next day, just a little
before the torpedo hit us. I then called the attention of himself and
Mrs. Hubbard to the extra watch which had been put on for submarines, and walked them forward to where two men were right at
the stern with glasses. Two were on each side of the navigating-bridge,
and three were in the crow's-nest, which is half way up the foremast.

He expressed surprise at this, for he was sure a submarine would
never make any effort to torpedo a ship filled with women, children
and non-combatants.

He mentioned the fact that there were no guns on board, and
that there was no place to put them. I agreed that there were no guns,
but pointed out that there were places to put them, and walked both
round to the places which were built with the vessel for the mount-
ing of guns if required . . .

We then parted to go to our cabins before taking lunch. On
finishing mine I went to the top deck, and was smoking with Rogers
[Percy Rogers, publisher of Jack Canuck] when I saw the torpedo
coming toward us.

We both sought the shelter of the companionway until after the explosion, when I saw another coming and again took shelter. After the second one we emerged, for the vessel took a terrible list right away.

I can not say specifically where your father and Mrs. Hubbard were when the torpedoes hit, but I can tell you just what happened after that. They emerged from their room, which was on the port side of the vessel, and came on to the boat-deck.

Neither appeared perturbed in the least. Your father and Mrs. Hubbard linked arms – the fashion in which they always walked the deck – and stood apparently wondering what to do. I passed him with a baby which I was taking to a lifeboat when he said, "Well, Jack, they have got us. They are a damn sight worse than I ever thought they were."

They did not move very far away from where they originally stood. As I moved to the other side of the ship, in preparation for a jump when the right moment came, I called to him, "What are you going to do?" and he just shook his head, while Mrs. Hubbard smiled and said, "There does not seem to be anything to do."

The expression seemed to produce action on the part of your father, for then he did one of the most dramatic things I ever saw done. He simply turned with Mrs. Hubbard and entered a room on the top deck, the door of which was open, and closed it behind him. It was apparent that his idea was that they should die together, and not risk being parted on going into the water . . .

There was a preponderance of women and children on board. This fact is accounted for owing to the number of wives and children of men belonging to the Canadian contingents (which were almost wholly composed of Old-Country men) who were going to England, where they could live cheaper and be near to the hospitals where their dear ones would be taken in case of injury.

Some of the horrors of the disaster can never be committed to print. I can tell you this: There were a surprisingly large number of women on board who were in advanced stages of pregnancy –

presumably English women who were going to their parents for the birth of their children.

I saw the corpses of four of these in the mortuary at Queenstown, and they had been delivered of their infants in the water, precipitated labor owing to shock being the cause. But can you in your mind conjure such a picture!

Because Great Britain is at war, there should be stretched out on the cold flagstones of the mortuary at Queenstown the bodies of four women in a condition which even animals respect, and this for the furtherance of the Kultur which Emperor William would impose on Europe, and America next, I suppose, were he not stopped (and he is stopped) . . .

Yours very faithfully,
Ernest C. Cowper

The Lusitania *sank in about twenty minutes. The exact number on board is not certain, but it is estimated that 1,201 people (123 Americans) perished and 764 survived. The incident influenced public opinion in the United States in favour of declaring war on Germany, which it did on April 6, 1917.*

DREADNOUGHT RN

More than 2,500 Canadian nurses went overseas, organized into a unit of the Canadian Expeditionary Force and enlisted as officers under their matron-in-chief, Margaret McDonald, the first woman in the British Empire to hold the rank of major. Five days after the Germans sank the Lusitania, *thirty-seven-year-old* **Nursing Sister Sophie Hoerner** *of Montreal described the atmosphere aboard the* Metagama, *which was carrying two thousand Canadian soldiers and 104 nurses. Later she wrote about her work at No. 1 Canadian General Hospital, near Le Touquet in France.*

Steamship Metagama,
May 12, 1915

Dearest Mollie:

Nearly a week since I left home. The time goes very quickly. Something doing every minute. Inspection every morning at ten. We have to have our buttons shining and our boots brushed. Drill at eleven by the Sergeant-Major. He wears a crown on his arm and a red cross. This morning we had inspection with our life preservers on, each girl given her post, and when the bell rings we are given five minutes to get there. Each doctor (he is an officer, too) takes charge of eighteen nurses and is responsible for them in case of accident. To-night all lights are blanketed and we sleep in the lounge room with our clothes on, all ready in case we are called, the officers and their men on deck. I tell you it is thrilling. I am having all sorts of thrills and bubbles inside me. Reported to-day that a spy was arrested in the 21st. Don't know on what grounds or whether it is true. I was sea-sick Sunday. It was hard for I was on duty with a nice boy, only nineteen, operated on for appendicitis; very bad case, gangrenous. He had an attack before he left, but was afraid to say anything for fear he would not be able to go. I said to him, "You took an awful chance, didn't you?' "Yes, I didn't care as long as I got there. I have been waiting 6 months to get there." He is getting on finely and to-day is out of danger, had the tube removed . . . To-day I am sea-sick again. Everybody is. We are pitching at a great rate, and it sounds like a wild night . . . Everybody is glad it is rough for they say the sub-marines can't get us. We have two British cruisers ahead of us. Sight land to-morrow evening in the Irish Sea . . . We heard about the Lusitania. Got a wireless and it was posted up. That made us all think a good deal. Lots of flirting going on and it is reported that two of the girls are to be sent back. I don't know whether that is true or not. I don't know which two. We have to wear our uniforms all the time. Muftie [mufti: civilian dress] was called in because the girls appeared in the most impossible costumes, some of them in low neck for breakfast (semi-demi), so we get up in the morning and put on our dress uniforms and wear them all day. Dinner is formal. Col. Birkett leads and his men follow, then the nurses two by two, like Noah and the animals, it reminds me of. Everything is by bugle call and red tape. Plenty of it is with us still. Miss McLatchy has been sick most of the time. She has a Miss Dineen assisting her. We call her the "Dreadnaught". There is a "Super Dreadnaught" who is huge; must weigh over three hundred pounds. She is one of the French sisters. The horrors of war seem very real to me now. I will write you from England. I am thinking how nice it will be to get back, though I wouldn't have missed this for the world. I am so glad to be part of this big movement.

Somewhere in France,
June 10/15

Dearest Carrie:

We are a summer camp under canvas and get patients every second night. Eighty-two last P.M. I was up till 2 A.M. on the emergency staff. A bugle sounds and in a moment the staff are helping the patients. Those that are able go right to the baths where the orderly bathes them, and they come to a clean bed, warmed, and are given a cup of cocoa and bread and butter. They are so grateful and want so little. My! The stories they can tell you. They are wonderful, so patient and sweet with one another and so gloriously cheerful. I have never seen anything like their spirit. No one could imagine the horrors of a war like this, unless they are here and could see for themselves. Of course a great many die, but the marvel is that so many who have the most awful wounds recover. We do little enough for them, goodness knows, but it seems to make the most wonderful difference. The hot soup we give them, the wash and change, and they go away different human beings. This is most interesting and by far the most worth while work I have yet done . . . One man last night at 1 o'clock said, after he had come from his bath, "Sister, this is Heaven. You said smoke?" "Yes, you can, all you like." I always keep a package of cigarettes in my pocket, gave him one, and he just had the time of his life. He had a shrapnel wound in his hand. What they must suffer, no words can describe. The wonder is, how they are alive at all . . . I had to cry the other day in the service tent at one awful case I saw, – a young man that had to lose both arms, had a thigh wound, and head. These are nearly all English, one or two Scots, no Canadians . . .

Now I must stop. I could go on and on, have seen so much already, and yet feel we have hardly started to real work. This is called a General Hospital, but it's not, for the men only stay three or four days and they are sent on to England or the base. I am sorry, for you don't get to know the men or see them much. Some of the cases can't be moved. Twenty went away yesterday. They are all crazy to get to England, even for a day; say they would go back to the trenches with a light heart if they could only see England again.

Nursing Sister,

S. M. Hoerner.

Sophie Hoerner received the Royal Red Cross decoration for her wartime service. She returned to civilian life in 1919 and married.

HELL'S CORNER

During the war more than nineteen thousand nurses, stretcher bearers, and doctors served in the Canadian Army Medical Corps. Half the nation's physicians and surgeons were in the service, among them **Major William Thomas Morse MacKinnon,** *who was on the scene briefly during the month of battles at Ypres in 1915. His letter, sent by a Mrs. T.B. Morse to* The Berwick Register, *Berwick, Nova Scotia, ran on June 30, 1915.*

Somewhere in France

[June 3, 1915]

At the Front

. . . But when the war is to end no one knows. The only tip I can give you is that when you hear of the Allies having taken Lille, you may count on the war being half over . . .

I have been up near the fighting line for several weeks in command of a section of a Clearing Station. We are working under canvas. I have forty-four big hospital tents for the accommodation of five hundred patients. My personnel consists of four medical officers and thirty-five non-commissioned officers and men. We live in tents and do our cooking out of doors.

During the recent active fighting we were very busy and several thousand cases passed through our station. On one busy day we dressed, fed and sent to the base 1036 wounded men. Recently, we have been working behind the Canadian Division, and several hundred wounded Canadians have passed through our hands. This is the first time a Canadian Station has worked behind our Canadian troops. The Canadians are now out of the trenches getting a much-needed rest. In the recent engagement they more than sustained the excellent reputation they made at Ypres.

A recent German criticism says that the Canadians are the best fighters in Europe today. They have certainly given the Germans a bad time of it whenever they have been in the lines. I was at Ypres for a day during the big fight in April. It was certainly a terrible affair. I was at the Canadian Field Ambulances, where the wounded are being brought in a constant stream from the front. I saw many of the victims of gas. The smell was so strong on their clothing that they had to be kept outside the buildings. Several died before they could be moved to a hospital. The noise of the guns and the clatter of the convoys going and coming to and from the front were terrific. Later in the day I went up to Ypres two miles away. The place was being shelled by the Germans, but we got up to what the soldiers called Hell's Corner. The city was in ruins. We did not find any wounded, but saw many dead horses in the streets and several dead civilians lying where they fell when trying to escape with a few of their belongings. As we were standing by the car a shell whistled by us and landed in a house about 40 rods away. We took the hint and left at once. Another shell followed and struck a house just at the moment we passed it. We put on more gas and did not wait to see the result. About a quarter of a mile further another landed in the rear of a house as we flew by. The occupants were all out in front with their household goods, waiting for an opportunity to get them away. It is a most pathetic sight to see the inhabitants leaving the danger zone. The aged are put in wheelbarrows or dog carts or sometimes even in baby wagons. Children, too small even to walk, are compelled to try, and you see them trotting along clinging to their mothers, who are loaded down with bundles of all kinds. Every kind of cart you can think of is brought into service. The stream of refugees sometimes extends for miles. When night overtakes them they sleep in the fields, if there is not shelter for them. Where they are going they do not know. Their only desire is to get away from danger.

At the hospital we see some awful wounds. Fine fellows, who have done their bit, maimed or disfigured for life, yet all anxious to recover and return to duty . . .

We have had a number of wounded German prisoners recently. One man had a broken thigh with bone protruding. Gangrene had set in and amputation was necessary. His last words as he went under the anaesthetic were "Gott strafe [God punish] England". He recovered and was sent to England.

Another convoy is coming in with more wounded, so I must stop.

> Major W.T.M. MacKinnon
> First Canadian Casualty Clearing Station
> British Expeditionary Force,
> France

GALS AT GALLIPOLI

In 1915 **Nursing Sister Patricia Tuckett** *of St. Marys, Ontario, was serving in the Mediterranean area, where the attacking Australians, New Zealanders, and Scots were attempting to take the Gallipoli peninsula from the Turkish army in order to control the Dardanelles strait and gain access to the Black Sea.*

[1915]

My Dear –

. . . Our life now consists of work, and incidentally, eat and sleep. We have had two innings recently. They were all in that big engagement at Gallipoli last Monday. I have charge of 25 tents with 8 patients in a tent so you can imagine how busy I am. The patients never groan and they will stand any operation nearly even without an anaesthetic. Of course they have the best medical officers that can be had . . .

. . . The natives here have just finished their Christmas season, called the Ramadon [sic]. The mosque is near our camp and I can see the Muezzin go up in the tower and chant his prayers to Mecca. They fast in this season from sunrise till sunset. The Muezzin goes up in the tower and lowers a flag when he sees the sun drop into the sea as it were and on the level a man at the gun fires it off when he sees the flag go down and you can hear all the children cheering and screaming because they all go to eat. They pray anywhere and at any time. They drop on the streets and turn to Mecca and pray for about 20 minutes.

I think I will soon be like the Mohamed [sic] women. They cover their faces up. My face is all tanned and bitten with insects so it needs to be covered.

The Arab children are the queerest. They go floating around on little donkeys. All the male children wear night shirts on the street and you cannot distinguish between boys and girls . . . We went to the quay in the motor ambulance last night and on one street corner the band was playing "You Make Me Love You" and a fearful creature was singing it in French. There is a great deal of French here. I will hardly know Canadian money when I see it. We are dealing now in piastres and milems, Egyptian money.

I would surely love to see a Canadian, but I suppose it will be a long time. All the patients here are from British Isles, Australia and New Zealand. They all say that I talk like a "Yankee" and I am sure they have never heard an American speak. Of course I cannot change my accent. I suppose you have heard that English expression "Swankey" I should say you were "swankey", of course Right Oh! and Cheer Oh! are very prevalent. When I tell an orderly to do anything he always says "Right Oh!".

Well my dear I must go to my slab and sleep. Give my best love to all the family. Letters are my only thing to live for now so write often.

Love,

PATT

Helen Fowlds, a nurse from Hastings, Ontario, enlisted in 1914 and four months later was serving in France with the Canadian Army Medical Corps. The next August, Fowlds was sent to a hospital on the island of Lemnos, Greece. At about the same time, the Newfoundland Regiment was on its way to Suvla Bay on the Gallipoli peninsula, where it joined the 29th Division of the British army and encountered enemy fire on September 20, 1915 – its first engagement since leaving Newfoundland almost a year earlier. Fowlds wrote home about the part played by two nurses in rescuing wounded Brits and Newfoundlanders from the shores of Suvla Bay and about the British retreat from the peninsula in December.

Lemnos
Sept. 23rd, [1915]

Dear Mother,

My fountain pen is rather on the blink so you must forgive the queer look of some parts and not attribute it to mental weakness. How I have blessed you for those two veils which arrived in good condition to-day . . . We can't buy anything on the island. A supply ship went to Malta over a week ago and we all ordered things but it may be six weeks before they come back – and it takes ages to get things from England and cheques are so apt to go astray.

I mentioned bandage scissors in my last letter – I'd love a pair and you can't get them in England.

Our meals are perfectly grand now. We have real butter – Italian and canned but good – a quantity of tinned asparagus that is almost as good as the fresh – canned fruit, sausages and altogether we make out very well. We have a real kitchen too instead of an open air fire and the cook can attempt a greater variety. Our teas are still a joy. Today a number of men from the Cornwall were over. They were in that famous [naval] battle off the Falkland Islands [in December 1914] . . .

Yesterday's mail caused a regular outburst of homesickness. One girl received a Western paper saying she was thought to have been on the Royal Edward [British troop ship torpedoed by the Germans on August 13 in the Aegean] and every one had letters in the same anxious strain and felt awfully blue . . .

I have [bugs?] again and Myra and I have hunting parties night and morning. We sing "Come ye disconsolate" – and it is really quite an event. I suppose that sounds awful to you. If you could send a couple of those nice cholera belts I should be glad, at present I don't need them but along about Christmas I likely will and they are unknown here except the red flannel things. And keep on with the veils – please.

. . . I am very happy here – we are needed badly and feel that our work is very much worth while, and we surely are seeing life . . . On the 23rd we admitted our first patients – Scoble and Brock came back at noon from the Delta, the hospital ship we came up on from Alexandria. The Matron was short four sisters and asked for four of our girls to go with them to the Pen. [Gallipoli] and back. At first no one seemed sure whether it was a desirable thing or not and I was really the first to say I was crazy to go – afterwards a lot offered and as the first cont[ingent] girls thought they should have first choice it was left to chance and one of the ship's officers picked two pieces of paper with names out of a hat. Scoble and Brock were the lucky ones. They had a wonderful time. Went right up to Suvla Bay – got the wounded straight from the shore via small lighters – ran into a field of mines, worked like the deuce and came home brimming over with stories . . .

Dec. 19 [1915]

. . . Everyone is so uneasy and upset these days. We are evacuating Suvla and Anzac and tonight will see the rear-guards off if all goes well and many are the prayers going up for them.

The famous "29th Div." came off several days ago. They have been in the thick of it since the first landing and practically none of the original officers and men are left. They came down here and the reinforcements went to Cape Hills where it is expected we are to "put on a show" – as they say.

We know a great many officers in the 29th and of course we are greatly interested. Their camp is next ours and is the camp – as they are the heroes of this end of the war.

We have been evacuating now for some days – trenches are mined, saps laid, guns spiked that can't be taken away – everything movable either brought off or dumped in the sea and of each regiment only [one] officer and 50 men remain as rear guard. History will take notice of this last week – for it will be one of the most extraordinary retreats.

Two weeks ago during the rough weather the rain collected and poured into the trenches of both British and Turks in torrents 7 or 8 ft. deep. There was practically no way out and the casualties were heavy. The men say it was the strangest thing – Both sides lost guns and everything and took to the tops of their parapets in their efforts to keep out of the water and not a shot was fired for hours.

The Turks are finding their position as untenable as ours – and while it seems that they must know of our retreat they are taking absolutely no notice. In one whole brigade there were not half a dozen casualties.

A Taube flew over the beach at Anzac and dropped bombs yesterday and the men think they must have seen what was doing.

The only thing possible to think is that the Turks are too busy getting out themselves or that they are appearing to be leaving in hopes that we will stay and advance.

Tonight is the last and what memories are in everyone's minds of the sadness connected with Anzac and Suvla – such loss of life, such glorious bravery and now it is all over and in vain.

With heaps of love
Yours always,
Helen

Nursing Sister Fowlds was awarded the Royal Red Cross for her war service. She returned to Canada in 1919 and married Captain Gerald Marryat of the Canadian Engineers. Of the 2,504 Canadian nurses in the Army Medical Corps, forty-six died, some when hospitals were bombed. Others nurses served in Canada or with the British forces or the Red Cross.

SPIES AMONG US

*A wave of anti-German sentiment swept Canada, resulting in the renaming of some towns and cities – such as Berlin, Ontario, which became Kitchener – and leading many German-born immigrants to anglicize their family names. This letter, by **A. Lonsdale**, appeared in* The Vancouver Sun *under the subhead "Would Shorten the War."*

[September 28, 1915]

Sir:

Canada wants money and wants it very badly for our wounded soldiers and their wives and dependents and there is no reason why the Germans and Austrians earning their living in this country should not be made to supply the amount required for this purpose. Everything in the way of money and goods that can be kept from Germany will bring this war nearer to a close. Canada can exercise great influence to bring about this result. Every week Germans and Austrians are sending money home via the States and Switzerland which money goes to enrich the war chest of Germany.

One sixteenth of the population of Canada is of German and Austrian birth, yet, with the exception of a few who have misbehaved themselves and have been interned, all these alien enemies have been allowed to work and earn money to the detriment of Britishers. According to the last census made in 1911, there are in the Dominion 129,103 Austrians and 393,000 Germans. If one-half of these alien enemies were to send home every week to their native country $5.00 they would be sending about $1,305,270 out of Canada. This is so much given to the German chest and helps to buy shrapnel to kill our boys at the front. Do the people of Canada realize this fact and what has the Dominion government done or going to do to stop this? The Dominion government has taken no steps whatever except to intern a few aliens who have misbehaved themselves. Every Britisher worthy of the name should see that as little of this money earned by aliens goes out of the country as possible.

There are two things which patriotism demands of Canadians (1) To see that no alien enemy is engaged in any work which can be done by a Britisher. (2) To refrain from buying anything which has been made in Germany or Austria.

Canadians are so accustomed to living amongst foreigners, one-half of the population of Canada being foreign born, that they still find it difficult to foster any feeling against their neighbors: unfortunately, we are too apt to forget and forgive, and that is what our enemies rely on. The time for false sentiment has gone. It is time to frustrate their knavish tricks and subtle devices . . .

It is the German government's method to send their people in thousands, who are nothing more or less than spies. They never lose their nationality. In our factories, works and banks and other manufacturing centres spies are to be found bought by German gold and sent over here to obtain information at any cost. They tamper with our employees, steal our ideas, imitate our machinery and forge British trade marks, in fact, the standard of commercial morality is one only equaled by their respect for sacred treaties, international conventions and other scraps of paper, everyone of which they have broken during the present war.

The Dominion government has a serious problem to face, but it must be faced, and we look to them to deal with it promptly. It is no credit to the Dominion government that they have allowed German papers by the score to be printed and published throughout the province and allowed German schools to be carried on.

Yours truly,

A. Lonsdale

Calgary, Alta.

WE'RE GOING OVER

The Canadian Corps was established after the 2nd Canadian Division arrived in England in August 1915. The division, commanded by Brigadier General Ernest Turner, trained at Shorncliffe under seventy-six-year-old Major General Sam Steele, a veteran of the Riel uprising and the South African War. **Lieutenant Duncan John Macleod Campbell** *was an employee of the Canadian Bank of Commerce in Medicine Hat when he enlisted on November 18, 1914, at the age of nineteen. He wrote to his father, Duncan John D'Urban Campbell, just before the 2nd Division crossed the channel to France.*

10/9 [September]/15
#79968
'B' Coy, 31st (Alberta) Bn
6th Bde, 2nd Divn Canadians
c/o Army Post Office, London

Dear Dad,

Well, at last we are going. Tomorrow till Wednesday, the 2nd Divn moves to France. We are not taking our own artillery though as their training is not completed. Gen Turner is in command, Gen Steele getting the South Eastern Command of the Imperial Army.

The King & K of K [Kitchener of Khartoum] inspected all the 2nd Divn & the Training Divn a week ago Thursday. Since then everything has been preparations for going. We have at last been issued with the webbing equipment, our kitbags are proud (normally we have everything down to our respirators, Neck shields, entrenching implements, first aid bandages, identification disks, etc.)

Everybody is in high spirits, all the more so as apparently we go to France and not the Dardanelles or Serbia.

Two weeks ago today (Saturday) I was going on a weekend pass when I got my six-day leave dated from the end of my weekend pass & went up to London where I stayed till Wednesday noon. I had a fair time, shows etc. Wednesday noon I went down to Twyford & stayed till Saturday afternoon. The Zepps have been at it hard. They hit the heart of London last raid right near the Bank of England & the G.P.O. [General Post office]. London looks fine at night with the searchlights all over. I saw the HorseGuards at Whitehall but never got as far as Buckingham Palace to see them change guard there . . .

Look Dad, if I happen to get killed, would you mind advising H.E. Lewis of the Can Bk of Commerce, Claresholm, who can then advise my friends whose addresses he of course knows. I think I asked you this before but I am making sure.

Also, in case of my decease will you please burn a packet of letters that are in the bottom right rear corner of my trunk.

Mother says in her last letter that Aunt Mabel & Uncle Colin hope I soon get promotion! The next time you are writing, tell them that I go to France as a full private of my own will & any promotion I ever take will be given on the field only . . .

Two men out of each machine gun reserve were given 110 shots apiece at the range & I was fortunate enough to be one of the two out of 'B' reserve. I never got my score but heard that it was very good. I am afraid, despite R.B. Bennett's promise, that we go to the front with only 4 MGs to a battn. We should have a least 16.

You would have liked to have seen the 6th Bde storm 3 lines of trenches the other day in front of Gen Turner. The 27-28 & 29th took the trenches & according to rules brought in by this war, the supports, the 31st, made the charge. The firing line & reserves preceded by bombers occupy the firing line & reserve trenches of the enemy & then the supports charge right from the support trenches

& take the 3rd line & any fortified works of the enemy. The support (3rd line) trenches are always the ones that require charging as the fire & reserve trenches are evacuated by the Germans when our artillery goes after them & our bombers clean the communication trenches & cut up any ones left behind. It is rather queer the supports charging the enemy support trenches.

Well, I must close, so with all sorts of love to all, I am

Your affectionate son

DJM Campbell

On the night of July 11, 1916, while attempting to capture a German at a listening post, Lieutenant Campbell was shot through the heart.

MERRY NOEL

*Born in Summerside, Prince Edward Island, in 1892, **Lieutenant Noel Adair Farrow** moved to Calgary in 1912 and joined the Canadian Army Medical Corps. He arrived in Plymouth in July 1915.*

Oct 21 1915

Dear Mother

. . . To day at noon I took a walk towards the Road & just as I reach the Guard House before turning into the Highway I heard the words Turn out the Guard, for a moment I was Lost I saw all the MP which means Military Police ajust their Selves from the Hap Hazard Position, to attention on looking up the road I saw an officer Speeding towards the Guard House very fast on his motor cycle. I thought something up so I stood stock still & before I could say Verne Farrow Ham [steel] twice a long string of motors appeared & who should be in them first staff officers & then the King of England, [seated] on his left the King of the Belgiums & in the next car Lord Kichner & other Generals. I looked with Eyes Wide Open & e'er a minute Had Passed they were all lost in the Distance. So I stood & Gased untill the sound of the Puffing Motors Gradually died away. Mother I

wished you had of been with me & you would say wer'nt we Lucky
to be here at the very minute He passed, but miles seperate us I hope
not for long . . . Mother I will say Good by for now Love to Father[,]
Maida & Verne Mrs. & Mr Stuckland. Your Dear Self

> No 2 Canadian Field Ambulance
> CAMC British Expeditionary
> Force 1st Canadian Division
> Some-where in France
> Oct 27/15

Dear Mother

I Left the Base last week & am now well up to the Front it is
Impossible for me to give you the exact Distance we are from the
Firing line. From tenth ave to Burns arena is within the Distance &
the Deaf can hear quite Plain. I am not in the country I left England
for. I left there & am now in [letter crossed out] if I were to write
Lieut H.L. you know the next letter I would use if I were to write
his name in Full. the Lieut from Kensington that is in the 6th
mounted Rifles you know the name I mean the next Letter used in
spelling His name out is the one you start to spell the name of the
country. Mother this is as much as I can tell you re my last move &
the above may be contrary to censors act, but I am sure the above is
within our scope . . .

> Dec 10/15

Dear Mother

. . . Mother the only Parcel I received from you was the Cake & it
Reached me ok I was up by the Trenches when I received it & it was
like a Thousand Pounds to me & I enjoyed every crum of it. I will
just explain Re Trenches. We <u>do not</u> go in the Trenches but we go
within one hundred yds of them & we are as you see in more danger
than the men in the trenches as we are out almost in the open & the
men are all Entrenched so you can see our position at times is a very

Dangerous one. We go up for two weeks & then we are back running Hospital & Dressing Station for four weeks & then we go up again . . . The motor Ambulances do not come up where the men are in the Day time as it is to Dangerous & sometimes they come up at night. so you see we are in the Danger Zone all the time . . .

Dec 25/5 [1915]

Dear Mother

Xmas Night & I am just behind the trenches & about three hundred yds from German trenches. So you see I am quite close to the Enemy . . . last Evening I was down at our advance Dressing Station & I & another fellow walked down the Road about two miles & we done our Xmas shoping, my wealth being six cents 60 centimes in the Currency of this Country. So you see I was by no means wealthy but I purchased 12 Gum Drops which cost me four cents & two chocolats they were very small ones . . . so after making the above purchases I wended my way home. One would hardly believe that I would walk four miles to spend six cents, but it being Xmas Eve I decided to keep the old custom . . .

Your Loving Son

Noel

Farrow completed his pharmacy degree at the University of Alberta School of Pharmacy in 1920. He was president of the Canadian Pharmaceutical Association in 1950 and ran a pharmacy in Calgary until 1970.

WIRER GOING OUT

*Telegraph operator **Charles Sprague** of Belleville, Ontario, enlisted in September 1914. Overseas he served with the signal company of the 1st Canadian Division. He wrote to his brother James in Chicago.*

Bus Farm,
Belgium Dec 19/15

Dear Jim, –

Just a few lines let you know how we are getting along, my eyes are kind of sore yet from the gas attack which was launched against us at 545 this morning about five miles up the line near Ypres on the [censored] Division front (English Divn) I have an idea that the German are concentrating great forces on our front here in Flanders, also they are busy on their gas tanks again. from 355 am till 420 am, there was terrific rifle fire, (the English mad minute) then at 535 am a cannonade broke out, seemed as if every gun on the British front was firing at once, one continual deafening roar. I went up on top of the hill to see the glare and red flashes, this kept up till after 8 oclock without interruption. The gas must of been pretty strong for we felt it here five miles away. Of course the wind was blowing the right way. The first thing I did was to get my gas helmet for we expected a gas attack along our front (Canadian Divn) from reports which came in over my wire, it appears the Germans were repulsed, not being able to gain one inch of ground. The wind veered around and blew the gas back into the German line. this and the precautions we had taken in cases of gas attacks, with a terrific rifle and canon fire stopped them. They are going at it again up on our left, probably a second try at it, however you can rest assured Jim we are here waiting for them and will give them one warm reception if they try to advance. Our front along here is swarming with guns. We have more than they have now. It used to be the opposite way, once upon a time. That was at Ypres. I think Xmas will see some heavy fighting. Their aeroplanes were busy today over our lines, and our anti air craft guns were kept busy trying to shoot them down . . .

Where we are here, you can look over into the German line and see the ruined town of Messines, (where the London Scottish made their famous charge.) the front Line would be a mile from here, we are pretty safe. the only thing that would get us would be shells and as far as that goes they might throw a hundred without hitting the farm, we have them going over our heads and bursting away down in the fields, you see a big cloud of smoke then a roar, dirt flying all over, those are precusion shells. then there are time shells which burst in the air on time fuse. I was living down in a little dugout, but it caved in while I was on pass to Blighty (London) about a month ago, good thing I was away at the time or else I might have had a cross with an RIP on it, (rest in peace) in one of those little grave yards with little wood crosses, said Flanders being dotted with them every where. I am in an old barn now, built a (lay me down to sleep) out of some old boards and some hay with a little canvas, then I enclosed it all in, with some canvas I hustled not far from here, so you see I feel as if I were in a Pullman standard sleeping car, when we are in a place some time, we can fix ourselves up pretty good, of course Jim we are all Lousy, you get so after a while to not mind them a bit everyone out here get that way, its funny to hear the new troops, when we ask them, are they Lousy, then they look at you with that disgustful look, one week out here, then they are like the rest of us . . .

Bye the bye, my little Job is to work a cable wire which is run off of cable carts on the fly, connecting up the three brigades, I work the wire from Brigade to Division, and many interesting little things pass over our line, the Divisional operators are mostly all C.P.R. men, the three of us here are all CPR men. I am on duty nights now, pretty hard to stay awake, but a person cannot go to sleep for an attack may be launched against us any time, the whole country behind the firing line is connected up with wire, we do not use flags, they are too slow, then another thing as soon as you start to wig wag, you are shot down. they tried it down at Ploegsteert and lost two officers in ten minutes.

We have men on hand night and day, and as soon as a wire goes down, out goes our men to repair it no matter how bad they are shelling, this is the reason we never lost Communication during Ypres, our men out all the time repairing, stretches of over a hundred feet of wire being carried away by shells. Now I think I had better wind up and take a wink of sleep. they are still going at it up on our left.

Wishing Eva and yourself a Merry Xmas and a happy New Year
I remain
Charlie

... Me thinks up yonder a great storm is brewing, Is it going to be Ypres over again, let them come and come soon, my rifle hangs above me and us signallers can fill the gap if necessary.

We've got the pig skins beaten Jim its only a matter of another year, sticking tight standing pat.

Sprague served with the signal company of the 1st Canadian Division until the end of the war. (A letter concerning his brother, Melburn Sprague, appears on page 131.)

EXTERMINATE THEM

The year 1916 began with a new commanding officer for the British army – Sir Douglas Haig, an inflexible, unimaginative, old-fashioned officer, of whom British prime minister David Lloyd George said, "We could certainly beat the Germans if only we could get Haig to join them." The trenches extended from Switzerland north to the sea, and large portions of France and Belgium were still held by the Germans. Over the winter fifty thousand Canadians soldiers were holding the front south of the Ypres salient, with units alternating in support trenches, in the front line, and in reserve. In February a German offensive at Verdun almost destroyed the French army. **Barlow Whiteside,** *the McGill University medical student (see page 75), served in France at a Canadian hospital near the front line but so much wanted a transfer to the Princess Patricia's Canadian Light Infantry that he asked his sister to write to Sam Hughes, the Canadian minister of militia, on his behalf. When his clergyman father objected, Barlow responded.*

[February 1916]

Dear Father:

... The purpose of war is to exterminate the enemy, not to save our wounded. The wounded can be looked after by those who cannot kill the enemy, who are medically unfit to stand the strain, or by those whom it would be better for the state to save from the danger of being killed themselves, as fathers of families. If the medically unfit look after the wounded, then the fathers of families must kill the Germans, for every man is needed in his country's service.

So I, a medically fit man was doing that very thing, running very little risk under the shelter of the Red Cross . . .

You live three thousand miles away from the carnage. For a year I have been fifty miles away. You have not seen the wounds inflicted by the most hellish instruments that devilish people have spent their lives to perfect; bodies slashed and hacked beyond recognition; wounds that are wreaking, foul-smelling, gangrenous, loathsome, full of tetanus, decay and every disease. You haven't seen the wild, delirious eyes of the maniac, with a jagged piece of metal in the centre of his head; the helpless agony of the man with the broken spine; the raging, scratching grasp of the delirious at your throat; the furrowed brow, screwed-up face and stiffened body of one of Briton's sons whom the kindly hand of death has released from his agony. You have not seen one of these sons, as grand and manly a lad as you ever saw, able to repeat only the one word "Mother" for two weeks before death released him. You have not seen those who actually saw Canadians crucified in cold blood, a form of death to which the most debauched murderer would think too hideous even for him; or those who actually saw crimes committed on women too horrible to think of much less to mention . . .

Hoping God will bless you all . . .
Barlow

BEYOND EARTH'S SURLY BONDS

Canada did not set up a pilot training program until January 1917. Before then, Canadians who wanted to fight the war from the open cockpit of a biplane paid their own way to England and enlisted in the Royal Flying Corps (RFC). Historian Brereton Greenhous writes that by the summer of 1917 a quarter of the aircrew in the British

*flying services were Canadian. Eleven of them – including Billy
Bishop of Owen Sound, Ontario, and Donald MacLaren of Ottawa
– were among the twenty-seven elite in the RFC who shot down more
than thirty enemy aircraft. The most decorated Canadian during the
war was a pilot,* **Lieutenant Colonel William George (Billy) Barker.**
*Writing from near the French front, Barker told his parents in
Manitoba about his first flying adventures and warned his brother
Percy about the war.*

> March 27th, 1916
> Gunner W. G. Barker
> Machine Gun Section
> 1st. Batt. C.M.R.
> 8th Can. Inf. Bgde
> 3rd Can Div.
> B.E.F.

Dear Mother & Father

. . . I was recommended by my O.C. yesterday & this morning I went
before the Wing Commander & after asking me many questions he
recommended me for a Commission in the Royal Flying Corps . . .

I have done a lot of flying during the last three weeks and always
over the lines where we were shelled. I always flew with a young
Captain who sure can take a fellow's breath in the air. One day we
were coming home up about 9,000 feet well up above the white
clouds in nice sunshine. It was so odd – above us was sky & sun
below all we could see was the fields of clouds, but of course we
know the earth was 6 or 7 thousand feet below them. We were flying
along at about 90 miles per hour when suddenly with the engine full
open the pilot turned the plane nose down. There was a terrific rush
– down [we] dashed through the clouds and the earth seemed to fly
up at us. Slowly he righted her & I felt more at ease. You can imagine
what a nose dive is (not a plane down), but dive with engine full
open straight down. some sensation believe me. You know it is a terrific speed & the wires, wire rigging, etc. etc., sing & scream through
the air, also some noise, ha! ha!

The Captain & I were out on patrol over the lines today. Although it is Sunday we know no difference for if anything there is more flying.

We were up for two hours & I got one of my ears frozen for we flew high watching for German planes. Well as I was going to say we came back to our aerodrome at the same height & in front of a lot of spectators we did a spiral which is also some stunt . . .

I am enclosing some souvenirs of a wreck we had here. The reason I am sending them is that I used to fly in the plane that these splinters are from. I am not allowed to tell you all particulars but sufficient to say that two planes crashed together in mid-air up about 3,000 [feet] & dived to the earth. I was first on the spot and helped to pull the crushed men out from amongst the wires & twisted debris. I certainly never want to see such a mess again. The splinters are from the propeller & from the instrument board. The cloth is part of a Bulls eye we have [painted on] our wings to distinguish them from enemy planes. Keep these & some day I will tell you more about it. Must close for now.

I remain as ever
Your Loving Son
W. Geo. Barker

December 9th, 1916
Boulogne, France

Dear Brother:-

I rec'd your most welcome letter yesterday just in time too for this finds me at the above club [British Officers Club] on my way to England. Congratulations

I am going to learn to fly a very fast (130 m.p.h.) little fighter single seater scout & will then come out again to create what havoc I can.

I was very glad to hear what you had done. It is much better so. You see, Percy, it is like this – I am in it proper now & have settled down to it. Also I have done quite well & take this from me as soon as I come out again I will do enough for you & all our family & I think you have done the proper thing. Keep things going as best you can & never miss an opportunity of anything good if it comes your way. I also want you to keep Cecil [one of William's brothers, about seventeen at the time] where he is. I know exactly what it is like so exert every influence you can.

I might tell you that I have had some of it but it is different with me. I am hardened to it. It is just like going to school – all I do is to study how to kill the most Huns in the quickest way & believe me I have scored enough for one family.

Well, Percy, I suppose you have heard of my little souvenir, an M.C. [Military Cross] for the taking of Beaumont Hamel.

I will now close & will write again from Eng. – Soon.

Yours sincerely

W. Geo. Barker

Barker, whom the more famous Billy Bishop would call "the deadliest air fighter that ever lived," went on to win, among other medals, France's Croix de Guerre and the Commonwealth's highest military honour, the Victoria Cross.

MISSING THE DRAFT

From March 27 to April 16, 1916, the Canadians were engaged in the disastrous fighting of the St. Eloi craters. **Private John Wallace Ross,** *with the 47th Battalion New Westminster Regiment, wrote to his wife, Mabel, from hospital in England.*

[Monday, April 11, 1916]

Dear Girlie-

. . . Well Honey, the doctor took the stitches out on Saturday and I got up yesterday. It is healed up fine and hurts very little, only when I give it a twinge now and then. Well what do you think just as I finished writing the above few lines, in came five letters for me after sulking in bed for the past eight days with no mail.

. . . Well for the first event. Saturday the 14th Brigade was ordered to have 1300 men ready to leave on Sunday at 10 am for the front. They picked out either 250 or 350 from the 47th mostly out of B.Co. So, you can imagine how blue I felt when I heard that all my old chums were going and I was left laying on my back in hospital. Billy Myers, in the next ward, felt even worse than I did because he cried about it . . . Foster in the next ward, coughed his last yesterday and the ward seems very quiet today in consequence. It was pretty hard on his parents as they had already lost three boys at the front and he was all that was left to them . . .

I suppose you won't mind a bit because I missed that draft from the 47th. Well dear I am a fatalist – I think my landing in hospital is all mapped out in advance – and whatever happens is going to happen and can not be prevented. Just as I wrote the last few words one of the patients came in to tell me that our draft left for France about an hour ago so I guess with it passes out of my life a lot of mighty good chums and acquaintances as the chances are very much against ever running across them again. I hear that the chances are another draft will be picked out again shortly but nothing definite is known yet. I guess the old 47th will never get to France as a unit after all.

What I am very curious about is just who of my friends have gone and who is left. Its like breaking up a great big happy family and every body feels it very keenly.

4000 more Canadians blew in today to the camp here and 4000 more went to Shorncliffe. They all landed at Liverpool.

Well dear I guess I will close now. will write a good big letter to you next week so ta-ta for now.

Your Ever Ever Loving Hubby
With a Metagami full of hugs and kisses

Ross, who had been born in Peterborough, Ontario, and worked for The Peterborough Examiner, *enlisted from British Columbia, where he returned after the war. In the early 1930s, he was one of a group of newspapermen who started* The Vancouver News Herald.

SAVING PRIVATE ADKINS

In March 1916 the Canadian Corps, now three divisions, was moved into the Ypres salient to hold the line from Hooge at the apex of the bulge south to St.-Eloi, including Hill 62, Observatory Ridge, and Mount Sorrel, the only heights not in German hands. On June 2 the Germans demolished the Canadian positions with a fierce bombardment and explosions of underground mines. Their infantry then took Mt. Sorrel and Observatory Ridge. The following day, the Canadians recovered some ground, which gave them a better defensive line. **George Adkins** *was the youngest of three brothers from Westlock, Alberta, who signed on as infantrymen. Bill Adkins, with the 49th Battalion, was killed in action May 7, 1916. George and Martin fought in one of the several actions of the Battle of Mount Sorrel.*

June 5, 1916

Dear Mother

Just a line to let you know that we are both allright for which we must thank God for we have been through a terrible ordeal. I don't know if I am allowed to say much about it but you will see by the papers what a fierce fight the Canadians have been into. How we Mart & I came through without a scratch I can not tell as we have had terrible losses. It has been simply awful I cannot describe it in words but I know there has been nothing worse in this war. We did our [?] days in allright and were bombarded pretty heavy all the time but did not suffer much. Then we came out for a rest. The next night they broke through and we had to go back. We had to make a charge in broad daylight but they were ready for us and opened up an awful fire on us we took what cover we could get in old trenches and were there all day. They opened up again two or three times in the night but we kept them back. That night we were supposed to be relieved but the relief could not get in so we had another awful 24 hrs. during which they sent over the terrible high explosives & shrapnel but we held firm. Two or three times they nearly landed one in our trench. The force of the explosion threw us down and I could'nt hear nothing but ringing in my ears. I was hit on the head about four times but my steel helmet saved me. Then I had a bullet go right through a mess tin strapped on my back. I am going to keep it as a souvenir. But I wasn't very frightened although the strongest nerves could'nt stand it for long while the shells are bursting around & above. We had to stay in that trench for 8 hours without water & no food but about two dry biscuits each. It was up to our shoe tops in water and we got all stiffened & cramped up. We were thankful when the relief came at last. Of course we had some very close shaves but God must have been watching over us and it made one think about that. The wounded were very brave and bore the pain and suffering like heroes, and some had ghastly wounds. I expect to be home soon now then I can give you a good account of it. We were so tired when we got home that we just fell down and slept for a long time. I will close now as I am pretty shaky to-day through nervous strain & loss of sleep etc. . . . . I think we are out for a good rest now.

Good by with love

George

Several days later in a night attack, the 1st Canadian Division regained what had been lost on June 2. The British official war history called the battle "an unqualified success," at the cost of eight thousand Canadian casualties. After June 27, 1916, when Martin Adkins died in battle, officials moved George out of the front lines. He survived the war.

SINISTER SYMPHONY

Barlow Whiteside, the clergyman's son and former member of the medical corps (see pages 75 and 112), had won a transfer to the Princess Patricia's Canadian Light Infantry (PPCLI). During the Battle of Mount Sorrel, as the PPCLI fought fiercely in Sanctuary Wood, Whiteside witnessed the death of the regiment's command-ing officer, Lieutenant Colonel Herbert Buller, who was kneeling on

the parados, the wall behind a trench, when he was shot and killed.
Later Whiteside wrote to a McGill University friend from hospital
in England.

[July 1916]

My Dear Ted:

Your letter just to hand, and I was awfully glad to hear from you,
also that you have been making the good old T.N.T. Hope you
make lots of it, for that is surely the stuff to put the fear of God
into Fritz if anything will. I transferred to the Pats as an infantryman. I saw more life in the time I was there than I would in the
fifteen years in the Medical Corps . . . I thought you might like to
know of some of my experiences up the line. Well, they were pretty
well focused into the three days, June 2, 3, and 4, as [we] had an
easy time before that . . .

We went into the trenches for an eight-day shift on the night of
May 31st . . . Two of our companies went into the fire trench and
two in support. I was in a support company. The part of the trenches
we were in is in peacetime a forest on a large bluff. Thousands of
trees are of course shattered and splintered by shells or killed by
incessant machine-gun fire. Thousands still remain, however, and
they were a mass of the most beautiful foliage I ever saw. Nothing I
know of can compare in beauty with the simple grandeur of the lux-
urious foliage of the trees in France . . . The next night, over the
whole of that fire-swept zone not a single tree had a clump of leaves
larger than a man's hand . . . On the morning of the 2nd we were
awakened by the persistent bursting of heavy shells here and there
along the line. At 8:30 we got up with a jump and went out. One
would think that the floor of heaven were made of shells, and that
it had given way. Every size and shape were coming our way – 9.2,
5.9, 4.5, Sausage, Whiz Bang, Silent Lizzie, Whistling Charlie and
others we did not know about. We could hear the big ones coming.
They came incredibly slow; we could hear the dull boom of the guns,
then in five seconds or so away from the distance would come a low

sighing sound, rising and falling like a slow tremelo on the bass chord of a violin, increasing to an unearthly moan till with a shriek, swish, bang it would land in front or behind, a huge column of smoke, dirt, mud, stones, would shoot high in the air and fall for hundreds of yards around, and we would wait for the next. It was never long in coming . . .

About 1:30 the bombardment increased to an indescribable intensity, and shrapnel began bursting overhead. Through the din we could hear bullets whistling over the trench with a sound like the strings of a violin touched sharply and the beating of a gigantic bass drum. Word came down that the Germans were coming over, and we all got up and went back up the trench. The colonel was ahead up on the parapet waving on his men – a hero to the last. The bombardment stopped as suddenly as it had begun. Instead the air was cleft and cut and sawed by millions of machine gun bullets. What they saw going on up the trench seemed to madden the fellows. We passed a man with a hole through both ankles, walking towards us. Another with both legs shot off at the hips, fast bleeding to death looking at us in mute appeal as we stepped over his mangled body. And then – but what's the use – there were hundreds, one as bad as the other . . . I say we were maddened. It was not bravery nor bravado, nor patriotism, nor fear of being shot that drove us on . . . I think it was animal instinct and vengeance that prodded us on . . .

At midnight Fritz used a different signal [to announce a new shelling], thousands of star shells shooting up to a great height from the same spot at the time. It was a glorious spectacle, exactly like a mighty fountain of fire, the points of flame falling for hundreds of yards around. It was seen a score of miles behind the lines. The spectacle was magnificent, but the bombardment that followed beat all that preceded. I got mine just before relief on the night of the fourth . . .

Barlow

Barlow was one of the four hundred PPCLI casualties in this engagement. He sustained shrapnel injuries to wrist, arm, shoulder, and knee.

PETITE BOMBARDMENT

The Royal 22e Régiment, a French-Canadian battalion known as the Van Doos, was the only unit that Sam Hughes, the bigoted Canadian minister of militia, would allow to be formed along linguistic lines. Its members, attached to the 5th Infantry Brigade (of the 2nd Division), acquitted themselves superbly throughout the war. Among the battalion's founding officers was an upper-class Montreal legal student named Georges Vanier, who later became its commanding officer (and, decades later, Canada's governor general). A lesser-born member of the Van Doos, identified only as **Henri***, was with Vanier in the Ypres salient in the spring of 1916. Henri wrote to his mother in French.*

7/5/16

Dearest mother,

I received your letter this morning, I am very happy to learn all the good news that you tell me. I am still healthy, it is raining this afternoon we had good weather all last week if it hadn't rained we would certainly have had a water shortage but since it is raining things will be a bit better. I will return to the trenches tomorrow evening, I hope it will be better than last time, I will be there for a few days and then I will go to the rear, which is pretty well the same thing, because the shells fall there even more than in the trenches.

The last time we were caught in a little bombardment we had to stand-to all night long. Father Dion said Mass at 2 in the morning in a dug-House [dugout] and I tell you, it was not pleasant. Dear mother I do not want to tell you the dangers we run when we are there, one bit of bad luck and you've had it; for example I'll be in a trench and a shell will fall, you might very well get it right on your bean fragments will fall all around you, on your head, etc., you're very lucky if nothing happens to you and so it goes ordinarily one is always in danger and then there's the wiss-bang, that's a shell, it falls on the dug-Houses, it isn't very big but it makes a big bang it can demolish pretty well anything and then there's the coalbox that's another kind of shell for communications trenches or to wreck earthworks but it's just like the others it kills people and then we have the German sausages, I think that's the one that does the most damage and makes the biggest bang, it demolishes the trench and then before we can see anything down come the explosive and regular bullets, then the aerial torpedoes and the bombs and grenades, that's hand-bombs, and I could list many others for you as well. Now imagine there's a big bombardment all of that together and it lasts 2 or three hours if it makes a huge racket all the while we're in the dug-houses and happy the man who is (as the English say shellproof) I tell you dear mother when one is trapped in all that it makes us think about many things, and especially the good Lord. That's when we see our life before us oh! dear mother there is fire everywhere, rushing about the cry of the sirens when there is a gas attack, it is hell. I can't say any more than that, perhaps you will think that I am telling you lies but it is real: to be able to describe a huge bombardment acompanied by a gas attack, I am absolutely certain it would frighten you, believe me dear mother, it is unspeakable and if I am not wounded today or killed it is because of your prayers I am sure I could have been wounded five thousand times [and] I haven't been others are dead others wounded if I am not called to die here I will see you again I knew a Belgian who was in the army right from the beginning of the war and who took part in the biggest battles who was wounded 9 times and one night took a bullet in his chest was seriously wounded, he died 4 days later, he was sure that he wouldn't die it took only one shell to tell him otherwise, and then we have one chance in a hundred not to be skinned alive, 8 months at the front without even a scratch. I'm not the only one, there are many others but the war isn't over. The best course of action is to ask for prudence plenty of courage and a heart-felt prayer to the good Lord for your son who loves you always.

Henri

BAD BEER AND NO BEER

In exuberantly misspelled letters to a Mrs. A. Hogg and a Miss L. Hogg, **Private Stanley Rippingale** *of Peterborough, Ontario, mixed his observations of French urchins and English farming women with wry comments about a laggard chaplain and the effects of Prohibition on some of the folks back home.*

Sept. 7th, 1916
London, England

Dear Friend

I hope you are quite well and all at home we are well as this leaves us. I was very pleased to get your letter. I am glad to hear that Lizzie has pass. I exspect that hands are very hard to get, and we heard that in the west they are paying from five dollars up. In England there are no thing but old men and women to do the work. they help in every way, they are on the stacks, hoeing and even driveng binders. On the 5th we had a fifteen mile of a route march with our packs, on to a place called Lydd we started at 3.0 oclock and got their at 8.30. the camp here is the cleanest camping ground I have ever seen every where is like a lawn. We will not be here very long for we are here for a firing course, we get up at three in the morning march 2½ miles to the ranges with our packs and rilfes come home at ten for breakfast and go back at one to eight at night; at the ranges the fireing is like we get at front laying down in trenches, with packs on and with gas helmets, and while we are are shooting, there is a heavy battrey firing big hundred pounders over our heads and I tell you they whisle though the air. I exspect we will be sent to France next for the battalion is broken up into dralfs [drafts]. . . . I [am] longing to get to France to have a crack at those big Germans. my cousin has been there twice and was wounded one in the knee and one in the rist we went down to see him he showed us the bullet wound in his rist and you can see where it went right through and broke the bone, and the bone had not set right and he had to have it broke again and set. He said that he dose not want to go back any more . . .

Some Where in France
25/10/16

Dear Friend Lizzie

I hope you are quite well I am as this leaves me. I was very glad to get your nice letter I gess you have heard that we are in France. Our Battalion the 93rd was broken up into dralf [draft], I am in the 20th Canadian Batt. We have been in the trenchs and came out saft & sound, I thank you very much for the socks they were great. I put them on in the trenches, for out here it is getting cold sharp frosts at night, we keep our boots on all the time in the line you are not aloud to take any thing off, and you can not very often get a wash for the water is very hard to get to trenches. I gess Peterboro will have a hard time to get another battalion.

I do not think you would not [sic] to live in this country it so dirty and untidy. The Frence kids very ragy and they are hungry they come around us and ask for bully beef The houses are in ruin here, and there is very few in-habitance just a few to keep the hotels open the beer is not very good so the boys do not like it, in the trenche we have lots of company with the rats and crums for you can-not keep yourself clean for we sleep in old stables, and barns, we can-not wash our clothes for we have now time, we get a bath and a clean change of clothes. We are not like the slacker afraid to do there little bit . . . Major Frost the chaplian would have a lot more to tell the Peterboro people if he had a few weeks in this country instead of England. Out here we do not now Sunday from any other day I gess the old home town looks just the same only a little quite. What will they do with the hotels now it is dry will they turn them into stores. It will go very hard with Ethel Waterman, but I hope she will soon recover all-right. I hope you like going to Normal [teachers' school], and I wish you the best of Luck . . . I spent my birthday in France the 14th of October, I think Mr Sage could let one of his boys do his bit by enlisting.

Well me and Ben are still to-gether and we are taking a Lewis Machine gun course so I gess well be put in the machine section I think this is all now Write soon I am all-way glad to get a letter from Peterboro

I remain Yours Truly
Stanley Rippingale

Stanley and his brother Benjamin died together on July 16, 1917. They are buried side by side at Aix-Noulette communal cemetery extension.

SING SING SING

Rowland E. Brinckman, an architect born in the Irish county of Kilkenny, enlisted at New Westminster, British Columbia, with the Irish Fusiliers of Canada. He wrote to Mabel Ross of West Vancouver.

121st Battn C.E.F.
Bramshott
Hants
Sept 21st 1916

Dear Mabel

Ta muchly for your delectable epistle, it sure was good to hear from you again, your letters are guaranteed blue-banishers alright . . .

I've got two more choruses which probably haven't reached Vancouver yet – one is a sequel to Sister Susie and I was a little Vague about the words.

"Six short soldiers scrubbing six short shirts
Six short soldiers scrubbed & scrubbed,
   "   "   "   rubbed & rubbed,
   "   "   "   sang this song
Their singing surely shows

That six short soldiers scrubbed six <u>short</u> shirts Sister Susie Sewed or something –

The other one I want you to sing at your lustiest whenever Mother looks depressed – one tune is very like that of "Henry the Eighth, I am"

"Pack all your troubles in your own kit bag & Smile Smile Smile. Find a Lucifer and light a fag and smile, boys, that's the style What's the use of worrying; (pause) it never was worth while <u>SO</u> Pack your troubles in your own kit bag & smile smile, smile.

b'aint un purty? (That's the Somerset for aint it pretty) Well Mabel I can hardly think of anything to tell . . .

Suffice it to say that I hate this place The weather is rotten, the parade hours worse and the (so called – by courtesy) food is wusser yet! However I am told the trenches are nearly as bad so the experience may prove useful if we ever get there –

Someone is just opening a parcel of real food so good bye in haste or I shant get any

Love to all
Rowland E Brinckman

Mabel Ross's family never knew Private Brinckman. He is not listed by Veterans Affairs Canada on its war memorial Web site, indicating that he survived the war.

THE BLOODY, STUPID SOMME

The officers in charge referred to it as The Big Push; the enlisted men called it The Great Fuck-Up. It was a series of futile conflicts fought near the Somme River in northwestern France from July 1 until late November 1916. Sir Douglas Haig, the commander of the British forces, directed this show – with horrific consequences. As Paul Fussell says in The Great War and Modern Memory: *"There was a hopeless absence of cleverness about the whole thing, entirely characteristic of its author." On the first day the 1st Newfoundland*

Regiment, fighting with the British forces, was almost annihilated at Beaumont Hamel; only ninety-one of its 801 officers and men survived. The Canadian Corps moved to the Somme battlefield at the end of August and fought numerous engagements throughout September, October, and November. **Private Stephen Dalton,** *a London-born emigrant to Canada, signed up with the Canadian forces on March 1, 1915. He wrote to his fiancée about the final decisive action in the Battle of the Somme, in which his battalion and five others captured Desire Trench on November 18, 1916.*

Nov. 22.11.16
S. Dalton. Po 410257
'B' Coy. 38th Batt. C.E.F.
c/o Army Post Office
London, England

Miss May Curtis
41 Laurier Ave. West
Ottawa, Ont.

My Dearest May

Just a few lines to let you know that I am O.K. and still kicking. We are resting again after another few hard days work. By the time you get this letter, you will have heard of the good work our boys have done, and the name they are getting for those at home & Ottawa. It was a great piece of work, and I wish I could tell you all about it. We certainly work hard this trip, as we had to make our name, and live up to the motto, we received at home. We have been traveling around about two years before we got the chance to let Fritz see what we were made of. and what we had in store for him. "Poor Nelson" [Lachance], he got killed in the advance his was killed by sharpnel [*sic*], we were about half way over to Fritz's line, when he got hit, he died a hero's death, you must go over and stay with Irene for awhile, as it will be a hard hit for her. Give her my deepest sympathy, and tell her I could do nothing for "Nelson" as he was away up the other end of the line to where I was, but I made inquiries after him as soon as, we had dug ourselves in again, and his chums on the machine gun told me that he had been killed on the way over, I had no chance to try and find his body, or I would have buried him for her. There will be quite a few homes that will be sad after this, I did not receive a scratch, although I had several narrow escapes, I am glad to be having a rest now, we had a very hard time in our new line, and when we were relieved, we had to come out over land in broad daylight, and under shell fire but we all got out safely, or at least all that was left of us, and how we did, was a miracle. Well love if we can pull through like this all the time, we may still live in hopes of seeing home once more.

I am yours lovingly
xxx Don xxxxx

NOT TO HARROW YOU

Bombardier **William Rowat**, *who was among the survivors of the Somme slaughter, recalled the events of September 15, 1916, for his parents in Athelstan, Quebec, when he was on leave in London. Rowat lived in Huntingdon, Quebec, after the war, working for the Department of National Revenue.*

Dec. 28th, – 1916.

Dear Mom & Dad

. . . My leave expires on Sunday, when I will cross the channel once more to the land of strife and carnage, only, I hope, that my stay there this time will not be so long as my former ones. As you must know from reading the papers the Canadians spent quite a number of months on the Somme front, and I have been in a good many of the battles which took place at Poziers, Courcelette, Martin-Puich and Thiepval. How I ever came through them all with out a scratch is a mystery to me, save that the hand of God has guided and protected me through every seeming death trap. I recall one terrible night, that of the 15th of Sept., when I, along with two officers and 15 signallers were detailed by the Colonel to establish a line of communication from the front line back to the batteries and H.Q.S. At twelve o'clock midnight, we set forth wending our way single file through pitch darkness toward the distant flares that arose from time to time denoting the front lines of friend and foe alike. We eventually arrived within a few yards of our destination, only to come under a terrible rain of shell fire from the enemy's field artillery. We immediately began to run out our wires with the utmost speed, and after much falling and tumbling through shell holes and over dead and mutilated bodies, we arrived at a badly battered support trench, where we established an intermediate station, leaving three signallers and a telephone to test out the lines and repair them when broken by shell fire. We then continued our line up to the forward trench, where we were suddenly attacked by a company of German bombers. Two of our men were killed outright, one officer left in a dying condition and the other, a very plucky fellow, though wounded in the left arm, drew his colt and shot down three Huns. A company of our own infantry came rushing up at the critical moment and the Germans were either killed or taken prisoners. We then established a terminal station in the regained trench and, after crouching there for 5 or 6 hours, under a nerve trying bombardment, which put many around us out of action, we were ordered to prepare for the attack. By this time everything had become quiet and an ominous stillness prevaded the atmosphere, then with a crash that would have made ordinary thunder seem insignificant, the thousand or more giant guns of our grand army belched forth fire, our machine guns situated in rows behind the front line, opened up a tirade that would make one think that a thousand riveting machiners were at work. The Irish Navy (Tanks) now made its appearance and with a blood curdling yell, infantry, tanks, and all went bang into the German lines, carrying all before them. Such is an attack, dear mother, and although I could fill many pages with like experiences and tales, I will refrain from harrowing you with things that are terrible as hell can possibly

be. We are out of action now, and will not be sent into any hot places
this winter, so hope to come through all right.

Love

Bill.

*The Somme was the most massive battle in human history. On the
first day 57,470 British were killed, wounded, or missing in action.
By the end of the battle there were 24,000 Canadian casualties
(8,000 dead), 620,000 British and French killed or wounded, and
670,000 German casualties. The Allies' gains on the ground were
insignificant.*

TO WELCOME A HERO

*In a letter to his brother and sister-in-law, Melburn Permenus
Sprague, a carpenter from Belleville, Ontario, told how his legs had
been broken when a shell exploded near him. Germans overran the
trench where he was lying in his dugout, and while shelling and fighting continued for the next four or five days, enemy soldiers gave him
water from time to time and splinted one of his legs. Finally German
Red Cross workers carried him to a dressing station and later transported him to a hospital where "the German Doctors and orderlies
used me good." He was repatriated because of the extent of his
injuries and by November was in hospital in England, recovering
from the amputation of his right leg. When it became known that
Melburn was to return to Belleville, C.B. Scantlebury wrote to a
local newspaper.*

[December 15, 1916]

Dear Mr. Editor:

Our townsman, Melbourne [sic] Sprague, a young man of noble
character, who has been fighting for us in France with two other
brothers, all sons of Mr. and Mrs. Edward Sprague, North Front St.,

is on his way home with the Eighteen Hundred disabled soldiers being returned to Canada.

Melbourne fell on June 2nd at Battle of Zillebecke, lying for five days and as many nights, helpless, with only his dead comrades as companions, until picked up by the German Red Cross attendants, placed in a German hospital, starved and butchered by those heathens. Both legs having been severely broken, the one thigh improperly set and is to be treated here after his return. The other leg amputated in Germany, improperly cared for and a further amputation of four inches in an English hospital.

Truly Melbourne has given more than his life for undoubtedly death must have been something hoped for amidst his misery.

I address this letter with the hope of enthusing our citizens towards the giving of this young man a grand reception upon his return. Nice receptions have been given those returning and all credit to our enthusiastic Mayor but he must in this matter have abundant assistance of both men and women, everybody should turn out, crowd the main streets and not watch the procession pass as they would a funeral, although we could all remove our hats with good grace. The reception at the stations have been fine but the people on the street fall down. More cheering and enthusiasm is needed and still more. I have found it an awkward trial to alone commence a rousing cheer, one feels so conspicuous, particularly when so few join and I would suggest that some officially appointed committees be placed [?] two or three at 100 yard intervals along the Main street for the very purpose of creating enthusiastic enthusiasm by just mingling with the crowd and inciting them to cheering and so arrange that one group pick up the cheering, from the next and thus follow the procession.

Furthermore if the ladies, who are always doing so much to help, would organize to be at certain positions along the route of procession and hand the hero as he passes a bunch of flowers, I fancy it would be very pretty and much appreciated, in fact organization would not be necessary, the more the better, if ladies would only feel free enough to do this and why should they not?

Surely it is not necessary for a lady to have met the hero to inspire this act of courtesy to one who has been fighting for us and who returns a cripple for life, crippled for the sake of others.

This or some similar programme should be arranged for every returning soldier, it seems to me, for every man who enlists virtually gives up his life for you and I and we never can repay the debt. I also think a hearty demonstration on such lines would greatly aid recruiting.

We may have recognized our returned soldiers quite equal with other cities, I believe we have but let us put other cities to shame in the future, let us give our boys each and all a grand reception such as they will ever appreciate and never forget.

Respectfully,

C. B. Scantlebury.

Private Sprague was welcomed with a "monster demonstration" capped by a procession through the city for which he sat in the mayor's decorated car. The local paper reported, without demur, that the bands played "When Johnny Comes Marching Home."

FLIGHT OF THE TUMBLEBIRD

Barlow Whiteside, *the McGill University medical student who moved from the hospital corps to the Princess Patricia's (see pages 75, 112, and 119), could not return to the infantry after he was wounded at the Battle of Mount Sorrel, and so he transferred to the Royal Air Corps.*

[Shoreham-by-Sea, January 1917]

Dear Father:

... I came here on the 12th to learn flying. This is a beautiful summer resort on the sea shore near Brighton, the great English spa. I had my first flight the day after I arrived, and several times during it I thought for certain it would be my last. The pilot was an expert airman who could do anything in an airplane, from looping the loop to turning sideways wing-tip over wing-tip. He can go up a few thousand feet, turn off the engine and come down in a whirling nose-dive to a few hundred feet from earth, recover and go whirling off like a mad mullah. He got the wind up me properly. He would dive within a short distance of the earth, and all that was within me would try to stay behind. Then he would swoop up like a hawk and all that was within me would turn as cold as ice. Then he would do a vertical bank, or turn, and I would find myself looking up to the horizon, down to the horizon, and with the earth on one side and heaven on the other. Then with a diabolical smile on his face, he would turn round, stop the engine, whisper sweet nothings in my ear, let go the controls and ask me how I felt. When he saw terror written sufficiently large on my other-wise noble features he would turn round, make a few more heart-breaking turns, a swoop or two, and ask me again. At last I told him, I felt very much like an over-ripe teased salmon, and had enough. So he nodded and came to earth in triumph. The second time up was much better and the third time quite common-place; so I don't mind it now at all . . .

Barlow

A veteran of more than fifty night raids, Flight Lieutenant Whiteside earned a Military Cross and bar, which he received from King George V on September 25, 1918. After the war, he stayed in England and became an instructor with the Royal Flying Corps on large Handley Page planes. In April 1919 he was readying for a round-Britain flight in preparation for a cross-Atlantic attempt when his plane crashed just after takeoff from Andover. His last letter home had ended: "God bless you all."

DOUBLE-CROSSED

William Patrick Ross *was a clerk at the Royal Bank in Vancouver when he enlisted in 1916. His many long letters to his parents,*

John and Elizabeth Ross, describe his training at Camp Hughes,
Manitoba, the troop train trip to Halifax, the voyage across the
Atlantic, and the camp at South Seaford in Sussex, where he had a
good Christmas before being sent across the Channel. A few months
later, recalling the Battle of the Somme, Private Ross recounted a
rumour that resembled the tale of the crucified Canadian (the sup-
posed victim was often also British or Scottish). Whether true or
not, these rumours demonized the enemy and induced caution in
the troops.

South Seaford, Sussex
Jan 3/17.

Dear Mother: –
. . . I do hope you had an enjoyable Xmas in spite of my absence . . .

I received a splendid box from messrs. Harrod & Co. of London
on tuesday. It was contributed by the staff of the Royal Bank of
Canada and sent out by the Royal Bank, London.

Am enclosing a list of the articles which were in the parcel. The
parcel must have cost full £1 ($5.00). All the articles are splendid the
cutlery being silver plated.

100 Cigarettes
1 lb. Chocolate
½ lb. Muscatels
2 lb. Genoa Cake
1 Balaclava Helmet
1 pair Gloves
2 pair Socks
1 Tooth Brush
1 tube Tooth Paste
1 tablet Soap
1 stick Shaving Soap
1 Towel
1 Knife, Fork & Spoon
1 pack Playing Cards
Christmas Card.

The cigarettes, chocolate, and cake were of a high grade. We will make short work of the eats, but won't have to buy smokes for a good long time. We all smoke a little indeed they say it is absolutely necessary in the trenches, so we might as well get accustomed to it. Am going to get a pipe and break it in . . .

As Ever
Your loving son
William

Somewhere in France
Sept 9th 1917

My Dear Dad:~

Sunday once more and it has been a splendid day. A clear blue sky without a cloud in sight, reminds me of this time last year. I was then busy harvesting and the weather throughout the period was exceptionally warm.

Just fifteen months today since my enlistment. Seems more like fifteen years, during this short space of time. What shall the next fifteen months hold in store for us all? God grant that it may see peace restored to the tumultuous world . . .

Am beginning to despise the German race more, day by day. Have just been reading of another of their fiendish acts. During the advance on the Somme, a certain battalion was following close on the heels of the retreating Germans. One of the British officers went into a church in the captured zone and found a black cat, tied by wire to a crucifix, squealing piteously. He called one of his men and told him to cut the wire and release it. No sooner had he cut same when a terrific explosion shattered the crucifix, and blew both man and cat to pieces. Surely this is a good example of their fiendish crimes. They are very fond of setting traps, of every conceivable nature but we are pretty wise to their stunts now and will be mighty wary henceforth . . .

Am still at the school and having a splendid time. Have learned a great deal on Bombing and Grenade work, which makes me much more proficient in the section. Have now lots of confidence in handling them, while before was rather wary of using same . . .

As Ever

Your Loving Son

William

Ross would return to the trenches and fight at the Battle of Passchendaele in 1917, where, his family was told, he was wounded. Not until March 1918 did they hear from an officer that on the night of October 26, William was with his company in a shell hole behind the firing line near Zonnebeke, Belgium, when the area was bombarded. The officer wrote that "no identifications were secured of your son, from which it is assumed he was blown to pieces." Mrs. Ross wrote in her diary, "I can't help wondering why God had him blown to pieces, such a death for such a good lad as he was. I am in torture always."

#1 FOR BISHOP

When **Captain William Avery (Billy) Bishop** of Owen Sound, Ontario, finished his flight training and joined 60 Squadron of the Royal Flying Corps near Arras, France (facing Baron von Richthofen's "Flying Circus"), he had a good chance of surviving for eleven days – the odds that faced every other rookie pilot. Instead, he kept shooting down enemy planes for months, earning the Military Cross, the Distinguished Service Order, and the Victoria Cross. After his wedding in Owen Sound he returned to combat, and in twelve days in 1918 reported twenty-five kills, bringing his total to seventy-two. He was ordered back to England, promoted to lieutenant colonel, and assigned to help form the Canadian Flying Corps. Bishop wrote to his then fiancée, Margaret Burden, about his first dogfight in which he was "tail end Charley," the most dangerous position in a flight of four planes.

France
March 25; 1917

My Darling,

I am writing this in a dugout 300 yds from our front line, after the most exciting adventure of my life. Four of us were doing a patrol when we encountered 3 Huns. I opened fire on one and another opened fire on me. I hit mine I think, for he suddenly fell out of control and I dove after him. I must have been going over 200 miles an hour so you can imagine how fast he was falling. I poured another 60 bullets at him and followed him vertically down from 8000 to 600 ft then he regained control and headed over the lines, and the infantry report that he crashed on the other side of the line.

My engine then oiled up and stopped. I was 600 ft over "No Mans Land" and glided into a field which has only been captured for two days. It was a narrow squeak. I tried to start my engine again but it refused, so I am stuck here for the night. I am so anxious to know if the Hun really crashed, for if he did he will count as one machine for me. I hit him I know for I saw my tracer bullets enter his machine.

Much love my dearest. I didn't tell you but I have again been recommended for a flight commander

Billy

Bishop's record has been challenged by Canadian military historian Brereton Greenhous because so few of his victories were witnessed by others. Of forty-seven claimed kills while Bishop was with 60 Squadron, Greenhous argues, three are demonstrably false and eleven are highly suspect – but not Bishop's first one.

SOMEWHERE AMONG THE CLOUDS

*In 1916 **Charles Cecil Hendershot** left Kingsville, Ontario, and found a job in a Toronto factory making salves and creams. That summer, just after his eighteenth birthday, he wrote his mother that*

recruiting officers had approached him in the street but that he would rather commit suicide than join the army. By spring he had found another option.

Toronto Sunday
[April, 1917]

Dear Mother,

You know how badly I have been wanting to enlist. Well I am going now. I think it far better than waiting until the Militia Act comes in force, and it will be in force soon. There are two fellows in the Factory that are in the home guards and they hear all the latest. They say that it will be in force in May. Don't think I have been worked up by any recruiting officer because I haven't been stopped by one for 6 months but all my chums have gone now and I am going for sure. I do not think it right for you to persist in me not going when I feel it my duty and have made up my mind to go. I know how you would feel but just think of hundreds of mothers that have given their only sons. They certainly would feel considerably worse than you would. This Flying Corps is the best thing that has turned up yet. There is no mud to be standing in no rats or bugs to bother with and no lying out in a field wounded beyond help. Think it over. If I come home I will come home whole not with a leg or arm off (maybe both). The next best thing is the Signalling which I will go into if you will not sign those papers right away.

There is very little danger of a flying machine falling.

Well make the best of it. Don't think I haven't showed any consideration in what you have done for me because I have. I have been at you for a long time to enlist and you have shattered my intentions, so now is time to put down my foot and go.

Well Good Bye
With Best Love

By the end of April, Hendershot had been accepted into the Royal Flying Corps (RFC) and was learning to fly at Camp Borden, Ontario. He advised his older brother, Warren, to apply to the RFC "because it is the only branch for a decent fellow." He sent Warren this account.

Camp Borden Saturday
[July 1917]

Dear Bro,

. . . I have passed my instructors test now. I passed it yesterday. I told you about a spinning nose dive. Well I was doing a stunt (a stall) that is point your machine up straight in the air and she will loose speed and fall back on her tail that is slide back on her tail. Then her nose drops and she takes a dive. Well I was up in the morning and did three stalls and in the afternoon I did three more and on the last I went into a spin. I pull her out tho'. When I came down the captain told me it was great work. The aeroplane fell about 600 ft and made 3 complete spins before I got her out. Do not tell mother this because she will worry but there is no danger if you are high enough . . .

Oct 16/17

Dear Mother,

. . . We were up again this morning on a bombing raid. We were supposed to bomb a town. I was on a D.H. [de Havilland] 4 and was supposed to escort the others. Tonight I had a crash, didn't hurt myself but broke the machine. It is the first crash I have had and I certainly do feel down hearted about it but what is the use of worrying, the government has lots of money . . .

I am certainly glad that I am going over this time of the year and on the D.H. 4. There is very little fighting in the Winter time and by spring I will be considered an old pilot . . .

Best of love to all
ChasH.

Lieutenant Warren Francis Hendershot followed his brother into the RFC in August 1917 and arrived in England near the end of the

*year. The brothers, in different squadrons, were attempting to be
united when Warren wrote his parents on black-edged stationery.*

London, February 11/18

Dear Mother and Father,

At last this cruel war has come home to us. I cannot tell you what a
shock it was to me. I had been in London the day before and had
just got back when the major sent word that he wanted to see me, I
thought is [*sic*] was about the application I had made to be transferred to Charlie's squadron but when I got in the office he said,
"Hendershot I have bad news for you." I was almost stunned and
couldn't imagine what it was until he handed me the telegram. All I
said was "My God" and of course he told me I could go to Amesbury
right away so I caught the first train and landed there that night. I
saw the major of the squadron and he told me how it was thought
the accident occurred. It seems as though Charlie had not been well
the day before and had remained in bed for the day and Wednesday
morning he went down to the camp early. There was a 50 mile gale
blowing and he took a pupil up. Charlie in the front seat and the
pupil in the back seat. You know you should never instruct from the
front seat of a BE2E unless the pupil is ready to go solo. Well Charlie
took the chance and the pupil ran the machine. They had only got up
about 150 feet when the pupil turned down wind and the machine
lost flying speed and started to spin to the ground. It seemed as though
Charlie tried to correct it but the pupil grabbed the controls and they
both crashed to the ground and were instantly killed. Poor Charlie
pitched forward and struck the front cowling with his chin and his
neck was broken. The funeral was held Saturday afternoon and it was
a fitting funeral for one who died doing his duty. The casket was draped
with our flag and was carried on a gun carriage, which was lead by
100 New Zealand troops with arms reversed. On each side of the carriage a mounted officer rode. The pall-bearers were six of his chums.
The funeral services were held in the English church and he was laid
to rest in the church yard. He certainly was well liked by all the officers

and men who gave him beautiful flowers. I saw him in his casket and he looked just as though he were peacefully sleeping but the poor boy is in a sleep that knows no awakening . . .

I am

your loving son

Warren

Warren Hendershot saw action in France in 1918. He returned to Kingsville, married, and settled in Harrow, Ontario. In June 1940 he enlisted in the Royal Canadian Air Force as a temporary squadron leader in the reserve. The body of Second Lieutenant Charles Hendershot was removed from its initial resting place in England and shipped home for burial. He was nineteen when he died. In total 23,000 Canadian airmen served overseas and 1,500 gave their lives.

THE VIMY GLIDE

In 1917 the Canadian Corps proved its efficiency, winning battles at Vimy, Arleux, Fresnoy, Hill 70, and Passchendaele. The four divisions fought side by side for the first time to capture Vimy Ridge, an eleven-kilometre-long escarpment rising to a height of 143 metres, which the Germans had held for two years and which the British and French had earlier failed to take. The Canadians gathered intelligence by raiding enemy trenches and photographing them from the air. Lieutenant Colonel Andrew McNaughton, a McGill University scientist, took theodolite bearings on gun flashes to pinpoint and destroy the German artillery. The troops practised what became known as the Vimy glide – a precisely paced advance behind their own artillery's creeping barrage. Each man knew his task that early Easter morning when he climbed out of the trenches. The 1st, 2nd, and 3rd Divisions achieved their objectives on schedule, but the 4th came to grief on Hill 145, which was eventually taken at sunset by the Nova Scotia Highlanders, in their first battle outing. By April 10 the Canadians held Vimy Ridge. **Captain Claude Vivian Williams**

*had finished his second year of medical school at the University of
Toronto in 1915. He volunteered for an infantry battalion, which
was disbanded in England to form the Canadian Machine Gun
Depot, where he trained as a machine-gun officer. He went to France
in 1916 and was almost continuously in the line until June 30, 1917.*

April 15, 1917

Dear Mother & All:

Just came in from sending a cable to you reporting "All Well". They
say you will receive it to-night. I thought you might be a little anxious
after seeing the account of the battle in the paper. The papers over
here are full of it: The French especially wish to congratulate the
"gallant Canadians" for capturing the "Vimy Ridge". There is no
harm in mentioning this as the papers have given very detailed
accounts of it, saying where we were and what part we took in the
offensive. It was absolutely the finest thing I have ever experienced in
my life – wouldn't have missed it for anything – there are of course
lots of sights we are trying to forget as well as we can. A battle is a
grand thing when you see pictures of it and descriptions, but they
only show up the bright side of the affair but we see the shady side –
the horribly mangled dead, and mutilated wounded, at first one feels
an absolute nausea at these sights, but in the excitement soon reaches
a surprising callousness and never thinks twice of them . . .

I can tell you a few of the incidents which may be of interest.
The attack was at daybreak, we had to lie in the open trenches all
the night; the morning turned out a grey cold and drizzling, everybody shivering and chilled to the bone, I managed to "snaffle" a
couple of dry-outs for the fellows about an hour "before we went
over". So with a few minutes rest and a good show of fun everybody
felt in good spirits and eager to get after Fritz.

At the arranged time to the absolute second our artillery opened
up – the most wonderful part of the "show". It seemed as far as one
could see and hear was one line of artillery flashes, from the sharp
barks of the "pip squeaks" to the dull earthquake boom of the 15"
naval guns. We had to shout in one another's ears to give orders.

Fritz immediately put up his S.O.S. signals ("prepare for attack, send up reinforcements"), the sky was alight with his orange coloured flares, one after another, all along his line like a fire work display. Behind his front line was our barrage, one continuous line of bursting shells and smoke, it seemed impossible for a soul to live under such fire. When our time came we jumped "over the bags" with our guns and advanced over the shell torn ground, the men as steady as on parade. Fritz was some time "coming back" with his artillery but finally awoke to the situation. Our artillery however outnumbered his by more than two to one, with hundreds of our "silent guns" which had never fired a shot before and whose sole duty was counter battery work, to silence Heiney's guns. His barrage was feeble, he did make things a little inconvenient for a time at one spot, [by] putting over gas shells. We were all choking, coughing, our eyes flowing rivers of tears. I got the section out of this without a casualty however; we kept right along at a steady walk following up the "creeping barrage" which kept getting hotter, but soon we spotted a gap in this barrage, worked right there – still not a casualty. Everywhere now dead Fritzes and our wounded, some limping out, dragging themselves along and some waiting in shell holes for the stretcher bearers to come up. These bearers did wonderful work running from spot to spot binding up wounds for the fellows until they could be carried out. The ground kept getting worse and worse, there wasn't a spot but where one could put one foot in a shell hole, and another anywhere around but in another, shells flying everywhere. We passed a town we had seen on the map – nothing to show where it was but the wall of one lone house.

As we passed over the deep dugouts Fritzes would jump out by the dozens running like hares to our rear, every time they passed us throwing up their hands calling out "kamaradi" but never slacking their pace – they were absolutely frightened out of their wits. Finally we got to our objective and found the Bosche had in a great many cases already retired. Their dugouts were full of revolvers, clothes, food and everything just as if in a great many cases he had been eating a meal. He never expected we would get that far, hundreds were captured as they tried to get away. That night we were sleeping in Fritz dugouts. We were eating sausages, smoking German cigarettes, cigars and tobacco. We also sampled his black bread and good butter. There is absolutely no truth in the rumour that the German Soldiers are starving in the trenches – they had all kinds of provisions and of good quality. What we did when we were actually there I cannot say. It was bitterly cold and snowing much of the time. None of us had a warm minute all the time we were there.

My section captured some Hun prisoners, brought them down to me, I was talking to some of them, they said as soon as they were in danger their officers ran away and left them to their fate. They were a good looking crowd and appeared to be well fed. The O.C. was pleased with the work of the section. The men were excellent and everyone deserved a medal, there was not a shirker in the crowd. We got 2 German Machine guns and turned them on Mr. Hun: Our men all know how to use his "gat". In the entire action I only lost one man, who was wounded – it was wonderful luck. We got out of the action with lighter casualties than any of the rest of the Company . . .

Love to all,
"Claude".

Williams received the Military Cross for his "conspicuous gallantry and devotion to duty" at Vimy. After a period in England recovering from trench fever and gas poisoning, he returned to France in the Canadian Machine Gun Corps in March 1918. He was repatriated in September and returned to medical school.

A CROSS AT VIMY

Captain Thomas Carlyle McGill was the accountant at the Kingston, Ontario, branch of the Canadian Bank of Commerce when he enlisted in 1915. He served in the Signal Corps with the 3rd Division. He wrote to Charles Foster, who edited the pamphlet Letters from the Front, *which followed the fortunes of Canadian soldier-bankers throughout the war.*

6th July, 1917
France

Dear Mr. Foster

. . . Have you seen in the papers that a cross has been erected on the highest point of Vimy Ridge by the Third Division to commemorate the loss of our men in the battle? I was at the ceremony and greatly impressed. There were only about one hundred there altogether. It took place at twelve noon. Sharp on the tick of twelve all the big guns in our area fired three volleys at the German lines as a salute, while the men all present presented arms. Then the ceremony began; a hymn, a prayer, a lesson, the Lord's Prayer, a dirge by the pipes, the funeral march by the band and then 'God Save the King.' I have never seen men stand straighter or with their heads more proudly lifted, for each felt that a little bit of his own heart was buried there too. During all the ceremony we stood with our backs to the German lines, clearly visible below us though a mile or so distant, and between the cross and them; but when we sang 'God Save the King' we turned our faces again to the front. The bands had been warned to play softly lest it draw fire upon us, but, when that came, discretion was thrown to the winds and I hope our challenge reached them. Then we saluted the cross and left it there, looking down towards the trenches we took that day on one side and on the other across a mile or so of valley towards the present front lines. Altogether it was a very satisfactory little ceremony, and one felt less poignantly as he passed a little wooden cross which read, 'Here lies an unknown Canadian who fell in action, 9th April, 1917.'

[T.C. McGill]

After Vimy, McGill fought at Passchendaele, Amiens, and Cambrai, and in Siberia in 1918 and 1919. For his services there, he was appointed a Member of the Order of the British Empire. He was demobilized in 1919 and returned to Canada. Vimy was a landmark victory in Canadian military history, but the price was heavy: one casualty for every ten who went into battle – 10,602 wounded, 3,598 killed.

NATURE WINS BACK

Lieutenant William Livingstone of Big Bras d'Or, Nova Scotia, wrote to a girlfriend, Marietta MacDonald, telling her of the aftermath of Vimy.

France August 1st. 1917

Dear Mame,

. . . Yesterday I took a walk over our old front, where we spent last winter but the line is now well in advance of that and what a change what was bare shelltorn ground is now covered with wild oats waist high and a profusion of wild flowers hiding the hideous barbed wire entanglements and trenches until one in places has got to be careful to avoid falling into them a complete mantle of beauty as though nature is striving to cover the sordid ugliness of it all. I visited the enemy trenches that we raided Christmas morning. I entered some of the dugouts luxuriously furnished with everything they desired stolen of course from the French houses behind their lines. On my way back I could not help feeling a bit saddened as I found the cemetery where we laid so many of the old boys away . . .

ever yours

Billy

Livingstone survived the war and lived to an old age. He did not, however, marry Mame.

LEO'S LUCKY LEAVE

In 1917 Haligonian Leo Keating was a signalman at an artillery camp near Richmond, England, close to the Scottish border. One weekend

he was on a pass and – as he told Luke Feetham, his best friend back
home – he had a surprising adventure.

> Tuesday, August 21st 1917
> No. 1 Section
> No. 11 Can. Siege Artillery
> Raffey Camp
> Horsham

Dear Luke

. . . Well here is how I started out last Saturday afternoon with no special place to go to. I had a week end pass Mason or Fry did not. Well we went to Rich[mond] – from there we took a buss (a small auto to hold about 10). This auto was going to the small town of Reeth a distance of ten miles off. The road lead thru the valley of the Swale and by books I have read, it is described as being the most beautiful drive in England. It sure was beautiful. Well we arrived there had supper in a hotel and I was so charmed with the place that I told Mason and Fry that I was going to spend my weekend there. There was no buss going back Sunday so I had the pleasure of walking thru the most beautiful valley in England 10 miles long all alone (no not all the way). Well Mason and Fry left at 5.15 and I was there alone in a small town and I thought that I might as well make the best of it. In the town there was two small shops a church and a few house, some town. On a bench by the village green there was a middle aged lady and two young ladies both 17 so they were about the only ones that I felt like asking a few questions concerning the light heather clad hills and castles that surrounded the small village . . .

Within ten minuits I found myself walking up the road with the two young ladies one the daughter of the lady with us and the other girl a college friend . . . we had worked up quite a friendly conversation and to my surprise the lady (Mrs. Thompson) asked me to say at her home for the week end. Well Luke I was alone and believe me that certainly touched a soft spot in my heart. At first I thanked her and told her that . . . well you know how I felt but she asked me again so I said I would. When we arrived up along the moores (is that the way to spell moores) and she showed me where they lived, well I almost fainted. It was some home believe me. It remined me of homes you often see when you pass along the road on a dark night and the electric lights are lit in side and everything looks to nice to touch. Silk curtains and the best of rugs, furnature, silverware . . . Well I said to myself I'll make the best of it. The first thing I know she told her daugh[t]er (Dora) and Hazel her college chum who was spending a week with them to go in and put on their brogues (heavy low shoes) and to take me to the top of the highest peak. So like a flash they were in the house and out, they came with their heavy jersies on and each with a walking stick also one for me. (Some class) They were a picture . . . The three of us after climbing for an hour or so arrived on the highest point of land in that part of the country. Luke I must try to cut this short or I will never stop. Well from the top we could see hills and valleys as far as the eye could reach and all those hills were clad with heather. The sun was but an hour high and their I stood admiring the beauty of the surroundings (now Luke you know I would not look at the girls)[.] Miss Thompson decided that we go down the other side to the river so we did. Some life in those girls. Believe me. Well Luke we had to walk about two miles arou[n]d the road when we go[t] to the river before we got back to her home. Well I went in was introduced to her father and we had a talk and then supper. Luke such a tabel. Everything was sparkling and you can imagine how I felt after eating like a savage for five or six months but Luke I got along as cool as a cucumber. After supper Dora, Hazel Dora's brother, his boy friend (both college fellows) and I played cards and believe me I certainly did enjoy myself. At 10.30 we went to bed and Luke some room I had, everything seemed too clean to touch. Well I slept great and when I awoke I could see thru the pink silk curtains the sun just rising above the heather clad hills. After breakfast Miss Thompson and I went for a long walk down thru the village and far off over the moors. She told me the whole history of all the places of interest (nothing else). We arrive back just in time for dinner (5 courses) "O" yes I forgot to mention that the maid had shined me boots in the morning. The custom is that all

hands leave their boots down stairs before going to bed and on rising
in the morning the maid has them polished (some fuss ha ha)[.] Well
Luke I will not say anything about the dinner but I conducted my self
all right. After dinner Mr. Thompson passed the cigars but not for
mine. Cigars are too much for me. Miss Thompson, Hazel the two
young fellows and I went down to the river and gathered mushrooms
and had a splendid time. We went back to the house and I go[t] ready
to leave it was then 3.30. Well Mr & Mrs Thompson are splendid
also their beautiful daughter. I thanked them and they insisted on me
spending my leave with them. Believe me they really meant it . . .

Poor Miss Thompson, she felt kind of down hearted when I left
for we had such a time. She wanted me to stay a week and she promised me that she would take me every place. But you know what a
soldier gets when he breaks his pass . . .

Luke don't let anyone read this but you can imagine the time I
had last week and far away in the north of England in the valley of
the Swale . . .

Leo

ELMER'S TUNE

*Lance Corporal Elmer Belding of Saint John, New Brunswick, a
bank clerk when he enlisted in March 1915, was one of the original
Dumbells, a troupe of Canadian soldier-entertainers funded by the
YMCA and brought together in 1917 from various units to entertain
the troops. The troupe took its name from the 3rd Division's insignia
– crossed red dumb-bells.*

France
Sep. 23rd 1917

Dear Dad:-
. . . This is my third year away and it seems ages. What a kid I must
have been at 19. I feel like 29 now, worse luck . . .

I am still doing France by motor-lorry. We have played at Brigade

Hdqs, Division Hdqs, Corps Hdqs and Army Hdqs. We have only to go to G.H.Q. and play to Haig and then we will have done the lot. Generals from Brigadiers up have laughed at our show and we are getting quite at home among brass-hats.

At present we are playing without the services of our Captain [Merton (Mert) Plunkett] who is senior officer for our Division in his line. We miss him very much but still we "carry on". We would show if we all were sick. Our comedians are splendid and we enjoy ourselves by just listening to the hearty laughter of the boys in front. It often lasts for some time. The show is strictly clean and we have had many compliments on that account. The temptation to get smutty is too much for some parties but our Captain is strictly onto his job in that respect.

He is also strong against anything in the wet line. I still keep to my old line, no booze for me. Funny thing is that I can be in the midst of it and never have the slightest desire for it . . .

Love to all

Elmer.

The Dumbells' biggest production was a full-dress "HMS Pinafore," which played for thirty-two days in Mons just after the war ended. On Boxing Day, 1918, Belding wrote that he was being sent to England for an unspecified operation, after which he expected to be home.

BATTLE FOR WARM BODIES

In May 1917, after attending a war conference in London, Prime Minister Borden returned to Canada convinced that conscription was needed to sustain the size of the Canadian Expedition Force, which had been eroded by casualties and a waning flow of volunteers. Borden invited Wilfrid Laurier, leader of the opposition, to form a coalition government that would support conscription; Laurier refused, knowing that French Canadians were vehemently against it.

Nevertheless, the Military Service Act *became law in August 1917. Later in the year the government enfranchised all soldiers and their wives, mothers, and sisters. Two letters from Canadian soldiers in Europe talk of the "hell" of battle, but come to different conclusions about conscription. One of three brothers in the service,* **Private Orville Deville Fleming** *of Vancouver, was in the 7th Battalion of the Canadian Infantry when he wrote to his wife, Louise.*

May 29/17

Dear Jid,

I am just off fatigue at our temporary base. I left the front the 19th of April very sick, but am feeling better and expect to go up the lines soon. "When I get home" will tell you all about affair here and my hospital experience. The soldier fellows of all nations are getting horribly fed up on this thing, and matters are so complicated you cannot tell how long this affair is going to last. Fritz says he is going to send us Canadians home on a fishing smack, and if it lasts a great deal longer he may come closer the mark than we think. The Allies will win without question but at an awful cost . . .

If they attempt conscription in Canada do all you can against it. Australia knew better, and Canada will regret it if she passes such an act, although I am satisfied the people there will force an election before standing for it . . .

Hell is not a nice place and when we get out of it there will be a sigh of relief reaching unto high heaven. In the meantime you are all in my mind constantly. I re-live old scenes, failures and small successes over again, and so often manage to forget my surroundings . . .

Watch the papers. Fritz is going to get hell this summer . . .

With sincere love

O.D.

Four months later, **Private Edward Sargent,** *from the Bancroft, Ontario, area, wrote home to urge his three brothers (one was only sixteen) to enlist. None did, perhaps deterred by Edward's death on October 30, 1917.*

Sept. 3, 1917

Dear Mother:

. . . I would like to give you a little idea of our place at present but as you know mail going out from here is censored so I can't say to much, but I hope I will be back before long and tell you what it is like some times, but I could give you a brief description of it . . .

Well you said they didn't like conscription much in Trenton but perhaps if they were just where I am just now, they would think of it a little more serious. It is no pleasure trip but the Canadians always have done fine here and made a name for themselves that will never be forgotten, but the few boys that are here can't live forever, and if there are no more come for reinforcements what are we to do? We can't loose [sic] our name now so we will just have to stick to it that's all. George may not like this but I can't help it, he is able to come and help a brother. I say to him come as I said before it is no pleasure trip they are coming on but it is for right and I think we should have help over here. Words can't explain the Hell we go through here some times to fight for freedom and right, and we are getting nearer to our object every day, so I hope this wont offend anybody and if it does I can't help it for everyone of the boys here will say the same thing. I hate to ask a Bro. to come out here for I wish they hadn't to come, but they are needed and they shouldn't wait for conscription, so if you want to send this to the paper you can do so. It is my plain opinion so tell the boys around there to consider it serious for this is a big affair and no easy job, but it has to be done, so I guess I will say good-bye for now.

I remain with love and best wishes,
Your Son,
E.B.S.

The election of December 1917 returned Borden as the head of a coalition government of Conservatives, some Liberals, and independents. Conscription was applied on January 1, 1918, but had so many allowable exemptions that of the 400,000 men called up, 380,000 were able to appeal. Finally, in March 1918, with disaster *looming in Europe, the government cancelled all exemptions. That Easter there were riots in Quebec. Of the conscription crisis, Pierre Berton wrote: "Here were sown the seeds of a future separatist movement . . ."*

THE PASSION OF PASSCHENDAELE

Another Allied endeavour to break out of the Ypres salient and reach Belgian ports began in late July 1917 and petered out in early October, after the British had failed to take Passchendaele. Stubbornly refusing to abandon the attempt, British commander Sir Douglas Haig ordered General Arthur Currie, commanding officer of the Canadian Corps, to submit plans to take the ridge. Currie protested; he could see no strategic reason for the effort, which he (accurately) predicted would cost sixteen thousand Canadian casualties. Haig would not relent, and Currie conceived a series of battles with the objective of advancing the four Canadian divisions gradually. The fighting began on October 26 and ended on November 10, when the Canadians were securely in possession of their goal. On October 30, the Princess Patricia's Canadian Light Infantry, in the 3rd Division, fought through deep mud, icy water, and heavy enemy fire and took Meetcheele, a destroyed village on the road to Passchendaele. **Colonel Agar Adamson** *wrote to his wife.*

Watou, 2nd Nov. 1917

My dear Mabel,

We got out late last night and this morning trained back about 20 miles where we are under canvas . . . We are quite uncomfortable and wet, but the rest and quiet is wonderful. The 160 men we have left are cheerful and at this moment singing. Lt. Puley of ours, who goes on leave, takes this . . . Puley is a most gallant fellow and was in it from the very moment we went over. He will give you a list of our casualties and if you draw him out, tell you how magnificently the men behaved, but he won't do it at one of your round table tea parties . . . at the moment, I must struggle with 9 letters to next of kin of killed officers, including Majors Haggard and Sulivan, besides honours and awards and as you may well imagine, a great many other painful and pressing details.

The ground we gained and held against two counter-attacks and continuing artillery bombardment is of some importance, as the ridge we took is a commanding one and I do not expect the Army (although they ordered us to do so) thought we would be able to hold it, even if able to take it. The higher authorities are themselves out in expressing to us their appreciation of our efforts, but I cannot help wondering if the position gained was worth the awful sacrifice of life.

Get Puley to tell you of our being gassed coming out, of how Mackenzie of the Machine Guns, when all officers of No. 3 Company were killed, lead the company against a series of pill boxes and was killed, also how Lt. Christie and Sergeant Mullin behaved, also how a Corporal took charge of No. 3 Company when Papineau and Haggard were killed. My love to you.

Ever thine,

Agar

Before the attack and minutes before he died, Major Talbot Papineau of the Princess Patricia's Canadian Light Infantry said to his fellow officer, Major H.W. Niven, "You know, Hughie, this is suicide." It was: of its 600 men, the regiment suffered 363 casualties, of whom 150 were killed.

STILL TODDLING ALONG

William Alexander MacDonald described for his sister, Mary, in Glenwilliam, Prince Edward Island, his trauma at Passchendaele.

Devonport Military Hospital
Devonport,
England
January 5 [1918]

My Dear Marie,
At last the cloud of mystery which has surrounded the whereabouts
and welfare of your brother is lifted.

It was on the morning of November 6 that my company "went
over the top" in the attack on Pasachendalle [sic] Ridge, the capture
of which once more brought such laurels to the Canadian arms.

I was always in the machine gun section since I came to France.
Our section went in 10 men and the corporal. Just after we jumped
out of our trench one of the boys "got it" through the stomach. He
was carrying a machine gun and I instantly took it. I just went about
a 100 yards more when "thung" a ringing sound in my ear and I fell
in my tracks as a result of a shot fired by Bosche snipper [sic]. I
dropped in a shell hole still retaining my senses but doubting very
much whether or no my wound was fatal as it bled profusely. It dis-
couraged me very much to see one of my chums, Dan Ross, Valleyfield
(machine gun, too) laying there quite dead, shot through the head.

Dear Marie, you can't imagine the misery. There was a pool of
water in the shell hole red with Ross' blood and my own. I really
thought and hoped my end would come any minute, but then I suddenly realized how sweet life really was and I just determined I would
try and live. I lay in this miserable shell hole for hours afraid to try
and look up for fear "Fritz" would have another try at me. At last
one of our own boys came along and I called him and told him to
get the stretcher bearer. He bandaged me and started me for the
dressing station and then more misery. The mud was actually up to
my waist and several times I sank right down in it but of course there
was a lad helping me, a kid about 17 and a good kid he was. The
dressing station was 2 miles away. But alas new dangers awaited me.
In order to get to the dressing station I must go through the enemy's
barrage. This I did and oh! what gruesome sights: pieces of arms,
legs, intestines, hearts, etc., scattered out just like so many leaves.

Ah! what a pity – all good Canadian blood. Now here was the danger spot and I did not know what second one of Fritz's big shells might come and hurl me to destruction. One landed a few yards away, a piece of shrapnel hitting me in the right shoulder and knocked me. I thought "all was up" and the lad lifted me and found that I could still toddle along. (It's wonderful what one is able to do when it's a matter of life and death). The pain was awful. At last I arrived at the dressing station where I collapsed. They carried me 3 miles to a casualty clearing station where my wounds were attended to better. It was feared that the right shoulder blade was broken. I was shot under the right ear, the bullet passing exactly under the entrance to the right ear and coming out about ½ inch from right eye. I arrived at 3 S Hospital Calais, November 8. There I stayed 2 weeks until I contracted erysipelas [an infectious skin disease] in head and face. I was immediately sent to 30 Isolation Hospital. My first 10 days there was nearly obliterate. I seemed to be in a stupor. At last I came around. The erysipelas vanished. After a bit the head wound healed up. The ear is treated still and is pretty deaf but not as deaf as it was. The doctor tells me it will be normal through time. My recovery then was marvelous. My appetite came back. I really believe I had the best nurse in the service, an English nurse, Sister Cooper, of London, England who has had a great deal of experience and took a great interest in my case. She sure did a great deal for me.

After Christmas I came back to 3 S and yesterday struck this place. It is an English hospital. There are no other Canadians in my ward. I think I'll like it. So you can see there's no cause of alarm or worry on your part. Of course you can't expect a broken shoulder blade to mend in a hurry. As a result of erysipelas my hair is all coming out. Now I will close. I think you'll make out my writing, my right hand is very shaky. So good bye, love to all. xxxx

William

Private MacDonald became a physician and practised in northern Alberta while raising a family of three with his wife, Margaret.

ALEX'S FUNERAL

Lieutenant Colonel Alexander T. Thomson (see page 72) was wounded twice in 1915 but returned to the trenches that October and fought in 1916 and 1917, receiving the Military Cross, the Distinguished Service Order, and the Croix de Guerre (France). In June 1917 he was given command of the 4th Battalion, becoming at twenty-nine the youngest commanding officer in the Canadian Corps. He was killed by a sniper's bullet on November 19, 1917. **Lieutenant Douglas Cameron Thomson** *learned of his brother's death eight days later.*

> France
> 29/11/17

My Dear Father,

. . . I know papa that Alex's death will be a great blow to you at home. I can hardly realize yet that he is gone. I came up the line and was just going out to look for his Battalion when they told me. Ever since I left home he has been the best of brothers to me and I looked on him more as a father than anything else. He was everybody's friend and ever since I have been out here I never heard a word against him. He was always praised by everybody as a "man" and that is everything in this country where an officer or ranker must show himself as a man or a mouse.

He had a great funeral papa. It was the largest ever given to a Canadian in France. It was attended by General Currie, General McDonnel[l] and Brigadier General Loomis with eight Colonels of the first Division acting pall bearers. He is mourned deeply by the 10th Battalion and the whole of it was there. The 4th were in the line but they brought part of it out. They also had officers and men representing every Battalion in the Division . . . I was over to his grave yesterday and there is no cross on it yet. The 10th Battalion are having a nice one made and it will be ready in about a week . . .

Your loving son

Doug.

Doug Thomson was bombing the enemy in Buissay Switch on the evening of September 2, 1918, when he was hit by shrapnel from an enemy grenade and instantly killed. He was awarded the British War Medal and the Victory Medal.

EMPIRE IN PERIL

*A real estate agent and militia member in Victoria, British Columbia, in 1914, **Arthur Currie** commanded a brigade at Ypres in 1915 and then the 1st Canadian Division, which he led to the victory at Vimy. In June 1917 he succeeded Sir Julian Byng as commander of the Canadian Corps. Forty-two years old, pudgy, but a brilliant tactician, General Currie was Old Guts and Gaiters to his men, whom he strove to protect by thoroughly organizing and planning operations. Following the difficult victory at Passchendaele, he wrote to J.J. Creelman, Esq., D.S.O., in Montreal (possibly John Jennings Creelman, a lieutenant colonel who had commanded an artillery brigade).*

Canadian Corps Headquarters,
30th November, 1917.

My dear Creelman,

. . . I am glad to hear you say that in your opinion the opponents of the Military Service Act will not have an opportunity of upsetting it. I feel that any interference with its provisions, or any delay in its operation will mean the death of this Corps. I feel that months have already been wasted, and even if the men who are being called up now are got into training at once we shall need them very badly before they will be fit to send. If they don't come at all within three months I feel that this Corps may still consist of four Divisions, but of probably only nine Battalions each; in six months, it would probably consist of only two Divisions, and in a year from now not more than one. It would suffer not only by reason of its loss in numbers but in the loss of morale of those remaining. The men who are here now are committed until peace is declared. If no others are sent to help them they can look forward to nothing else but to be killed or permanently maimed. Many of our men have already been wounded three or four times, yet the exigencies of the service demand that they be again sent to the firing line.

The death struggle is approaching, and if Canada neglects to put forth her full strength in that struggle such an action can be considered not only a desertion of the men in the trenches, but a desertion of the Empire as well. The Empire is fighting for its life, and must see this thing through. If we do not play our part, we cannot hold up our heads in honour at its conclusion, no matter what that conclusion is. Furthermore, I believe the withholding of men at the present time might have a great influence on the situation in Australia and South Africa. I believe the fate of the Empire is at stake, and I cannot believe that the people of Canada for one minute understand the true situation. I know that they have been deceived. They have been constantly told that Canada has raised 450,000 men; they assume that these men are capable of taking their places in the firing line; they have all studied arithmetic, and when they add the number who are serving in France to the number who have become casualties, and subtract that total from this 450,000, they naturally conclude that there must still be a couple of hundred thousand available for service. What they have not been told is that out of that 450,000 probably 100,000 were no use. If they add to that 100,000 the number who disappear through sickness and what we call the normal wastage, they will find that there are at the present time very, very few available for reinforcements.

You know I have always done my best to keep politics out of the Corps, and I shall continue to do so . . . I cannot take any action to influence the present election, but if I thought the situation in Canada was serious enough to possibly prejudice the successful operation of the Military Service Act I would be disposed to tell the people of Canada how serious the situation is, even if by so doing I had to give up my present position . . .

I thank you for your congratulations <u>re</u> the Passchendaele battle.

I can tell you briefly what the situation was when we were called upon to undertake that task. Others had repeatedly failed to take the Ridge, and it was imperative that it should be taken or much of the previous fighting would count for naught. In order to make sure of success, the Commander-in-Chief called on the Canadian Corps, and I am proud to say the Corps delivered the goods. The obstacles that had to be overcome in the way of defences of the Bosche and bad communications on our part were simply staggering. The fellows have never worked so hard or fought with such grim determination. This has been a wonderful year for the Corps. It has fought continuously and has never once failed, a record I am assured which is enjoyed by no other similar formation . . .

Yours ever,

[Currie]

HALIFAX'S PASSCHENDAELE

No Canadian city felt the impact of the war as much as Halifax, the last port Europe-bound soldiers saw and the one that received the returning wounded and prisoners of war. Infantry posts, blockhouses, artillery guns, searchlights, minefields, and anti-submarine nets protected the harbour. It was a base for the Royal Navy's ships, for the Royal Canadian Navy's motley collection of craft that patrolled the coast and swept the harbour daily for mines, and for merchant ships carrying food and supplies overseas. Although sabotage was an ever-looming possibility, the explosion of December 6, 1917, began in an accident – a Belgian relief boat, the Imo, *struck a French steamship as it was drawing up to a terminal in Bedford Basin. The* Mont Blanc *was loaded with picric acid, guncotton, TNT, and flammable benzol, which lighted when the ships separated. The captain and crew fled, but firemen boarded the ship and were fighting the flames when the* Mont Blanc *blew.* **Lieutenant James Calder Munro** *served with the First Searchlight Battery in Halifax.*

[Halifax, December 19, 1917]

Dear mother,

This is a dreary letter indeed and I have spent most of it in bed making up lost sleep. This is the first rest we have had since the explosion.

Yesterday I obtained a pass from the chief of Police & in the P.M. McLean and I went all over the devastated area. It is a terrible sight. Just a mass of charred ruins where once was beautiful homes. The people did not have a chance in the world as their houses just collapsed like a pile of cards. The whole place is strewn with pieces of the ship chain & armour plate fully a mile away from where the explosion took place. At No. 2 pier where I am working a piece of armour plate came through the roof & bent a six inch steam pipe all out of shape. The roof is 10 inches thick and made of reinforced concrete. The pier is almost a mile from where the explosion occurred. This will give you some idea of the wreckage that was flying around. There is not a trace left of the ship itself . . .

The other night I was talking to some undertakers from Toronto who were staying at the hotel. They got a car and took me down to Chebucto Road School which is one of the largest morgues. They had buried 150 unidentified dead from it that day but there still was about 150 bodies there and they were coming in all the time and are still coming in. Practically all the bodies were in such a condition that they could be identified but no one had done so as yet and they were burying them as soon as decomposition set in. They showed me the embalming and washing process. Every body had a coffin and each one was thoroughly washed – that is providing they were not too badly charred. I saw a row of about 20 little babies from the Protestant Orphanage and it was a sad sight. I don't know what will become of all the homeless people. At present all the theatres and halls are full of them and there are thousands being cared for in Windsor, Truro, Sydney and other towns . . .

No attempt has been made as yet to rebuild homes. Temporary shelters, huge affairs but these are only temporary buildings, but I suppose it is all that can be done under the circumstances. The situation is more serious than most people here in Halifax realize. Not only are we up against the problem of looking after the homeless and wounded, but there is a conjestion [sic] of traffic and a serious hold up in the water transportation. Yesterday the I.C.R. [Intercontinental Railroad] lost 32000 [3,200?] feet of dock frontage alone. Also the dry dock is a complete wreck. As Halifax is the premier port in Canada especially in the wintertime the effect will be greatly felt.

The reconstruction going on at present is being all financed by public subscription practically.

Well heres wishing you a Merry Christmas

lovingly Calder

The explosion destroyed about two and a half square kilometres of the city, killing more than 1,400 people immediately. Six hundred more died later of injuries. Thousands were wounded (some bore blue scars for the rest of their lives), and six thousand were left homeless. Unable to find shelter in public buildings, people nailed boards over the broken windows of their homes and tried to stay warm while a bitter blizzard struck the city.

PRINCE OF GOOD FELLOWS

*In 1916, before he went overseas, **Sergeant Leonard James Chase** of Nova Scotia was travelling by train to New Brunswick. He got into conversation with another passenger, Reverend Harry S. Handel, the chaplain of the New York and Brooklyn Fire Department, and agreed to write the chaplain when he arrived in England. A correspondence developed, and soon parcels began to arrive from Handel for C Company of the 5th Canadian Battalion, of which Len was quartermaster. Among the gifts were baseball bats, gloves, balls, and uniforms. Just before Christmas 1917 came a large wooden box stamped: "Greetings for some boys 'OVER THERE' from a few of their American friends."*

France
Dec. 30, 1917

My dear Friend:

The luckiest man in France is about to fail miserably in writing a letter of thanks for a couple of boxes which arrived to-day, one by parcel post and the other by ration train. "Oh" such Xmas boxes.

My thoughts are running riot to-night, so you are in for an awful letter. If it seems terribly disjointed, please excuse. I am just a big bunch of excitement and joy. I want to reach out and shake hands with you or call on the 'phone and have a good long talk. How you did it all is beyond me. The time, money, patience, and work you must have spent. The whole thing is just one big sentence, "A real man who loves his fellow-man." . . .

The Xmas box that came by parcel post was in perfect condition, as they all have been. It was a dandy, just the things that are useful, thoroughness seems to be a habit with my cowboy, fireman Chaplain. He's a wonder!!! Coming up from the ration dump I had the big box right up on top where every one could see and read, and I'll say there was a proud boy riding right with it. From the expression on some of those who saw and read, I was an envied man . . .

We were like a bunch of kids and I was the biggest kid of the lot. Never, since I was a wee kiddie getting up early on Xmas morn to see what was on the tree, have I been so excited at Xmas time. I wouldn't have traded places with the King, nor would I trade your friendship for that of the King. I say this in all sincerity.

You have given me the best coat in France. It's a perfect fit, really too good for this life. I showed it to one of the boys, an Indian, who was born on the shores of Hudson Bay; he said it was made up better than any he had ever seen and would be just the article for the north country. He knows a skin when he sees one too, and says I have a dandy collar. This is true; I, a Q.M. have a better coat than the majority of staff officers out here, and it's a cinch I wouldn't trade any of them . . .

After I had taken the articles addressed to me out, as well as the wristlets, which I am giving to the boys at H.Q. who drive the cars, I turned the rest over to Capt. Forbes; he sorted them into four piles, then the Platoon Sgts. drew for them; they, in turn, numbered everything and had the men draw for them. In this way every man in C. Coy, as well as some of H.Q. received some article . . .

If I have failed in this letter, forgive me and in doing so, know that there is a bunch of boys not a thousand miles behind the line who have voted Chaplain Handel the Prince of Good Fellows.

Will close now (I am forced to); hoping to hear from you soon, I remain.

Your friend,

Len

To mark his fifteenth anniversary with the New York Fire Department, Handel sent more goodies in a second wooden box, which the Chase family still has. Len Chase was repatriated in the fall of 1919. Three months later he went to New York to meet a ship carrying a darling ninety-pound French woman, Marie Louise Poiriez. They were married by Reverend Handel on January 5, 1920, in Brooklyn. Their marriage lasted fifty-three years and produced four children.

OF SOAP AND SUNSHINE

Corporal John Cannon Stothers was a teacher living in Toronto when he and his younger brother, Carman, enlisted in January 1916. John, who signs himself Cannon, wrote to another brother, Stephen.

France

January 12, 1918

Dear Steve:

I'm marking time preparatory to going to our platoon dinner, for which I've been sparing my appetite all day. The boys are standing around and criticizing and finding fault with the Management of the

Supper. There are the usual arm-chair critics and censurers. But withal, I feel confident that we will have at least a "good feed". I will probably tell you about it tomorrow, when I finish this letter.

I got the parcel from home last night, with the kidney . . . In all I got four parcels last night and am thus able to be the donor to the dinner of 5 boxes of candy, a fruit cake, some sugar and cocoa, and a couple of packets of raisins, all of which have proved, for I've already seen the table, a wonderful addition to the menu, and garnishment of the table . . .

There's one thing I can't understand about, and that is the way Jack Canuck [a newspaper] knocks the YMCA. I can't say anything but good about the "Y's" over here. They usually have so many things distinctly Canadian, like Old Chum & Hudson Bay tobaccos, MacDonald's chewing, Tuckett's cigars, maple sugar, and Canadian brands of chocolate bars. They are to be found almost everywhere from the base to the front line, in all manner of places from tents to dug-outs. In those in the battle zone, you can procure free coffee and tea. I never hear any knockers among the troops especially when they are lining up [at] some old "sap" or cellar, filling an empty milk tin with steaming tea. Then they stand around and blow on the hot liquid and swap stories or just talk & jolly each other . . .

Our billet here is in the attic of an "Estiminet" on the banks of a canal filled with dirty looking water in which we perform our ablutions when time and the spirit prompts us to wash. The attic is large, airy, and windowless. The roof is of tiles with frequent air spaces and chinks where roof and supporting walls meet. As I write, the candle flares and flickers in the draught. I'm cross-legged like a Turk or a sailor, and my feet would super induce cold in a refrigerator. My mind is a blank except for an air space through which some vapours (vapidity perhaps) of thought waves percolate, the substance of which I'm translating to you now . . .

Sun. Jan. 13 A.M. [1918] – Before Church
This morning we were up early before daybreak. There was a touch of frost in the air, and the mud was frozen to a stiff semi-plastic

hardness. As I passed our billet, I noted in the cold and semi-darkness that a dog was chained in his kennel on the opposite side of the canal, a huge, heavy jowled, dun coloured dog. He lay there, shivering and looking out on a bleak and cheerless world. His lot I thought, was a hard one, denied as he was his freedom, freedom to romp and run. The picture touched me in a vague disquieting way.

An hour later I was washing on my side of the canal and, as I rubbed the soap into a thick lather, I looked up and saw the self-same dog fast asleep with a glint of sunshine on his face. He looked the picture of peace and the atmosphere of a bright Sunday morning was tranquil. The waters of the canal looked less dark as they rippled by, where an hour ago was cold, darkness, and a dearth of comfort and happiness, there now seemed brightness, joy, peace. What a difference a little sunshine makes!

The dog flicked his ears & "changed position right"; the sun rose higher and higher; hens clucked and moved about industriously; the waters almost sang; the church bells chimed in the distance and mingled with gurgling of water flowing over a nearby dam. It was a picture, pleasing and cheering, and it refreshed me more, perhaps, than my ablutions in the questionable waters of a canal flowing through the heart of a town.

Don't think I'm wound up in giving this poorly executed sermonette. I should now point a moral as a fitting conclusion to this rhapsodizing, if so it may be termed. But you see, I still have an imagination, stultified perhaps, yet an imagination and as such, cherished even over here . . .

Our platoon dinner was a success. We had a good feed and lots of merriment, songs, music, and speeches. Our platoon Sergeant is a card. He has been out here thirty odd months and is merely Sergt. because of good work in the line. He can't give a command – at least not in a Military way. He usually has a chew of tobacco bulging in his cheek. He is by no means smart in appearance. The other night he was giving the orders for next morning . . . "I want every man right up on the palms of his feet" . . . While occupying the chair last night in charge of the program he got up and said, "The next in the

line of Bull, will be a speech by so & so". Everybody roared. His
face was a study . . .

Yours in F.L. & T. [Faith, Love & Trust?]

Cannon

Reg. # 681036

*John Cannon Stothers remained in Europe with the army of occupa-
tion until 1919. Carman, who fought at Vimy and was wounded in
a trench raid in June 1917, recovered from his wounds in Canada.*

A WAR OF NERVES

*The first case of shell shock was recorded in the winter of 1914–15.
By 1918 twenty specialized hospitals and many rest homes in
England were treating the thousands of men whose symptoms
included bizarre ways of walking, hysterical paralysis, and hair that
stood intractably on end. Initially some doctors argued that only
degenerates and weaklings suffered neurasthenia, as it came to be
called, but that argument was heard less often when it became known
that officers were more likely than the men to break down. Shell
shock was rarely mentioned in letters home.* **Private Robert George
Duncan** *of Sandwick, on Vancouver Island, a stretcher-bearer with
the 102nd Canadian Infantry Battalion, used the term in describing
with unusual honesty his reactions to stress and comparing his
stamina as a twenty-four-year-old with that of older men.*

France

15.1.18

Dear Mamma & Papa, –
Yesterday's mail brought me two letters from you, all about the election and Mamma's first vote. I'd have given a lot to have seen the look
on Mamma's face when she first exercised her "prerogative" . . .

The older men although they boast they are as good at fifty as
they were at twenty-five when in civil life soon find out their mistake

after a few months here. They have not got the come-back that a younger man has, he may stand a few of the rough bits better than the youngster but the strain soon tells on him. After the taking of that trench in which our battalion first distinguished itself over a year ago I was in such a state that had I been a man of forty-five I do not believe I would ever have got over it. We were relieved after a very trying day at about eleven at night (after four days of it on bully and captured rations) and had to make about six miles back to reserves. Naturally we were exhausted before we started our trip out and we had to go through a veritable ocean of mud, all the time Fritz was throwing all he had at us. When we got about three miles of it over we were met by the band who had been sent out to guide us in and they seeing that we were all in foolishly tried to encourage us by telling us we only had a hundred yards or so to go. I knew better but I was so exhausted that I was almost delirious and I began counting my steps. I would count to ten or so and then forget that I intended to count so I'd start in again and count perhaps to fifteen and then forget again. All the time the boys were falling out one by one but I still kept plodding on counting my steps when I could remember or telling the guides what I thought of them in the strongest language I knew about fooling us about the distance. We finished the trip at six a.m. six [men] only of the three companies got in without falling out, the rest were scattered all the way along the road. The cooks had a hot breakfast for us and we ate like wolves but all the time we ate the lot of us cried like babies. I'll never forget the way the tears rolled out of my eyes and I couldn't have told you why I cried excepting that my nerves were completely gone. The quartermaster was there with blankets and told us to take one apiece so just to prove I wasn't shell shocked I took two because I knew there were a lot of the boys who didn't come out for their issue. I beat it with my blankets to a little shelter and slept the clock around and woke up not a bit the worse for the experience. That same trip cleaned out nearly every one of our men over forty . . .

Yours lovingly
Robbie.

Working at a regimental aid post near the front during the attack on Bourlon Wood on September 27, 1918, Duncan was hit in the abdomen by a machine gun bullet and succumbed to his wounds in a casualty clearing station.

NATIVE BROTHERS IN ARMS

Corporal Mike Mountain Horse – *Miistatosomitai, in the tongue of his Alberta Blood tribe – was one of more than four thousand natives from across Canada who volunteered in the First World War. Among them were fifteen Inuit from Labrador who joined the Newfoundland Regiment; thirty descendants of Metis who had fought with Louis Riel in the 19th-century North-West Rebellion; and one in three of all able-bodied first-nation men in Canada – including three hundred Iroquois from the Six Nations Reserve in Brantford, Ontario. Not surprisingly, many of them proved to be superb scouts and snipers. Mountain Horse, who had attended an Anglican boarding school and became a scout for the North-West Mounted Police, joined up in May 1916. He was wounded twice at Cambrai, northern France, where in late 1917 the British used a concentrated force of 240 tanks and broke through the supposedly impregnable Hindenburg Line. Convalescing, Mountain Horse wrote to his family.*

[February 21, 1918]

. . . I am now in an English hospital for wounded Colonial soldiers; all we have to do is to get well, and at the present time I am getting along fine, although they've told me that I've got to stay for another two months before I am again fit for active service. I hate the idea of staying here doing nothing, and offered to go with the first draft leaving for the trenches. The officer in command said he admired my pluck, but he could not take me, so I am doomed to stay in this place for some time. We all had to behave like men in France, and I think we did so, although well knowing the nature of the men facing us. I got a slight scratch from a Prussian Guard during an engagement in

No Man's Land; the fellow caught me with his bayonet, on the outside of my arm, but I proved superior to him, although he made it hot for me for a time. I received the Xmas parcels from Good Old Macleod [Alberta] Red Cross, and I want to thank them for them very much. I am rather lonely, although I am amongst good friends – I have not talked Blackfoot for over six months.

Mike M. Horse
R95041, D. Company, 21st Reserve,
Bramshott Camp,
Hants, England.

Mountain Horse's brother Albert (Flying Star) had been the first in the family to enlist, in the first week of the war. He was gassed three times, once with chlorine at the Second Battle of Ypres. As he wrote to a minister on his reserve, "Oh it was awful . . . I don't mind rifle fire and the shells bursting around us, but this gas is the limit." Sent home, he died a day after arriving in Canada, in November 1915, of tuberculosis lodged in his gas-weakened lungs. The remaining brothers, Joe and Mike, then joined up. Joe, an industrial-school grad and interpreter, was wounded three times. Mike survived his time overseas and came home to work for the Mounties. He later wrote newspaper articles and a book, My People the Bloods. *"The war," he wrote, "proved that the fighting spirit of my tribe was not squelched through reservation life."*

FLOWERDEW'S CHARGE

The anticipated German offensive of 1918 began on March 21 with an assault that routed the British 3rd and 5th Armies and allowed the enemy to advance rapidly westward. Only a few Canadian units took part in the initial fighting, but the Canadian Cavalry Brigade fought at Moreuil Wood, helping to stall the seemingly inexorable German march on Amiens. One hero of that battle was **Lieutenant Gordon Flowerdew,** *an Englishman who had emigrated to Canada* *and settled for a while in Walhachin, British Columbia (where he earned a certain notoriety as the postmaster who put thirteen sacks of eastbound mail on the westbound train). Flowerdew served in Europe with Lord Strathcona's Horse. On March 30 Brigadier General Jack G. Seely directed mounted squadrons against the Germans in Moreuil Wood. Flowerdew led about seventy-five horsemen, who fought with sabres against rifles and machine guns until the enemy broke and retired. Flowerdew wrote this brief note to his mother just before the battle.*

[March 30, 1918]

My dearest Mother

Have been a bit busy lately, so havent been able to write. I managed to borrow this card–Havent had any mail for some days, so we are very keen to see the papers. The weather is still very good, but very keen at night. Have had the most wonderful experiences lately & wouldn't have missed it for anything–Best love to all

Your affectionate son

Gordon

The official account, written for Flowerdew's Victoria Cross citation, says: "Lieut. Flowerdew was dangerously wounded through both thighs during the operations, but continued to cheer his men." An unofficial account had him galloping up to General Seely, saluting and saying, "We have won, Sir," before collapsing. He died the following day. Seventy-one Canadians received the Victoria Cross, the British Empire's highest award for bravery. Three recipients lived on the same street in Winnipeg, which has been renamed Valour Road.

WHO KILLED THE BARON?

Wilfrid Reid (Wop) May *was born at Carberry, Manitoba, in 1896 and served in the Canadian infantry in 1916 before transferring to*

the Royal Flying Corps. During his maiden combat flight on April 21, 1918, Lieutenant May faced off with the fabled Red Baron, Manfred von Richthofen, whose score was eighty downed planes. In this letter, written decades later, May recalled the encounter for a writer. (His nickname, Wop, was a young playmate's attempt to pronounce Wilfrid.)

3867 S.W. Marine Drive
Vancouver, B.C.
March 5th 1950.

Donald Naughton, Esq.,
133 Center Street,
Mt. Vernon, N.Y.
U.S.A.

Dear Mr. Naughton:

. . . A driver and tender was sent for me and we started off to our squadron which was then situated at Bertangles, approximately 12 miles west of Amiens. The driver was a good chap, and on the way to the Squadron we got on a party, and arrived 2 or 3 days late. When I did finally report to the Squadron I was paraded before the C.O., a Major Butler, who was very disturbed over the incident and would not keep me in the Squadron. He had arranged for my transfer back to the pilot's pool. I stepped out of his office and ran into an old school chum of mine, Roy Brown, in the Orderly room . . . I told him my difficulty, and he said he would see what he could do to fix it up. He went in to see the C.O. and arranged to take me in his flight and transfer one of his men to the flight that I was assigned to.

Roy took me under his wing and gave me as much training as he could, including aerial gunnery, which was cut short in England. He also took me over the lines to get me accustomed to anti-aircraft fire.

The time came that I was to join the flight in combat duty, April 21st.

Roy gave me my instructions which were to stay up on top when he went on down to attack enemy aircraft, and watch and see how things went. Roy was leader of the squadron this particular day.

We took off and I was outside man on the left of Brown's flight, we flew in V formation. There were 3 flights, approximately 18 machines. We went over the lines, approximately fifteen or twenty miles, and with the limited experience I had I did not see what Brown was going down on when he wobbled his wings to attack. I stayed up as instructed, circling, but for a long time I did not see any enemy aircraft or our own aircraft, until one enemy aircraft appeared just below me, which I let go as instructed. Another aircraft appeared below me, I did not let this one go by and went down and made an attack. I missed and followed him down. I then found myself in the middle of a swarm of enemy aircraft, I continued my attack and shot one aircraft down, which I was given credit for, having received confirmation from 2 members of my squadron.

The enemy aircraft were coming at me from all sides, I seemed to be missing some of them by inches, there seemed to be so many of them the best thing I thought to do was to go into a tight vertical turn, hold my guns open and spray as many as I could. The fight was at very close quarters, there seemed to be dozens of machines around me. Through lack of experience I held my guns open too long, one jammed and then the other, I could not clear them, so I spun out of the mess and headed west into the sun for home. After I leveled off I looked around but nobody was following me. I was patting myself on the back feeling pretty good getting out of that scrape. This was'nt to last long, and the first thing I knew I was being fired on from the rear. I could not fight back unfortunately, so all I could do was to try to dodge my attacker. I noticed it was a red tri-plane, but if I had realized it was Richthofen I would have probably passed out on the spot. I kept on dodging and spinning, I imagine from about 12,000 ft until I ran out of sky and had to hedge hop over the ground. Richthofen was firing at me continually, the only thing that saved me was my poor flying. I did'nt know what I was doing myself and I do not suppose that Richthofen could figure out what I was going to do. We came over the German lines, troops fired at us as we went over, this was also the case coming over the

British lines. I got on the Somme River and started up the valley at a very low altitude, Richthofen was very close on my tail. I went around a curve in the river near Corbie. Richthofen beat me to it and came over the hill, at that point I was a sitting duck. I was too low down between the banks to make a turn away from him. I felt that he had me cold, and I was in such a state of mind at this time that I had to restrain myself from pushing my stick forward into the river, as I knew that I had had it. I looked around again and saw Richthofen do a spin and a half and hit the ground. I looked up and saw one of our machines directly behind. I joined up with him and returned to the airport.

It was not until later in the day that we found out that it was Richthofen, Brown had shot down. Brown was the one I had joined up with and returned to the airport. He told me after that 2 enemy aircraft were on his tail and he just happened to come out over Richthofen and myself. He fired one short burst, the bullet was found to have entered his back, near the shoulder, and went down through his heart or near his heart, killing him instantly. It was proved that the bullet could not have been fired from the ground, and Brown was given official credit.

The Australians came to our Squadron and tried to talk us out of our claim, they said that Richthofen pulled up and an Australian gunner on top of the hill, who was firing at him at the time, shot him down when he had pulled up at a fairly steep angle. However, the autopsy proved this was not possible and I am sure what happened is when Brown hit Richthofen, he fell back and pulled the stick back, went into a stall, and spun in. The only part of the spin that I saw as I mentioned, was approximately a spin and a half.

With reference to the official medical report, the way that you have it down does not add up. The one bullet is correct. It entered in his back and went down through or near his heart. If it had gone in and come out higher it would have substantiated the Australian machine gunner's claim, however, there is no doubt about it, the official report gave Brown credit . . .

When I saw Richthofen spin in, and looked up behind Richthofen, Brown was directly behind him but at a higher level, we were all going in the same direction. I did not see the two aircraft Brown had on his tail, I think probably they left him at our lines.

Richthofen was not noted for coming over our lines, I think he followed me over because he was so mad he could'nt shoot me down. He did not hit me with any of his fire, the only bullet holes I had in my aircraft when I returned to our base, was from the ground up, through the wings and fusilage. It was remarkable that I was not hit any time during that fight . . .

Richthofen was buried at Bertangles Cemetary and given full Military Honours. I also believe that he was buried in a lead coffin. However, I did not attend the funeral. Our squadron dropped messages on a German airport advising that Richthofen had been shot down, where he was buried, etc. I also believe that we dropped flowers . . .

With kindest personal regards.
Yours sincerely
W.R. May.

Captain Arthur Roy Brown wrote to his father: "There were eleven of us and twenty-two of them as nearly as we can make out. It was the most terrible fight I have ever seen in the air . . . It is bound to have a great effect on the Hun especially when they lost their best fighter and their stunt squadron was defeated." In the fights to follow, Wop May shot down eighteen German fighter planes and was awarded the Distinguished Flying Cross. After the war, he became a bush pilot in the Canadian north, performing other feats of aerial daring, such as the first non-stop flight from Edmonton to Winnipeg and a flight in a blizzard to deliver an antitoxin to Fort Vermilion. In 1931 May founded a northern flying service, which he sold to Canadian Airways Limited, where he became the superintendent. Canadian Airways was later folded into Canadian Pacific Airlines. May died in 1952.

BRUTALIZING CIVIL POWS

The following letter was addressed to the consul general of the Swiss Republic, Beni R. Iseli, in Montreal, with the request that it be forwarded to the Imperial German Foreign Office on Wilhelmstrasse in Berlin.

[April 1918]

We, the undersigned Civil P.o.W. feel it our moral duty against our fellow prisoners at the Morrissey Detention Camp, to give the Imperial German Foreign Office the following notice:

On April 2nd, 1918 we were sent from the Morrissey Detention Camp to the Detention Camp at Vernon/B.C.

We can testify under oath, that since the middle of January 1917 German and Austrian Civil P.o.War at the Morrissey Detention Camp at different times have been cruelly treated by guards and especially by the Camp-police. Some fellow prisoners have been arrested on false charges and taken to the guardroom by the camp-police. On the way to the guardroom and inside of the guardroom they were hit with fists and kicked by guard or Camp-police. Several of those prisoners fell sick in consequence of such ill-treatment, especially No. 335 and 188. No. 335 is at present in the isolate hospital in a hopeless condition (tuberculosis). Both these prisoners were with some others put into close confinement in April 1917, because they refused to do work outside of the wire fence, work which was not for the interests of the inmates of the Camp excl. While in the cells, they were treated in the most brutal manner. Other civil P.o.W., who refused to do such work, were often sentenced to close confinement too, and during their time in the cells brutally treated and forced to do the most degrading kinds of work for the guards under the threats of bodily punishment if refusing to comply. Some prisoners, who called the O/C's attention to the condition were told that the prisoners were liars.

In spite of the fact, that we have told this to the Swiss Consil, Mr. S. Gintzburger, during his first and last visit he paid to the Camp during our stay there, on August 24. 1917, and notwithstanding our vain efforts to keep in touch with the Consul the treatment of the prisoners has not materially changed since that time. Only a few days before we lest [sic] the Camp on March 28th. 1918 prisoners were brutally treated by the Camp-police.

The civil prisoners at the Morrissey Camp are not allowed to lay down on their bunks during the daytime, even if they feel ill, tired and hungry, without a permit of the medical sergeant, who gives his opinion whether the prisoner is sick or not. Prisoners, found on their beds at daytime, were punished with as much as 6 days in the cells at half rations and in spite of their feeling unwell immediately arrested and forced to do humiliating work for the guards in the guardroom. Anybody refusing to do this was threatened with bodily punishment.

We have done everything possible to better the conditions of our poor German and Austrian fellow-prisoners, who are detained at the isolation barracks or at the hospital. Fresh milk, the chief-nourishment for sick people, is not to be had at these hospitals and when we received $100, – from a Mrs. Schroeder, Winnipeg for the benefit of the Camp, the prisoners resolved, that this money should be used to buy milk and other proper food for the sick. The Camp Medical Officer, when told of our intention, replied, that no fresh milk were obtainable even if we paid for it ourselves.

In this matter we do not expect any help from our legal representatives, the Resp. Consuls of Switzerland or Sweden. During the week of Febr. 24. 1918 we requested the Swiss Consul, Mr. S. Gintzburger, in 15 different letter, to at last visit the Camp, but up to this time we have received no answer whatever.

Therefore we sincerely request the German Foreign Office to immediately cause the necessary measures to be taken by the Imperial German Government, to put an end to this ill treatment. Furthermore we beg the I.G. Foreign Office to make these facts known to the K.& K. Austr[o]-Hungarian Government, in order that similar steps may be taken.

We declare voluntarily, our willingness to support these our statements with an oath.

Very respectfully

[Signed by 32 men]

Canadian authorities rounded up Canadian residents who did not have Canadian citizenship (among them 8,500 Ukrainians) and detained them with German prisoners of war in twenty-four camps across the country. There were 137 POW deaths in Canada during the First World War.

HEDGE-BIRDS WHISTLE

Max Aitken (Lord Beaverbrook), who was in charge of the Canadian War Records Office in London, originated the idea of bringing Canadian artists to Europe to record in paintings, prints, and sculpture the Canadian contribution to the war, which resulted in 850 works of art, now gathered together as the Canadian War Memorials Collection. Among the artists were A.Y. Jackson, Maurice Cullen, Arthur Lismer, and **Frederick Varley**, *a Briton who was living in Canada at the onset of the war while his wife remained in England.*

3rd C.C.D.

Canadian Camp

Seafard

May 3rd, 1918

Dear Wife, my little pal,

. . . At present I paint every day, learn the ways of fighting – understand gas masks and the meaning of a helmet, and have heard the scream and whistling of exploding bombs as they cut the grass near by – All the boys I have met are wonders – giants of strength and good to look upon. They have all been two and three years in France and are training newcomers in the art of murder – Many of them are the Princess Pats men and a more amiable sympathetic lot of men I have never met . . .

I went with [Maurice] Cullen last night after mess to a valley about 3 miles away overlooking Alfreston and I could do nothing else but marvel. Never have I seen such beauty and grandeur so combined – It was as fine a sermon as I have ever had, and if you could have stood by me and seen the same glories we would have had real Communion – Someday love, we shall be able to do these things – On the coast near here are a range of white cliffs, called the Seven sisters, just west of Beachy head, crowned by velvety grass – of hues like that of a faded green satin carpet – rolling inland, wave after wave of undulating hills where one frequently sees the "dew-pools" of the Sussex downs; a perfect pasture land for thousands of sheep. Everytime I look at those marvels of hills with their great white sides facing the sea, I wonder if the scene is real. But in the evening after a rainfall I swear they are not real. They float intangibly in a pearly atmosphere. Delicate gold and rose have painted the cliffs, and sapphires are in the dreamy hazy sea. Yes, and the valleys down to the beach are satin carpets. Seabirds wheel around, mingling with the blackcoat crows and their discordant screeching accentuates the whole magic of the place. Blackbirds and thrushes flood the air with their full throated warblings – somewhere inland a cuckoo calls and even after sundown, skylarks from on high pour down their trills into the valleys – Just over the cliffs a pale yellow moon is climbing above the vapours. I wait until it reaches the clear air and a faint ripple of silver catches the booming waves, and then, my love, I take you by the hand and journey back to realities feeling a peace beyond all understanding – Sleep well, little wife Night night . . .

Your very affectionate husband
Fred.

UNADULTERATED PIFFLE

Lieutenant Frederick Donald MacKenzie and his brother, Robert, students at Queen's University, joined No. 5 Stationery Hospital, a unit raised by the university, and later obtained commissions in the artillery. Don wrote to Wilma Robertson.

29/6/18
France

Wilma dear –

How am I going to thank you for those beautiful maple leaves, or for the thought that prompted you to send them? They are perfect. Such delicate form and tint & they were in a perfect state of preservation. If there is any other national emblem just quite so sweet & beautiful I should like to know about it . . . you know Wilma (or do you?) that the things that make war such a Hell are not so much the physical as the mental. To a fellow without imagination the most of this war is one grand picnic – its the deadly monotony that kills, the strain on the nerves, the little irritating things, the surrounding coarseness & brutality, the uncertainty, the vagueness of the future & even of the present, the lack of any definite thing to look forward to or work for. The physical difficulties are nothing. Frankly I often envy the fellow who comes out & gets it on his first trip. He's lucky in comparison with the fellow who is compelled to stick around for a few years & is pipped in the end, although he (the latter) may be more fortunate than the man who doesn't get it at all.

The whole business gets one so fed up at times – well its just like a long sickly swell at sea or a good rough roll, first your afraid your going to die & then your afraid you aint. Thats "Seasickness" . . .

This is rather a pessimistic letter – will have to pick up, eh? You said something in your other letter about the fighting in the first big offensive being beyond description. From this point of the line it looked very much like a blame good foot-race. Of course the "press" had some wonderful description but the war correspondents must hold their jobs & their copy generally furnishes humor for the troops in the field . . . There are a great many people who write pure unadulterated piffle about things that never happened and about some things that do, to their people at home forgetting that those at home are not in a position to judge and sift the truth and (I hope) forgetting or failing to understand that those at home waiting are having the more terrible time . . . We all have certain strenuous times, but I know people (officers & soldiers) whom Canadians on the other side of the water thought were suffering so terribly in the big offensive – what were they doing – eating strawberries & cream in one of the most beautiful parts of sunny France. Others who were sent up to take part in the big resistance in the north came back from the fight not because they wanted to but because it was over & they weren't needed. They hadn't had as good food (chicken, fresh eggs, butter, milk etc) since leaving home. We have had the most wonderful time since Fritzie started his big push in the spring, baseball, football, cricket, horse shows, athletic meets – by the way (this is now Sunday the 30th) the big final athletic meet for the Canadian Corps is to take place tomorrow July 1st and it is to be the biggest & most wonderful Canadian athletic meet held in or out of Canada in the last ten years. How's that for a line? Oh no, we don't think much of ourselves, just read that newspaper clipping. I believe Mr. [Robert] Borden is to be on hand tomorrow in order to drop the odd tear as he tells the boys the Govt. is behind them to the last man (not meant to include himself or members of his cabinet). Well if the people are willing that he should spend their money that way – c'est la guerre . . .

Jessie wrote & told me she voted Union – my only comment was, that the Govt. expected the women to vote for them or they wouldn't have given them the franchise. She had done the expected . . .

Yes I think there will be another winter of war, although there are many things that only the higher command know (and they wont tell) that one can hardly judge. But if the Americans send over some more men & that other aeroplane by next spring, we should be able to give old Heinie a kick in the neck next summer. Do you know, Wilma, I've had a terrible time since the U.S. entered the war [in April 1917] upholding their ability etc. So very few people will take them seriously.

The Canadians, generally, hope to see them do good work, it's the European people who have to be shown. It did look for a long time as though they were willing to sacrifice their money & everything else but their men. I only wish we could form up an army with American troops – nothing in Europe could stop it of equal size . . .

Always
Don.

In 1918 the Dominion Day sports event, which the Canadians held every year of the war, took place at Tincques, a village near Arras. While planes flew protectively overhead, fifty thousand soldiers watched and participated in track and field events, soccer and base-ball games. The day ended with a musical revue by a group called the Volatiles. Donald MacKenzie married Wilma and became a teacher at Neepawa, Manitoba, and a member of Parliament from 1935 to 1945. His brother, Bert, lost his left foot in the battle of Amiens.

MOM'S GAS ATTACK

Not all the correspondence from overseas during the First World War dealt in human misery. **Private Harry Scott** *of Morden, Manitoba, was only sixteen when he joined the 196th Infantry Battalion in 1916. Perhaps because of his youth, he served in the relative safety of England, from which he sent this missive to his mom.*

London
July 15th/18

Dear Mother,

I received the birthday parcel a few days after the big day but that didnt matter so much. There was four of us all gathered around to have a feed. I took an old army razor and opened it. When I got the cloth part off and had one half of the car[d]board lid open three fellows fainted. (I am trying to break it easy.) I staggered back across the room then rushed to the windows. I at last got enough courage up to finish. I very gingerly picked the different things out till I came to four very <u>rotten</u> eggs then I prayed for a gas mask. I have gone through some awful odours in cookhouses but that took them all. I threw them out and then cut the cake. There was one piece whereon an egg reposed all the way over. We watched to see who was to have it. I managed to miss it but we all had to hold our noses as we ate it it was agony. We also devoured the maple sugar and soda biscuits they had a faint perfume – but not quite as bad. The butter at the top of the jar had a queer taste but we all pretended that we did not notice it. The sugar was alright. The parcel would have been a grand success on the western front as a gas attack if the wind was blowing the right way . . .

Well I must close now. Still fat and long.

Love to All

Harry

REVENGE AND VICTORY

In early August 1918 the entire Canadian Corps was moved in secrecy 112 kilometres from Arras to positions south and west of Amiens for a major attack alongside British, French, and Australian troops. The Canadians code-named their operation "L.C.," for the Llandovery Castle, *a Canadian hospital ship torpedoed by a German U-boat in June as it was sailing to Britain with ninety-seven medical staff and crew. (Although many escaped to lifeboats, they were shelled by the submarine or drowned; ninety-one perished, including fourteen nursing sisters.) Between August 8 and 11, the four Canadian divisions fought parts of fifteen German divisions and penetrated well into German-held territory, taking Amiens. Then began the final hundred days of rapid Allied attacks and advances, during which the Canadian Corps cracked the Drocourt-Queant defence line and captured Cambrai, Valenciennes, and, on the last day of fighting, Mons.* **Corporal Jack Stratford** *had been in the lines near Arras in late July, conducting night raids and bringing back German prison-*

ers, when the transfer of the Canadian Corps to Amiens began. He wrote to his sister.

October 25th 1918
Bramshott Hospital

Dearest Mayden,

. . . Well we settled down then and held the line until about the end of the month, and one night the Imperials came in, unannounced, and relieved us, and we went out and systematically got lost. We marched for miles then we got in busses and got back, then we'd have a ride on the broad gauge, then a ride in busses, then another march, then another march, always at night and all night. Well on August 7th we were in the wilderness, but where we didn't know. However it turned out that we were in front of Amiens, a few kilometres from where Joe [their brother] was buried. I tried to get over to see his grave but I couldn't get away, as we were to go over the next day, August 8th. We were shown airmens' photos of the ground we were to go over and everything was explained . . . Oh, Lordy, Oh Lordy! you never saw anything like it in your life, and I can't tell you what it was like, nor no one else can. I'd go back and do it over ten times though, just for the fun of it.

Well old dear the 1st Division made a record, and the 10th Battn had the final objective to take and I was with the 1st platoon to gain the objective so saw some things worth doing, and seeing. 8 miles deep (the way the crow flies) in 8 hours, taking prisoners at the rate of 30 per minute. This record has not been equalled by our allies or the enemy since the war started, so you see we did do things that day. The Division on our right was an hour and a half behind us, and the one on our left was 6 hours later. That night we could see Fritz bringing up re-inforcements, and the F.G.H. [Fort Garry Horse] came up and dismounted and came into the line with us. I met lots of officers and men who knew Joe and we had some great old chats. As we were in the country that they and Joe scrapped in before.

The next day at noon the 2nd Division and cavalry went through us, and relieved us. This picture I'll never forget, as we were in a position where we could see for miles, and the way the infantry and cavalry went through, shells breaking, men and horses dropping, our men going ahead and Frits prisoners coming back, ambulances, artillery, tanks etc. moving up – by jove it was some sight, and there'll never be another like it. We moved out that afternoon and over to our left flank and went over there three times in the next week. Went through and relieved the P.P.C.L.I's once. Well we came back from there and went back to Arras and in and over on September 2nd [the Drocourt-Queant attack]. This was a tougher scrap than the 8th August and we killed lots more Germans and captured more stuff, but it took us 3 days to go the same distance we went in 8 hours down south, but we got there just the same. We were in that trip 8 days and three times over the top, then we came out and had two week's rest and back again into Cambrai. This was a hell of a scrap, I was in for 7 days and over the top 3 times, and left the Battn in supports, and very much under strength. Gee, I'm about the oldest man in the battn now, and when I left there was hardly a man outside the O.C. and a few of H.Q. officers that I knew, and I went all through the three scraps without a scratch. Pretty lucky or I miss my guess. I didn't bother much the first two scraps but that last Cambrai show I sure did think at times that my number was up, but here I am you see, all in one piece and going strong . . .

Your loving bro.
Jack

Of the eight brothers in the Joseph Stratford family of Brantford, Ontario, five signed up for service overseas. Harold caught tuberculosis and was sent home. Arthur served in Africa and survived the war. George joined the Princess Patricia's Canadian Light Infantry and was killed in 1917. Joseph, who was awarded the Military Cross, was killed at Amiens in 1918. Jack Stratford survived the war but was disabled by exposure to gas and died at the age of forty-five. His letters and those of his brothers were used by their great-nephew R.H. Thomson in his one-man show The Lost Boys.

NO TO WAR

Private James Ernest Brown also fought in the action that pushed the Germans eighteen kilometres back from Amiens. Born in Ontario, Brown was a thirty-year-old single farmer in Alberta when he enlisted in the 89th Battalion at Calgary in January 1916. He wrote to his mother in Castor, Alberta.

August 18/18

Dear Mother –

Rec'd yours of July 26 today and thought I would answer it "tout suite" while I have a chance . . . Of course you know all about what has happened in the last ten days. It was certainly the most successful attack I have seen pulled off yet and let us hope it helps to bring the end nearer. But the more we see of war and its results the less a man wants to see of it and the more he feels that we have got to win and put an end to the idiotic delusion that war is a method of settling disputes. But war is inevitable so long as there are armies and there will be armies (peace time) so long as there are men fools enough to allow themselves to be used by other fools to satisfy their wish for pomp and show and yet so long as any powerful nation will allow itself to be fooled into believing that war can settle a dispute and insist on keeping an army other nations will be forced into keeping armies too as the only way to meet force is with force. Therefore the war must not end until Germany is willing to disarm or the world would still have to be an armed camp. Along this line we have produced a great many men who have attained and exert power that they never dreamed of before the war. Many of these men are serving well others are impediments but to all militarism has been so kind that they are carried away by the glamour of it and will insist on carrying on after the war. These men we must watch. If we force Germany to discard militarism we must discard it ourselves as quickly as safe for so long as we allow ourselves to think of might even as a last resource as a way of enforcing right we are laying the foundations of another war. We must therefore learn the lesson ourselves as well as teach it to Germany. We must not allow ourselves to listen to those who will preach "let us not be caught unprepared again["]. Peace when it comes must be such that there will be no nation armed against us then we must disarm ourselves. Think of war as a means of settling disputes and you will have war I think is just as true as the motto "Honi soit qui mal y pense". It is only those who have seen war who know what a calamity it is. If the boys when they get back could and would express their opinion of it. But you know how thoughtless and indifferent the average man is. He will soon forget all he has seen and let it go at that. I don't think I make my meaning very clear but there has got to be a world wide change in national thought as well as a political house cleaning in Canada if we are to reap the full benefit of the war . . .

Weather is very dry and roads dusty.

As Ever

J E Brown

Brown returned to Alberta, married, and had at least one child.

THANKS FROM A POW

As the war wound down, Germany allowed some Canadian prisoners of war to be relocated to internment camps in the Netherlands. **Private David H. Borden** *of Canard, Nova Scotia, offered belated thanks to women in Berwick, Nova Scotia.*

The Hague, August 28, 1918

The Ladies of the Berwick Red Cross
Dear Friends. –
Mrs. Harris told me some time ago that you were paying for my parcels in Germany, but, owing to restrictions on correspondence, I have been unable to thank you.

I arrived in Holland about three weeks ago, under the agreement of 1917, for the internment of officers, N.C.O's and invalids in neutral countries. Needless to say, the change is very much to our liking. In the lagers [stores] of Germany, British, Italians, French, Belgians, Russians and the rest, are all herded together in close, smelly barracks. Here we are billeted in empty houses and hotels, two or three in a room. The food, well, the German rations were not fit for pigs and we were compelled to live entirely on our parcels, except when we succeeded in stealing a few vegetables.

As for treatment, I want to forget that, until I get a chance at a German again. You may be certain that no ex-kriegsgafangener [prisoner of war] will forget or forgive Germany in a hurry. Our papers don't print half enough regarding them. No matter what agreements they make for better treatment of prisoners, they always find some way of dodging around a corner. Thousands of newly captured men are kept working close to the line, until they either die of starvation or are killed or maimed by shell fire. I know one sergeant, who was thirteen months under our own hellfire, and finally came back with one of his arms useless.

If it were not for the British Red Cross not one prisoner in ten would ever leave Germany alive. In Saltan Lager, Russians and Italians are dying at the rate of ten a day. The French and Belgian prisoners are fairly well looked after, but the British are away above all. In all the large lagers, relief committees receive parcels of food, clothing and medical comforts for the new prisoners. Each new prisoner gets a parcel every tenth day until his own parcels come through. Then as far as food and clothing is concerned, he is far better off than his captors.

We have been hoping to hear that the new agreement for direct exchange of all prisoners had been ratified, but so far we have been disappointed. There's no use saying we're not homesick, though its really more the desire to be doing something. It's no joke, sitting on the bench, when the game is a tight one.

I started in to tell you how deeply grateful all the boys are to the women of the Red Cross, and instead, I've been burdening you with more of our troubles. As a matter of fact, my vocabulary is too limited to say all I want to. So until I see you in person, I will just say, "Thank you" for all of us.

Very sincerely yours,
David H. Borden

ON THE LAM

Captain Edward [Tod] Bath was raised in Oakville, Ontario. (The family home, Belair, still stands on Bath Street.) He was taken prisoner on April 24, 1915, following the gas attacks on the Canadians at Vimy and was interned in camps in Germany and the Netherlands. When he wrote his mother, Alice Ruth Bath, from Holland he was waiting to be sent home.

Hotel Klanderÿ
Leeuwarden
Sept. 12 [1918]

Dear Maither
. . . Now I will try to remember a few more pleasant incidents of prison life. Poole & Medlicott were caught the third day after the wire jumping stunt were brought back & given two weeks jug in the meantime we were fixing up another stunt of dressing up as russian & french orderlies & going out in the early morning to feed the pigs which were just outside the second wire but in view of the sentries & two days after they were released we pulled it off. We got up about five oclock put on our civilian kit with orderlies uniform over it succeeded in dodging the sentries in the building & got into the kitchen where we hid our rucksacks under the pig food, a gunman came in while we were there but didn't notice anything wrong as soon as he had gone the six of us Poole, Medlicott, Voelker, Hilpern, Pramberger (the little russky) & myself walked out with big buckets of pig food on our shoulders said good morning to the sentry who very kindly opened the gate for us & we smiled a little sm[i]le of relief & walked

into the pig pen, once there we hid behind the pigs slipped off our uniform & got out the back without being noticed then we divided into two parties & went in opposite directions Hilpern, Pramberger & I got to the road & walked back in front of the camp greeting the same sentry again as we went by. We walked quietly on until we were out of sight of the camp & then when the way was clear beat it hell bent for election to a wooded hill we went up hill & down dale through the thick woods for about ten miles when we came to open country & there were a lot of farmers working in the fields so we picked out a thick spot & lay up for the day soaking wet & very cold at 10 a.m. had a biscuit & a raw oxo cube at 4 p.m. a biscuit & piece of chocolate, very thirsty, an old boar paid us a visit. We didn't like it's looks at all fortunately it scampered off on seeing us, 8.30 biscuit, raw oxo cube, & tot of rum start walking at 9 p.m. have great difficulty in finding roads through the woods finally get to open ground & go across country, arrive at small river about 3 a.m. which we drink nearly dry come to another river at daylight which we wade, the farmers were all out working but there was no cover in sight so had to keep on finally lay up about 8.30 in small clump of trees not very good cover but the best we could find, raining hard, cold as blazes p's feet beginning to get blistered same rations as the day before, position 2 kil. N of Sielen, start at 9 p.m. pass through Buhne whistling "der Vaterland". Very bad road to Natzungen, passing through a woman shouted to us to halt, went like the devil for about a mile & then lay up in a field to see if we were followed. After about 20 minutes start off again, p. in agonies with his feet & thirst & keeps saying "Oh gentlemen, gentlemen do not take such long steps & I can keep up with you". Reach a wood just before daylight where we decide to lay up. Nearly walked on a family of boars who started grunting & snorting which didn't make things more comfortable for us but we were too tired to pay much attention to them & flopped where we were, it had rained all night so were still soaking wet. At daylight we went farther into the woods for safety I found exactly what we wanted most, a small stream, we had our little spirit stove going hard in about five minutes & soon after had a heap big meal of two cups of thick cocoa & a biscuit heavens how good that hot drink was it was the first we had had & we had been wet ever since starting, at noon & in the evening we had hot oxo & a biscuit & started off again a little after eight it rained very little that night & we found our roads without much difficulty so managed to cover a lot of ground & daylight found us opposite Driberg on a high wooded hill, when we lay up we didn't notice that there was a road & a few houses just a little farther on, during the morning some youngsters came into the woods quite close to us & started playing hide & go seek, the little devils were all around us but fortunately a bad thunderstorm came up which drove them away before they had seen us, about 5 p.m. we were so wet & cold that we couldn't lie still any longer so we started off keeping in the woods as much as possible at eight oclock we stopped for something to eat & then did physical torture to try to get warm until it was dark enough to go on the roads. We passed through Allenbeken just after starting but took the wrong road out of the town & had to come back & get on the right one after following it for about a mile it ended in a blank wall of trees & very thick underbrush we tried to go through it but found it impossible as we couldn't see six inches ahead of us so had to come back we spent three hours looking for a road going in our direction but had no luck, at about one oclock the rain started coming down whole water so we gave it up in dispair & crawled under a little bridge to wait for daylight . . . Started off through the woods about noon we came to open country again but it was raining so hard that no one was out in the fields so we carried on & got a few mangles on the way which we put under our belts about four oclock we came to a fairly large stream in the woods where we stopped for a couple of hours & shaved each other had a good wash & a big meal & then started on again & kept going until five oclock the next morning. During the night we almost walked slap bang into a gunman training camp about 25 miles north of Paderborn it happened to be just ten oclock & the "lights out" bugle blew when we were not 50 yards away we made a big detour . . . at five oclock we were looking for a place to lie up when a woman passed us on a bicycle it was still pretty dark & we hadn't seen or heard her, as soon as she had passed we made tracks for a small wood but as it got lighter we found that it was not thick enough for our purpose so decided to try a bigger one across the road. Just as we were crossing the road we heard a wild shout of Halt!! & saw two men trying to jump off their bikes & put their rifles to their shoulders at the same time with the result that one of them took a dive into the mud he picked himself up again told us to put our hands up & then asked us if we had any papers, & what we were doing, Pramberger (who spoke perfect german) spun them a long yarn about our going to work on our cousin's farm at the next town but it wasn't good enough & we had to come along then when we saw the game was up we told them who we were they took us to a little pub & locked us up . . . sentries arrived from Münden to take us back . . . Voelker & Poole . . . had been caught the third day, Medlicott had run for it when they were caught & was still out . . . Medlicott was brought in later in the day he got as far as Münster where he was collared by a detective, we were all kept locked up for six weeks . . .

Cherroh

Tod

Heading northwest in the direction of the Netherlands, Bath and his pals covered about eighty kilometres. Harry Medlicott, a British lieutenant, travelled about 160 kilometres and was caught sixty kilometres short of the Dutch border. A famous escape artist, Medlicott was shot in May 1918 after surrendering on his tenth escape attempt. Edward Bath caught the flu and pneumonia and died in England on November 23, 1918.

THE PITY WAR DISTILLED

*Donald Ross, only son of **Mabel Ross**, wasn't yet eighteen when he signed up in 1916. Shot through the foot on Easter Monday, 1917, at*

*Vimy Ridge, he crawled a mile on hands and knees to a first aid
station. During his fourteen months' recuperation in England, he
became engaged to an English woman who called him Smiler because
he smiled, danced, and whistled and was "the happiest boy in the
world." Private Ross was sent back to France in August 1918. He
died when he became lost behind the lines and entered German-held
trenches. His mother wrote one of his friends.*

Grafton, Ontario
October 23, 1918

Dear Friend Conners,

My Friend Conners is the way my Dear Son Donald Ross spoke of
you when he wrote me the last letter he ever will write to me, said
letter being dated "somewhere in France Aug 30th." He was killed
Sept 2nd, I believe the day you were wounded. You know I do not
know what your name is but believe Donald mentioned it in his letter
but I do not want to read the letter just now if I do I shall not be able
to finish this letter to you. I am very sorry to know you are wounded
then again if not dangerously so I am glad as you will be safe for
awhile at least and now I am going to cry out a mother's sore heart
to you for some little news of my son's death or at least something
about his last days or hours on earth.

Ah if you only knew how I want to hear something about him
you see he wrote me the Friday before he was killed and he said like
this – my old friend Conners is Sargent and I am going in his
company so do not be surprised if I get a stripe myself that is if I am
lucky enough to stay here long enough to get one. And as I have
nothing except the cable and a letter from a Chaplain by the name of
Jackson who put another man's name and number in the letter he
wrote about my boy's death so you see it had very little interest for
me. So I just made up my mind I would appeal to you for news.
Perhaps you can give me some details and if not get into connection
with some of the boys who were near him when he fell and also try
and have his little personal effects sent to me they are as nothing to

anyone else but ah how precious they would be to me his Mother anything touched by his dear hands.

Ah Connors may you never have that longing to see anyone that I have to see my son for I am so lonely for him and have been waiting for so long and now ah now I must wait all in vain and I loved him so. Please do all you can in this for me and I shall give you a Mother's blessing.

We are holding a Red Cross concert hear Monday night Oct. 28 and Kate went down to see if Frank Mallory would sing for us. Our Minister Rev. Le Bonnie got your address from Paddy Gale so I will get it from Mr. Bessner tomorrow and send this off to you hoping and praying that you will be able to write me some news any little thing about him even the fact that you spoke with him and how he looked etc. etc. would be a great source of comfort to me.

Now I will close and I do hope this awful long selfish letter will not tire you too much and that you will try to send me some little news.

Hoping this finds you as comfortable as can be and trusting you to do what you can for a poor lonesome mother. I will close with best wishes.

Mrs. Hugh Ross
Grafton Ontario Canada

Mrs. Ross's letter was returned unopened; Conners, or Connors, was also dead.

HISTORY IS BUNK

*Even before the war ended, the soldiers and the historians were at odds. **General Sir Arthur Currie** wrote to Lieutenant Colonel Harold Daly, in Ottawa, to complain about the first official Canadian war history, written by Major (later Sir) Charles G.D. Roberts, a leading Canadian man of letters.*

Headquarters, Canadian Corps.
26th October, 1918.

Dear Harold,

. . . I am glad to hear you speak so kindly of the Corps. It is very gratifying to us all to be told that the people of Canada are satisfied with what it has accomplished. Naturally I am prejudiced, but I believe it is hard to estimate the exact value of the results of our attacks. You, no doubt, have seen a copy of my recent Order, in which I set forth what the Corps had accomplished since August 8th. It is a truly marvellous story, and the half has not yet been told.

We were the spear-head of the attack at Amiens, and in the battle of Arras and the battle of Cambrai, formed the flank to the big attack of the Third and Fourth Armies. I venture to say now that this flank attack by the Canadian Corps will form one of the most interesting subjects for future study by military students. A flank attack is always a hard attack, and in this case our flank was exposed for twenty-five miles. The Germans fought us exceedingly hard all the way, for whenever the Canadian Corps goes into a battle he seems to throw a far higher proportion of men and ammunition at us than he does at any other part of the front. He assumes that if he stops the Canadian Corps, everything else stops. This is a point that should be remembered by the people of Canada when they think of the casualties the Corps has to sustain, but yet, in view of all we have accomplished, I do not think anyone has any right to complain of the casualties.

You probably have not heard very much of the Corps since the battle of Cambrai, but because you have not you must not assume that we have been out of the line and resting. I said that in our advance on Cambrai, we had our left flank exposed for twenty-five miles. After being relieved in front of Cambrai, we went to the western edge of that flank and began to roll it up, and tonight we are half way through the City of Valenciennes, much further east than we were when we left the Cambrai front. In this operation we have released more than fifty thousand French civilians, and you can imagine their joy at that release. We have now left far behind the area of trenches, shell-holes, dug-outs and barbed wire, and I hope never to see them again. The country we are now in is a very clean one with good roads, nice villages and towns. Every man has a good billet, and most of them are in beds. The populace are exceedingly kind, and to be able to release them has been an inspiration to all our men. They are hearing from these people's own lips what it means to be under German rule.

I am glad to see that the temper of Canada is to fight this war out to a finish, and that peace when it does come must be a peace that will last for many, many years. We do not want to have to do this thing all over again in another fifteen or twenty years. If that is to be the case, German military power must now be irretrievably crushed. This is the end we must obtain if we have the will and the guts to see it through. To me the present situation is one fraught with much danger. I hope that when we make peace there exists in Germany a form of Government which possesses some stability. We do not want to make peace with a lot of Bolshevists, and there is a danger of Bolshevism becoming rampant in Germany. Furthermore, if Bolshevism does appear there, it may easily spread to France and England, and we might go from the frying-pan into the fire . . .

When the Prime Minister was here last summer, I protested against this book known as "Canada in Flanders" being styled the Official story of the Canadian Expeditionary Force, but apparently all to no avail. I stated my reasons very clearly in a letter to Sir Edward Kemp [minister in charge of overseas military forces], a copy of which letter I sent to the Prime Minister. All that was done with my letter was to hand it over to Lord Beaverbrook, who wrote to me saying that in finding fault as I did I was casting aspersions on one of the most noted Canadian writers, namely, Charles G.D. Roberts who, as you know, is another writer of poetry and fiction. I cannot help whether I cast aspersions on Roberts or not, but I do say that Volume III of "Canada in Flanders" bears no more resemblance to the true story of the period it depicts than a mutton stew does to the sheep itself. I am afraid, though, that it is too much to hope that things in England will ever be run satisfactorily.

With all good wishes, and hoping that before another October comes around that I may see you again in Ottawa.

I am,

Ever yours faithfully,

[Currie]

11/11/11

The final twelve hours of the war were perilous, poignant, and surreal. Armistice negotiations had begun in early October of 1918; Kaiser Wilhelm II had been forced to abdicate on November 9. On the night of November 10 and into the following morning, the 42nd Battalion (the Black Watch of Montreal) and the Royal Canadian Regiment captured Mons in Belgium. At 5 a.m. the armistice was signed in a French railway car, with fighting to cease six hours later. Canadian battalions continued to advance towards their objectives that morning, although it's not clear why Private George Lawrence Price, a Nova Scotian, crossed the Canal du Centre in the village of Havre, where at 10:58 a.m. he was killed by a sniper. Two minutes later the guns were silenced. **Captain Waring Gerald Cosbie,** *a surgeon with the 58th Battalion, described the reception in Mons.*

Mons

13-11-18

Dear Father,

I am writing this on a series of cards to give you some idea of what this famous old place is like, and now that the war is finished we are allowed to write more freely of what we are doing.

We received orders to go forward on the morning of the 11th towards Mons, and it was when we were marching up the road that we received the news that the armistice would start at 1100 o'clock, So the Colonel and I road on ahead with a groom to this place. It having been taken at 200 am by our division.

We certainly received a wonderful reception, something that I shall never forget, for as soon as we reached the outskirts the people were crowding about us, so that we could not even trot, throwing flowers on us, and in front of our horses on the road, and crying "vive les canadiens", "long live our deliverers". It certainly was thrilling, but made one feel like a frightful hypocrite.

All the houses were decked with Belgian and French flags and buntings, and people at every window when we reached the square in front of the town hall it was packed with people cheering, and singing and dancing. Everyone's wildest imagination could not have pictured a more stirring or glorious demonstration for the day of victory and peace.

I had often hoped to be either in London or Paris on this day, but that could never compare with being in Mons, the place where Britain started and ended the war, and to think that our own division had the honour of taking this place.

The bells in the cathedral started to play the marsellais [sic] and then the Belgian anthem first before 1100, and then representative companies from the brigade which took the town, marched into the square with bands playing and colours flying. The Montreal Highlanders made a tremendous impression on the people, as they marched past the General, with the pipes sculling out the "cock o' the north". Everyone seemed to go wild with excitement.

Cutherbert [sic] Robinson marched past with the detachment from the P.P.C.L.I. after the infantry came the guns and cavalry, this latter the 5th Royal Irish Lancers were here at the first battle.

In the afternoon there was another big march past in front of Gen. Currie, who presented the Corps pennant to the City Fathers. Every time the bands played either the Marseillaise [sic] and the Belgian anthem, all the people would sing at the top of their voices. It was a glorious day, and very orderly for in spite of everyone except those on duty having a holiday and wine and beer being gratis, the men behaved themselves perfectly . . .

Now we are preparing for our triumphal march to the Rhine. That of course will be the glorious finale and after the winter we should be turning our facing [sic] toward home. As yet as you may imagine it is hard to realize that it is all over, and when one wakes up it seems strange to think that never again will we listen to the ominous whine of a shell or on going to bed, not to be waked with the crash of the odd bomb . . .

Best of love to all at home
Gerald.

CROSSING THE RHINE

On November 18, 1918, Canadian troops in Mons began a four-hundred-kilometre march to Germany. On their journey they passed grateful Belgians, such as the inhabitants of Nivelles, who dug up eight thousand bottles of wine for them. A toss of a coin gave the 14th Battalion the privilege of leading the 1st Division over the Rhine and into Cologne on December 4. At the bridge at Bonn, General Currie stood taking the salute as the twenty-nine-kilometre-long column of the 2nd Division marched past. **Lieutenant James Chalmers McRuer,** *who became Chief Justice of the High Court of Ontario, described the occasion for Mary Dow, his fiancée in Toronto.*

Dec. 11, 1918

Dear Mary

At last, the day has come, that for so long was a mere dream and matter of jest – the day we should enter Germany. Not many of us ever imagined that we would be here, but we are here.

We moved all day yesterday and this morning we crossed the border at 9:20 a.m. We travelled down a road for about 300 yards that divided Belgium from Germany. All there was to show the frontier was a pole painted black and white in the same spiral manner as a barber's pole. It seemed strange to go along the road for those few yards and on the right were our friends and on the left our enemies. A small Belgian flag hung from one of the houses on the right, but from the houses on the left there was no sign of life except for some children peeking through the fence in the rear of one house.

We turned off into the wilds of West Prussia, which is much like Muskoka. We travelled a long time before we saw anyone. Presently we passed a number of men of all ages working on the road. They stood back and regarded us with an indifferent curiosity. By this time the feeling of strangeness had worn off and we settled down to go on our way in a perfectly indifferent manner.

No bands played.

Your ever loving,

Jim

It's estimated that, worldwide, the war cost $186 billion and that 8.5 million people from more than twenty nations lost their lives. Canada sent a force of almost 620,000 overseas; nearly 60,000 died and nearly 173,000 suffered non-fatal injuries. The war cost Canada $1.6 billion in 1914–18 dollars. Not as a colony of Great Britain but as a sovereign nation, Canada signed the 1919 Treaty of Versailles, the peace settlement imposed on Germany, and won membership at the League of Nations, the organization formed to ensure that the Great War would be the war to end all wars. A Canadian soldier-scientist calculated the future more accurately. Lieutenant Colonel Andrew McNaughton, who would command the Canadian Army in the Second World War, predicted: "We shall have to do it all over again in another twenty-five years."

THE SECOND WORLD WAR, 1939–1945

"I have no nerves left, Laura"

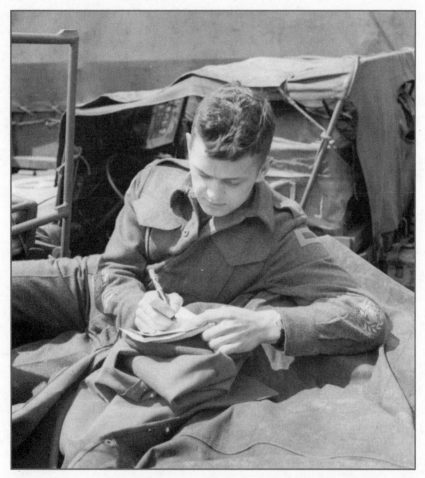

Company Sergeant Major D.D. Perkins of Ottawa, serving with the Royal Canadian Army Medical Corps, writes home from his Jeep in France following the D-Day invasion at Normandy.

U nlike the enthusiasm in 1914, when Canadians reflexively signed up for service overseas, there was little allure in 1939 to sailing off to another world war. The Great War had introduced the horrors of trench battle, poison gas, and the new weapons of air-planes, submarines, and giant armaments. Few romantic notions lingered about fighting the good fight. The people of Canada, along with most Europeans, hoped that Germany would stay its hand and not throw down the gauntlet of full-scale war.

We had come through a devastating decade. Although the bur-geoning economy of the 1920s had lured more Canadians off the farm and into the city – expanding the middle class – a global depression gripped most of the world in the 1930s. One in four Canadians was jobless, and millions went on relief, lining up for soup kitchens, labouring in work camps, riding their lives away in boxcars. Only recently had there been glimmerings of an end to the economic downturn.

Although many Canadians were dubious about the efficacy of war, some still clung to a muted vision of democracy vanquishing dicta-torship. Oral historian Barry Broadfoot quotes one veteran in *Six War Years*: "If going out and killing millions of Krauts to get Hitler off his goddamned pedestal is a high moral purpose, then I'm all for it." Yet too many of the men signed up simply to escape poverty, hungry for "three hots and a cot" – food and lodging.

After the First World War, Germany's middle class had also been hit hard by mass unemployment and currency inflation, which gave rise to extremist politicians. Among them was Adolf Hitler, a failed artist who'd won an Iron Cross after being gassed and wounded in that war. During the Great Depression, Hitler repositioned himself as the anti-Semitic, anti-communist führer of the largest party in the Reichstag. By 1933 he was chancellor of a coalition government, and a year later he pulled Germany out of the League of Nations, already weakened by the defection of the United States and an increasingly warlike Japan, which had taken over Manchuria and later invaded northern China.

Many Germans, still nursing collective wounds from their defeat in 1918, were eager for vengeance. Hitler was soon given dictatorial powers and employed the Gestapo secret police, a propaganda ministry, and a renascent army to help pursue his dream of a Third Reich, an empire that would rule for a thousand years. As early as 1936 Winston Churchill, a British member of Parliament, allied himself with Jewish, leftist, and unionist members of organizations such as the Anti-Nazi Council to warn the world about Hitler. A German accord that year with Italian dictator Benito Mussolini created the Rome-Berlin Axis. Both Germany and Italy helped fascist leader Francisco Franco to victory in the Spanish Civil War (during which about half of the 1,600 Canadian volunteers died while fighting for the democratic Republicans). In March 1938 a compliant Austria, infiltrated by National Socialist cabinet members, yielded to annexation by its expansionist neighbour Germany. The kindling was in place, poised to flare up into an all-out European war.

Britain and France were hesitant about reigniting hostilities with their old foe. Prime Minister Neville Chamberlain and Premier Édouard Daladier favoured placating Hitler, even when the Munich Pact of 1938 sacrificed much of Czechoslovakia to Germany. Canadians were generally sympathetic to this appeasement policy.

Social historian George Woodcock noted: "British-born Canadians made up a much smaller proportion of the population, imperialist sentiment had died away and even English-speaking Canadians were affected by the isolationism that in the 1930s was strong in the United States. And Québécois and Acadians were as reluctant as ever to become involved in the quarrels and causes of Europe."

In this tense atmosphere Canada, despite its financial woes, was increasingly standing on its own feet. In 1919 it had become an independent charter member of the League of Nations, and in 1931 Britain's Statute of Westminster formally ended Canada's colonial status. Canadians had a more conscious sense of themselves as a distinctive people, no longer linked inevitably to lands across the sea. This self-determination would soon be tested.

By the spring of 1939 Germany had occupied all of Czechoslovakia, and Italy had seized Albania. Britain and France abandoned appeasement and allied with Turkey, Greece, Romania, and Poland in an anti-aggression coalition. Germany and Italy then formalized a full military alliance, and in August the fascist Hitler signed a non-aggression pact with the communist Joseph Stalin, the Soviet Union's dictator. No longer at risk of having to mount a military campaign on two fronts, Germany invaded Poland on September 1. The British and French governments declared war two days later. "EMPIRE AT WAR," *The Halifax Herald* declared.

Mackenzie King's Liberal government maintained Canadian neutrality for one long week. On September 10 Parliament was recalled and Canada joined the Allied cause, agreeing to send soldiers overseas to fight Germany for the second time in a generation. This time they would typecast their enemy mostly as Jerry and Krauts (rather than the Great War's Fritz and Bosch), and would face new foes: the Italians they dismissed as Wops, and the Japanese as Japs or Nips.

To mount a new expeditionary force, Canada had to play catch-up. The nation had only about ten thousand full-timers in the three services. C.P. Stacey, the Canadian army's official historian of the Second World War, summed up the nation's woeful state of readiness for war: "Canada had no troops ready for immediate action, except for local coastal defence against very small raids. The tiny Permanent Force did not constitute a striking force capable either of counter-attack against a major raid or of expeditionary action. The Non-Permanent Active Militia, with its limited strength, obsolescent equipment and rudimentary training, was incapable of immediate effective action of any sort against a formidable enemy. The two forces together constituted a useful and indeed essential foundation upon which, over a period of months, an army could be built. They offered, however, no means for rapid intervention in an overseas theatre of operation."

The 1st Canadian Division sailed in December 1939 to begin training in England. They were welcomed by King George VI, who that spring had made a drum-beating, seven-week royal visit to Canada with Queen Elizabeth – the first such tour of any reigning monarch – and who had been received with great warmth. In a letter to the troops, the king wrote: "The British Army will be proud to have as comrades-in-arms the successors of those who came from Canada in the Great War and fought with a heroism that has never been forgotten."

The Royal Canadian Regiment, the Royal 22e Régiment (the Van Doos), and the Princess Patricia's Canadian Light Infantry (PPCLI) – the three Permanent Force infantry battalions – were the guts of the division. A 2nd Division was held in reserve at home. Together they formed the Canadian Active Service Force (CASF) under the command of fifty-two-year-old General Andrew McNaughton, the First World War artillery officer and later chief of the general staff. A popular choice, he would continue to earn the admiration of his troops. In June 1942 Canadian Seaforth Highlander Bob Tweedie wrote home: "The news that our much thought of General McNaughton being raised as a candidate for second front Generalissimo is swell. The boys respect his ability tremendously and would do any job he asked."

Andy MacNaughton and his counterparts in the Royal Canadian Navy and the Royal Canadian Air Force had a long, laborious travail ahead of them. They had to arm their men and women, physically and mentally, for a new kind of war.

THE DRUMS OF WAR

Gladys Arnold was an adventurous, thirty-four-year-old Saskatchewan reporter when she went to Europe in 1935 and began writing for The Canadian Press. She became the news agency's full-time Paris-based correspondent. Travelling in eight countries during the next six years, she observed the clouds of war building. She wrote to her mother back home.

[Paris] mid Sept 1938

Dearest Mother:

Just another little note as I did not get time to post my letter. Things at the moment look bad in Central Europe but I doubt very much, if we can get by the Congress of Nuremberg without war, that we will have anything this year – at any rate by the time you get this letter the destiny of Europe will be decided – if Hitler persists we will have war certainly – if he realizes his folly and that England and France mean business this time and will not allow Czechoslovakia to be touched (not so much for the Czechs. But because if Czechoslovakia crumbles before the "Great" Germany, as they persist in calling it now, all central Europe will go – Hungaria, Romania – Yugoslavia will crumble before the pressure – and Germany will dominate Europe – it will only be a matter of time then until France and England will feel the force of the Prussian-Nazi heel – so if they will save themselves they must save Czechoslovakia). On the other hand if we get by the Nuremberg congress it will be too late in the season to declare war this year – if Germany makes war it must be swift – without mercy and finished in less than 10 weeks – she hasn't the economic possibility of holding out during a long war . . .

. . . one thing we do know – Hitler must announce the future of Germany and of Europe next week at the congress and what he says there he must follow – because it is his promise to the people and he dare not promise what he cannot carry out – otherwise, like all dictators, he risks his own future.

Well, we will see – at any rate France is calm although I have several friends in the army here who have had their vacation cancelled. Everybody is alert but there is no sign of panic, of emotion – the french are at their best in face of danger . . .

Love

Glad

xxxxx

Arnold's hope was dashed within days, as British prime minister Neville Chamberlain tried to head off war by allowing Germany to swallow Czechoslovakia. Canadian prime minister Mackenzie King approved of the appeasement.

A REAL GOOD FIGHT

Hitler was not appeased for long. A year later, after he attacked Poland, Canada sent the first 7,400 troops to train at the dreary British army garrison town of Aldershot, amid the Hampshire heaths in southern England. As soldiers in training endured the cold and damp of a British winter, their senior officers enjoyed better conditions. **Ernest Sansom**, *a Great War veteran from New Brunswick, joined the headquarters staff of the 1st Division and was soon assistant adjutant and quartermaster general (the top administrative and supply official) at the Canadian military headquarters in London. He wrote faithfully to his wife, Lucy, in Fredericton.*

Wellesley House

31 Jan 40

Precious One, –

. . . When I got back tonight Ernie Wolford reported a bit of a fight in a pub last night which occurred when a couple of British Military Police attempted to arrest a couple of our men who had had a few glasses too much beer. One of our Mounties was there but apparently the British police thought he was not handling the situation strongly enough and undertook to do some arresting. Result some broken; heads, 14 doz glasses a windsor chair glass panel in a door some tables and a few plate glass windows. Reserves of police were called and which added fuel to the flames until our provost reserve (RCMP) arrived and dispersed the crowd. One man however spent the night in gaol with the civil authorities. Command Headquarters are greatly concerned and have to submit a report and take such action as may be considered necessary. It must have been a real good fight from what I can gather. The only danger is it may start a feud between our people and the British Military Police which would be unfortunate . . .

All my love
Your own Sammy.

Sansom later led two battalions that embarked for Norway in 1940 to try to counterattack the German forces that had captured the port of Trondheim, but the mission was called off as too dangerous. Two years later, Sansom became a lieutenant colonel commanding the 2nd Canadian Corps. When his unseasoned troops performed badly during Exercise Spartan, a dress rehearsal for a potential invasion of Europe, the British wanted to dismiss him, but General McNaughton resisted the pressure. At war's end, Sansom was inspector general of the Canadian Army Overseas.

WHERE'S THE BEER?

A "phony war" (or "bore war," as the British called it) lasted until the spring of 1940. No British or French soldiers were killed as Germany focused on the nations of eastern Europe. Canadian forces trained and underwent endless exercises. **Helen Lambart** *stayed home in Ottawa to work for* Canadian Aviation *magazine while her brother Arthur joined the Royal Air Force and brother Edward, the Royal Canadian Artillery. During the war years, she reported to them from the home front, as in this undated letter to her younger brother.*

[Ottawa]
March 15. [1942?]

Hiya Eddie:

This letter isn't going to leave for several days yet, but I'll start it now and I guess it will be a long one . . .

Life on the home front: We really know, now, that the war's on. The civilian just isn't considered, these days, which is as it should be. But I forsee that the time will come when restrictions will have to be relaxed a little bit. Its alright now, when everyone has something extra on hand, and can make do, and the stores have reserve stocks. But I think that eventually the situation's going to be pretty tight. Nearly everything is hard to get now. It's almost <u>impossible</u> to buy firewood – even in the country.

For instance: honey is hard to get; very few stores have any jam on their shelves; biscuits in a big A&P store last Saturday just didn't exist. I asked the man. He laughed at me: "You'll have to come on Thursdays if you want biscuits, lady." Beer just isn't to be come by. The liquor stores almost always have the sign out "Beer all sold". On Saturday, half an hour before the beer store opened, 27 people were lined up. Its just impossible. At the Chateau tavern you can only have one quart – and there are <u>no</u> small bottles. And half the joints are closed for lack of beer entirely. I heard a lad report that Standish Hall was closed last Wednesday, for lack of beer. The liquor shops are constantly crowded, though the prices are terrific with the new taxes. Good whisky (26 oz) now costs $4.85, the 40s cost $7.25 if you can get them. At Laura Secords they'll only sell you a measly half-pound of chocolates – about 12 candies – at a cost of 35¢. No elastic in the shops.

Worst of all for the ladies – there's now no Kleenex to be had, anywhere. We're lost without it. Not a shop has any – and everyone's asking for it. If any comes, . . . they'll be a most terrific crush. To get your tubes of shaving cream for the "Kelly box" I had to scout around and find empties to turn [in]. I found an old tube of glue, and an old cold cream tube. If you want more tubes, send back the empties for me to turn [in] for new ones. I'll send as many new tubes as you want if you'll supply the empties . . .

You can only get one pat of butter at a hotel or restaurant, and only one cup of coffee or tea, and only two lumps of sugar and you have to ask for it – usually. Everything is a line-up. They've taken off all the chair cars and diners etc. between here and Montreal and Toronto on account of the tie-up of freight traffic, and the coaches are jam-packed . . .

March 18 (after lunch)
I meant to go over at this time for some beer, but I can see from my window that there are about 50 people lined up outside the store, and I'm not going to get into that jam. Its three weeks now since I've been able to get any beer. The other afternoon when I went around they had a sign up: "Sorry. Today's quota of beer sold out". Its no joke. What there is, I guess, goes to those willing to stand in line for it . . .

(Interjection – the beer shop across the street has been open for 50 minutes. The line-up is all gone. I guess the beer is, also.) . . .

The liquor ration in Quebec province has just been cut in half. I think there's going to be a riot about this beer question . . .

Love – HE.

DUNKIRK'S WAKE

That spring, the German blitzkrieg ended the phony war with a vengeance. On May 10, 1940 – the day Winston Churchill succeeded the disgraced Neville Chamberlain as British prime minister – Germany's Wehrmacht invaded the Netherlands, Belgium, and Luxembourg with thirty divisions of Army Group B. Within two days forty-five Group A divisions were in France, and by May 20 they had reached the English Channel. The two groups pinned down the British Expeditionary Force (BEF) in a pocket around Lille, western France. Hundreds of thousands of Allies retreated to the channel port of Dunkirk. In one of the most heroic actions in naval *history, nearly nine hundred vessels of all kinds – many manned by civilians – ferried across the English Channel between May 27 and June 4, 1940, to rescue some 350,000 Allied troops, including 70,000 French soldiers. **Edward Lambart**, the brother of Helen in Ottawa (see page 210), was among those Canadians sent in afterward in a failed attempt to back French forces still battling in western France.*

1 Fd. Regt. R.C.H.A.
Base Post Office
CASF
England.
July 2/40.

Dear Bro[?] –

Thanks for your last nice letter from Toronto. I envy you like any-thing being up at Blue Sea [Lake] now lying around in a bathing suit on nice warm rocks. I wish I was there even for a weekend now.

In case you haven't heard much about the movements of the CASF [Canadian Active Service Force] we were not at Dunkirk . . . We did get across to France tho landed at Brest [on June 12 and 13]. We went inland about 300 miles, spent one night in billets and came right back because the frogs had given in. So the whole BEF [British Expeditionary Force] and the 1st Brigade of the CASF made a dash for life for Cherbourg, Brest and Bordeaux. After quite a while we got on board a transport and got back to Plymouth where we had sailed from with the best hopes a week before. So here we are back here again at Aldershot, still waiting to do something . . . The people here are still or even more so united and waiting. The factories are really going full blast too. Nearly every night there are air raids on some part of the country. We [hear] the Bosch quite often and a woman was killed in a house just down the road by a bomb. Everyone is expecting a real air raid every night – not just 2 or 3 bombers but 2 or 3 hundred which is the way our wall paperhanger–corporal [Hitler] does things. The fellows from France say the air is literally black with them. We'll win tho – we've got to. The country is seething with guards everywhere and all the commons have been ditched so aircraft can't land. Straight roads have concrete pillars on both sides for the same reason . . .

"Mine Kampf" is funny as anything. Best to you both –,

Affect.

Eddy

Italy's Benito Mussolini declared war on Britain and France on June 10, 1940, and invaded France the following day. Paris fell three days later, and the French government of Paul Reynaud signed an armistice with the Axis powers on June 22. Marshall Philippe Pétain, the vice-premier, took over as France's puppet leader, based in Vichy. Canadians were now the only major ally the British had.

MAKE LOVE AND WAR

Hitler intended to destroy the Royal Air Force, which the German Luftwaffe outnumbered three to one, and then paralyze England with saturation bombing. The Battle of Britain began on July 10. Canada's No. 1 Fighter Squadron was the first unit of the Royal Canadian Air Force to help the British contain the Luftwaffe. Meanwhile, other Canadians were already serving with the No. 242 (Canadian) Squadron of the Royal Air Force – among them pilot **William McKnight** *of Edmonton, who won a Distinguished Flying Cross (DFC) as a leading air ace in the first two years of the war. A party-animal who smashed the neck of a bottle and drank the liquor straight, he loved women.*

[July 18, 1940]
Royal Air Force.
c/o Canada House.
London S.W.

Dear Mike:

. . . I've been sick in bed for four days now and to-day is the first day I've been allowed to do anything at all and the M.O.'s [medical officers] even put a time limit to writing letters. Everything seemed to go wrong with me all at the same time, stomach, ears, throat, eyes etc. or in other words I was more or less useless to anyone. The Doc. says it was about two months of no sleep and less food that did it then sort of coming back to a civilized life just floored my system and I was left sucking a hind tit. I should be out in another four or five days though I hope so as the "Blitz" is just starting again and I've got to keep Turner from hogging all the fun. We two are the high scorers in the squadron so far having got twenty-three between us – nine for Stan and fourteen for me – so we have a pretty keen competition going on and neither one of us likes to be off duty when the other one is on as we're both afraid we'll miss a chance to get something. This game is damn good fun when you're fighting bombers as they're just like picking apples off a tree but fighters are a hell of a different proposition and keep you moving like greased lightening. Its a funny thing this fighting in the air before you actually start or see any of the Hun you're as nervous and scared as hell but as soon as everything starts you're too busy to be afraid or worried. We've had several fights with Colonel [Carl] Schumachers squadron – its supposed to be in the same class as Richt[h]ofen was in the last do – and I don't mind saying that they're about the finest pilots I've ever met. We generally manage to come out even-steven with them but a lot of the other squadrons haven't been so lucky. We had rather a funny thing happen one day – you may have read about it in the English newspapers – anyway we were chasing a hun bomber – five of us – when we lost him in some bad cloud – however right after this we saw about nine Me. [Messerschmitt] 109's. so we jumped them thinking we'd get a couple then slip off into the clouds. Right after this however the sky just poured 109's and some bloke, who must be the personal ace of the luftwaffe jumped me and succeeded in shooting away nearly all the machine except where I was sitting before I managed to dive into a cloud. Well anyway after we got home (three out of five) we found out that about eight Jerry squadrons had pooled their resources for the morning and we'd tried to jump about eighty machines.

We laugh like hell when we think of it now but it wasn't so funny then. Still the odds are always in their favor for some reason or other and we're always fighting like the underdog. I suppose you have heard about my decoration by now – it all happened by a mistake one day and things I'd been doing before. I got separated from the squadron and was sort of pissing about on my own – you know, boots shaking, knees knocking etc. when about fifteen Ju: [Junkers] 87's. came out of the clouds and started to bomb the fleet. I got four and luckly chased the rest off but the funny part is that while I was doing this the rest of the boys got jumped by 109's as usual right above me but on top of the clouds – so while I was having all the fun they were keeping everything away from me. We've only got five of the original twenty-two pilots in the squadron left now and those of us who are left aren't quite the same blokes as before. Its peculiar but war seems to make you older and quieter and changes your views a lot on life. – you also find out who are the blokes worth knowing and who aren't and I haven't met one yet who wasn't worth knowing. I expect soon they'll have most of the chaps [at] home in the army though I can't see what good an army is going to do now that we've only got an island left to defend. I hope you'll pardon me if this letter seems to ramble but I'm trying to remember things I think you might like to hear and also throw in a few of my own view-points. You'd never believe it but the last time I was in France I lost twenty seven pounds – I almost looked like an overgrown kid when we arrived back in England. I enjoyed our last stay in France – I had a hell of a nice Parisian refugee with me and the brass hats pulled out so fast we all had our own private cars. This girl and I – her name was Maryna – took a flat in Nantes and had a hell of a time for about two weeks. All the boys kept dropping in every night and we'd all B.S. and listen to the radio and eat then bog off to bed (after the lads had gone). It was sure marvellous and I certainly miss it now – I tried to smuggle the girl back on one of our bombing planes but one of the few big noises left in France caught me and raised merry hell. It was too bad because she was certainly one first class femme – she had been to university and was a modiste until the hun started towards Paris when she had to evacuate and then I ran into her. Oh well, I suppose I must have been fated for a bachelor – I can't fall in love anymore like I used to, I get all worked up for about an hour then I just lose interest . . . The real funny thing is the doc. has stopped my drinking everything except beer as my stomach is in such bad shape . . .

Ever your friend
Bill

McKnight received a bar to his DFC, *having shot down eight aircraft from August through November. He died when his Hurricane was hit during a fighter sweep over France on January 12, 1941.*

ENGLAND SHALL BE FREE

In August Germany focused the aerial fury of its Blitz on London with daytime attacks and then night raids right through the following spring. **Georges Vanier** *was a veteran of the Van Doos regiment in the First World War, an esteemed infantry commander who was wounded twice, yet insisted on returning to his battalion. Serving as a Canadian government representative in London, he knew what he was speaking about when he wrote the editor of* The Times.

Sept. 13 [1940]

Sir, – After the "All clear" sounded this morning I thought of the words of a devout Englishwoman, Julian of Norwich: – ". . . He said not: 'Thou shalt not be tempested, thou shalt not be travailed, thou shalt not be distressed'; but He said: 'Thou shalt not be overcome.'"

Therefore, in this hour of trial, let us pray not that we be spared suffering but that we be given the strength to bear it. This is a prayer that God, faithful to His promise, must answer. Thus we shall not be overcome and England will live.

Faithfully yours, GEORGES P. VANIER
Office of the High Commissioner for Canada, Canada House,
S.W.1

By mid-September Private George Garbutt of Calgary – serving with the 2nd Canadian Infantry Brigade – was reporting on the Blitz: "The planes zip over at night and drop their eggs by the light of flares. When fires start, they can see better and keep it up all night. It's sure tough on the civilians." It was tough on Canadian service people, too, as Major John MacBeth of Ottawa explained in a letter to his family.

February 1, 1941.

Dear Family,

I'm wondering how to give you my impressions of England without making a lecture trip. But perhaps I could start a news review like this . . .

The <u>first</u> experience that must be faced by the newcomers is, of course, the black-out. It is almost impossible to describe the agony of picking one's way around the streets with a flashlight whose aperture is about the size of a dime. On clear nights it is bad enough, but on the foggy, overcast nights such as we have in the winter it is just too much trouble to go out unless one has to. It was a novelty for a while but the novelty turned into a nuisance. The <u>second</u> thing that they must be taught is the bombing. But time will do that for them. Sometimes that, too, is impossible to describe. I heard a recording made by an engineer from the CBC of a bad night – or rather of several bad nights with all the sounds off-stage, and unless you hear it, no words of mine could describe the noise, depending upon nearness of the blitz. This decides the <u>kind</u> of noise that smashes on the ear drums. Then, again – and I'm not joking – it depends how heavy a sleeper one is. I have slept through many raids. London is a pretty large place, after all.

Last fall, we were in several heavy raids. One of my stations was on the edge of a particularly juicy target area. The order of appearance would be something like this. <u>First</u>, Wailing Willie . . . the local air raid siren, screaming away, tearing the blackness of the night with its shrieking. <u>Second</u>, the sound of engines "upstairs". The Jerry planes have a sound all their own and there's no mistaking them. <u>Third</u>, the searchlights stabbing round like the Northern Lights. I used to feel homesick when they did that, for I always went into a trance when the Aurora was turned on. Sometimes, it used to light up our ski trails for the homeward journey! <u>Fourth</u>, the ack-acks – anti-aircraft guns, little ones with a bark like a terrier, big ones with a throaty growl; flashes on the ground from the guns; fire-flies in the sky from the bursting shells. Sometimes, a patter on the roof like hail – shrapnel and shell splinters coming down. <u>Fifth</u>, the bombs; big ones, little ones, incendiaries, flares, screams, whines, bangs, crumps, bumps, swish, whoosh – the San Francisco earthquake. Windows rattling, flashes from the explosions, a blast of air down the street. Sirens of the A.F.S. wagons – Auxilliary Fire Service – men who deserve three Victoria Crosses each. Whistles of the policemen standing on point duty, shooing people and motor cars off the streets. <u>Sixth</u>, the silence. Cats creeping around seem to be stamping their feet. Cigarettes are lit behind carefully-cupped hands. <u>Seventh</u>, Wailing Willie blowing the All Clear. Police toot their whistles again. Traffic starts to flow, diverted here and there. People ooze towards the nearest pub, for an Englishman must has his beer. The talk about football, cricket, Winston Churchill's latest speech. They "Lor"; they "Coo"; they "Blimey"; they go home. It's just another night in the front line for them . . .

They're a tough race . . . the British, and a patient one. As Churchill, the idol of these people, says, "The war may go on for a few years, but whether it's 1941, 1943, 1944 or 1948 we will get them, eventually. We will fight on even if London is a pile of bricks and rubbish. We will fight to the last man and the last gun."

And the Cockney swallows his beer and says, "Coo, 'e's a one, ain't 'e?" . . .

John

NURSES AND LEAD SWINGERS

Nearly five thousand Canadian nurses went overseas during the war, serving in all three branches of the military, not just in the army as in the First World War. The army nurses were the first to go, sailing the North Atlantic in convoys, always wary of attack from German vessels. In England they worked in Royal Canadian Army Medical Corps hospitals in Basingstoke, Bramshott, and Taplow. One of the original contingent was **Elaine Wright** *of Montreal, who joined the corps in October 1940 as a lieutenant (nursing sister).*

OVERSEAS SERVICE
No 1 Gen. Hosp,
Feb. 24/41.

Dear Folks at Home:

One of our nurses is going home & I am asking her to take this with her & mail it in Canada. It will get there much quicker & I might be able to tell you a few things I otherwise couldn't . . .

To begin at the beginning, we were on the "Pasteur" & it is a lovely boat. There were 3 other boats with us, all troop ships, one British battleship the Revenge, & 2 cruisers. The war cruisers were the sinister looking boats! Our escort left us about ½ way over & the convoy (Do not mention this to many people as it is very important) from this side was to meet us in a day or two but we missed it & came in alone. Our last day out we met a convoy going to Canada & it was a wonderful sight – right on the horizon. Four planes came swooping down on us & kept circling & dipping over us. Were we thrilled. They were a bit worried about us one day as a boat was hit 25 mins. sailing distance behind us but we knew nothing about it till later . . .

We are stationed at Marston Green but <u>do not</u> put that on any letters. We are really just outside the village . . .

Yes the people talk with quite an English accent & they find some of our expressions amusing. I will never get used to hearing a big well-built man saying "Ta, ta." & "Oh my deah!" It sounds so sissified . . .

We are well organized here for air raids & the wards are well equipped for incendiary bombs. We are going through the gas chamber to-morrow [where nurses briefly took off their gas masks to learn how to identify poison gases by odour] & have had a couple of more lectures on it. Nothing is being left to chance. There are several gas detectors around & well watched.

The general impression just now is preparedness for the invasion attempt very shortly. Whether or not it will really come no one knows, but the whole country is being prepared. With the system of spotters, fire watchers, home guards, etc, it is hard to imagine they would get far if they did try to invade . . .

You asked about the patients but there is not much to say about them, I haven't been looking after any but sick officers & am now with the nurses, & a couple of English girls who had their appendixes out. Almost all the patients get up, & about half are to be boarded back to Canada, a lot of lead swingers among them. A lead swinger is one who complains of something he hasn't got, in other words there is nothing wrong with them except the desire to get out of the army . . .

Love to all

Elaine.

P.S. Am very glad to get any letters, even if it is about ordinary every day things.

Wright later nursed Canadian soldiers during the Sicilian and Italian campaigns. She married Lieutenant Peter Webster in 1945.

IMPRISONING OUR OWN

Federal law in wartime allowed the detention of Canadian citizens as well as enemy nationals. As early as September 1939, Canada's Directorate of Internment Operations opened its first prison camps for civilian internees in Petawawa, Ontario, and Kananaskis, Alberta. Before Japanese Canadians were interned, suspects with German backgrounds had been rounded up and, after Italy entered the war in June 1940, so were some prominent Italian Canadians. **Antonio Rebaudengo,** *a CPR machinist who had emigrated to Calgary from Italy and become an agent of the Italian consular*

*office, helped thousands of his countrymen settle in the city. He was
a member of a Fascist Club in Calgary, a social group that disbanded
when Mussolini allied Italy with Germany. In 1941 Rebaudengo was
detained in internment camps for his "pro-Fascist activities and sympathies." He wrote to his wife in English and then to his family in
Italian (here translated).*

[1941?]

Dear Angiolina,

The last few days I suffer a crisis, that I never felt before. it is impossible to write the cause of this, I got no appetites I can not sleep, I am
restless and very nervous, I do not feel to talk to any one, my moral
is going down. I will give my life to be free, to be with you, and hold
you, I feel the desire to join my leeps with yours. With the sweetes
love of Joy and orgasm, my heart never before love you like now . . .

10 March 1941

Dear Family,

As I mentioned in one of my preceding letters, writing has become
problematic and I will list some of the reasons for this. I have found
that I jump from one topic to another, not making sense, believing
what is not true because the pen is free to write what it wants even
when the brain thinks otherwise because after 9 months of imprisonment one cannot be expected to be in the right frame of mind and
then remember, one of the ten commandments "do unto others as
you would have them do unto you" . . .

*Rebaudengo was released in 1943. After the war he again worked as
an agent for the Italian consulate, assisting immigrants to Canada.
Meanwhile, **Muriel Kitagawa** of Vancouver was one of about 21,000
Canadians of Japanese origin forced from their homes on the Pacific
coast under Canada's War Measures Act. The government, fearing
that they threatened the nation's security, sent them to work in camps*

and small towns in the interior of British Columbia, and in other provinces – while confiscating their property to dissuade them from returning after the war. Muriel was a writer and a mother of two, expecting twins. She wrote to her brother in Ontario.

March 4, 1942

Dear Wes,

. . . We are Israelites on the move. The public is getting bloodthirsty and will have our blood Nazi-fashion. Okay we move. But where? Signs up on all highways . . . JAPS KEEP OUT. Curfew. "My father is dying. May I have permission to go to his bedside?" "NO!" Like moles we burrow within after dark, and only dare to peek out of the window or else be thrown into the hoosegow with long term sentences and hard labour. Confiscation of radios, cameras, cars and trucks. Shut down of all business. No one will buy. No agency yet set up to evaluate. When you get a notice to report to RCMP for orders to move, you report or be interned. "Who will guard my wife and daughters?" Strong arm reply. Lord, if this was Germany you can expect such things as the normal way, but this is Canada, a Democracy! And the Nisei [second-generation Japanese Canadians], repudiated by the only land they know, no redress anywhere. Sure we can move somewhere on our own, but a job? Who will feed the family? Will they hire a Jap? Where can we go that will allow us to come? The only place to go is the Camp the Government will provide when it gets around to it. Ah, but we are bewildered and bitter and uncertain . . .

When shall we ever meet again if we scatter? Don't you dare come here!!! I'll lose you for sure if you do, then where will we be? . . .

The Nisei would have been so proud to wear the King's uniform! Even die in it. But not as Helots [the serfs of ancient Sparta], tied to the chariot wheels of Democracy . . . And you know that most of the people here call this a 'damned shame,' this treatment especially of the Canadian-born? It's just the few antis who have railroaded Ottawa into this unfairness. Talk about opportunists. Was there ever a better excuse for them to kick us out lock stock and barrel? . . .

So the saga of the Nisei begins. I, too, mean to survive this. This is the furnace where our worth will be tempered to white-hot resilience or not at all . . . Pray for us all, you who are in 'safe' areas. For me, whose faith these last few years is sorely tried and wearing thin.

Love,

Mur.

Kitagawa and her family joined her brother in Toronto, where she opposed the government's treatment of Japanese Canadians. Not until three years after the war did these citizens receive the right to vote, and it was another year before the government lifted the War Measures Act and the last of the wartime restrictions. In a redress agreement in 1988, the Canadian government formally apologized for its wrongful actions and pledged to ensure that such events would never recur. Muriel Kitagawa died in 1974, aged sixty-two.

BRIEF ESCAPE

The Allies began sending German prisoners of war (POWs) to other camps in the wilds of Canada. In all, about 25,000 POWs were confined in twenty-six internment centres and several work camps, mostly in Quebec, Alberta, and Ontario. Invariably, some tried to escape. The most ambitious attempt was at the secluded Camp X at Angler, Ontario, about six hundred kilometres northwest of Sault Ste. Marie. Here, during a night of freezing rain on April 18, 1941, twenty-eight of the 559 prisoners fled through a tunnel carved out of the sand, supported by floor joists, lit by homemade candles, and fitted with an air duct fashioned from milk tins and fuelled by a hand-operated fan. **Colonel Hubert Stethem,** *the crusty director of Internment Operations in Ottawa, wrote to a friend about the escape.*

Ottawa, April 28ᵗʰ, 1941

Major Norman Wells,
330 Bay Street
Toronto 2, Ontario.
Dear Major Wells:
. . . I am afraid the break-out at the western camp was due entirely
to negligence on the part of those responsible for the custody of the
prisoners. They have been given all kinds of suggestions and advice
and the regulations are very explicit, but, if regulations and instructions are ignored, then escapes will occur.

Unfortunately, I have no say in the selection of the personnel for
the staffs or guards. Many of the guards are, undoubtedly, beyond
the age of usefulness. I am enclosing two of a series of "Notes on
Prevention of Escapes" which are in the hands of all camp comman-
dants, and the escape in question could not have occurred had these
notes been studied and the action called for taken.

The trapdoors were not discovered because dust had been swept
over them, and the area under the floors had not been examined for
the storage of earth. Prisoners were in the possession of knapsacks,
and table knives had not been checked.

The above is for your confidential information.

As you probably know, the custody of the prisoners is entirely
the responsibility of the Department of National Defence, and my
duties are merely those of supervision and co-ordination of the
internment operations in Canada. Possibly, the system will be
changed in the near future in order to get more unified control . . .

Yours very truly,
H. Stethem,
Colonel,
Director of Internment Operations.

*By the end of their first day of freedom, eleven escapees were cap-
tured nearby. A soldier shot off the nose of one who appeared to be
fleeing. An Ojibwa guide led a search party through the bush to a*

cabin where a food cache had been found. The next day, a sergeant and a private spotted another cabin, where several escapees were sleeping. Ordering them to surrender, the soldiers shot four of the Germans as they emerged, killing two of them. All the remaining fugitives were rounded up within a week. Only two of them had got very far: pilots Karl Grund and Horst Liebeck travelled in boxcars on their way to the West Coast in the hope of catching a freighter to Japan. Near Medicine Hat, Alberta, a Mountie arrested them as they walked along a road. After the war, Grund returned to Germany and Liebeck became a businessman in Toronto.

DOCTOR AT SEA

Germany had wasted no time in commanding the Atlantic sea lanes. Ten hours after Britain declared war, German submarines – the dreaded U-boats (Unterseebooten) – torpedoed the British passenger liner Athenia on her way to Montreal, mistaking her for an auxiliary cruiser. On that first day of the war 118 people died, including the first Canadian service casualty, stewardess Hannah Baird of Verdun, Quebec. At times the subs worked in tandem with surface vessels, well-armed raiders that captured and often blew up Allied ships. **Surgeon Lieutenant A.G. (Gillean) MacKinnon** of Regina was one of eight Canadian medical officers sent overseas to work for the short-handed British navy in the spring of 1941. The twenty-seven-year-old graduate of the University of Toronto was aboard HMS Leith, a New Zealand sloop that served briefly as a patrol vessel in the Newfoundland Escort Force. It accompanied convoys across the North Atlantic and then handled traffic between Britain and Gibraltar. During the summer the Leith was patrolling for a convoy northwest of Gibraltar when a wolf pack of U-boats attacked. As the Leith's censor of outgoing mail, Dr. MacKinnon was mindful of security in this letter to his parents.

September 10th 1941.

At Sea

Dear Mother and Father:

It seems a long time since I've written to you or had any word from you . . .

As for me I have been very much in the thick of things since I last wrote but am none the worse for it and getting quite a kick out of doing my small share in this business. Naturally I cannot begin to tell you our activities or whereabouts but suffice it to say that I've seen lots of water and some land that I hadn't seen before. It is good that [I] realize that my meagre abilities are of some use here and that I can help with the war effort and at the same time practice my chosen profession. (The Ship is rolling rather a lot hence my jumpy writing.) On our last trip I was transferred from Ship to Ship to attend to casualties and actually spent the last week at sea in a corvette looking after two chaps with badly broken legs. Fortunately I was able to bring them both into port alive and in fair condition and they'll be all right after a spell in hospital. Right now I have a chap aboard with pneumonia, who was sent over to me from one of the smaller Ships. He is a Newfoundlander, from Conception Bay. Today his temperature was normal for the first time. He has been ill over a week. His recovery can largely be attributed to Dagenan [a sulfa medicine] the "miracle drug" of which we carry fairly large stocks on board . . .

The war seems to be going well for us doesn't it. The submarines seem to be in line for congrats these days also the RAF. It looks as if the Germans were going to be faced with a winter campaign in Russia. It will give us extra much needed time to draw on our resources and gird ourselves for the scraps that will come next year . . .

I'll say goodbye for now with much love to you both.

Gillean

The week-long encounter with the U-boats was "a tremendous engagement – we were safeguarding a large convoy of merchants ships coming from northwest of Gibraltar," Dr. MacKinnon recalled. "We lost perhaps fifteen or more ships. One ship was full of nurses and ATS [Auxiliary Territorial Service, the main British women's service] and they were lost, every last one of them. It was heart-rending." He left the Leith after a year to return to Canada, where he and his wife raised three daughters and he worked after the war for the federal Veterans Affairs department. Of the eight Canadian doctors who went over to work with the Royal Navy in the spring of 1941, only four survived the war.

RUSSIA, WITH LOVE

*Despite their mutual non-aggression pact of 1939, Germany attacked the Soviet Union on June 22, 1941. In Oakville, Ontario, **Norah Egener** was pining for her lawyer husband, who had just left her, pregnant with their second child, to serve overseas.*

June 29 [1941]

Dearest Fred:

It is about 11:30 Sunday morning; Master Waide is playing in front with his wagon, just having been bathed and a clean new sunsuit and his white shoes on. He is so tanned, you would be pleased to see him looking so strong and well . . .

They are organizing a women's auxiliary unit to go overseas. If I didn't have the babies, I could go with it and be near you. But I know you wouldn't let me go anyway, would you? And watching over your babies means more, I guess, darling. In the days and years to come it will, anyway . . .

Britain has not been receiving much bombing lately since Russia seems to keep the Germans busy. However, it is hard to say how Russia will fare. I miss our chats after dinner at night over the war, news, etc. Loads of love and kisses and hugs.

Norah and Waide

In July Britain and the Soviet Union signed a treaty that promised British aid to the Soviets. By September Kiev in the Ukraine was captured, Leningrad was under siege, and German troops were soon converging on Moscow.

NATIVE SOLDIERS

Although the federal government refused to recognize treaty Indians as citizens, more than three thousand of them served during the war and more than two hundred died. Their white brothers-in-arms soon came to respect them; as historian Fred Gaffen pointed out: "Most Indian recruits were familiar with firearms and the outdoors. Like their ancestors, many were excellent marksmen. Indians served in a wide variety of roles in the army, navy, and air force." Canadian historian **George F.G. Stanley** *was a captain during the war, retiring as deputy director of the army's historical section. (He went on to create the basic design of the Canadian flag and to become the lieutenant governor of New Brunswick.) Stanley wrote Gaffen a post-war letter about his experiences with native soldiers from eastern Canada.*

Dear Fred,

At the Training Centre at Fredericton in 1941, I had a number of Micmacs and Maliseets. They were excellent as parade ground soldiers. I even used a platoon of Indians as a guard-of-honour for the opening of the Legislature. They put on an excellent show – good coordination and very steady. They were well motivated because they liked and respected the officers and non-commissioned officers under whom they served. I think it was a matter of winning their respect; and doing so by fairness and understanding . . .

The Indians were, however, always on the alert to take offence. They seemed to anticipate that the 'whites' would not like them and would treat them badly. It took time to overcome this attitude. Perhaps I was fortunate in winning their cooperation by defending one of them in a court martial. The Indian was absent three months and charged with desertion. My defence was based on two points.

(1) The Indian's cultural background was different from ours. He was not used to working with others and spending long periods drilling and training for war. His idea of fighting was to take a rifle and go off to find the enemy. His cultural pattern was not based on group discipline which he found boring. So he went absent without leave until the Army was ready to send him overseas to fight.

(2) My second line of defence (and probably the most effective) was the fact that he was picked up on his reserve still wearing a uniform. Desertion requires proof of intent to desert. The best proof of intent would be the discarding of the uniform. Since the Indian, when taken into custody, was still in uniform, it was obvious there was no intent to desert. I scolded the military police for taking three months before they thought to go to the Indian reserve. Where else would an Indian go but back to his reserve?

The court gave the Indian two weeks confinement to the guard house. Since he had spent eleven days awaiting trial he had to spend only three more days in the clink. After that, my stock with the Indians was pretty high.

One night I heard a row in one of the barrack blocks. I went with my Company Sergeant-Major. I found a group of Indians and whites just about ready for a battle. On the floor was a drunken Indian boy. The white corporal said the Indian had returned drunk and disorderly and he had ordered him to be escorted to the guard room by two privates (whites). I asked the senior Indian present what he had to say. He said the young Indian was drunk and should be taken to the guard room. What they were afraid of was that he would be beaten up by the white escort. I told the corporal to appoint an escort of one white man and one Indian to take the boy to the guard room. That solved the crisis. Indians have so often been beaten up by whites that they were suspicious of white soldiers and white officers . . .

George Stanley

After the war native soldiers received few of the benefits, training, or jobs their white counterparts were offered. Although they fought for fair compensation for decades, the federal government offered the 1,800 surviving veterans and their spouses a "compassionate package" only in 2002. Some accepted the cash offer; others decided to take their case to the United Nations' human rights committee in Geneva.

AN ANGEL FROM HEAVEN

*In 1940 the Royal Canadian Air Force (RCAF) formed its first squadron of air cadets, in Vancouver. A local university freshman, **Jim Whalen**, became its first wing commander and in June enlisted in the RCAF. He was one of the initial candidates of the ambitious British Commonwealth Air Training Plan designed to prepare Australian, New Zealand, and Canadian as well as British air crew at Canadian bases for overseas service with the Royal Air Force (RAF). Of the 131,000 flight crew in the program, 73,000 were Canadians. Whalen lost his commission as a pilot officer after twice flying his Harvard under the Ottawa–Hull bridge but was soon in England piloting Spitfires. On September 17, 1941, his 129 Squadron had a dogfight over France with Luftwaffe Me (Messerschmitt) 109s.*

Sept. 17/41

Dear Mother,
Well I suppose that you want to hear all about the Gerries that I shot down. I was on a sweep leading Green section when I saw a Me 109F about to attack my number two. I turned after him and shot him down and then lost our Squadron. I was going to head for England when I saw a Squadron above about ten to twenty miles inside France. I didn't know who they were so I headed towards them. When I was close enough I saw that they were Me 109 E's. About 12–15 flying in formation. I attacked shooting down the first Gerry. I missed the next then damaged a third, who might have crashed,

and was going to shoot at a fourth when my ammunition was finished. I could see nothing but Gerrys around me and I beat it for England as fast as I could go doing all kinds of queer manouvers to keep the Me 109's away from me. That was my first fight and yesterday I had my second. We were on a sweep just crossing the coast when 90+ Me 109's attacked us. I had a couple of unsuccessful brushes and being separated from the rest my number two and I started to fight our way home. We were attacked by four Me 109's and over the channel, we took on two apiece but mine headed for France. I lost my number two then and was heading home when I saw two of three Me 109's that were attacking a damaged Spitfire. I attacked them shooting the first down and damaging the other and was then attacked by the third Me 109. He hit out for France after a slight scrap and I returned to base. The pilot of the damaged Spitfire said he thought I was an angel from heaven when he saw me coming to help him. Well my bag is now

      1 Me 109 F shot down

      2 Me 109 E's shot down

      2 Me 109 E's damaged

      Give my love to everyone . . .

Whalen didn't tell his mother that, with his fuel almost gone, he'd been forced to crash-land on the English coast. Four days later, on another sweep across the English Channel, he was in another battle in which one pilot was killed and a second shot down and captured. In April 1944, now a flight lieutenant in India, Whalen was leading six Hawker Hurricane bombers to defend the hill town of Kohima from the Japanese when his plane did a barrel spin after dropping bombs and crashed in the jungle. He received a posthumous Distinguished Flying Cross.

DEATH OVER THE DESERT

In November 1941 Britain launched an offensive in Libya, which became one of the major battlegrounds in North Africa after the

Italians entered the war. En route to India, Jimmy Whalen had stopped over briefly and flown Curtis Kittyhawks on an anti-submarine patrol over the Red Sea. The Kittyhawks were one of two aircraft flown by the No. 112 Squadron of the RAF's Western Desert Air Force; the other was the P-40 Tomahawk. The crews painted the nose of their Tomahawks with fearsome shark's teeth, which inspired the sobriquet "the Shark Squadron." Forty of the squadron's 226 pilots were Canadians and Americans who'd joined the RCAF. Among them was a jug-eared veteran of the Battle of Britain, pilot officer **Jean-Paul (Sab) Sabourin** *of St. Isidore de Prescott, Ontario. In this letter, translated from French, he recounted his second sortie over the Libyan desert, on November 22, 1941.*

112 Squadron, Middle East.
22/11/41

Dear parents,

. . . At the moment I am in the desert. We have about one quart of water per day for drinking and washing. We have had a few sand storms. My head is still full of sand, in spite of having washed my hair yesterday. I needed a gallon of water. I was forced to land in a sand storm. I missed the landing strip and hit a tent. I damaged the aircraft but fortunately I did not hit anyone . . .

. . . Since we have been here we have shot down some Italians and Germans. Yesterday we got two unfortunate Italians. We were twelve against two. When it was my turn to attack . . . there was nothing left but flames . . .

I can't wait for this war to be over and to get back to Canada . . .

November 27, 1941

Just about an hour after finishing my last letter, I was shot down by anti-aircraft fire. As the machine was on fire I had to bale out. My parachute opened at two hundred feet so it goes without saying that I did not have the time to disengage one of my legs which was caught in the lines. I landed on my head. But since my head is almost as hard as the rocks on which I fell, I got out of it with only a cut on the head and nearly a week's leave. I'll have my stitches out tomorrow and will return to the desert where we are very busy at the moment.

At present I'm in Cairo. Today, I went to see the pyramids and took lots of photos . . .

On December 5 Sabourin's Tomahawk was among twenty-two RAF aircraft from two squadrons defending against about seventy-five German and Italian dive-bombers and fighters.

6/12/41

Back again in the desert, I did not waste any time to avenge myself of these . . . Germans who shot me down. In a few minutes I shot down three enemy aircraft and damaged about four others, which probably didn't get back. Since I was all alone in the middle of a dozen machines, I could not follow to see what happened to them. I had only one cannon shell in my machine. They were all around me. Our squadron got 10 in all. As the total for our squadron since the beginning of the war was 99, we celebrated our century yesterday evening with a total of 109; we don't know who had the hundredth . . .

If I can catch a few more Germans or Italians I may have a chance of getting a decoration. In any case I try to do my duty and I have the satisfaction of getting my own back for the blood I lost in the desert . . .

Good bye and see you soon,
Jean-Paul

The Allies downed twenty aircraft, the Axis eight. Four days later Sabourin was up again, but this time six RAF planes were hit and he had to force-land when his engine failed. "After that show," he wrote home, "the CO said I should get a rest and be posted to England. Instead, I was posted to a training school here to let the green pilots get my experience." He was killed in September 1942 in a dogfight with Stuka dive-bombers over the western desert.

A VC IN HONG KONG

On December 7, 1941, Japan launched an attack on the American Pacific Fleet in Pearl Harbor with 353 planes and 31 ships. The surprise strike killed more than 2,400 service people and civilians and wounded nearly 1,200 more while destroying 188 planes and demolishing or damaging eight battleships. The next day the United States, the Commonwealth, and the Netherlands declared war on Japan, which then began to launch invasions of Thailand, Malaya, and the British crown colony of Hong Kong. It was in Hong Kong that Canadians – one tenth of the 20,000 Allied forces defending the colony – had their first major battle of the Second World War. Among them was **Company Sergeant Major John Osborn**, *a British-born infantryman with the Winnipeg Grenadiers. Several months earlier, he had written to one of his five children in Manitoba.*

9 Apr 1941
From Dad

Hello Old Man
Very pleased to hear from you again, and sorry I couldn't answer before, no I didn't like those kisses from the cat, but a smell of that Rabbit cooking would be very nice. So you are quite a swell, with your Air Force suit, whats the matter with you all have you gone Air Force crazy. Say listen Son, your Mother tells me you have been a bad boy, whats the matter with you, you know you promised me that you would be good, and look after Mother for me but it doesn't look as if you are. You had better buck up or I'll be coming home and use my stick again. Gee you and John sure must have grown a lot. Fancy weighing all that much. John sure will be a big man now he has so many ties won't he. Well Old Fellow I guess this about all for this time So will close Hoping to hear that you are a good boy again

From your old Dad
and Pal
Jack

The Japanese invaded Hong Kong late in the dark of December 18 through a pivotal gap in the centre of the island, where Brigadier John K. Lawson had his headquarters. The First World War vet, a Permanent Force officer, was the first senior Canadian commander to die in the war. That morning Jack Osborn had led his Winnipeg Grenadiers company up Mount Butler and captured the hill at bayonet point before being forced to fall back. Covering his men as they retreated, he ran a gauntlet of gunfire. That afternoon his company was surrounded by Japanese soldiers tossing grenades. Osborn caught several and threw them back. When one landed out of his reach, he yelled a warning to his mates and flung himself on the grenade as it exploded, killing him. He was the first Canadian to receive the Victoria Cross in this war.

NEVER OUT OF MIND

*All the Allied troops were either killed or captured in the Battle of Hong Kong. Some Japanese soldiers were ruthless in victory, raping women and torturing men before killing them. Survivors were sent to prison camps horrific in their living conditions and in the brutality of guards. For the folks at home, having spouses, siblings, or children behind the barbed wire of a foreign camp was like being in a perpetual prison of the mind. **Jean Rose** was the mother of Jack Rose, a telegraph operator from Vancouver with the 10th Fortress Signal Company. At the insistence of the Japanese censors, she wrote in block letters.*

13TH JAN. 1942
2356 WEST 14TH AVE
VANCOUVER.

SIGLM. JACK. ROSE
K34771 HEADQUARTERS FORCE
TAKEN PRISONER AT HONG KONG
MY DARLING SON JACK
    SO FAR WE HAVE RECEIVED NO LETTER FROM YOU. I DO HOPE
THAT YOU ARE RECEIVING OUR LETTERS. DARLING I HOPE YOU

ARE WELL AND IN GOOD SPIRITS. I PRAY FOR YOU EVERY NIGHT,
MY DARLING YOU ARE NEVER OUT OF MY THOUGHTS. I SOME
TIMES FEEL THAT I CANT GO ON ANY MORE BUT I AM GOING TO
CARRY ON & HAVE ONLY ONE THOUGHT IN MIND TO SEE YOU
AGAIN. DARLING HOW I WILL TAKE CARE OF YOU WHEN YOU
COME HOME. FOR MY SAKE KEEP YOUR CHIN UP. SAY YOUR
PRAYERS EVERY NIGHT. DARLING I AM GOING THROUGH IT WITH
YOU. EVERY ONE KEEPS ASKING ABOUT YOU. MAY GOD BLESS YOU
& TAKE CARE OF YOU. I AM SURE HE WILL HEAR MY PRAYERS. I
AM PRAYING FOR A LETTER SOON. DARLING I LOVE YOU SO
MUCH THAT IT HURTS.

MOTHER

*To outfox the censors in one of his few letters that reached
Vancouver, **Jack Rose** referred to a tough jail back home.*

MARCH 16, 1943

DEAREST MOTHER AND FATHER: –
AT THIS WRITING I AM HIGH IN MORALE, HOPING YOU AND
DARLING SISTER DOREEN ARE THE SAME. I AM PRAYING THE
DAY WILL COME WHEN WE WILL BE TOGETHER AGAIN. I HAVE
RECEIVED NO LETTERS FROM YOU AS YET. I WOULD LOOK
FORWARD TO A NICE HOLIDAY IN OAKALLA AFTER I GET HOME.

YOUR LOVING SON,

JACK

A FLYPAST OF CHRISTMASES

*In 1941 **Donald McCulloch** was a twenty-one-year-old flying officer
with the RCAF's 61st Squadron, whose dangerous missions took him
over Germany. On December 14 this youngest of four sons wrote
his mother in Kelowna, British Columbia.*

No. 2 DEC.
14/12/41

Dear Moms,

. . . I shall wire on Xmas day, my first away from home. Remember those other Christmases, Mother. The many preparations; – the Christmas cakes, the Oregon grape & holly dug from under the snow, – walking miles through bushes to cut a suitable tree. (I can remember one such occasion when we set out down the South tracks, you & Mary pulling me on a toboggan. Then when you had cut down a tree, I, who had been a spectator & an idle one at that, burst into tears "because it wasn't big enough"!)

Remember the excitement over the ceremonial decorating of our tree. The ancient dust covered boxes were brought forth from the cellar where they had rested peacefully for a year. They were opened & 4 anxious children examined their contents critically; choosing this, discarding that. The endless lengths of faded tinsel, & the contrastingly glittering newly-bought-that-week. The dozens of ornaments, the miniature Santa Clauses, Adam & Eve, the strings of tree lights (which varied every year with Dad's replacements). All of these had to be placed in a pre-decided order until the finished tree was to everyone's satisfaction.

Then there were the four "streamers" to be hung from the corners of the dining room and parlor.

Christmas Eve!

I would lie in bed, wide awake at first, listening to the passing sleigh bells; sitting up now & then to glance at the spotted snow on the verandah roof near my window.

The shimmers of light from the street lamp had silvered it through the branches of the old chestnut tree. Whilst our cat would be purring from where he lay near the pillow (smuggled to bed at the last minute). Later on I would drowsily feel my stocking hanging from the bed post. Empty now, in the morning I should find it bulging with wonderful mysteries. And best of all there was Xmas day to come; Xmas day when one carried the "little tree" & presents over to Grannie's, Xmas day with its parcels to be unwrapped, explored & appraised. The carols, the millards of nuts, sweets, cakes, feasts – a wonderful day. The most wonderful of a child's year!

Yes I'm afraid that Christmas has been "the Christmas past" for years now: But its memory has lived in every succeeding Xmas & has been the true source of enjoyment. Indeed in this one to come the memory of those gone by shall be significant above all else.

Mother and Dad I thank you for those glorious spontaneous Xmases; for what they meant to that child; and what they mean now to this slightly older edition of him.

All my love,
Donald.

Six months later, on June 24, 1942, his family received a telegram that Donald McCulloch was missing in action; on October 17 another letter confirmed that he had been killed over Germany, where his body was buried.

A BIT OF A JAM

The Americans' entry in the war emboldened the hard-pressed Allies. The Royal Canadian Navy's fleet remained concentrated in the North Atlantic, while the British Royal Navy (RN) also waged war in the Pacific. Among the Canadians in the British service was **George Tidy**, *a graduate of an advanced wireless course at the University of Toronto, who had joined the Royal Canadian Naval Volunteer Reserve in 1940. Transferred to the RN as a shore-based radar operator, he then served aboard HMS* Exeter, *a 7,630-tonne cruiser that in 1939, in the first major naval battle of the war, had been badly damaged fighting the* Graf Spee, *a German battleship. Refitted, the* Exeter *was doing convoy duty in the Java Sea off the Dutch East Indies in early 1942.*

H.M.S. EXETER
C/o. G.P.O. LONDON
Jan 30/42

Darling Mom:

In my last letter you were worried that letters might be few & far between for the next while. We are doing a great deal of sea time with very few opportunities to send of[f] mail . . . & none has reached us since Christmas.

I suggest you ignore any rumours that Exeter has been sunk. It seems that various people are a bit anxious to get us out of the way but they have been nowhere near it yet. That doesnt say that it would happen, since times are rather difficult now but there is no use in worrying unduly.

Well, the old B.E. [British Empire] is in a bit of a jam now. I think the English & Yanks have been fools to bully the Japs into fighting now. A bit of delaying (appeasement) would have given a chance for preparation.

I have read a report that a vote on conscription is to be held (or I suppose has been held by now). I hope the answer is yes. There are too many slackers at home. I could name a few myself.

I expect things are a bit different now with the Yanks in. Gasoline rationing, no new cars and all that sort of stuff. With plenty of flag waving across the border. Well, such is life, things can't get much worse now (my fingers are crossed).

Suppose I sound pessimistic. So does everyone down here, fighting as we are in a pretty hopeless situation. However theres always a silver lining etc etc . . .

Your loving Son
George

On February 27, 1942, in the Battle of the Java Sea, the Exeter suffered damage to her boiler room as the Allied squadron fought a superior Japanese force. The next day, after reporting three enemy cruisers ahead, she was never heard from again. George Tidy's mother was told he had been killed in the sinking. A year later, she received a brief letter.

[Spring 1942]

DEAR MOTHER

I AM NOW IN A PRISONER OF WAR CAMP IN JAVA. MY HEALTH IS
EXCELLENT. I AM CONSTANTLY THINKING OF YOU. IT WILL BE
WONDERFUL WHEN WE MEET AGAIN.

   I AM LOOKING FORWARD TO HEARING FROM YOU. I HOPE
YOU AND ALL THE FAMILY ARE WELL.

YOUR LOVING SON
George

*Tidy was one of forty-six surviving officers and 610 sailors. On
September 16, 1945, he wired his mother: "Free at last. In good
health and uninjured. We expect to leave in three weeks to a month.
May be home for Christmas." He was discharged as a lieutenant
commander and after the war worked for the Defence Research
Board, retiring in 1973.*

HONEYMOON FROM HELL

***Danny and Ann Jensen** had just been married when they sent this
note to Danny's army buddy, Staff Sergeant Les Grant. Both men
served with the 1st Canadian Engineers. Danny had been raised on
an Alberta farm; his new wife was English.*

[July 1, 1942]
St. Agnes Hotel
Neva Road
Weston-Sup[er]-Mare

Dear Les,

Danny and I have spent our wedding night and Sunday, fighting fires,
climbing roofs and smashing down doors, in short Jerry has blitzed
us pretty badly two nights in succession. We are both hoping for a
rebate of our bill at the end of week, for saving the hotel from
destruction, if it hadn't been for Danny & I the hotel would have

been burnt to the ground. Sirens are just going again, oh hell what a honeymoon! Jerry gave us all she had, incendaries were dropping like hot-cakes, we couldn't get help from any of the folk, so he and I set to and put out about 10 incendaries fetching the water ourselves and pumping, and dropping bags of sand here and there, Jerry even had the nerve to machine-gun us. You must excuse my scrawl but I feel dead to the world bed at 5 am each morning, not so good. Will give a good account of ourselves when we return, providing Jerry will co-operate and let us. Cheers.

Danny & Ann Jensen

For the Allies the late summer of 1942 was among the darkest stages of the war. As well as renewing the Blitz on London, Hitler had ordered raids of revenge on British historic towns, such as the seaside resort in Somerset where the Jensens honeymooned. Meanwhile, in North Africa, Field Marshall Erwin Rommel's Axis forces were invading Egypt; in Russia, Stalingrad was besieged; and U-boats were sinking ships off North America at an unparalleled pace.

THE DIEPPE CATASTROPHE

It was code-named Jubilee. Military historian Jack Granatstein called it "a disaster, a jubilee of death and destruction." The Canadian raid on Dieppe – a day-trip resort on the northern coast of France, about a hundred kilometres across the English Channel – was a tactical catastrophe. Both the Soviet Union and the United States had been calling for more pressure on the western front, with the Americans even considering a full invasion before year's end. The idea of a quick foray across the channel to test the defences of a fortified port appealed to military planners – especially General Harry Crerar, acting commander for the Canadian Corps in Britain, filling in for an ailing General Andrew McNaughton. Canadian troops, bored with their practice warfare, their morale at low ebb, were anxious to prove themselves in combat. The 2nd Canadian Infantry Division *was chosen to make the raid under Crerar, with the backing of British Lieutenant General Bernard L. Montgomery – the legendary, volatile Monty. On the night of August 18, 1942, 4,963 men from the 2nd Division and the 1st Canadian Armoured Brigade, along with 1,075 British commandos and fifty American Rangers, were poised for a full frontal assault on the beach. Eight destroyers and a gunboat would accompany them. Although seventy-four squadrons of fighter-bombers did cover the amphibious assault, no large bombers were sent in first to weaken German defences. And instead of attacking before dawn, the raiders landed in daylight. **Private Ernest Ludkin** was there with his local regiment, the Royal Hamilton Light Infantry. Three days later he recounted the disaster to his girlfriend, Gail Owen, from a hospital in England.*

No. 1 Can. Gen. Hosp.
Horsham,
Sussex
Sunday 22/8/42

Hello Darling,

As you see I am writing this in hospital so please forgive the writing as I am still shaky yet. I've got a bullet through my face under my left eye coming out close to my ear. In my right leg they dug out a lot of shrapnel from a four inch mortar. Darling, Dieppe was plain hell for six hours. Let me start from the beginning. On the evening of the 18th we started away on the mother ship. We were due to land at 4.50 on the beach at the Casino. About four o'clock planes suddenly shot off in the sky. An enemy army bomber had spotted us. After an exchange of shots she was left burning. By this time we were greatly excited. Just before dawn our bombers went in and you should have seen the flak going up. All of a sudden we saw one bomber going across (it was now almost daylight) and streams of flak going up & after him. Then "Tail End Charlie" opened up with his machine guns firing tracers. We all yelled as one, we were so damned excited, "Give it to him Charlie" & he did, silenced him. By this time we were nearly in. Just before we hit the beach the mortars opened up on us and hit the A.L.C. [landing craft] next to us blowing it in halves. Most of the men drowned right away. They carried so much, the weight took them down. Then we grounded, the door went down and we charged, and what a shambles. I might say that the R.H.L.I. [Royal Hamilton Light Infantry] had the hottest spot to take, the Casino, where we landed. It was like a fortress with machine guns etc. in every window & they let us have it. Anyway we lay on the beach and peppered it with all we had, while they did the same to us and lobbed out stick grenades Molotovs [incendiaries with flammable liquid] and what have you. I was laying alongside Major Wilkinson, who incidentally is badly wounded, when bang, I got it. It slapped me back a few yards and I took cover under a disabled Bren carrier. Then the others took cover and and "R" boat came up and smashed the Casino with its pom-poms etc. Now to the right of the Casino but about five hundred yards back was a high cliff, I'd say about 200 ft. Every house up there was full of machine guns and snipers and by this time the soldiers were practically lying in rows along the open beach. Well the enemy opened up, and honestly dear, the slaughter was teriffic. I still had my head under the carrier trying to stop the blood, every once in awhile taking a shot. Four guys to my right got killed one after the other so I pulled one of them towards me as a shield, and I pushed stones under the carrier up to the axle to stop the bullets from coming through. By this time a tank landing craft pulled in to my right but the mortars got direct hits on it and it was burning furiously. Some of the wounded managed to get to it. Capt. Skerrett was there with nothing on. Incidentally he got killed by a shell getting back on the boats as did a lot more. Interruption. General Roberts and a bunch of staff officers with photogs etc. have been around chatting with us and taking pictures, so maybe you'll see me. I'm laying in bed with a big slab of bandage on the side of my face, the left side. Anyway, to get back to the story, by this time the mortars were exploding round us dangerously close and men were dying hard. By eight o'clock three hours had elapsed, it seemed like three years, and a couple of heavy Canadian tanks managed to get ashore. Gee, we cheered them. They opened up with their six pounders which finally resolved itself into a duel. They worked fine about ten rounds, the blast was tremendous, and then the enemy mortars let us have three or four salvos. All this time they never let up on us with their machine guns and them damned snipers. If one bullet skimmed across my back a hundred did, how they missed me, I'll never know. About nine o'clock about a hundred commando reinforcements landed behind us, but they went down screaming, riddled with bullets. At the same time a mortar landed behind me & killed a couple of them and I got parts of it in the back of my leg. By this time honey, we were feeling kind of beat. One thing I've forgotten to mention, the Spitfires, they were magnificent, you've probably read all about what they did by now. Anyway, to make a long gory story short, around eleven the assault landing craft were seen approaching land to pick us up again. Boy, did we cheer, we'd done a good job, but at a sacrifice. As far as I know there's only about 62 of us left out of about 700 and only 8 officers. Now came another test, getting back, on the boats as they were now being dive-bombed. Suddenly two Spitfires shot across the edge of the water laying a smoke screen and we waited, tense until we were enveloped in it and we dashed across the beach to a tank which was on the waters edge & got it between us and the snipers. It didn't do us much good as we were now in a crossfire of machine guns. Then a dive bomber came out of nowhere, bombed the boats, missed, saw us huddled on the beach and turned his guns on us. We instinctively ducked and prayed, and he missed us. Then I was in the water up to my waist, then my neck until finally I reached a boat. Bullets were pinging around, mortars exploding, but somehow or other I got on, and the damn thing was flooded. We began bailing with helmets when, bang, a mortar blew the boat in halves, and we found ourselves in the water again. Thank God, I had my Mae West on otherwise I wouldn't be here now, but somehow or other I managed to make another boat, which also was flooded & finally we got a mile from shore, where a motor launch took us wounded off. From then on, almost to the coast of England it was a series of dive-bombing and machine gunning attacks, because, although we had dozens of Spitfires with us, the odd one will keep getting through.

What a glorious sight it was to see the coast of England again. I have a correction to make dear, it has now been learned that 220 of us are back. Look for me on the films. The news reels were round this morning and I am the first guy being wheeled out in a wheel-chair by a nurse. You can't miss me as I believe I'm the only one with my face bandaged.

Well dearest, am getting tired now so will have to close.

I still love you honey,

Cheerio,

Love & Kisses,

Ernest

P.S. I left everything behind, but managed to retain one of your pic-tures which I have propped up here.

Nearly 3,500 officers and men were left behind on the beach at Dieppe: 907 killed, 586 wounded, and 1,946 captured. A mere 2,200 returned. Recriminations soon began about the abysmal planning and appalling loss of life. The possible benefits of the raid were to discourage American forces from invading France that year and to encourage Canadian generals to improve the training of their troops. But as Jack Granatstein wrote, "The limited salutary results of Dieppe were much overshadowed by the casualties, the suffering, and the horror." Ernest Ludkin recovered from his wounds, and went home to marry Gail Owen in 1945 and raise a family.

A DIEPPE POW'S ESCAPE

Private Roy Tuer *was part of Ontario's Essex Scottish (now called the Essex and Kent Scottish) Regiment that hit the main beach at Dieppe in tandem with the Royal Hamilton Light Infantry. German fire kept him and his comrades boxed in; only about a dozen reached* *the promenade across the shingle of the beach. Within thirty minutes of landing, as many as 40 percent of the 550 men were dead or wounded; in the end 121 were killed. In late 1942 Tuer wrote his parents in Windsor, Ontario, from an internment camp in France.*

Hello Dad:

Well I've finally gotten into a position where I can write again. I'm in the very best of health, happy and not eating too bad either (Thanks to the Canadian Red Cross).

Well it's a long story, as you probably know I was in on that raid on Dieppe on August 19. It was a pretty hot nine hours, too, I might say. I went out swimming at 11 a.m. but I had to come back to the beach at 3 and I was captured by the Germans. During that time I was in two boats, both of which were sunk. Then the Germans put us on a train (40 to a box car), and took us to a temporary camp near Chartres in occupied France. We stayed there for nine days, living on a fifth of a loaf of bread and a bowl of soup per day. The evening of the 28th they put us back in our box car, gave us a loaf of bread and a half tin of meat per man, then they went on to tell us that that was our rations for four days and that we were on our way to Eastern Germany.

We moved off about seven with a machine gun on every second car and a rifleman on each car. They had cut two holes about one foot by three in the side of the car for ventilation, and they had covered the opening with barb wire. As soon as it was dark, I tugged and pulled until I got the wire loose, and about eleven I went out feet first. The train was moving too fast so I had to walk along a steel rod until I reached the middle of the car, there I crawled underneath on to a plank that was fastened to the bottom of the car. And about 10 minutes later a chap from Drouillard road named Rufus Parent came asking to join me. We stayed on the plank for about ten minutes, then when we slowed down a little, I jumped off and Parent followed.

We laid flat on our faces until the train had passed, then we found our directions from the stars and headed for Spain, via unoccupied

France. Next day a French farmer gave us a road map and some old patched clothes, and we started out for the border, about 200 kilometres away. We were then near Versailles, and seven days later on the 4th of September, we crossed the line into unoccupied France near Vierzon. Boy did we ever have hot feet after that walking!

We saw quite a number of German soldiers, but they took us for farmers in our old clothes. During that time we lived on fruit and bread and cheese and red wine, given us by French farmers. We hid in a woods about 300 yards from the border for about eight hours. During that time we were hiding, two German patrols passed 100 yards from us without spotting us. We slept in a barn in unoccupied France after crossing the line about 10 or 11.

We had only gone about eight kilometres in France when we were picked up by the French special police. We stayed in French jails until the 6th when we were taken to this prison. Now we are in an old castle on a mountain top, near Nice, in Southeast France in the Alps, only a few miles from the Italian border. We are only a few miles from the Mediterranean Sea, 2,500 feet up in the air. We are in a camp for internees and we're not prisoners of war any longer.

Of course we will be interned for the duration, but I would rather much be interned in France than a prisoner of war in Germany. It is just like Florida here, summer all the year around. There are about 160 people in this camp, including a Canadian airman from St. Catharines. There is a rumor going around that we will be leaving in a few days for another camp near Lyons a little farther north. If we had been able to get to Spain, before being picked up we would have been deported to England. The Canadian Red Cross looks after this camp pretty well, so I am not complaining. We get 50 English cigarets and a package of French tobacco per week. There really isn't much use sending parcels because they take months to get here, but if you want you can send over cigarets, and we are short of soap, needles and thread, but that's about all.

You remember Lloyd Lauzon and Jimmy Lauder don't you? Lloyd was in the same car as I was, he was not wounded. Somebody saw Lauder in a hospital in Dieppe and they say he was hit in the leg and shoulder. I am told that Doug Sheppard is in hospital, too, with several leg wounds. I was very fortunate in escaping without a scratch. Last week they had a little fun when they tunelled under the walls and 58 of the boys went A.W.O.L. As a result of that, we lost a few privileges and are being more strictly guarded.

Well, I really have nothing I can complain about, I am getting enough to eat for the time being, and we have been issued with enough clothing and things to keep us going for awhile. I am told that the worst thing about these places is that they get monotonous as hell after a while. I am getting writer's cramp, so I will have to lay off for awhile.

So long Dad, your son,
Roy.

GOING TO HELL FAST

*Among the RCAF's forty-eight squadrons, totalling 94,000 men over-seas, was No. 405, formed in April 1941 as part of the Allies' Bomber Command to target German cities, U-boat bases, railway lines, and enemy troops. The bombing raids became controversial because of the huge numbers of civilian deaths. But the airmen themselves were always a heartbeat away from oblivion. **Flying Officer Ken Canning** of Dunchurch, Ontario, was a wireless operator and gunner with the 405 who maintained a long, confessional correspondence with a friend from his hometown, Don MacFie, an air force sergeant with the 423 Squadron.*

"1ST CANADIAN BOMBER SQDN"

405 Sqdn.
Topcliffe, Yorks.
Oct. 2nd. 1942.

Dear Don:

. . . Maybe I've always been a bit high-strung & nervous but lately my nerves are going to hell fast. Last night we lost 3 "kites" and about the last of the fellows that was with the Sqdn. when I joined are gone. Old Jack Jennings is the only chum I have left here now, of course you meet new fellows all the time but it's never the same. To size the whole thing up Don. I haven't a Chinaman's chance in this game, although I think Providence is on my side . . .

"THE KILLER SQUADRON." 405 R.C.A.F.

Oct. 19, 1942,

. . . You asked me once to tell you something of what I was doing, well it's hard to write about but I had the worst & shakiest "do" I ever want to have the other night. I suppose you read in the papers of how the Kiel [German naval-yard] defences were swamped by us one night about a week or so ago well from what I saw they were a long way from being swamped. We got lost somewhere near Kiel and in doing violent evasive action our compass stuck. We flew for about 15 minutes heading for Berlin & thinking we were coming home so that meant we had to come all the way back across Germany again. We were stooging along about 18,000 [feet] dodging "flak" & searchlights when we must have ran over some big city because everything they had opened up on us. There were anywhere from 60 to 100 searchlights on us & so the skipper did the only thing possible & stuck the nose down. We went down from 18,000 to between 150 & 200 feet & it took two on the stick to pull out. Even machine guns were giving us blazes so the pilot told the gunners to open up & we put out 7 searchlights in about half a minute. Well we flew the rest of the way so close I thought we were cutting grass & to end with we had to hit for the nearest aerodrome in England with only 15 mins. gas left & our hydraulic system all shot to blazes, so many holes in us we looked like a sieve. I tell you Don stay on the Coastal [Command] there's a heck of a lot more future in it . . .

Your pal,

Ken

On average, for every hundred aircrew on Bomber Command, half were killed in operations, another nine died in England, and twelve became prisoners of war. Others were injured; only about two dozen survived unharmed. Canning was not one of them. On the night of January 27, 1944, he died on a bombing mission to Berlin. His friend Don McFie returned home safely to Dunchurch. During the war the Royal Canadian Air Force (RCAF) flew 41,000 operations and dropped 126,000 tons of bombs, an eighth of Bomber Command's total. The RCAF death toll was 3,500, and another 4,700 officers and men died in other Bomber Command squadrons. In all, 17,101 members of the RCAF were killed in the war – nearly the same total as the Canadian army's combat losses in Europe.

A FLEET GOES DOWN

Late in 1942, German troops marched through southern France intending to capture the French fleet, fourth-largest in the world. When the Vichy government refused a British plea to join with the Allies, the French navy scuttled as many as ninety of its warships and other vessels in Toulon harbour to prevent Germany from using them. **Gladys Arnold**, *The Canadian Press correspondent (see page 208), wrote home about it.*

Nov. 27, 1942.

Dearest Mother and Arnold:
You are perfectly right Mother – I am a louse and whatever else you will – there is no excuse – even if I am busy I should not be that much so and – so I make a new resolution . . .

But, as you know, the events of the past two weeks have been so drastic, so wonderful and at the same time so worrying for the United States state department policy – playing around with Darlan [commander of Vichy France forces] and the other fascists – that we have gone to bed every night after midnight entirely exhausted.

Today came the climax – the sabotage of the French fleet. What a magnificent and heroic gesture: When Andre Philip was here he told us that the harbor was mined and that the Germans had always kept a certain air fleet observing the ships constantly ready to pounce if they left. Finally after they marched into unoccupied France they strengthened the air armada to so many planes ready to sink the ships at the slightest move. He told us that the day would come when if they could not slip out their fuel would reach a place where they would not be able to keep up steam – and at that moment the Germans would take them if they could – then we would see what the men on the ships really thought for at that moment they would make a desperate effort to show their real will. Today was the day.

Can you imagine these men? Can you see those thousands of sailors brought up in such a strict tradition of the sea – to leave their ship or disobey their commander is harder for sailors than for any other force. But when they heard the Germans were moving toward Toulon they began. First the great ship Strasbourg blew up – then 15 others. The second lot did not go off at once and the soldiers and sailors in Toulon fought off the approaching Germans to give the ships time. Some tried to get away – some were sunk – two at least are known to have escaped. Then more blew up – finally the sailors deliberately turned their guns on one another and blew each other up. They have more than redeemed the honor of France – for it is one thing to go down in a battle at sea in the heat of a fight – and another to prepare the ship you love to blow it up and yourself with it. Another thing to deliberately turn the guns on one another – Many of the sailors and captains went down with their ships. The shore batteries manned by Frenchmen turned on the ships and finished the rest and in their turn blew themselves up including munition dumps. This is one of the greatest acts of heroism in history – and we got the short wave programs from Algeria and Morocco – also from the BBC as they broadcast to France and the speech by de Gaulle. It was wonderful and tragic at the same time. They understood so well in England where they really know what it means to scuttle a fleet of

63 [*sic*] ships. No one dare say now that the French are not brave – or that there can be any doubt about where they stand. And how foolish for Darlan to tell them to leave. He knew they could not – but it shows that the men have heard de Gaulle who told them that if they could not sail to scuttle and die like heroes that their country might live. This he told them 10 days ago – and these are the instructions which they have obeyed.

It is a terrible thing – they say the whole port of Toulon is demolished and the harbor clogged with ships and burning hulks and the bodies of the men who died with them. But it is a glorious page in French history and no one now will dare to say that they are not with us. Also perhaps now Washington will have the grace and the decency to recognize de Gualle and the people of France – and have done with Darlan, Petain and the rest of the traitorous crew. What a blot on their own honor. Today I am glad I am not an American. But I hope my own country will not be long in recognizing as it should the true expression of the people of France. They may lift their heads again – for now the fleet is no longer a menace and a pawn – and many British ships which had to keep constant watch for the Vichy fleet – will be released to help in the battle for Tunis and the whole mediterranean. One thing is sure – France has earned her place at the peace table and if there be a free man anywhere who does not raise his voice in her defence and to help her at that moment – then he is not worthy to be called a man – or free.

In London all flags are flying at half mast for the French sailors tomorrow. I called External Affairs and said that I thought that we too should do honor to these men who have so given their lives and they said they thought it a good idea and would give it every consideration – and try to arrange it too . . .

Will try to do better my dears really – forgive me.

all my love and kisses,

Glad

XXX

WHO NEEDS AN ENEMY?

*Edis A. (Brud) Flewwelling, a twenty-four-year-old captain in the
4th Anti-Tank Regiment of the Royal Canadian Artillery, wrote to
his "pretty cousin" Mary Teed of Saint John, New Brunswick, about
his commando training.*

Dec. 8/42

Dear Mary:

. . . After two weeks of fun I was sent on a course for a month and
a half with the commandos, at their training school. They nearly
killed me, but I made up my mind if they could take it I could. We
did three main things, if we weren't running we were crawling, if we
weren't crawling we were swimming in nearly ice water.

The first day they made us crawl seventy five yds down a hill,
twelve at a time, under fire of live rounds.

We were told to keep in a strai[gh]t line, if we got ahead we
would get shot, if we got behind we got it, if we raised our heels or
our heads we got it. They said our chances of getting to the bottom
were pretty good if we ob[e]yed all rules. Well we started, I looked
behind once to see bullets just missing my heels and in front they
would just about take the grass from between our fingers. They were
fired over our backs from all directions every once in a while they
blew the earth up in front of us with explosives buried in the ground.
I never hug[g]ed the ground so hard in my life. To give an example
of how close they were one chap raised his head to see in front if he
was going short, I am afraid he raised it for the last time, they shot
him through the fore head. One day we got in a river from one P.M.
till seven with water most of the time to our neck we were training
in how to go through enemy posts. Other days we crawled down
sewers. I was in one where I only had enough room to breath, when
I [had] hit the top my chin was in the water. We crawled about fifty
yds through that one. We slept out never had dry close on for the
whole course. There were times when I wished I could of been shot I
was so tired. We went on an eighteen mile scheme one day and got

H___ if we slowed down to read a map – every thing on the double. We had to do two miles in twelve minutes with all weapons and full pack . . . The hardest thing was every morning while the cold dew was still on the ground, we ran about two miles till we got warm (full equipment on) then went to a lake where on the shore was a large tree with three ropes hanging down from a limb, from the ropes to the water and about four feet out were coils of wire. We had to get a rope run away back and swing out over the wire and drop into eight feet of the coldest water on earth. I never did such awful things in my life. We were scaling a cliff one night (pitch black) we had sixty feet to climb every once in a while a flare went off we had to stop moving if the instruct[o]rs saw us they fired a machine gun at our feet. During one climb I heard a scream, (really awful) and a chap went down twenty feet to break his back.

During the course twenty two were shot, as all the time we used live rounds. One broken back four broken legs and a lot of others injured and fifteen were returned to their units . . . I learned a lot of tactics which I am to instruct in my Regt.

After I returned a week to the Battery, I was sent on another course from where I am writing. I am at the College of Science [in Stoke on Trent] to study the science of all Artillery equipment. They have special engineer Proffers and a few English army captains. The school is the most modern building I have ever been in. I really enjoy it but I am getting awfully soft after the other course . . . At the college we have tea at eleven and again at three finish at four thirty and get home in time for tea and dinner at seven . . .

Love
Brud

The new gun he mentioned was an anti-tank weapon, the seventeen-pounder. From late 1943 through spring 1944, Flewwelling saw active duty in Italy and took part in the liberation of the Netherlands. After the war he remained in the service and achieved the rank of major before retiring. He also served as the mayor of Saint John.

CHRISTMAS WITHOUT JEAN

Ed Brunanski, a lanky Saskatchewan welder, had been hopping freight trains for four years before joining the air force in 1940. He became an airframe and engine master mechanic in Yorkshire with the RCAF's 428 Ghost Squadron. It was named for the bombers' countless hours of night action and the destruction they wrought; its badge was a death's head in a shroud. On Christmas Day, 1942, Sergeant Brunanski was in no mood to mix with his mates – as he told his schoolteacher wife, Jean ("Jelenka," a Hungarian pet name), whom he'd married just before leaving Canada more than a year earlier.

#428 Sqdn R.C.A.F.
R.C.A.F. O'seas
Dec. 25th [1942]

My Dearest Wife Jelenka, –
Sweetheart you can't realize even if you understand what a Xmas day Ive had. I don't feel no self pity & I'm not asking for sympathy – but I can't sit here by myself and even make myself believe that it was Xmas day today.

There are four boys sleeping in this hut with me and it seems they all live near-by as they left last night to spend Xmas at home. This morning I woke up in a cold & miserable hut to find myself alone. There isn't much else to say – I went and had a wash and shave and then sat around until it was time for dinner. Im enclosing the menu so there is no use in describing what we had [the meal included roast turkey with forcemeat stuffing, braised ham, brussels sprouts, roast potatoes, Christmas pudding, custard sauce, mince pies, cheese, biscuits, celery, fruit, cigarettes, beer, and minerals]. The officers served us. But you can't make a man happy by giving him a good meal. This afternoon I sat around read a couple of story books then I went over & had tea – cookies cake and tea, sat around some more until seven when I went down to the mess hall where they were holding a dance. I watched a couple of dances and came back.

Now here I am sitting in silence that is almost eerie – broken occasionally by some outburst of song as the guys pass down the road to the dance after being to the pub (beer parlor). I hope no one envies me in my solitude . . .

Next Xmas morning when we wake up please remind me of this one darling so I can look back upon it without any resentment and to enjoy that day even more so to appreciate its fullness with you by my side. Okay hon? . . .

Goodnight sweetheart and may God keep and bless you – and please darling don't be like me but keep smiling eh.

Forever yours with all my love
Hubby Ed

xxxxxx&
a big one X
for Xmas

Brunanski missed another Christmas with Jean, but they were reunited in Ottawa in November 1944. Four years later they bought The Wakaw Recorder, *a Saskatchewan weekly newspaper, which they ran together for twenty-six years.*

ALWAYS A BRITAIN

By 1943 the tide of war was turning in favour of the Allies. Montgomery had defeated Rommel in North Africa (where 350 Canadian officers and non-commissioned officers served with British forces). The German 6th Army would surrender to Russia in early February, and Africa would be cleared of German troops by May. In January, **Flying Officer Maurice Park,** *a pilot with the RCAF, was on leave in England, far from winter-white Winnipeg, where his wife, Mabel, was expecting their first child. He wrote to the friends who would be the infant's godparents.*

Overseas, January 28/43

My Dear Alf and Janet:

Received the cigarettes, and believe me, they are a treat – I have not been able to accustom myself to the flavor of foreign brands. Many, many thanks for your kindness.

At present I am on leave, am enjoying a rest in the South of England. Spend my time sleeping, reading and walking about the country side, enjoying its beauties, even at this time of year it is green, and flowers may still be seen in the gardens. Another week of this leisure, then back to a new station and a different type of aircraft, even larger than those I have been flying. From all indications, I may eventually end up on the four engined jobs, and am quite happy about the whole thing. Of course, everyone would like to fly fighters, but I know my limitations and have no hopes of that. If I were only ten years younger!

Enjoyed my short stay in Ireland, it is truly the Emerald Isle. The tree trunks are green, the stone fences and cottages are covered with green fungi, the fields are a soft paddy color. The country roads are narrow and twisting, tree bordered, two wheeled horse drawn carts join along them. In the cities you see horse drawn hansom cabs with silk hatted drivers perched proudly on the box, it is a page from the past. One of the amusing sights was a taxi drawn by a single horse, the cabby had built a seat on the radiator. The old and the new were certainly wedded in that case, thanks to the gasoline shortage!

There are also a great many cars using natural or coal gas for fuel. They look queer, have huge fabric bags mounted on a rack on the roof. All that is required for conversion is a special type of carburetor. They also have buses which generate their own gas from anthracite, every hour or so the driver stops and shovels in a bit more coal. It is an economical means of propulsion apparently, though I have no idea how it affects the engine.

I spent a few days in London on the way down here, and was properly impressed. They still feed the pigeons in Trafalgar Square, artists still peddle their canvases on the sidewalks, people still go fishing on weekends. Bomb damage is apparent yet not too disfiguring

– I think it has removed a bit of eyesores. The general impression I get is that you could bomb these people every day and it still wouldn't disturb their equanimity, they will continue to go about their business, when it is all over they will erect bigger and better edifices in place of those that have been destroyed. You know damn well there will always be an England . . .

All the best, and thanks again –
Sincerely, Maurice

Park was co-pilot of an aircraft patrolling for U-boats in August when it was shot down by German fighters; all nine Canadians on board died. He never saw his daughter, Maureen, who had been born in March.

THE BACK-DOOR TROT

Amy White of Fenelon Falls, Ontario, was a nurse who joined the Royal Canadian Naval Nursing Service in December 1942. She went overseas to HMCS Niobe, a Canadian naval base near Greencock, Scotland, where she rose to be sister-in-charge of the hospital.

ROYAL CANADIAN NAVY

Feb. 7th 1943
3 a.m.

Dear Mother & Dad –
Do you remember in the last war how anxious you both were to get overseas? and how disappointed you were when Sam Hughes wouldn't let you? Well, my greatest dream has come true, & now your daughter has been chosen to go. The draft came thru to-day & I'm so excited I have the back-door trot. There are six of us going, we don't know when, but we get embarkation leave & I'll be home for a couple of days . . .

April 7th 1943

. . . We have had a very busy week. Two ships in with their quota of sick. I was on 4–12 last week & we got seven in one lot. The comings are so secretive that we get no warning. The ambulance just pulls up at the door & disgorges . . . I didn't get off until 2.30, and the time changed that night, & I had to be back on at eight, so I went short of sleep. Thanks to sulpha the patients are all better now. With this double day light time the evenings are really long . . .

Lots of love & kisses

Amy

In 1943 Canadian nursing sisters were sent to the Continent to treat the wounded of the Sicily campaign; others went to Algeria; nurses in two other units served in Italy. Seventeen Canadian nurses who lost their lives during the war are honoured in the Book of Remembrance on Parliament Hill. Amy White received an honourable discharge from the nursing service in November 1945.

LIGHT AND DARK

Private Jack Powerful Griss *of the Royal Hamilton Light Infantry was a prisoner of war in Stalag VIII B near Breslau, Poland. He sent a lighthearted letter to his wife in Montreal.*

Nov 7th/43

Stalag VIII B

Dear Olga. I had two letters yesterday, one from you and one from Elsie (Aug 23rd). Glad to hear that you are all well. I also received more cigarettes from the R.H L.I. Womens Club. I suppose that the time this reaches you it will be Xmas. Under these circumstances I wish you all at 5162 the best for the season. Let us hope that we shall all be together for the Christmas 1944. Well dear this life goes on – we are still very crowded. I am mucking in with the Aussie again and his cooking is not so hot. The other day he made some fish cakes with a tin of salmon and potatoes, but when he was frying them they started to vanish so I said after, they, the fishcakes were down to the size of a shilling [we] better eat them raw. I was over to the Canadian compound last night and we were all saying that it was opening night in the Maple Leaf Gardens for the hockey season. Won't it be grand to have those days back again. Oh well we have our Canadian Football League going here. Cheerio dear love to all

your Jack

Griss's correspondence with the War Claims Commission after the war presented a far different picture of his incarceration.

7 Attlee Street,
New Sudbury, Ont.
January 7, 1953.

Thane A. Campbell, Esq.,
War Claims Commission,
Ottawa, Canada.

B. 38187 Griss, J.P. – R.H.L.I.

Dear Sir,

With reference to press notice, attached, I wish to make claim for maltreatment during my service with the Armed Forces during World War II.

Taken prisoner during the Dieppe Raid August 19, 1942, and sent to Stalag VIII B (later called Stalag 344), I was one of the Canadian P.O.W. who were tied up with rope (our hands were tied) on October 8, 1942. Ropes were used until November 20, 1942, then handcuffs and chains were used. Was sent to hospital in February 1943, where I was operated on for hernia, contracted in action. Later sent back to Canadian Compound and chained up again. Handcuff treatment continued until November 18, 1943. In February 1944 was transferred to Stalag II D, at Stargaard in Pomerania. Further mal-treatment experienced was from February 1st, 1945, on hunger march from Stargaard, across Germany to Hanover, then back to Schwerin (77 days of near-starvation and hardship). Unable to travel farther, due to complete collapse of my bowels, I was sent to hospital at P.O.W. Camp at Schwerin, but no medical treatment was available. After liberation was flown to England and hospitalized at Aldershot, Hants.

Yours truly,
Jack P. Griss

NAOMI THE RIVETER

To replace the men who joined up, tens of thousands of Canadian women went to work in factories. As Canada's Imperial Munitions Board of Canada reported, "Twelve months ago no thought of woman labour was in the mind of any manufacturer. Experience has now proved that there is no operation on shellwork that a woman cannot do . . ." Among the women making shells, ships, tanks, aircraft, and artillery pieces was **Naomi Turner** *of Vancouver, a twenty-year-old shipyard worker who had fallen in love and lived briefly with a private named Hugh.*

[June 1943]

My Darling Hugh:

. . . It was so lonesome at night when I was on day shift I stayed on that shift for twenty-seven days and then I asked our foreman if I could go back on afternoon shift and he said sure if I wanted to. Now I'm back on day shift . . . Today when I had breakfast in the café the waitress told me there was no use waiting for you because you'd probably find another girl and I would never see you again, but I don't think you would . . . Oh by the way I didn't tell you I had another accident. I got one red hot rivet above my right eye but it's just about better now and on Tuesday I got a dolly bar slammed on my right foot and took the top right off my little toe. I can hardly get my shoe on and it sure hurt when I walked. It isn't as bad now but still sore. I hope the war will be over soon so I will be able to be with you always . . . I remain your one and only true love,

Naomi

Naomi Turner didn't yet know she was pregnant with Hugh's child. After their son was born, Naomi entered a marriage of convenience. Hugh visited her after the war and they conceived a daughter named Elaine, but on a trip to Edmonton to get his discharge from the army, he suffered an accident and had a leg amputated. Naomi never heard from him again.

HITTING THE SOFT BELLY

*In the summer of 1943 the troops of the First Canadian Army finally left England, where they had been playing at war, and saw extended action on the Continent. General McNaughton, who wanted to have his men fight as a single unit, was forced by political pressure back home to free the 1st Canadian Infantry Division and the 1st Canadian Army Tank Brigade to take part in Operation Husky, the invasion of Sicily. German and Italian troops were defending the island off the toe of Italy, the Allies' eventual target. Fooled by "the man who never was" – a body found on the shore with phony papers – the Axis believed their enemy would next be attacking the Balkans, not Sicily. On July 10 the Canadians under Major General Guy Granville Simonds, an astute but little-loved commander, joined the Eighth British Army under Montgomery and the Seventh U.S. Army under General George S. Patton. Overseeing the whole operation were British general Sir Harold Alexander and U.S. general Dwight D. Eisenhower. Three thousand ships and landing craft and two thousand aircraft made the amphibious assault, the Allies' largest offensive to that time. **Private Bob Hackett** of the Seaforth Highlanders of Canada was a bank clerk who had spent three and a half years in England training for battle. He wrote to his folks in Vancouver, the regiment's home base.*

August 1st, 1943.

Dear Dad & Mum: –

. . . All that afternoon we had ploughed through mountainous seas, and as we passed Malta, it seemed that the sea would never calm. The convoy started to grow as we moved, with ships of all sizes joining us. Boats the size of any small yacht you might see in Coal Harbour [in Vancouver] were being tossed about like match wood, yet they steadily steamed on with the rest of us. Gradually it grew dark, and, as we neared the Sicilian coast you could see a huge fire in the distance. This was caused by the Air Force to light the way to our objective. The job they did was very effective, both in a military sense, and from a point of beauty. Horrible thing to say, as many people in that town must have suffered from our bombing.

ZERO hour was approaching and the men slowly and silently moved to their boat stations. By this time the sea had calmed down, so that the assault landing craft could be launched without mishap. It was very calm and still, and the orders from the bridge rang out calm and clear as a bell. Finally, came the order "lower away" and down went the boats into the sea. I often wondered what went through the minds of those lads as they made way to the shore. The only sound to be heard was the chugging of the engines, which soon disappeared as the barges advanced towards the shore.

While this was going on, the Air Force was still very active, and searchlights and gunfire disturbed the tranquility of the night. Soon the air rocked with vibrations as the Navy (good old Navy) opened up with their big guns. We listened and waited attentively, as Zero hour approached, as we knew it was then that the landing craft were intended to touch down. We paced up and down the deck waiting for our turn to go in, and, at the same time waiting to hear of the latest developments on the beach. At last came the news we had been waiting for – Sugar Green, and Sugar Amber beaches had been secured with little opposition encountered.

The Navy then announced that our barge had drawn alongside the big ship, so down went a few of the boys and myself to receive the equipment as it was lowered. By this time the sea had started to act up again, and we had some difficulty with the loading. By the time all the equipment was aboard, daylight was approaching, and we pushed off for the shore. Everyone was a little excited, not knowing what to expect. We cocked rifles, slapped on Bren mags and waited. We were about ten miles out, and as we approached the beach, the sun came up revealing one of the most marvellous sights I have ever seen. Hundreds of ships of all sizes and description were scattered about the bay. A huge Monitor ahead split the silence with the terrific crack of its heavy guns. Occasionally, a few destroyers near by would join in the chorus, much to the discomfort of our eardrums. As we approached nearer to the beach, we could make out the figures of men running to and fro. Everything seemed under control, and in our hands, with the exception of a stretch of beach to the right of where we landed. There we could see smoke screens, and could hear the firing of automatic weapons, so that we concluded close hand fighting had been encountered. Soon we touched down, and rubber boats we had brought with us for the purpose of ferrying bombs to the shore proved useless on account of the big swell running. It was then decided to get the men off first by letting them wade in. The first batch to go in were a batch of English Pioneers, and of the whole lot two could swim. As you jumped from the boats the water rose to your hips, but as you advanced toward the shore it became deeper, and with the swell behind you, and handicapped by equipment, it was all the sturdiest individual could do to make shore. Three or four of us then decided to run a line from the ship to shore. We discarded our own equipment, and helped get the lads ashore. It was a tough job as many panicked, and I am sure would never have made it had we not been there to help them. One poor fellow near me did, and I am sure he went under a dozen times before I reached him. I grabbed him, pulling him to the rope, and at the same time he clutched me frantically, dragging me under with him. Finally I had to knock him out and dragged him by the feet with his head under water to the shore. He was absolutely purple, so I administered artificial respiration until he came around. I was pleased I had gone to this trouble as his face revealed such gratitude. Finally, after two hours in the water I got cramps and had to give it up. I went back on board, and the Navy were marvellous. They wrapped me in blankets, and gave me tea, which brought me around in nothing flat . . .

We are now moving amongst very mountainous country, and it is very difficult to spot the enemy, especially those deadly mortars of his. However, I am sure he finds our[s] just as deadly. The towns here are all situated on top of the mountains. The reason for this, I believe, is to escape the mosquitoes lurking in the valleys. All along we have been taking quinine to prevent malaria . . .

. . . One German captured recently said in summing up the fighting qualities of the British, that the English are good, the Canadians are good, but the "Red Patch" boys [Seaforth Highlanders] are just devils.

Bob

Hackett was slightly wounded during the Battle of Leonforte in north-central Italy when the man beside him was killed by friendly fire. Hackett wound up the war as a lieutenant and, after studying commerce at the University of British Columbia, became a successful businessman in Vancouver.

ABANDON SHIP

While Canadian ground forces battled through the sweltering, dust-blown Mediterranean island of Sicily, the Allied navies were turning the tide in the Battle of the Atlantic. In early 1943 specially built escort ships, accompanied by VLR – very long range – Liberator aircraft, had sunk nearly one hundred U-boats in four months. German naval commander Karl Dönitz pulled his U-boat fleet from the North Atlantic at the end of May. But danger still loomed for the small, fast Canadian corvettes that escorted convoys from North America to Europe. Warrant Engineer David Brenton, a twenty-nine-year-old Albertan, was chief engine room artificer, in charge of boilers and engines on HMCS The Pas ("the rammed") when it had a run-in with the SS Medina *("the rammer") on a convoy from Liverpool to New York. The encounter occurred on July 21 – not July 28, as he reported in a typed letter to his family back home.*

Letter from John to Mom and Pa, 5 Aug 43. Well folks, I have a letter chock full of news for you . . . So settle down to read about a nice little experience I had.

The enclosed cuttings, which I want you to save for me, are quite vague. However, the "rammer" was a large British Cargo-Passenger steamer, and the "rammed" was our little packet. Incidentally, please be careful not to repeat ships names, as such is not to be published. Here is the story, in all its detail. I may get some photos of it later.

We were Halifax bound, on the night of July 28. The main convoy was bound for New York, but a dozen ships had to be rounded up, to break away from the convoy, to go into Halifax. It was our ship's duty to round up these dozen ships.

The weather during the whole trip had been very foggy. Only short intervals of semi-clear weather would come to relieve us, And permit the convoy to be seen. The R.D.F. (Radio Direction Finder) was in use almost constantly. Often the fog was dense, and visibility only a matter of several yards. One couldn't be too careful, for the R.D.F. was only accurate beyond a mile or so. A ship at closer distance might record as being at any distance up to a few thousand yards. A whistle is blown regularly. Under such conditions, eleven ships were rounded up, and put upon their course for Halifax. The last ship remained to be instructed. The fog was so thick that using signal lights was useless. The best way to instruct him was by the Loud Hailer system. So we maneuvered to come in close to the huge vessel. Speed was slow, the R.D.F. range becoming lessened, as we approached. A few hundred yards remained. At such close range the whistle is not very much help, as it seems to come in all directions. Suddenly out of a dense opaque, loomed the massive shape of a huge ship. A glance by the skipper showed that a ramming was inevitable. In a split second, the orders were given for a "Full Ahead Hard to Port". The throttle was wound out to full, the ship shook and dug in for the hard pull. The stern swung away from the oncoming bow. It couldn't clear – it didn't. It struck, with a terrible crunching of steel, and splintering of wooden decks. Calamity was surely upon us. Such is an account as might be made from one on deck. The following is my experience.

As my cabin is located directly behind the engine room bulk-head, I am quite aware of any sudden changes in speed, or other variations in the noise of the machinery. It often wakes me during my sleep.

I had gone to bed, as usual with some clothes on. My life belt was at hands reach. My jacket, with a flashlight was at arm's reach. It was our last night at sea, for our ship was on the last lap of her last voyage before going in to refit. At long last, after twenty months of sailing, I was to get some shore time. The suitcase of parcels and toys for my baby boy was carefully packed, and ready to be carried ashore in a few hours. Soon, I would be back with my wife and baby. I slept soundly and contentedly, forgetting for the occasion, that we were still at sea, and in dense foggy weather.

In my sleep, I became aware of the sudden increase of the engine, but before I could arouse myself to even wonder why the unexpected change, a terrible jolt struck the ship. My body felt as though it were being rolled down a rocky mountain side. A deafening crunch and clash of twisted and mangled steel, with the snap and breaking of a million pieces of wood – and it lasted just a fraction of a second. I found myself sprawling upon a water-tight hatch door. That is where I came to. It was hard to think, for I was dazed and stunned. Salty water was splashing about me, so I concluded that we were hit. Around the edge of the hatch the water was forcing upwards – so I clamped down upon the dogs [grips]. My next thought was to go back into my cabin to find my life belt and flashlight. By now the water was around my middle. I did get into the door-way of the cabin, only to be driven back out by floating suitcases and debris. With each roll of the ship the water came higher. Now I was almost swim-ming. I groped in the inky darkness for the ladder, and climbed out. My clothes had been torn from me. All I had on was a torn pair of shorts. My next thought was to find a life belt. I knew where they [were], and I climbed up to them, on deck. I'm afraid I must have been pretty dazed and shaky, for I couldn't put on the lifebelt alone. However, someone put it on and secured it to me. Also, someone gave me a leather windbreaker to wear.

My next thought was to find out how much damage had been done. It was very dark, and I had no flashlight. I knew that the ship was going down rapidly by the stern, so I climbed up to the captain and told him what I knew of the damage. He ordered half the crew to take the lifeboats so I went back to the engine room, ordered the silent blow-off to be opened, and for the men to abandon the engine room. Then I went to the boiler room hatches and ordered the safety valves to be lifted and the feed pumps started and fed from the reserve feed tanks – and "Get out".

The roar of steam from the safety valves was terrible. One could not hear orders, and it was useless to give any. I don't mind telling – I was scared. I didn't know whether to stay with the ship to see if she would remain afloat, or to get away to the large merchant ship, hovering close by. I stood near the stern, watching her slowly settle, then someone grabbed my arm and hollered that there was room for me in the boat. So, I went, instead of staying with the ship. It was a mistake for me to have done that, and it has bothered my conscience ever since.

Still, upon that merchant ship lay safety, and a passage back to dear land. To remain aboard – well if the bulk-heads held – O.K., but if one suddenly let go, the ship would sink so rapidly that one would be lucky to get free of the drag in the water, as she sank.

We climbed aboard the merchant man, by way of a scramble net. No sooner had I climbed aboard, than the howling of the blowing steam suddenly ceased. The searchlights were now being played upon our ship, and I could see that she had ceased to sink further. Some of the boys remaining had done my job. They saw that the bulkheads were holding, so they closed the safety valves and silent blow-off. Imagine how I felt!

I yelled across to my captain to have the boat sent back for me. I picked out an ERA [engine room artificer] and a few stokers – and we returned to the ship. I was glad I did that. If I had remained on the merchantman, I would never have lived down such a feeling of cowardice.

When I was back on board, I got the sick bay tiffy to sterilize my cuts, and rig me out in rubber boots, pants and socks. Then a group of us gathered up the shoring from all over the ship, and spent one hour fitting it against the bulkheads, to make them more secure. The mechanical injuries to the ship I found to be limited to only the tele-motor lines, which had been severed. We proceeded at six knots, and steered by hand control. The merchantman and one escort stood by to guard us for the remaining forty mile trip into port . . .

. . . Now Mom, you and Lisa can rest assured that all your prayers for my safety have been answered. For surely, if you could see the hole in the ship, which came directly into my cabin, you would marvel how I came out alive, or even with[out] many broken or mangled bones. Only cuts and bruises were all I had to show; and to-day, a week later, I can walk about almost normally. Do you remember my cabin, Mom? The bow of the ship ploughed into it a distance of about eleven feet – which is nearly the whole length of the cabin! . . .

There is good news, Mom, now. I am a WE (Warrant Engineer) now . . . What is more, I am ashore, and will be for quite some time, I think . . .

Richard is perfect – and cuter, and funnier. I shall enjoy being home so much more . . .

It's a funny world, Mom . . .

Brenton became a well-known engineer for a mine and power plants in Alberta and fathered a second child. He died in 1959.

ON TO ORTONA

In July 1943 Benito Mussolini was overthrown and the Italian king had him placed under arrest, but the German troops in Italy refused to yield to the invading Allies. Canadian troops pushed north into Italy, where the new government announced its surrender on September 3, and met continued fierce resistance from the retreating Wehrmacht through the autumn. Now they were heading for Ortona, a seaport nearly depopulated because most of its men had fled to the mountains. In early December the Germans gave up the town of San Leonardo after bitter fighting. Ortona was only a few kilometres to the north. But first there was a long ravine called the Gully, where the enemy fought tenaciously for several days. Led by the Seaforth Highlanders and the West Nova Scotia Regiment, the Canadians breached German lines on December 13. That day Sergeant Alan Girling of Surrey, British Columbia – part of a mortar platoon of the Seaforths – laboriously began typing and then wrote by hand to his regimental pal, Bill Worton of Vancouver, who was behind the lines with jaundice.

K52568 Sgt. Girling W.A.
Seaforths of Canada.
Dec. 13, 1943.

Dear Bill,

I received your letter okay, and am glad to know thatyou have not forgotten us. We are dealing alright at present sleeping on springs in a Facisti houseand eating off plates. The battalion has done a good job at the front lately, pushing the Hun back and taking quite a few prisoners. We lost quite a few men and there were a large number of wounded. I am sorry to say that little Montgommery was killed by a shell that landed with in three feet of him. He was killed instantly. Windram got a piece of shrapnel through his leg, but it was not serious and he is still with us. Murphy, Winning and Street went down the line with Yellow Jaundice. Maybe you will see them . . .

Hi* – you Bill this is "royal" brother after being in this "do" they call your sickness yellow candy. The guys are looking at there eyes steady and wanting to go down the line instead of fighting tostayin the batty [battery] . . .

The swede and Harry and Duddle are sitting pretty back at F echelon and just chucklingg. they are L.O.B. [left out of battle for a backup force] . . .

Boy, you should have been with us the last couple of days, we sure had a hot time. We wer[e] up in the front line and the Hun was throwing over [every] thing but the kitching sink. We got in a couple of shoots that were not too bad . . .

(To hell with that phoney machine) Dec. 15 [1943] . . . too bad except for the base plate [of the mortar] sinking in. Twelve secondaries sure bat it into the ground . . . This is really war up here, Bill. Polly and Twyford were taken out on account of their nerves and Pratt is in pretty bad shape. I guess they are all too high strung. I'm a confirmed slit trench man now and put Soapy to shame when it comes to digging deep and fast. There are two detachments . . . and we go up in turns. We go up the day after tomorrow. I just rub the old goat's head and hope for the best.

I hope it is not long before you are back because now is the time we need good mortar men but just the same it is a good place to keep away from . . .

So long for now.

Alan

During the Sicilian and Italian campaigns, battle exhaustion – called "shell shock" in the First World War – was increasingly common. Canadian soldiers facing acute psychiatric collapse were often viewed with suspicion, particularly by Major General Guy Simonds. Historians Terry Copp and Bill McAndrew point out: "The Royal Canadian Army Medical Corps, especially, was committed to policies that placed the welfare of the individual soldier above considerations of manpower shortages, and Simonds, among others, criticized the army's policy." Military historian David Bercuson observes: "In the Italian theatre, men marched for days on end over bad roads, crossed rivers without apparent end, slept in the open in cold rainy winters and hot dusty summers, endured flies and disease, and witnessed the poverty and misery of the population. Combined with the tenacious and deadly defence of the German enemy, these conditions inevitably produced battle exhaustion in large numbers. The key breakthrough was to recognize . . . that battle exhaustion was temporary – a good sleep and a few calm days with food and rest usually restored a man's sense of balance and allowed him to return to his unit. In other cases, reassignment to other, noncombat duties was called for. In very rare cases, complete discharge was necessary."

GOING DOWN FIGHTING

In mid-December 1943 the Van Doos (the Royal 22e Régiment) suffered extensive casualties trying to clear a key crossroads on the way to Ortona. In the battle Captain Paul Triquet earned the first Canadian Victoria Cross of the Italian campaign. The Royal Canadian Regiment and the 48th Highlanders of the 1st Brigade from Ontario then took the crossroads. Ortona was the next target. Some military analysts now say the Canadians could have skirted the town altogether, but both sides seemed to consider it a crucial trophy on the road to Rome. On December 21 the Loyal Edmonton Regiment and the Seaforth Highlanders began house-to-house fighting, often mouseholing – blasting through a wall to enter an attached house rather than being exposed on the street. **Private George Lawton** *of St. Stephen, New Brunswick, sent his wife, Alice, letters with his own verses, including this one, from hospital in London (he'd been wounded in a later battle).*

Italy May 21/44

Dear Wifie,
I have done nothing but write and eat and of course make eyes at Nursie. I have some poems I would like to send home so I'll make this letter nothing but . . .

Seaforth of Canada
The Canadian Seaforth Highlands
With chips on their shoulders dyed red,
From Sicily's shore to Piscar's [Pescara's] back door
You will find their wounded & dead.
They said Ortona couldn't be taken,
They took it on Xmas day.
The fighting was hard from house to house,
And they lost a lot in the fray.
A lot of the Boys wont share
In the Victory day when it comes
But they know they went down fighting,
Taking with them lots of Huns.
They don't have to blow of their Glory,
Their deeds will live a long time
And the Seaforth Brigade will never back up
As long as the Hun's in the line.

Lawton was later wounded again, more severely. The shrapnel embedded in his body pained him until his death in 1993. By December 28, 1943, the Canadians had taken Ortona, which lay in ruins. In nineteen days of fighting in Italy, they had suffered 2,119 fatalities.

THE GENERALS JOUST

*While their men were routing the Wehrmacht in Italy, Canadian generals were warring with one another. **Major General Guy Simonds**, commander of the 5th Canadian Armoured Division, had been a favourite of both General Montgomery, leading the Eighth British Army, and Andrew McNaughton, who in December 1943 resigned under pressure because of his poor tactical judgment (including his handling of Dieppe). But Simonds was no friend of Lieutenant General H.D.G. (Harry) Crerar, who'd recently taken charge of the* *overall 1st Canadian Corps. Unannounced, Crerar had sent a captain to take measurements of Simonds's trailer, an action that precipitated a fresh feud between them and prompted Simonds to write this letter to Crerar.*

Headquarters
5 Canadian Armoured Division
15 Dec 43

Dear General:

. . . I do suggest that the implications which you attach to the incident are quite wrong and you have heard only one side of the story. Certainly, no discourtesy to you was intended, nor do I believe that the episode could be interpreted that way when you hear it from my point of view . . .

I did give Kirk a "rough ride". that is quite true, and I feel he deserved it . . .

In regard to your request for self-examination, I know I have a hot and quick temper. It is a characteristic of which I am not in the least proud. It is a fault I know, but it has always been with me and I am afraid always will be . . . I am impatient of stupidity, dul[l]ness and indifference – or gaucheness, and I know I sometimes lose my temper when I shouldn't . . .

. . . during the first evening's talk in my caravan, you accused me of "Thinking of nothing but myself" and "wanting to go home to bask in my newly won glory." I thought the remarks and the sense of others, unjust and uncalled for . . .

I am quite certain of one thing. I will not take troops into battle under your command if I have lost your confidence. It would be unfair to the troops and would prejudice a reasonable chance of a successful result. When that time comes, if you cannot express full confidence in my judgment and ability to handle my command in battle, I shall have to ask to be relieved.

Sincerely,
Guy Simonds.

Unimpressed, the politically ambitious **Harry Crerar** *responded by writing to Montgomery, mentioning at the end Brigadier General Christopher Vokes, who had led the 1st Canadian Infantry Division to Ortona.*

HEADQUARTERS

1 CANADIAN CORPS

17 Dec. 43

Dear Monty:

A number of actions and re-actions, on the part of Simonds since I arrived in this theatre of operations, nearly two months ago, have given me serious cause to doubt his suitability for higher command . . .

This situation does not worry me from the personal angle because I believe that I can still handle him, so much as it does should anything happen to me, or should a situation arise, which would remove me from Canadian command in this theatre of operations, Simonds being my potential replacement. My present judgment is that while he has all the military brilliance for higher command in the field with his tense mentality, under further strain through increased rank and responsibilities, he might go "off the deep end" very disastrously indeed . . .

I look forward to hearing from Vokes, if not yourself, how his troops have been doing. From such little information as comes my way in this island, I have reason to believe, however, that they continue to "produce the goods".

I shall be glad to hear from you soon. Kindest regards.

Yours ever,

HDGC

Bernard Montgomery *was not long in replying to Crerar.*

Eighth Army

21-12-43

My dear Harry:

I have your letter of 17 Dec. I have the highest opinion of Simonds. He tried to go off the rails once or twice when he first went into action with his Division, but I pulled him back again, and taught him his stuff.

Briefly, my views are that Simonds is a first class soldier. After a period with an armoured Division he will be suitable for a Corps. He will be a very valuable officer in the Canadian Forces as you have no one else with his experience; he must therefore be handled carefully, and be trained on.

VOKES is not even in the same parish; I am trying hard to teach him, but he will never be anything more than "a good plain cook".

I do not, of course, know what has taken place between you and Simonds. He is directly under my command for training and so on, but of course would deal with you on purely Canadian matters. If you have been sending him any instructions or directions on training he might possibly ignore them!! He gets that from me – verbally.

I suggest you discuss it fully with me when you visit Eighth Army. Come whenever you like.

Meanwhile: A Happy Xmas to you.

Yours ever,

Monty.

Crerar then sent a handwritten letter to Simonds.

8 Jan 44

Dear Guy

A great deal of trouble can result from a misunderstanding of motives. I was genuinely worried as to your "nervous tensity" on my arrival out here. It was because I have always been interested in your career, (and whether you know it or not, have many times intervened to further it) that I wrote you on 10 Dec to find out from you whether or not the incident which occurred really meant you were "on edge" and needed a change. That was my whole motive.

I could write you at length, and in some force, concerning your reply of 15 Dec. But, I do not think that such is worth while. I will, however, answer one of your implied queries. You always have had my confidence as a Staff Officer and Commander and if you had definitely lost that confidence you would not have had the <u>chance</u> to take troops into battle under my command.

I was going to delay until I saw you before saying this. However, I have today nominated you to command the first Cdn Corps in which a vacancy occurs – and it seems to me to be stupid to conceal this confirmatory evidence of my regard for you, from you. Keep this to yourself until the prospects become an actuality. And in the meantime, try to regard me with less suspicion than apparently has been the case during the last couple of years.

Yours,

H.D.G. Crerar

Crerar soon appointed Simonds commander of the 2nd Canadian Corps in Britain. Replacing him at the 1st Canadian Corps in Italy was Crerar's protégé, Major General E.L.M. (Tommy) Burns, who'd been dismissed in 1941 for revealing sensitive military facts to his mistress.

A WARMING THOUGHT

Captain Eric Harrison of Kingston, Ontario, was a history professor at Queen's University when he became historical officer for the 1st Canadian Corps, officially chronicling its advance through Italy. He was travelling with Charles Comfort of Toronto, one of thirty-one male Canadian war artists who produced about five thousand scenes of horror and humanity from the battlefront, and several female artists who depicted the home front. Among them were Alex Colville, Group of Seven co-founder Lawren Harris, Molly Lamb Bobak, and Harrison's wife, Elizabeth. Her paintings recorded the war effort in Canada, notably the loosening of sexual mores and social barriers. Writing Elizabeth during the Italian campaign, Harrison sent along a portrait Comfort had done of him.

As from HQ 1 Canadian Corp
CMF
24 Jan 1944

My Dear Darling,

Here is a drawing for you done by Charles Comfort. The address on the note-paper isn't that of the place where he made the drawing. Actually he did it in the open air in an orange grove, while I sat gazing at a stone fir tree on an adjacent ridge, thinking that I had been mistaken neither in my attitude towards war nor in my regard for you. These things are antithesis. War I hate; you I love. My loathing for war increases with my proximity to it. My love for you is advanced by my distance from you, but only because my appreciation of you is made poignant by my being away.

But the spring is not now far off, a lethal violent spring that must be the seed-time of our coming release from the evils of this struggle. You tell me of your snow. I can see snow from where I stand writing this to you. The sun shines upon it with Alpine brightness: there is the promise in the lucent distance of change. Every day passing brings us nearer to the time when you may do a sketch of me in a happier place than the orange grove. Even when you receive this we shall be so many weeks the closer to each other. What a warming thought to nourish that the passing days bring us closer to meeting.

I love you my Elizabeth.

Your Eric

In one letter Elizabeth wrote: "My God, there's going to be a lot of blood about when we do meet! Shall we tear each other limb from limb in our lusty passion or simply be content with lacerating each other with our nails . . ." After serving as a historical officer to Lieutenant General Harry Crerar, Harrison retired as a lieutenant colonel. Eventually he became head of Queen's University history department; his wife continued to paint and write. He died in 2000, she a year later.

THIS LITTLE PORCO

In late January the Americans established a beachhead at Anzio, a pre-war resort town on the Mediterranean's Tyrrhenian Sea, fifty kilometres south of Rome. The following four months saw some of the most savage fighting of the war in Italy. Inland, heavy winter rains and mud had stalled the Canadians, including Calgary's 14th Army Tank Regiment. Because of the inclement weather, the regiment billeted in houses a few kilometres from the Adriatic Sea. **Sergeant Grant Philip,** *whose nickname was Dan, wrote to his wife.*

B3858
Arm St Sgt Philip G.O.
Supply Sqdn 14 CAR
Canadian Army Overseas
Central Mediteranean Force
[March 18, 1944]

My Dearest Mumma

. . . I told you about the children around here and how they sing like angels, well the other day I took my washing to their mumma and discovered another little pie there about one year old. Therese, one of those fat happy babies that gurgle and spit and make "woofing" noises to be taken up. In spite of past experiences and all the discomforts of the loving I couldn't resist this one and soon we were all firm friends repeating "This little piggy went to market" on the baby's fat toes. Well when everyone including Grandma had learned it thoroughly then they wanted to know what it meant and was that a headache the way I butchered their language. With the aid of ready invention and much demonstration with the hands I finally offered this free and liberal translation as follows

Questa pogo porco portato vendi
Questa pogo porco casa mio momento
Questa pogo porco carne di pani

Questa pogo porco niente

Questa pogo porco portato "wee wee wee wee" distanta via casa mio

Anyway it pleased the baby (much too young to know better) and earned for myself the doubtful title "Pogo Porco" among a score or more of young street urchins about here so you see my reputation grows and like the rest I now want you to share this fame with me. In all truth however I must admit only the baby enjoyed it the bigger kids all think I am crazy . . .

I am closing now to spend a few moments before dreams with my old friend S. Pepys . . .

As Ever

Dan

The Calgary Tanks were on the move again by May 11, 1944. They supported the 8th Indian Division of the Eighth British Army as it advanced to Pignataro near Cassino behind the mightiest artillery barrage since the 1940 Battle of El Alamein in Libya. A thousand guns echoed in the Liri Valley as the combined Canadian, British, and French forces broke through the Gustav Line the Germans were holding 120 kilometres southeast of Rome. Grant Philip came home and fathered three daughters; he died in 1970.

IN VINO VANDALISM

*Not all the Canadians in Italy were as tender as Sergeant Grant Philip. **Captain William Bate** was a Toronto lawyer who went overseas in 1940 to serve with the 1st Canadian Brigade Group. He wrote to Wing Commander Colin Strathy at RCAF headquarters in Ottawa about Canadian hooligans in uniform.*

HQ 1 CBRGP
Fri. 14 Apr. 44

Dear Colin –

I've been intending to answer your missive of some months ago but have been bloody busy ever since my arrival in Sunny [?] Italy some 9 weeks ago . . .

. . . Most of our disciplinary problems in this base area can be summed up (if I may paraphrase) – "in vino vandalism". Our lads just can't cope with the cheap native white & red wines . . .

. . . Recently I was on a rape case that lasted 4 days. Personally I didn't think rape was possible in this amgotted [?] country. One of our lads – a full blooded Indian – got full of vino & allegedly assaulted a 54 yr. old wopsie on her return home 'from the milkman' (as the interpreter so charmingly expressed it). The pros[ecutor] produced a curious collection of exhibits, including a plan which a witness naively swore was a sketch of the alleged offence! – Here's another sample, that we had to deal with the other day – Two of our lads fell out of a route march across some of the nearby hills, ending up in a village wine-shop. The proprietor made the mistake of leaving the premises & his 7 mos. pregnant wife to their tender mercies while he came into town "to get food for the bambinos". Our fightin' troops got annoyed when the signora refused to entertain their joint & several advances. So then the lads proceeded to wreck the place to the tune of 16534 lire (the proprietor's estimate). By the time our provost had arrived our lads had practically captured the village singlehanded. – A couple of weeks ago I was on an F.G.C.M. [court martial] held about 30 miles away, where one of the pros. witnesses was the madame of the local brothel. I'll never forget the look of consternation on the faces of the Court when the pros. asked the old beldame to point out anyone in the room whom she had seen before. The waiting members (under instruction) looked most uncomfortable. Happily only the accused was for it. But enough of shop talk . . .

God Bless.
Bill

THE WHEELS OF MARS

In the spring of 1944 more than 75,000 Canadians were fighting the Italian campaign. The 1st Canadian Corps launched an attack on the Adolf Hitler Line, where the Germans had retreated a dozen kilometres to the west of the more heavily defended Gustav Line. **Corporal Robert Tweedie** *of Vancouver was maintaining wireless sets in radio cars with the 1st Canadian Signals Division as the troops breached the line and battled through the Liri Valley. Over ten days, he wrote to Laura, his girlfriend back home in Vancouver.*

May 25.44

Good Morning Laura Dear

. . . Very ordinary sort of a move today Dear. As we pulled into position we watched the infantry battling their way up the opposite side of the valley.

The big topic of the moment is the colossal nerve of McKenzie [*sic*] King as he climbs aboard the bandwagon. His ears should really be burning tonight! [On May 16 in London, King had been at the Commonwealth Prime Ministers' Conference endorsing a global organization "endowed with the necessary power and authority to prevent aggression and violence."]

Our route lay through Pontecorvo, which town had held us up for a few days. I should say what is left of Pontecorvo. Utter complete destruction presided over by the unmistakable & revolting smell of death. A few miserable starving civilians who managed to live through it all, watched apathetically as we rolled by. Bomb holes large enough to put a tank into had the roads & alleyways completely blocked. But the Engineers had worked miracles in opening up lanes to let us through. Caterpillars grunted & ground as they moved houses trees boulders and dirt. Even cars and trucks were ruthlessly pushed aside for the wheels of Mars.

Wednesday
10 A.M.

. . . I was chatting with Major Brown, the second in command and as the whole hideous stage of destruction & death was being set up we both agreed that it was all pretty silly. Like children playing games instead of grown adults of a supposedly civilized world.

Friday [June 2].

. . . I have no nerves left, Laura. They've been pulled out one by one and dropped by the roadside from Pachino in Sicily & Cassino in Italy. That was the last of them. Anyone who is unfortunate enough to have nerves doesn't last very long these days . . .

Now for bed kiddo. Cause there's no telling when we move again.

All my love Sweetheart
R.

P.S. I'm no gentleman cause I feel like howling.

Tweedie, wounded in battle, was sent to England, where he met a British nurse named Marjorie Eavis, who had made a hundred parachute jumps during the war, ridden camels, and been asked to join a sultan's harem. Tweedie returned home to marry Laura. After she died in the early 1990s, he returned to England to look up Marjorie, who had earlier visited the Tweedies with her husband. Now single, she accepted Bob's proposal and came to live with him in Sechelt, British Columbia.

THE ROAD TO ROME

Lieutenant Robert Hunter Dunn *of Westmount, Quebec, was a tank troop leader with the 8th Princess Louise's (New Brunswick) Hussars, which saw action in Italy starting November 1943 and found itself in the thick of battle as the Canadians supported the Fifth U.S. Army in the struggle to take Rome. In a letter to his father, Dunn mentioned* *fear in battle. The neuropsychiatric symptoms of battle exhaustion affected a quarter of all casualties in this assault, many of the men freezing or fleeing.*

14 June 44

. . . I am keeping very well – there is quite a lot of dissenting going around but it hasn't bothered me yet.

We are busy training for our next job whatever that may be. As you know our first action was very successful. We saw our first fighting on May 25 when we moved through a gap in the Hitler line. Some of his better troops put up a good fight but most of them were glad to give up. They had had enough and said so.

Our toughest show was crossing the Melfa River. We were heavily shelled while making the crossing and when I arrived on the other bank about 3 minutes behind the leading squadron some of our tanks had been hit. All the crews were saved although two were wounded. My job is to protect the Col[onel]. One of the officers of the knocked out tanks tried to attract my attention by firing his pistol at my tank. My driver saw him. He was pointing in the direction of the enemies fire but I couldn't see Jerry so I threw smoke to cover our group. I think the leading squadron knocked out all the anti-tank guns. The moaning minnies (large German mortar) started on us that night but cause no casualties – they are more frightening than effective.

I wasn't as scared as I thought I'd be and always could control my tank & its gun without hesitation. Guess it must have been our long period of training. Our worst moments seem to be when we are under shell-fire and we can't shoot back at him. Actually shellfire doesn't hurt a tank very much and our own casualties from shrapnel are when the lads were outside their tanks. Our own guns are very effective and we can blow down a house in about 20 seconds . . .

Hunter

Dunn and his compatriots helped the infantry and tanks of the 5th Armoured Brigade cross the Melfa. Two days later, the 11th Infantry Brigade occupied the town of Ceprano – opening up the route to

Rome. But Sir Oliver Leese, commanding the Eighth British Army, felt the 1st Canadian Corps under Tommy Burns had not acted swiftly and decisively enough. Leese placed the Canadians in reserve while the Fifth U.S. Army led the drive to Rome, reaching it June 4 to liberate the first Axis capital of the war. Hunter Dunn later served with his regiment in northwest Europe, and at war's end he returned to Gloucestor, Ontario. Some 3,300 of the corps were killed or wounded over three weeks; an estimated four thousand others fell ill or were injured.

WAITING FOR THE INEVITABLE

It would be the first frontal offensive on Fortress Europe since the disaster of Dieppe. British lieutenant general Sir Frederick Morgan and a team of British and American officers had been planning the invasion since March 1943. In January 1944 General Dwight D. Eisenhower – Ike – arrived to set up Supreme Headquarters, Allied Expeditionary Force, and oversee the assault. Eisenhower, a West Point graduate who'd trained tank troops in the First World War, had a meteoric rise in the Second World War after being named U.S. commander of the European theatre of operations. Canadian soldiers knew an invasion was imminent, as **Cliff Chadderton** *of the Royal Winnipeg Rifles mentioned in a letter to his mother. A news editor for* The Canadian Press *and a reporter for* The Winnipeg Free Press *before the war, he played for the Winnipeg Rangers, the farm team for the NHL's New York Rangers.*

Freshwater Bay
Isle of Wight, England
May 9, 1944

Dear Mum,

If you ever read this letter you will recognize the significance of the date. May 9, 1919 was of course my birthday.

I am sending the letter to Vic Peever and asking him to deliver it to you if for some reason I don't survive what we know now is coming very close – that is, the invasion across the Channel.

To say that I am ready for whatever comes is really the truth and I want you to understand that.

Unfortunately, there comes a time when young men have to deliver up the finest thing that God gave them: that is, their lives, but being pragmatic about it, although we were brought up to believe in the "greater being," you were the one who in a ward in the McKellar Hospital in Fort William brought me into this world.

I have so far had a wonderful life, thanks to you and Dad.

As a boy, we in our family had a taste of the good life. When the Depression came we sampled what millions on this earth had to face which would not be called the good life, but when we got it back again as Dad's business prospered again, we were able to appreciate what hard work, guts, determination and a good family can do.

I can hardly imagine what will be going through your mind if Vic ever has to deliver this letter to you. To a young man of my age going to war is a very selfish act. As you know I had several paths I could follow. One was hockey and that would have been short-lived, I am sure. Another was to go on to university. I could have followed the university path and in this regard I was attempting to decide whether I should take Dad's advice and be a veterinarian or take your advice and go into law. I guess without too much effort I had the marks that would get me to the early years of university and perhaps scholarships and everything would have helped.

The world changed all that for a young man like myself. We saw that we cannot let the bullies inherit this earth. I have often asked myself why I joined the Royal Winnipeg Rifles. One of them was Dad which of course was his choice and I know he was proud about that.

I could have had another path perhaps, but we will never know that now . . .

I will not make this letter too long Mum because there is no need. Between you and I it was always the unspoken word that really counted.

The mix of the Blackburn strain (your side) and the Chadderton strain certainly was more than I could have hoped for. You will realize that in a way I am getting on to the "gene line" but after all both you and Dad were very strong on bloodlines when it came to breeding the best springer spaniels in the world.

Nobody fooled me. I knew that when I told Dad that I was going to get married the first thought that went through his mind is that my wife would be able to carry on the line should anything happen.

Dorothy has Bill at home and I think I am particularly blessed because she has agreed to live with you and Dad and you can share everything that comes along.

Your loving son,
Cliff

Chadderton rose to the rank of captain, and in 1944, commanding his company four months after D-Day, he lost his right leg below the knee to a grenade near the Leopold Canal, which forms part of the border between Belgium and Holland. Back home he got involved with the War Amps organization, later becoming its chief executive officer as well as chairman of the National Council of Veteran Associations in Canada.

OVERLORD

The Allied invasion code-named Operation Overlord was set for dawn on June 5, 1944, but bad weather delayed the landing by a day. The raid on Dieppe had convinced Eisenhower and his fellow officers of the crucial need for many more and much-improved landing craft, better wireless communications, and tremendous air and naval bombardment to buttress the ground troops. The Allies began misdirecting the Germans to suggest that the landing in France would be at Pas de Calais, closer to England than the actual target, a broad stretch of beaches in Normandy west of Caen. Among the men sailing the rough English Channel to France on the night of

*June 5 was **Edwin Worden** of the Regina Rifles Regiment, which was
made up largely of farm workers collectively nicknamed Farmer
Johns, or just Johns.*

> 227027 Rfn E.O. Worden
> 1st Bttn Regina Rifles
> Can Army England
> Mon. 5. 44

To my darling wife:

How are you to-night? fine I hope. See darling I find it very hard to
write this to you. I only wish I could have seen you but I can say
this, I am fine and feel a 100 per cent for I know I have someone
waiting for me, who is very brave and knows how to smile.

We are going in to-morrow morning as I write this we are out on
the water so the big day has come. I often had wondered how I would
feel but I don't feel any differance, as I ever did befor thanks to you.
I know I can truthful say if it was not for you I would feel differant
but it is the love and trust I have for you and that will help me over
many a rough spot.

I am glad in away that it has come for it means you and I can be
together sooner something I have allways prayed for and I know you
have to. So promise darling you will not worry for I'll be allright
and home befor you know it.

Just you and Mum look after each other and time will pass swiftly.

Now befor I close I want to say again that I love you very much
and you mean the world to me.

So now darling I'll say good-night and God bless you till we meet
again soon.

> Yours forever
> Love
> Ted

P.S. Tell Mum that I am thinking of her too, and not to worry but
look after you. I am enclosing a message they gave us. good-night I'll
write as soon as I get a chance.

The Allied navies – including 110 Canadian ships and 10,000 sailors – contributed 7,016 vessels, from small landing crafts to massive battleships and destroyers, the largest modern fleet ever assembled. Air forces sent 11,590 fighters and fighter-bombers, many of them manned by Canadian crew; among the squadrons was the RCAF's 2nd Tactical Air Force. In all, more than 132,500 ground troops landed from the sea and 23,400 parachutists from the air. Their number included the men of the 3rd Canadian Division and the 2nd Canadian Armoured Brigade, to be followed by the 2nd Canadian Corps and the First Canadian Army, under the overall command of Lieutenant General Harry Crerar. The Farmer Johns suffered high casualties, including two company commanders killed and one wounded. Ed Worden's fate is unknown.

D-DAY DOCTOR

*In the early morning of June 6, 1944 – D-Day – the first Canadians to descend on the Normandy coast were the paratroopers of the 1st Canadian Parachute Battalion. They were part of the British 6th Airborne that joined two American airborne divisions to take key bridges and causeways inland. Then American ground troops landed at Utah and Omaha beaches while the British hit Gold and Sword beaches, flanking the Canadians at Juno Beach. The Queen's Own Rifles of Toronto streamed out of their landing craft at 8:12 a.m. in the first wave on the sector of beach code-named Nan, near St-Aubin-sur-Mer. Less than forty-five minutes later, **Dr. Charles Baker,** a major with the 3rd Canadian Division, landed with a field ambulance unit assigned to that sector.*

H.M.S. L.S.T. 409
[Early June 1944]

Lt. Col. M. R. Caverhill 22 Cdn. Fd. Amb.

Dear Sir:

I am sorry to be a bit late with my "recce" report. I'm afraid that this reconnaissance is taking me into a few odd and peculiar places. I am once again on my way back to England, dirty and unshaven, with a uniform dirtier than it was in 1940. There is also another difference in that there is no left sleeve in my shirt or battle-dress blouse. If it wasn't for the splitting headache I have, from the bits of metal in my skull and the pain in my useless arm I would be comparatively happy.

A [situation report] of Nan Red beach as I saw it, is a bit confusing.

I went across the channel in LCT [tank landing craft] 707 with a splendid Canadian officer as skipper. He was Lieut. C.J. Holland of St. Thomas Ont. We hit Nan Red beach at 08:55 on D day. The beach was being shelled, mortared and sniped. The tide was high and we passed over the beach obstacles: a mine exploded on our right and damaged the craft slightly. As we were coming in there was a ship on fire away off to our left. Just before we went in, an LCI [infantry landing craft] on our left went down. The ship's company waved good-bye as they slid under. Snipers' bullets began ricocheting in the craft. The skipper cursed the coxwain for staying on the prow but, oddly enough it was the skipper who got killed. As soon as the door dropped the armoured bulldozer and john trailer left the craft. I left the craft next with Major MacPherson and driver Etherington in my jeep ambulance. It was a dry landing, just as Lieut. Holland had promised us. Shells were bursting all around us. We moved a few yards and then had to stop in a traffic jam of S.P. arty [self-propelled artillery]. The beach was sandy but unfortunately had a high wall behind it. The beach obstacles were solid steel and each one had a teller mine tied on it. These were the new type mine and it was impossible to use a safety wire on them. I stepped on a mine but it did not go off. It was quite loose in the sand so I picked it up and threw it out to sea like a discus. There were several hundred men lying in the sand close to the wall. Some of them were wounded. Others were just sitting there waiting to get wounded apparently, because each shell burst picked off a few more. Major MacPherson and Major Chapman moved a few hundred yards to the west along the beach. Major Chapman's jeep was stopped by a groyne [a barrier to contain sand and shingle] about three hundred yards west. I was very much amazed to see all these men sitting on the beach. I asked an R.E. [Royal Engineer] officer why these men were not off the beach. He said that there was a belt of mines just off the beach and that we couldn't go east or west because of snipers and mines. The snipers couldn't see the men against the wall. The snipers were shooting sailors in the craft and the craft were replying with A.A. [anti-aircraft] guns. One German ran down to the beach and threw hand grenades into a craft. Someone killed the German with a sten gun.

I gave morphia to men lying in the sand. I dressed a lot of North Shore [New Brunswick Regiment] wounded there. Most of the men did not have shovels so we got them started digging holes in the soft sand with their hands. A shell explosion blew my hat off so I decided to move a bit. I went about fifty yards west and another explosion bent my glasses a bit and broke a man's back. About a hundred yards west along the beach there was a ditch through the barb wire into the mine field. This was just west of the sea wall. I think that this ditch was specially dug to be covered by rifle fire. I bent the wire back and crawled part way through. I was going to toss a coin to see whether I got killed by a shell or a mine but a shell explosion behind me made up my mind for me. It landed me flat on my face in the mine field. I ran along the ditch and was greeted by a rifle shot from the corner of a house off to the east about sixty yards. The shot missed me and I jumped into a bomb crater which happened to be in the edge of the ditch in a little hillock. The next shot covered my face with dirt. I thanked God for those fortress bombs [dropped by Flying Fortress bombers] and wished that they had been bigger than 100 pounds. It is amazing how small one can get if one really tries.

After a few moments I heard a burst of sten gun fire. Someone else was firing at my sniper. I raised my pistol with my tin hat over

my hand. Just as I reached the edge of the crater the shell-dressing
was shot off the back of my hat. I fired over the edge of the crater. I
heard a rifle bang on the cobblestones and someone running away.
Just then two beach riflemen came along the ditch. The three of us
ran to the gate of the house and round the corner. We couldn't see
anything but smoke. I posted the riflemen there as sentries and went
back to the beach. I got Etherington and the jeep and brought them
up through the S.P. arty to the ditch. I had no wire cutters so I
couldn't get the jeep through the wire. For lack of a wire cutter we
lost the jeep. Etherington and I crawled along the ditch. As we went
along I kicked up a mine. It was a dummy mine – just two round
pieces of tin with a block of wood between them shaped like a teller-
mine. There was a sharp steel spike on top of the mine about three
inches in length. I decided that this was a dummy mine field and that
it would be safe to bring the wounded across it. I went back to the
beach. A mortar bomb blew part of a man's head off and wounded
me in the leg. Etherington and I herded a few wounded up the ditch.
I remember particularly having a bad time getting a blinded North
Shore soldier through the wire. Next time I go to war I'll take a wire
cutter with me. Mortar bombs were coming over six at a time. We
got a few men up the ditch between each series of six bombs. Then I
had four men carrying a badly wounded man on a stretcher. A bomb
lit on the stretcher and killed all the stretcher bearers and the patient.
They were laid out just like a cart wheel. I was standing to the right
of No. 1 and he stopped most of the pieces coming my way. Two
pieces hit me in the head and covered my face and glasses with blood.
One piece cut into the chest piece of my flak suit and didn't hurt me
so please tell the boys that flak suits are a darned good idea. I was
stunned for a bit and did a bit of grovelling in the sand. Then I ran
up the ditch and hid in my bomb crater. A soldier hid in it with me
and he cleaned my glasses for me. After the next six bombs had gone
over I went back to the beach again like a darned fool. I was going
to drive the jeep off somewhere even if it was across a mine field.
The jeep was surrounded by S.P. arty and we couldn't move it. A
single bomb came over and lit right beside me. It killed two men and

knocked me down on my back. This time I got three pieces in my left arm and a few more in my face. I crawled under the jeep. A bomb set fire to the petrol on the S.P. arty. If the S.P. arty hadn't been carrying so much petrol on the outside of their guns they would not have lost four guns and burned up a lot of men. It was all started by a few small mortar bombs. I couldn't use my arm by this time so I crawled into my crater and stayed there. Bombs lit all around me but none of them touched me. The S.P. arty was burning merrily by this time. The ammo began exploding. It was about twenty yards north of me and although many pieces went past the top of my crater, none of them hit me. A sergeant crawled into my hole with me. My arm was soaked in blood and was stinging a bit. He cut my sleeve away dressed my wounds and gave me some morphine. The S.P. arty exploded and covered the whole area with smoke, fumes, burning cordite and burning petrol. The grass started burning all over the mine field and all around my hole. My face was scorched a bit. The sergeant and I decided to make a run for the house. Shells were exploding all over the place. A mortar bomb lit in the ditch in front of us. It didn't explode. The sergeant grabbed me or I would have stepped on it. We reached the house safely.

The men who had been unlucky enough to stay on the beach under and around the S.P. arty were burned alive. Some of them were probably wounded previously by mortar fire and could not move but I cannot for the life of me understand why they all stayed on the beach. As they burned up, they screamed blood-curdling screams that I can hear yet.

As the sergeant and Etherington and I made a run for it along the ditch, the ammo was going up continually. We ran around the corner of the house where I had posted the sentries. Quite a number of wounded had gathered there so we sat down for a bit and hid from the flying steel. Finally we got everybody down into a big cement basement under the building. We cleaned up the basement and made a small hospital there. [Driver] Etherington proved invaluable to me throughout the whole show. He is one of the coolest and best medical orderlies I have ever had. With S.P. arty exploding all around him he salvaged the mortar bomb case of serum and dressings from the jeep. The serum I think saved a soldier's life because he was practically dead when we gave it to him. Etherington and a gunner from the 19th [Field Regiment] did nearly all the dressings for me as I could only use one hand. The boys were very much afraid, of booby traps in the old house. A North Shore sergeant walked through a doorway and had his brains blown out onto the floor beside him. There was an old bed and a lot of junk in the basement which they were afraid to move. A couple of us with five or six holes in us decided that a few more holes wouldn't make much difference. We threw the junk out. Nothing happened.

We dressed everyone, laid them in rows, gave them morphine etc. The ammo explosions were dying down so Etherington and I went to look for our jeep. All that was left of it was two front tires and the two petrol tins on the bumper. We salvaged the petrol and then hid while more ammo went up.

As the ammo kept exploding and the petrol was burning everywhere, we couldn't go back onto the beach via our ditch. I took two stretcher squads and we sneaked west along a hedge and then across the mine field in single file. Half way across a sniper shot at us. We hugged the ground for a few moments. Then there was a burst of sten gun fire which I deemed to be in the direction of the sniper. Finally we ran for it and hid behind a wall. The wall led down to the groyne on the beach where Major Chapman's jeep was stalled. It was on fire. We put the fire out and Etherington backed the jeep around the end of the groyne. If you see Major Chapman please tell him I'm sorry I squashed his guitar.

We gathered up all the wounded from among the burning S.P. arty. Most of the men there were dead, including the engineer officer who had told me I couldn't get off the beach. Etherington put the fire out in a burning arty jeep and backed it into the water away from the main fire. Then we went along the beach to the B.D.S. [brigade dressing station] and reported the location of our patients. I sent

Etherington back to the cellar and told him to wait for the A.D.S. [advanced dressing station] to arrive. I dressed a few patients in the sand. The next thing I remembered I was lying in the sand and a patient was trying to give me a drink.

I reported to the Beach HQ on Nan Red beach that I was wounded and that I thought I should go to hospital. Just then an L.C.I. beached with some wounded aboard. I was sent aboard to see them. When I came out of the hold we were going Hell for leather for another L.C.I. that was sinking. We rescued everyone off that craft just before it sank. There were several seriously injured cases. When I finished dressing them we were alongside H.M.S. Waverly. The next thing I remember I was lying in the officers mess of H.M.S. Waverly talking to Commodore Ottway-Ribon. I was made very welcome by the officers aboard H.M.S. Waverly. I had several doses of morphine and eventually fell asleep. I slept about twelve hours. Then I attended a burial service for Lieut Holland and Pte Shaw. Lieut Holland (the skipper of my craft) had lost both arms and part of his head in a mortar bomb explosion.

About 16:00 hrs 8 June '44 all wounded were transferred from H.M.S. Waverly to LST 406 bound for England.

As we pulled away a cruiser was firing salvos at an enemy strong point.

I was ashore between five and six hours. When I left there were about thirty-five dead men on the shore and eighty or more wounded gathered up into a bunch at the house and another bunch near the groyne on the beach. The Commandos had not cleaned out all the snipers west of St. Aubin. The 8th Bde had taken objective "yew" [one of three areas targeted] but I did not get a chance to see Tailleville [a village near St.-Aubin-sur-Mer].

As I came away there were beached craft on every beach to the west of us as far as I could see.

I lost the jeep and all the equipment with it. I hope that loss did not bother you too much in the assault. If it is necessary I can send a statement to the Q.M. [quarter master] Capt. Scattergood for the write off.

I lost all my personal equipment and clothing and Etherington also lost his. When I get some clothing coupons I will get some clothes. I will make out a claim and send it to you for your signature.

As soon as my scratches are better I would like to come back to the unit if that is satisfactory to you. It is the best place for me in the army and I was quite happy there.

If you will be so kind as to ask the A.D.M.S. [assistant director] Medical Services to put in a special request to the R.U. [reinforcement unit] for me I may find my way back to the unit one day.

Give my regards to everyone in the unit. I wish them all the best of luck in the coming campaign.

Yours sincerely

Charles E. Baker

Major.

The North Shore Regiment and the Queen's Own Rifles had faced enemy gun emplacements that survived the early bombardment. They suffered heavy casualties in fire from a concrete bunker, which also destroyed several Sherman tanks of the Fort Garry Horse Regiment. It took the North Shores six hours, with armoured support, to capture Tailleville. The Queen's Own Rifles suffered more than any other Canadian unit that day. They were to land behind amphibious Duplex-Drive (DD) tanks, designed to float in ahead of the infantry. But the few that didn't sink in high seas didn't land until later. A German 88-millimetre gun mowed down two thirds of the lead platoon of one company, while another unit landed directly in front of an enemy position and quickly lost half its men. Despite these reverses, the Canadian contingent on that astonishingly successful D-Day had only half the expected losses: 340 killed and 574 wounded. Dr. Baker recovered from his wounds, went home to a fruitful career, and in his nineties was residing in a nursing home in Ohio.

WORTH FIGHTING FOR

Reports of the success of Operation Overlord spread quickly and gal-
vanized the Allied forces. Mary Hawkins of Montreal had joined the
women's division of the RCAF in 1943 and had been posted to England
to serve as an operations clerk in Lincolnshire and then as a map
clerk in Yorkshire. In 1944 she married George Buch, a lieutenant
with the Black Watch (Royal Highland Regiment) of Canada. **Mary**
Buch *wrote about D-Day to Marion Strong, dean of the women's res-*
idence at Macdonald College, Ste. Anne de Bellevue, Quebec.

June 6th, 1944.

My Dear One –

. . . I wish I might tell you what it has been like on the graveyard
shift of late. I got to bed at five this morning, and at six we all listened to the German News Broadcast suggesting that D-Day had
come. The official British report came some hours later. You in North
America will have awakened on the morning of June the sixth, 1944
to hear that momentous news. I wonder what the reaction is over
there. There is a tenseness here, combined with a relief that we need
no longer wonder "when" – We have had three hours' sleep since
Sunday morning and are standing by in case we are called . . .

. . . The previous evening in between a dozen little duties, such
as sitting in the Guard Room for a couple of hours (Duty Stooge,
they call it – the name is Joe) booking people in and out, I had a
report to write for s/o Findlay –: work-up of the outcome of the baseball series, account of a birthday party we had – details of our
Canada night last week. I sat listening to the King [George] broadcast, and as I stubbed out cigarettes, thought how crazy it was to be
occupied writing this, when the papers are publishing extra editions
and the radio blares forth news of world-importance. Then it
occurred to me that these very things – a baseball game, a birthday
party, the privilege of talking about one's country without fear for
one's life – are the very things that are being fought for – It's just a
thought – I think you know what I'm trying to say – It's just the

awful feeing that we get sometimes, that nothing matters – It goes
away again, with the realization that <u>every</u>thing matters – I had it at
the time of Hong Kong and Dieppe and during the desert-battle
months – I suppose you must have, too – many times – . . .

Good morning, Canada – (you're probably not even thinking of
morning, if it's not midnight yet over there – But I hope it will be a
good morning, when it comes)

My fondest love,
Mary

UTTER WASTEFULNESS

*While Dr. Charles Baker was among the wounded shipped back to
England, **Dr. Joseph Greenblatt** – a lieutenant from Ottawa who had
also landed on D-Day – proceeded through France with a field ambulance unit serving an artillery regiment of the 3rd Canadian Division.
He wrote to his fiancée, Fran.*

18 June 44
letter #24
Capt J. Greenblatt
14 Cdn Fd Ambulance
R.C.A.M.C. C.A.O.

Fran Darling –
. . . You know darling one of the main uncertain personal things that
I was worried about was what my reaction to fear would be like. I
might say that thank heavens I have been O.K. in that respect. At
times I have absolutely been terror-stricken yet fortunately I have
had sufficient will power to control that fear & carry on with my
work & not show external evidence of that fear to my men. Anyone
who says that he is not afraid is absolutely crazy & is a liar. That
experience of fear has been expressed to me by everyone from higher-
up to the newest private . . .

15 July 44

Letter #32

. . . Tonight a very young pilot was brought into my abode already dead killed not in an aerial engagement but purely on a social visit up towards the front & his vehicle got hit by a shell. Now this kid is a young bloke from Montreal whom I had once previously met back home. I have seen many casualties & some very very good friends have passed through my hands for preliminary patching up before proceeding to rear area hospitals but just now when it a slow time & one has time to think does the tragedy & utter wastefulness of it all strike home . . .

You mentioned a certain town that you hoped I wasn't around. Well that's exactly where I am right now. Not too healthy a spot either. One gets quite a bit of exercise diving into slit-trenches on the close ones . . .

All my love,

Joseph

Dr. Greenblatt was in Caen, that "certain town." The Canadians and the British had been pushing south towards it since D-Day. The North Nova Scotia Highlanders of the 9th Brigade and the tanks of the Sherbrooke Fusiliers attacked Buron and Authie, near Caen. The towns were held by the 12th SS Panzer Division of the Hitler Jugend *– teenaged Hitler Youth troops – and a Panzer-Grenadier regiment led by Kurt Meyer, a veteran commander from the Eastern Front. On June 7, 1944, Meyer ordered twenty-three Canadian prisoners executed. (He was later found guilty of war crimes by a Canadian court martial and received life imprisonment.) After six days' fighting and 2,831 casualties, the Canadians were removed from battle for two weeks. Back in action, the 3rd Division seized Buron and Authie and the next day, July 9, they began moving into the rubble-ridden streets of Caen, fighting seven Panzer divisions in the sector.*

THE POOR BLOODY HUN

Peter Griffin was the younger brother of William Griffin, a pilot who escaped from France after Dunkirk. Peter witnessed the initial bombing of Caen by the British Bomber Command. He had landed on D-Day with the elite 1st Canadian Parachute Battalion – Canada's first airborne unit – as part of the British 6th Airborne Division in the Normandy invasion. He wrote to his married sister, Margaret Norman.

Tuesday June 20th 1944.

My dear Marg,

Thanks very much for the letter – I got it today. Your brother continues to lead a charmed life up to two days ago when we were finally pulled back into reserve. Up till then for 11 days I've been leading the most amazing life right from the moment we took off from England. In the first two days I had fun blowing up two bridges and was completely cut off from our own troops with my party.

We finally made it back without loss and things began to take some logical shape. From then on we fought Jerry at every turn and Marg we literally slaughtered them. The 6th Airborne Division can be rightly proud of itself as most of the fighting we did was without supporting arms. The thing that shocked me was the 51st Highland Division. Three different times our Division restored a situation for them. If you could have seen our lads come up to help them out one occasion and call them yellow b . . . ds when the Scotties threw their weapons and equipment away and fled. The answer to that one is the Highland Div have been used to much different type of fighting in N. Africa.

A shell landed 20 feet from me the other day when they attacked my company! Not one piece touched me . . .

At the moment I'm quite near a chateau and a count and countess live in it called Rohan-Chabot. They know Guy de Lesseps and saw him last in 1939. A nephew or brother or something of hers called le Compte de Begassiere married a sister of Uncle Jacques! Damned strange world we live in. The old girl gave me a few bottles of wine and cognac so I gave her soap, cigarettes, candy and a flashlight . . .

July 8 1944.

. . . I really take my hat off to the [Field] Ambulances. They work only a matter of hundreds of yards behind the forward troops and perform major operations two minutes after wounded are brought in, under shelling and mortar fire. I'm sure the number of lives saved compared to the last war is tremendous.

We are still in reserve having a good rest. Last evening I sat smoking a cigarette beside a river watching 2300 tons of bombs being dropped on Caen 6 or 7 miles away. What an incredible sight it was – the poor bloody hun! News came through an hour or so ago that the attack had reached the outskirts of the city . . .

July 18 1944.

. . . For some unknown reason I've been awarded the M.C. [Military Cross]. I have no idea what it is for, no citation as yet, but in any event there it is. Monty came to our division and made the preliminary awards. He pinned the ribbons on us and had a few pictures taken among which the last is interesting to note. He called the medallists around him in a semi-circle, in that very informal gesture of his, sat in the middle, with me two places from him on his left. He's having an autographed print made for each one of us. There were four other awards in our Bn. He has quite a soft spot for the 6th Airborne division and spoke to us at great length. He told us what an important job we'd done in securing the left flank of his beachhead and subsequent bridgehead.

We've been wondering all along why its so important, on such a high level, until this morning at 0530 A.M. when 1500 bombers of the R.A.F. and American A.F. came over and dropped their loads on Troarn and Fauborg de Vaucelles, just south of Caen, and a three

Corps attack came through our very own little left flank. A total of 9000 tons is expected to be dropped to-day and its going on right now. The bridges we are securing are just teeming with armour going up to the battle. Warships are lying offshore engaging Jerry coastal batteries and other counter battery tasks. 660 medium and field guns constitute the artillery effort.

Two other Corps put on a feint attack elsewhere last night. The prisoners are streaming in past us, most of them paralysed by our bombing effort. Our own casualties are starting to come in, but these troops got too far ahead of schedule and got caught in our own fire. It's a little too early yet to say, but word has it that this is the greatest effort by any army so far this war. We are all feeling very proud of our left flank . . .

Aug 28 '44

What a merry pursuit of the Jerry we've had for the past two weeks. All the way from the Bois de Bavent to Pont Audemer this side of the Saine, where I believe, the 6ᵗʰ Airborne Division has now completed its task set prior to first moving. What the form is now is not yet known by small fry such as myself, but I believe the big decision regarding our future employment in an airborne role is being made and if parachutists and gliders we remain, then back to England we'll go.

Best Love

Peter

After great success, the Parachute Battalion returned to England in early September. It later fought in the Battle of the Bulge in Belgium before moving on to the Netherlands and Germany. Griffin won the Military Cross for his courage during the Normandy landing and at a battle in late August at Dives Crossing. He came home with the rank of major.

"LES CANADIENS SONT LÀ"

Charles Bradley was fifteen in 1939. When he later falsified his birth record and joined Montreal's Black Watch (Royal Highland) Regiment of Canada, his grandmother prevented him from going overseas for a year. But he arrived in England in 1943 and was with the regiment during the Normandy offensive – and the assault on Caen – as part of the 2nd Canadian Infantry Brigade.

17 July/44

Dear Mom,

This letter will probably be cut to pieces by the censor, but I don't care what happens, guys like that don't worry me a bit any more. After what I've been through, the chaps in my own outfit killed and wounded, who were my pals, and after the amount of Jerrys I've killed, which was a good amount, I don't care a hoot what happens to me, or do I care what those guys who stay behind the line have to say. As you have read we have taken Caen. We were the first ones there who stayed, and were not pushed out by the Jerry. That's a fact no matter what you read. We were an hour in the centre of the town before we seen any Limeys . . .

It cost us more than 60% of our unit. We entered the town [Buron, near Caen] at dawn and fought all that day and night. We were the first company in the town and there was not much left of the Co[mpan]y, when we got to the town. We fought our way through to the other side of the town and dug in. All that afternoon we fought off counter-attacks, and the ground in front of us was piled with German dead; all that time we were under very heavy mortar fire which knocked out a lot of our boys. By night time Jerry was surrounded and just about cleaned out. During the night two other chaps and myself sneaked out to the rear of a Jerry position with two Brens, a rifle and a flock of grenades. At dawn our boys chased him out and when he came out of his trenches me and my two buddies just mowed him down; we killed 38 Jerrys between the three of us. That completed the capture of Buron which by then was just a pile of rubble. There was a lot of our own dead around, but there was 6 Germans to every one of ours dead. We then advanced till we got to Caen; that is, the centre of Caen. We did not see much after that: a few shells and the odd sniper to knock out. All in all it was a tough show, but the Canadian soldier again proved that he is the best soldier in the world . . .

In one town, his memory of the NHL's Montreal Canadiens proved vital.

6 Sept. 44

Received your letter from Meaford [Ontario], also received 1000 cigs, which came in quite handy. I guess the newspapers have really been going to town in the last few weeks with the news from France. Jerry is retreating so fast that we have been riding tanks from dawn to dark trying to catch him. It's really quite the thing to go through these towns; we are always the first troops in the town, and the French people go mad with joy when they see us. No sooner do we enter a town, than every house has flags of the Allies and France, and they just plaster the tanks with flowers. I had quite an experience of my own a few days ago. We had been traveling all day and about 8 o'clock we stopped just out-side of a town by the name of Bethencourt-Sur-Mer. We were to stop for the night, but we had to find out if there were any enemy there or not. So our platoon officer, sergeant, and myself were told to take a jeep and to recce [reconnoitre] the town; we put a machine gun on the front of the jeep and I got the radio set. The idea was to go like the devil right to the centre of town and if nobody fired on us, OK, but if we were fired on to come back. We set off across the open field on to the road and right in to town without no trouble. We stopped at the town centre, got out and did not see a soul; we did not know what to do; we could not go back with a report like that, and yet there was not enough of us to look through all the houses. I then remembered the old Canadian hockey team's song, so I roared as loud as I could "Les Canadians sont là." Well, it worked swell; in five minutes the streets were jammed tight with French people. All I did for the next hour was kiss beautiful girls and drink wine. Just before dark the Mayor of the town gave a speech in front of the town population over which there was a lot of cheering although it was all mud to me; he then pulled out a very important looking document which stated who the first three Allied soldiers were to enter the town with all our particulars. It is to hang on the wall in the City Hall forever, so the Mayor said; it was all very thrilling, and the wine we had made it that much more so. I only wish that war was always like that . . .

Love,

Charlie

After the war, Bradley recorded an account of the campaign to liberate Caen, describing it as "the No. 1 battle as far as the Canadian Army was concerned; it was the fiercest we had in the 2nd War, as far as casualties were concerned." More Canadians were killed and wounded in taking the city of Caen than on D-Day itself. And, by mid-July, battle exhaustion accounted for one quarter of non-fatal Canadian casualties in the Normandy campaign.

FOR HOME WE FIGHT

Corporal Tom Quinn lived up the street from the Robertson family in Burnaby, British Columbia, before going to war. In writing to Mollie Robertson (now Mollie Manifold), he mentioned Operation Overlord's "45 days of invasion" but focused on the imagined life of one French family, so like his family at home.

> K46560 Cpl T. Quinn
> "C" Sqdn 27 C.A.R.
> Cdn. Army Overseas
> July 21st, 1944

Mollie,

. . . This is being written in an empty shell scarred house in the suburbs of a French town. Perhaps empty is not a good word to describe it for although the people who once lived here are gone their spirits still remain. I felt their presence when I stepped into the room, their living room I guess it was, and looked at the tables and chairs, at the sideboard full of old china and glassware, and dozens of odd little ornaments that have been handed down from one generation to another.

I felt their presences even more keenly as I looked into cupboards full of clothes and clean linen, and bed clothes, into drawers full of all sorts of odds and ends, full of the story of their lives, school books, scribblers, pencils, all the little things you'd find in your own drawer at home. And now I think perhaps that it is not the spirits of the occupants of this house but the spirit of my own home that is in this room.

I looked in the bedroom upstairs and the tears smarted my eyes as I looked at the tiny cradle with the doll tucked neatly away under the little quilt, as if small hands had done it only last night.

The long years rolled back and I saw my sisters tiny hands tucking the quilt around the silent occupant of that cradle and heard my sisters voice telling it to go to sleep, that she'd be there in the morning.

The ghosts of the past filled the room to overflowing so I left.

This house has taught me one reason why we fight, – to preserve the mainstay of civilization – the Home.

So Mollie please write to me even if you have nothing to say (that sounds very Irish) for your place has always been like a second home to me, and a letter from home renews our determination to get this war over and done with so that we can get back to the things we love.

> Goodbye for awhile.
> Tom

Mollie wrote to Tom again and again. And he did come home to live in British Columbia.

VICTORY AND SURRENDER

As the Allied armies advanced inland from the beaches of Normandy, they enclosed the German Seventh Army, leaving a fifty-kilometre-wide opening, south of Falaise, towards which the Germans retreated. The Canadians were charged with closing the Falaise Gap. They took Falaise on August 16, 1944, and five days later linked up with a Polish armoured division to plug the gap – but not before thousands of enemy soldiers and senior officers had escaped, prolonging the war. **Lieutenant Colonel Paul Baillargeon** *fought at Falaise with Quebec's Régiment de la Chaudière, part of the 3rd Division's 8th Infantry Brigade. Two days after the bittersweet victory, he wrote (in French) to a padre back home.*

Overseas, 18 August 1944

Major Philippe Tanguay
Camp Valcartier, P.Q.
My dear padré,
I am naked, my HQ has been bombed and I have lost everything. I saved nothing but a shirt-tail. Sansoucis was killed in this bombardment. His two legs were sliced off and he died on arrival at hospital. Wounded: Louis Labrecque, Pierre Taschereau, Jean Miller; St-Jacques was killed. We had a bad time of it. We took part in a major advance on Falaise. We advanced for three days, working with our friends the tanks, and we made good speed in spite of the very hilly terrain.

The old hands are quickly disappearing. You'd no longer recognize the Regiment. I'm lucky still to have Lacasse, Lemaire, Cadorette. Poor little Lagacé had a dreadful fright yesterday. I sent him off with a message, he took the wrong route and found himself on enemy land. He rushed back, and thanked me for having given him a new motorcycle the day before. He's a good sort, very devoted.

L'abbé Huot has been offered the chance to return to Canada. I told him that as long as he enjoyed good health, his place was here. I believe that he understood. He has had to work hard, and often in very unpleasant conditions, so I'm going to have to help him buck up. Boulard and Gauthier are now captains. Rioux will also be one within a few days. I am promoting as many members of the Regiment as I can. Today I learned that we have closed the trap, and taken 100,000 prisoners. I hope it is true. I told you that I had summoned Desautels and given him the boots. I believe that he will write better articles in the future (if he is capable of it).

My greetings to all. I hope that your mother has recovered. I will read your letters to the boys. Hoping to receive word from you shortly,

Sincerely Paul

THE INEVITABLE CIDER

The South Alberta Regiment had also been on the move towards Falaise. At one point, its men could see a long column of German soldiers ahead. Although reduced to a complement of 120, they killed, wounded, or captured 2,900 of the enemy. **Lance Corporal Robert Henry Goodyer** *was with them and wrote to his parents and wife in Winnipeg.*

August 20th 1944

. . . Now let me describe the events of the past few days. I don't often get time to write because we seem to be always moving, digging slit trenches or eating or sleeping and not much of the latter. I've been on guard 4 times in the last 8 days, having to take my turn like the rest.

We are steadily advancing at the rate of about 2 miles per day. A few days ago our convoy passed through some lovely wooded country like you see north of Montreal. At the time, there wasn't an artillery shot fired and you wouldn't know there was a war on just a few miles away.

Our group of vehicles harboured for awhile in an apple orchard in a little village we had captured the night before and the French population came swarming to greet us, shaking hands all around and saying, "Les Boches caput!" We had a few extra cans of bully beef which we handed over to them and they were pleased as punch. From my meagre knowledge of French, the Germans had confiscated their food and looted their houses and they hadn't had anything to eat for about a week. I knew a little more French than most of our fellows and acted as interpretor. In return for our gifts of food and act of liberation, an old wealthy-looking gent asked if we would like some cider so I was delegated to fill up one of our water tins. The gent took me around to his house and stable and filled up the can with cider. Then I had to drink his health and that of his wife and friends. The cider is nothing to rave about though, I've tasted better stuff in England. But every single French family seems to have a cider barrel.

Yesterday was our field day, though. Our regiment's tanks went into a village and cleaned it up and pretty soon, Jerries by the hundred came out of hiding in buildings and woods and gave themselves up. I had to go up to this village to fix a little radio trouble in one of our tanks so stayed to watch the fun. The prisoners were quite a nondescript lot of every nationality. We herded them back to our H.Q. where some of the boys on hand helped to search them and line them up, etc. Our padre and M.O. were there to attend the wounded and they did a marvelous job. One or two of the prisoners could talk a little English and they said they were glad to get out of it all and said the war is lost for Germany. It should be over soon.

It was quite a field day all right. Our regiment must have taken a thousand prisoners all day. And we marched them down the road in bunches with us riding behind in a beep [a Jeep] with a machine gun trained on them. So you can expect me home any day now . . .

. . . We hoped to catch up to our tanks which were away ahead but after travelling all day we made only about 25 miles so we decided to hunt for a barn. I asked a farmer alongside the road in my best French if he had a barn where four of us could sleep, so he took us to his house insisting that we sleep in a spare bed-room he had. I was the interpretor and we got along famously. We met his wife and large family of boys and girls. He begged us to eat with them and we had duck and milk and some bread he made himself and the inevitable cider. We gave them some of our canned bully beef and a little tea in return. They were very hospitable and gave us an invitation to return. Needless to say we slept very well in the soft beds. All this happened on my birthday so I was particularly enjoying myself. In the morning we rose bright and early and after a lot more travelling finally found our regiment. I could go on and on describing our advance and our experiences but here we have no more space . . .

This was Goodyer's final letter from France. He died on October 28, 1944, aged twenty-five. In the battle at the Falaise Gap, the Germans employed the Nebelwerfer, a mobile smoke-shell mortar that in ten seconds launched six rockets with a range of 6,700 metres. Nearly 1,500 Canadians were killed and more than 4,000 wounded in taking the objective. John English, a retired Canadian military officer and professor of history at the University of Waterloo, argues that the generals leading the Canadian divisions were "mediocre performers" who failed to effect plans developed by Montgomery and Simonds. In the Normandy campaign from D-Day until late August, 5,021 Canadians died and 13,423 were wounded. Among the casualties were more than 160 Canadian and Polish soldiers killed and about 250 injured by friendly fire – bombs dropped by American aircraft. French and American troops liberated Paris on August 25, 1944.

THE GUNS OF AUGUST

*In southern Italy that August, **Alexander Ross** of Embro, Ontario, had joined the 17th Field Regiment of the Royal Canadian Artillery, which had come through the assaults on the Gustav and Adolf Hitler Lines. The non-commissioned officer was just in time for the battle at Monte Maggiore, a village in rugged hills of the Apennines. On August 24 the 1st Canadian Corps took over from the 21st Polish*

Corps on a front passing through Monte Maggiore. The next day, Ross was in the thick of it, as he later wrote to his brother.

[September 1944]

Dear Burns,

. . . At times I couldn't see my own guns for the dust caused by high explosives bang on our position. Obviously Jerry knew where we were to the last yard, but thank heaven his guns were not always accurate; many of the rounds meant for us exploded up the slope among the olive trees. But it was at night that I found the shelling even more unnerving than in the day. And it was during the night that Jerry really dusted us off – set the camouflage netting on one of our limbers on fire. It was a real effort for me to leave the safety of the dugout and race over to the gun to offer assistance. Inside the limber, its doors open, were rows of cartridges filled with H.E. [high explosives] and, round about us, exploding mortar bombs. I was damned scared and perhaps not very helpful, but I'm glad I managed to show, as initial impressions mean much, as you try to justify your existence in a regiment as seasoned as ours. Fortunately no one was hurt.

For a time I worried lest I became 'windy' but gradually I simmered down although I still got awfully close to the bottom of a slit trench when Jerry was right on target with his mortars or his guns.

I must give great credit to my gunners; big prairie farmer-types, strong and spare of speech, gun-centred, who waited defiantly for their turn. It's just as well they were not the ones who found two Italians in the village above us who had maps, binoculars, a mirror, and radio set for directing the German fire on us. No damned wonder the fire was so accurate. I heard we shot them . . .

Alex

Ross later fought in the Netherlands and left the service in 1946 as a captain with a Military Cross. Back home in Ontario, he became chairman of the English department at the University of Guelph.

A BUGGER OF A JOB

In October the Canadians were with the Eighth British Army trying to breach the Gothic Line, a heavily fortified stretch of German defences running from the Adriatic to the Tyrrhenian Sea across the Apennines of northern Italy. The first phase of the offensive was the battle of Rimini, one of the more crucial (but little-known) battles of the war, fought by 1.2 million men with thousands of guns, tanks, and aircraft. It was a giant pincer manoeuvre by the British and Canadians on the Adriatic and the Fifth U.S. Army in the Apennines. **Lieutenant Fred Egener** *(see page 228) led a platoon of B Company with the Perth Regiment, a motorized infantry that acted like a mobile shock troop to accompany tanks. The regiment was the first to crack the Gothic Line. He wrote to his wife.*

Sept. 19/44
From the Gothic Line to Rimini

Dearest Norah:

. . . This narrative will be dotted with "I's" from start to finish. That is because it is not intended to be the story of the battle nor a part of the history of a unit, but simply all that I can recall of what I personally saw and heard . . .

The unit had begun its move from Spoletti after an early breakfast on Aug. 24 . . . This movement was a slow one, the unit moving up behind the units of another division that was pushing the fighting line back to the Foglia river and the main Gothic defences . . .

The area was at the bottom of the steepest hill I think I've ever had the pleasure of coming down. It was not a regular road, but a track enlarged by our use and the dust lay heavily upon it. I thought several times that we would slither down the pillar of powder . . .

Since no one knew where we were headed or what echelon we were to join, prudence led me to order the carrying of small packs and blanket. It was prudent all right, but what a bugger of a job.

When we reached the end of our trail, we were exhausted and that completely. I believe I have never been so dead beat . . .

It was here that the matter of the packs really began to tell. The road seemed intent upon going straight up to heaven, and though we quickly peered around each bend as we came to it, believing the summit must be revealed, we were not rewarded until we were nearly too tuckered to be appreciative . . .

When we saw the position we were in on the morning of the thirtieth, we were pleased for we surrounded a sturdy farm building that was set quite picturesquely on the gentle slope of a spur that ran off onto the top of a lesser hill . . .

Just about 10 o'clock I found everyone retired to bed. Norm Root told me Lt. Cook had had to go to hospital sick and that I was to go up to the company. I moved fast; roused Wawro, put on my essential kit and then the two of us started out for the next town . . .

When I arrived there were numerous vehicles crowded about and five or six prisoners could be made out standing under guard by the house wall . . .

Shell fire came down . . . intermittently during the night, but it was aimed at harassing the road more than demolishing the house so that, except for the odd bit of shrapnel striking the forward part of the house, the fire did not come dangerously close to us.

Just as the darkness was beginning to thin out, the colonel decided to go forward to recce [reconnoitre] for a headquarters on the north of the river. He took Wawro and I with him . . . We set off quickly to get benefit of what darkness was left, for it was lightening rapidly and we knew we had open ground to cover that was under enemy observation . . .

As we came along the road, the height of Mont[e]cchio lay before us on the left. It gave the enemy complete observation of the road and was within easy range. But although it was now light, no fire came at us from the feature and we reached the road junction quite easily and there used the deep ditch for cover till the company showed signs of activity.

Sgt. Reid showed me the platoon's positions and then shared his slit trench while he told me in detail what had happened the day and night before.

By now the Jerries on Mont[e]cchio had become active and were sniping particularly at the tanks . . . The snipers were accurate. I saw one tank lumber down the hill to a safer point where its crew were able to get out the tank commander, who apparently had been shot through the head while observing from his open turret.

More tank units began to move up the road . . . At the same time the Irish came up the road, cut through our position and proceeded up the slope to line the ridge. It was the right moment for Jerry, and he quickly brought down the shell fire on the road junction. Baker company got its full share of this. One shell that landed right on top of company headquarters instantly killed a wireless operator, wounded CSM [Command Sergeant Major] Sheardown and wounded another man.

Crouching in Reid's slit trench, I got the odd piece of spent shrapnel that fell into the trench, but no more . . .

Major Snellgrove led off company H.Q. and I came next, leading 12 Platoon. We were in the tank harbour area proceeding north from the main road and commencing to climb up a shallow draw leading to the top of the ridge when shells landed right in amongst us. I had been going along trying to see some of everything that was going on, at the same time searching the ground for hollows, furrows, folds or ditches that might give some cover . . .

I had just sighted one narrow, shallow ditch when I was in it and the shelling was on. I shall never know whether I dove into that ditch or was blown in, for I didn't consciously hear the shell that landed on top of the platoon, catching nearly eleven in a standing position, killing Cpl. Dube and wounding L/Cpl. Droshner . . .

The effect of the morning's trials on the men was all too apparent. They were nervous, hesitant, reluctant to go on. Nothing was said, but the major paused here and the platoons moved in closer and individuals found better spots of ground.

It is amazing what can be found to get one below the ordinary ground level: the ground turf where a tank had turned in its tracks, a grass-grown furrow where once a plow had ditched the ground, the gouges spring water had taken from the land, and the innumerable folds not normally visible to the eye, besides the more obvious ditches, banks and stream bottoms, give more hiding spots than one might expect . . .

Fifteen or twenty minutes after the shelling, we moved off up to the ridge . . . We had proceeded to a point from which we could see north and east, and there we halted . . . The men spread out on the track, which here was sunken, and removed their equipment. It was a welcome rest.

Peters pointed out a trench cutting off at right angles from the road, the entrance barred by the limb of a tree that had been drawn into it. He wanted to go into the trench but thought the limb might be booby-trapped. I got well to one side and jerked out the limb and then went on up the track on some errand or other.

When I came back, it was to be passed by platoon members proudly escorting back seven Jerry paratroopers Peters had found when he investigated the trench . . . It was just the same when we later investigated a similarly concealed trench system on the other side of the track and took out another nine paratroopers, including an officer. They were well-equipped and armed . . . If these troopers had sallied out when we were taking it easy in the road, they might well have taken the whole company for a mighty serious loss . . .

So long-winded . . . I tired of the task of setting down the detail. Writing what I did gave me a chance to blow off some of the excitement and desire to talk of what had happened. As you see, the narrative covers to Sept. 1 . . .

Fred

The Canadians breached the Gothic Line and reached Rimini on September 21. Bill McAndrew, a historian at National Defence Headquarters, said: "The Gothic Line was arguably the finest single action of the Canadian corps during the entire Second World War." Although it was a victory for General Burns, the officers under him criticized his command. General Crerar tried to protect him, but Burns was replaced by Major General Charles Foulkes as commander of the 1st Canadian Corps.

CREATING ZOMBIES

In 1942 a plebiscite had shown more than 70 percent of Quebecers opposed to and 80 percent of other Canadians in favour of conscription. Prime Minister Mackenzie King's government passed a bill authorizing compulsory service "if necessary." Two years later, after the heavy Canadian losses at the Falaise Gap and in the Italian campaign, Defence Minister James Ralston strongly supported conscription. King replaced him with General Andrew McNaughton (now relieved of his overseas command and back in Canada), who favoured voluntary service. **Norah Egener** *wrote to her husband.*

Nov. 5 [1944]

My dearest Fred:

. . . Gen. McNaughton, the new minister of defence, said at a press conference that the men who have been away for a long while would have an opportunity to come home – I hope it means you. Mr. King spoke tonight on the reinforcement problem. He admitted they had to have more infantry reinforcements.

The government is still going to adopt the voluntary system, and he gave plenty of reasons, facts and figures why it was better than conscription . . .

Didn't you say, when you went active, something to the effect I was not to go around with my hatchet after people who weren't in the army or navy or air force, it was their own business etc? Well, I've tried to do what you told me ever since you went away. There are lots of people I could get mad at and feel bitter about and don't. I feel you went because you felt it was your duty and I agreed, so I'll stick by that . . .

Norah

Later that month, the prime minister agreed to send conscripts overseas – though fewer than thirteen thousand ever went. They were nicknamed Zombies because they were supposedly mindless beings.

After four years overseas, Fred Egener returned home to Norah and
to a legal career that eventually led to a family court judgeship.

DIGGING UP INTELLIGENCE

Homer Thompson was a professor of archaeology at the University
of Toronto in 1942 when he enlisted in the Canadian navy. Because
of his background – he spoke Greek and on a Rockefeller Foundation
fellowship had helped excavate the ancient city of Agora in Athens –
he was seconded to the British navy. He was soon working for British
Intelligence from a station in Bari, Italy. He began as staff officer
(intelligence), special operations, in the office that received, collated,
and distributed all naval intelligence affecting Allied special opera-
tions in the Adriatic. He was focused on Greece, Yugoslavia, and
Albania, the base from which Mussolini had tried, and failed, to take
over Greece (though by April 1941 the Greek mainland was in
German hands, while Albanian guerrilla forces were fighting the Axis
powers). By mid-1944 Thompson was reporting on enemy naval and
shipping targets to the Balkan Air Force, a new local command coor-
dinating all air, sea, land, and special operations across the Adriatic.
Throughout his posting, he wrote to his wife.

Bari, Italy
October 17, 1944
Letter # 40

My Dearest DB,

. . . After a long wait, I was cheered yesterday by your #38 of Nov.
19, 1943, which like a good fruit cake, survived the months very well
and had even acquired a heightened flavor through the lapse of time
. . . You will have rejoiced in the liberation of Athens. And you may
well indeed have rejoiced more than we did; for at this close distance
our anticipations were not a little clouded by the fear of the civil strife
that might follow. The tension in most parts already liberated has
been very great, but in the capital itself there appears to have been no

trouble as yet. Here as in Patras, the Germans seem to have been undecided about the policy of demolition. The quick work of the locals and of our own people on the spot also had much to do with saving so many of the public utilities and preventing the maximum amount of damage to the harbour. You will have read with horror of the sad end of Kokopi [?]. You may, however, take some satisfaction from the fact that the enemy is taking a most terrible beating these days from our ships and planes at sea, from the Antartes [Greek partisans] and our planes by land, – a grim and incessant pounding. I have had a little something to do with the planning for that part of it and must admit that I'm not much restrained by sympathy for our victims, – they are certainly reaping a whirlwind.

Though you may hear little of it the war continues grimly on in our own narrow sea. I have had long talks to-day with the commanding officers of a flotilla and Coastal Forces who a few nights ago in the course of a 5 hour battle wiped out an enemy convoy, sinking at least 9 of his ships at the cost of a little superficial damage to our boats and a few wounds among the crews. I'm much struck by the decided superiority of our people in this type of fighting which calls for an extraordinary combination of skill and training, quick thinking and dash. These blows should be especially effective right now for his landlines are almost hopelessly cut and he wants to evacuate as much as possible by sea. It's simply fantastic how he finds the spirit to keep up this unequal fight. From interrogation of prisoners, however, it's quite clear that his present desperate courage has a sort of religious basis. A good portion of German soldiers still regard the Fuhrer as a divine being and also feel that Heaven simply wouldn't allow the defeat of Germany – that would be inconceivable [sic] wrong. Many others are buoyed up by the hope of still other secret weapons. The flying bomb, I suspect quite apart from the material damage it did to us, undoubtedly propped up German morale for several months. I'm wondering what effect the knocking out of the prop may have . . .

Much Love

H

In December 1944 civil war broke out in Greece. Lieutenant Thompson was captured in Athens as a prisoner of war by Greek communists who were trying to gain control of the country (the Democratic army eventually won). After a few hours, and after threats to have him shot, the rebels befriended Thompson and took him through the city, dodging gunfire, to the American embassy. He later filed an intelligence report on the war to the British. Returning to Toronto, he then moved to the Institute for Advanced Study in Princeton, New Jersey, and directed the Agora excavations in Athens for the American School of Classical Studies.

A FOOT CLOSER TO HOME

*On September 1, 1944, the 2nd Canadian Corps had crossed the Seine River and was advancing towards the English Channel. That morning the 2nd Canadian Infantry Division took control of the port where they had suffered such an ignominious defeat two years before: Dieppe. That month the British liberated Antwerp, Belgium, but the tenacious Wehrmacht still held the estuary of the Scheldt (or Schelde) River between that major European port and the North Sea, eighty kilometres away. Through October and into November, Canadians waged a fierce fight to open the river. **Rifleman John McManus** of Renfrew, Ontario, who called himself Arnold, was wounded in battle, as he explained to his wife, Anna.*

From John James McManus, R.F.M. No. C6340 . . .
B.L.A. [British Liberation Army]
October 23rd, 1944.

My dearest Wife,
I am here in Belgium in a big convent boarding school. Two buildings of the school have been given over to the Canadians for a field dressing station. On the afternoon of Oct. 21st I stepped on a German mine and got wounded in the leg. I was carried on here and operated on. Unfortunately I have had to have an amputation halfway between

the knee and the ankle. The army doctors and nurses are very devoted and are taking wonderful care of me. I am very cheery and full of hope and courage. I am not taking my mishap to heart for modern science can do wonders, and my artificial foot will be almost as perfect as my natural one, please God. – In a couple of days I expect to fly to England, and as I have always said I'd be home for Xmas I am keeping my word. I am looking forward to seeing you all again and to enjoy the comforts of our new home. I want you to keep up your spirits and not to trouble about me for in a very near future I shall reach you safe and sound. Please forward this to dear mother and tell the boys I shall be skating with them one of these days. God bless you – my fondest love to you and the kiddies –

Your loving

Arnold

Sister Agnes, an Irish Sister in the school, has written this for me. She sends you her kind regards and will pray for you and me. If it is worth while to write another letter before my return I shall write it myself.

Love again.

Arnold.

With General Harry Crerar ailing in England, General Guy Simonds was acting army commander and chief planner of the Scheldt Estuary offensive. By October 16, 1944, the 2nd and 3rd Canadian Infantry Divisions, supported by the 4th Canadian Armoured Division, had seized the entrance to South Beveland, an isthmus north of the estuary. By month's end the entire Beveland peninsula had been won. The Canadians went on to attack the strongly defended island of Walcheren at the end of a long, slender causeway. They were supported by assaults from the sea and Royal Air Force bombing from the air. The 52nd British Division then propelled the advance, and by November 8 the Germans yielded. Twenty days later, with the English Channel swept for mines, the first Allied convoy entered Antwerp, led by the Canadian-built freighter Fort Cataraqui. *The Battle of the Scheldt was over – at a cost of 6,367 Canadian casualties.*

UNDER HELLFIRE

Dr. Joseph Greenblatt (see page 299) continued to accompany the 3rd Canadian Division from France into Belgium and then advanced into the Netherlands, where his field-ambulance unit faced heavy shellfire. He wrote to Fran, his fiancée.

19 Oct 44
Letter #62
#23 Cdn. Fd Am.
R.C.A.M.C. C.A.O.
B.W.E.F.

Hello my Dearest –

. . . Remember in the second last letter I told you that I had some rather horrific experiences just lately. Well about three nights ago I had the climax of the whole show. For some reason or other Jerry decided that my position was the most important target in this whole area & therefore from 9.30 p.m. to 6.30 a.m. every three to five minutes he dropped one in a radius of 50 yards from my position. He scored four direct hits on the house in which I was sleeping & shook me up no end & then dropped two on the barn I used for working in. Naturally he caused casualties amongst my boys – one killed and five wounded – but what was the worst thing is that in the middle of all this one had to stand up all the time & work in the middle of all this. I could hear the boom of the gun in the distance then you would wait for two seconds & then the shriek of the shell coming in your direction would freeze your blood. The inclination was of course to duck under cover & you would look at the patient lying so helpless & terrified on stretcher seeking protection & fortitude from you & you knew you couldn't leave him. So you worked as quickly as you could & tried to pacify the poor defenceless bloke all the time those horrid missiles would come at you. I don't think I'll ever forget that night – it lasted for a year of time. However that's life & has to be expected.

The other day I applied for transfer to a General Hospital because

I find I am a little nervously exhausted & rather unnaturally weary & would like a chance to get away from all this for a time. I feel that I could stand a good rest. No doubt though nothing will come of my application as I feel that my luck is not very good right now. Oh well the hell with it . . .

Yours
Joseph

Military historian Bill McAndrew, a former infantryman, says that ten thousand battle-exhaustion casualties passed through Canadian medical units – half in Italy, half in northwestern Europe. By the end of 1944, when manpower was short, "standing courts-martial routinely awarded sentences of two to five years at hard labour for a variety of offences; many of them to battle-exhaustion cases." Dr. Greenblatt, who took his field-ambulance unit on to Germany, survived the war and returned home to marry Fran.

ON ICE

*As the sixth Christmas of the war approached, Canadian prisoners were still languishing in German prison camps. RCAF **Flight Lieutenant Ian Fowler** of Castor, Alberta, had been on patrol along the Danish border in 1944 when his disabled plane crashed near Groningen, the Netherlands. He was imprisoned by the Germans in Dulag Luft camp and Stalag Luft III, site of the Allies' Great Escape in early 1944. Fowler wrote a* Kriegsgefangenenpost *– a prisoner's letter – to his fiancée, Dorothy Pemberton, in Edmonton.*

Dec. 22, 1944

My own darling Pem. This has indeed been a red letter day for me dear for I got four letters this AM two of them from Pem, an air letter of September 28 & one of Oct. 2nd containing a snap taken in Banff this summer and gee its absolutely wizard dear – its boosted the old moral[e] no end. You know dear I've been longing for such a photo for ages it seems & I might say you can't send too many for my liking darling. Reckon the boys in the room are really envious of me now & I can well understand for I'm a very lucky lad. Glad to hear about the coffee spoon too dear for I hope we two will be setting up house shortly after I get back. We must lay our plans together though dear & oh what a time that'll be! There are 3 small ice rinks in use around the camp now & the 4th, a much larger job is to be ready to-morrow. So I borrowed Eski's skates this afternoon & really enjoyed myself for ¾s of an hour. Then the first hockey match is planned for Xmas day & boy I'll be right in the thick of things. Be the best thing that happened to me for months. We got our Xmas parcels today (½ per man) & they contain turkey, pudding, sausages, sweets, etc. – which will make for a grand bash on Monday. Fondest love dearest,

Your Ian

Released in 1945, Fowler married "Pem," studied chemical engineering at the University of Alberta, and worked for Imperial Oil until retiring in 1986.

A CWAC IN EUROPE

Women back home had pressed politicians to let them join the armed forces. Ottawa agreed to the formation of the Canadian Women's Army Corps (CWAC) in August 1941 and formally melded it into the Canadian army the following March. The RCAF already had a Women's Division, and the navy would soon launch the Women's Royal Canadian Naval Service. The CWACs had a collar badge showing Athena, the helmeted goddess of war, and a cap badge with three maple leaves. Although much of their work was secretarial and clerical, some women did ciphering and decoding and even vehicle maintenance. The first 350 to go overseas served in Canadian military headquarters in London from November 1942. Among them was **Kathleen Robson** *of London, Ontario, who had taken a mechanic's course before joining up but wound up doing office work – until*

early July 1944, when she was in Normandy in the wake of D-Day.
By September she had followed the Canadian army to Belgium. She
wrote her family and a friend.

Brussels, Belgium

27 December 1944

The Germans are advancing. We have been so long and so far chasing
them that it is hard to believe. A lot of people prefer to think it is a
trap. We see beggars on the streets with packs getting out of the city.
The civilians are nervous and keep asking if we think it will be
serious, as if we knew. They should ask General Patton. Second
Ech[elon] moved to Alost because of the V2s and flying bombs. Last
night they were strafed and glass was broken in windows by bullets.
Some were cut by glass. Last night here a plane dropped incendiaries
on Avenue Louise and another fighter flew down Avenue Longchamp
and strafed the houses. It is only about four blocks away. The civilians are very worried. One lady in a store said that when the Germans
came before they took all her stock and what would she do this time.
Parachutists dressed in American uniforms have been dropped at
Ghent and a chap from there told me that doors are always banging
from blasts of V2s and flying bombs. It is a wonder they don't go
after the Headquarters here in Brussels as they must know where
they are . . .

The zombies [conscripts] have arrived and are at Antwerp. What
a reception. After London, it isn't too bad – bad never having seen
London or lived during old fashioned raids or the flying bombs, they
must be finding it very strenuous. Needless to say nobody is wasting
any sympathy on them . . .

6 January 1945

Dear Ruth,

. . . Have made some good friends nearby and went out for supper
tonight. Madame Surrys apologized because all she had to serve was
eggs – I haven't seen an egg for about two years now and forget what

it tastes like. (Correction, we got about one a month in London.) Her maid's husband had caught two Germans last night just outside the city. One was wearing an American uniform and another a British uniform which aroused suspicions as it is rare to see them going around together.

She also told us about a friend of hers who was trying to collect her Aunt's estate. The point is they can't prove her Aunt is dead as they can't find the body. These people were late in leaving before the Germans came in 1940 as the old lady was very sick. They finally persuaded her to leave and loaded the car with treasures including a special carpet. The old lady died in the night and they didn't know what to do with her so they rolled her in the carpet and put it on the top of the car. They finally found a place to stay and when they came out to the car in the morning someone had stolen the carpet! It is almost time to make tea for my two officers. We brought the tea habit from England and now are simply lost without our afternoon and morning teas . . .

Kathleen

Of the 21,624 CWACs in the war, about three thousand served overseas. None died in battle, but a V-2 rocket wounded four in Antwerp in 1945. That June, Kathleen was working in Bad Salzuflen, Germany, next to Sergeant Edward Roe. They were married in the fall (her wedding ring was German-made) and by year's end she was safely home in Ontario. The Canadian Women's Army Corps was disbanded in 1946.

A BROKEN HEART

*Women in the Canadian Red Cross Corps were also in Europe – as cooks, transport drivers, ambulance drivers, and nurses' aides. At twenty-three **Lois MacDonald** was working for a life-insurance company in Ottawa, where she'd been the city's junior badminton champion. In 1943 she left her comfortable middle-class life to go*

overseas with the corps; "I felt as I did not have any brothers, I had
an obligation to take part." She worked as a hospital aide in England,
France, and Belgium. Dodging bombs in London while juggling an
American boyfriend and the Canadian fellow she later married, Lois
grew up quickly. She sent this letter home from Bruges, Belgium.

March 15th, 1945.

Dearest family: –

Here it is my 25th birthday, and also my day off, so am being very
lazy . . .

Have been lying here – doing a bit of thinking – and will try to
give you an inside glimpse of our work at the hospital . . .

To do our job properly and perfectly – one would need to be a
Master of Psychology, a glamour girl, a Comedian, a Dorothy Dix
[an advice columnist], a Florence Nightingale, a Santa Claus, a fount
of Wisdom and Information, with the patience of Job, all rolled into
one. This must sound like a pretty tall order, and I don't mean that
we attain all these standards – on the contrary – I'm afraid Laura,
Sheila and I probably fall short on most of the requirements, but we
do try, and one certainly learns by experience.

To learn how to handle people, to get the most out of them – to
do as much as possible for the boys – without letting them impose.
To let them treat you as a sister or girlfriend, and be gay and friendly,
but be able to slap them down if they get fresh. To know when and
where to offer sympathy – strangely enough – very few really want
it. Understanding goes a lot farther. They like to be babied and
spoiled and get extra favours – and are very easily pleased. If you
remember that they like Winchesters rather than Sweet Caps, or
remember their names, or ask about their favourite son or daughter,
or even if you only make a special trip back to the Ward, with a
chocolate bar or gum, when they are coming out of an operation.

It's only the ones who haven't completely grown up or accepted a
set of values and proper outlook on life, who want sympathy. Most of
the lads are young and strong, and while it breaks your heart to see
them maimed, disfigured or handicapped – it's fatal to let them know

– because they accept our reaction to their loss of limb or disfigure-
ment – as the reaction of their loved ones when they get home. If we
can look at them, straight, and regard their loss as unimportant, and
even joke about it – instead of looking at them, with eyes averted from
an empty sleeve – they lose their self consciousness and soon laugh
about it too. Perhaps it's laughter from a sense of relief – as the thought
of going home and being stared at and pitied, really scares them . . .

They tell us the strangest and most hair-raising tales of their lives
and loves. Some true enough, but very often embellished with extra
details. You get a much broader outlook on life, and realize that
everyone has troubles and greater ones than any small worries you
might have at the time. You develop the ability to laugh at almost
anything and acquire a new philosophy of life. As Sheila so aptly
puts it, "Why worry? It won't even matter in ten years!" We offer
advice to the lovelorn, sympathize and laugh, too, when their gal at
home turns off and marries a Zombie [a conscript]. Tell them to keep
writing, even if they are not receiving mail, because we are absolutely
sure the folks at home are writing faithfully. Sometimes we write
them letters ourselves and toss it in the Ward mail so that they will
at least get something when the mail is being distributed . . .

Just knowing these lads – watching them day by day – seeing
how much they think of each other – how kind they are and ready to
help – yet their complete independence, their courage, their pride in
their own Regiment, their ability to get the very most out of life, and
their constant thought and goal – Canada and home. It really restores
your faith in human nature. We really do little for them, in return
for what they have given us . . .

Much love, my dears.

Lois

NOT OVER YET

*From November 1944 until early the following year, Canadian
troops were inactive while 500,000 Americans and 55,000 British*

defeated 600,000 Germans in the Battle of the Bulge – named for the enemy salient in the Ardennes region of Belgium. By spring 1945 the European war was winding down. The Allies were close to victory in Italy, and the Russians had retaken the Soviet Union and most of Poland. The Americans were about to invade Iwo Jima as a launching pad to bomb Japan. Meanwhile, Field Marshall Montgomery was planning a massive assault to clear the enemy from the Rhineland and drive into western Germany. **Wilfred I. Smith**, *an Acadia University student from Port La Tour, Nova Scotia, had trained as an infantry officer and had gone to Europe in time for D-Day through a scheme called CANLOAN. He joined Britain's Wiltshire Regiment (4th Battalion), where he became second in command of a platoon in charge of flamethrowers. After being wounded near Caen in July 1944, he returned to the front in January. As a platoon and company commander in the Battle of the Rhineland, he got a quick education in leadership.*

[April 1945]

Dear Mom and Family: I am about ten years older that I was when I wrote to you last and have been commanding a company in action most of that time. The CO has suggested several times that I take promotion and Philip wanted me for his 2 i/c [second-in-command] so Capt Bennett was transferred to another battalion to make a vacancy for the next battle. It turned out to be the hardest day we ever had, fighting our way about ten miles on foot along the out-skirts of Bremen where the main defences were, taking 16 subse-quent objectives, and capturing the commandant of Bremen, his HQ complete and a total of 1000 prisoners. At dusk we were about to pass thru another [company] to go on to the final objective and Philip went ahead in a carrier to interview the other company commander. I heard a volley of shots and the carrier came speeding back with Philip's dead body and I was commanding the company under severe shelling and sniping. I was standing beside the colonel a few minutes later when he got shot in the leg but insisted on carrying on. The next minute a shell burst beside us and he fell, hit on the back. One of my sergeants volunteered to help me carry him across the open to the nearest building, during which the C.O. was hit again and I was in command of the battalion until the second in command came up. We then pushed on, getting consolidated about 2 a.m. and at dawn we went on again in a pouring rainstorm to take six more objectives. I've had wonderful cooperation ever since and the other lieuts give me all the obedience and respect they did Major Colverson. Please don't worry about me as I am absolutely fit and happy as a lark. I'll at least have something to remember – or forget – about this war (which isn't over out here).

During February and March 1945, in a grim battle of attack and counterattack, the Allies cleared the territory between the Maas and the Rhine Rivers. By February 10, Canadians and Americans broke through the Siegfried Line, the complex of fortifications along the French-German border, but it took another month before they eliminated the final pockets of resistance. About 90,000 Germans died in the Battle of the Rhineland; Allied forces had 23,000 casualties, including about 5,500 with the 2nd and 3rd Canadian Infantry Divisions and the 4th Canadian Armoured Division. Wilfred Smith went on to participate in the disarming of Nazi Germany. In peacetime he earned an M.A. in history and was Canada's dominion archivist from 1970 to 1984.

FREE AT LAST

*As the Soviet army advanced through German-occupied territory, prisoner-of-war (POW) camps in the east were evacuated and POWs were forced to march west through bitter winter weather. Among them was **Lorne Goat** of Montreal, an RCAF wireless operator and air gunner who went overseas in 1941 and was shot down over Germany the following year. He was held in Stalag 344 near Breslau, Poland, until early 1945, when he and his fellow prisoners from at least eight nations went on a death march to Stalag IXA near*

Frankfurt. Fed meagre rations of black bread, they barely survived. But at the end of March, American troops crossed the Rhine and liberated their camp. A few days later, Goat recounted the ordeal to his girlfriend in Montreal.

Apr. 3/45

Betty darling –

Well sweetheart, its me again, but this time I'm writing not as a P.o.W., but as a free man, a man who does not have to jump when a German says anything to me. Gad, but its a wonderful feeling knowing that within a few weeks I'll be back in England, then Canada, home & with you for the rest of my life. The great day is getting closer, honey, & its making me feel better each hour. I've written mother & dad to-day, so if you get together you'll both get news of the march, which we did from Stalag 344, Lamsdorf to Stalag IXA Ziegenhain, covering 515 miles in 39 days, and it wasn't any picnic. The main trouble being lack of food. You know that I weighed about 195 pounds at 344, but now I'm just about 150 pounds, my legs, hips, arms, knees, chest, look like those of a skeleton with skin on. I'd be ashamed to be seen & thats the truth, back at the Club. But lets get off the bad news & talk of something pleasant – mainly food – the thing I've been thinking of for weeks & months. Heres something I want you to do for me, it's this – will you make a good batch of those delicious date squares & send them to me at Aunty Vic's address in Glasgow . . . I've asked mother to send me a parcel of clothing and food, something like I used to get before I was shot down . . . The Yanks, who liberated us on Good Friday, March 30, 1945, are treating us as best they can, giving us smokes, food, sweets etc, gad they're a great bunch of fellows. Oh yes, darling, send some smokes to me in Blighty also. Just think, I'm a free man after 949 days of being a Prisoner of War. Its a wonderful feeling . . . Remember I'll love you always in the future as I have in the past. So long for now.

Always your,

Lorne xxx

Lorne Goat married Betty Hopley in 1946 and they had three children. He was a chartered accountant in Montreal until retiring in 1984, when the Goats moved to Calgary. After Betty died, he remarried.

BIG DAY, EH?

George R. de Long, *from Barss Corner, Nova Scotia, joined the army at twenty-six in 1941 and, after serving in the Forestry Corps in Quebec and Scotland, transferred to the RCAF. As a wireless operator/air gunner, he was shot down in January 1945 and became a POW at Stalag Luft I in Germany. He didn't learn until his release that he had earned his commission as flying officer. He wrote from Bournemouth, England.*

C-93037

F/O G.R. de Long,

(Ex P.O.W.) R.C.A.F. Overseas

May 15, 1945.

Dear Mother,

I hardly know just what to say now that I've finally got the opportunity of writing what I like . . .

We were liberated by the Russians on 1st May. The Germans pulled out that same morning and were we happy! We were right up on the Baltic at "Bart[h]" about 10 miles from "Stralsund" and we had been "sweating out" JOE [Soviet leader Joseph Stalin] and the [Russian] break-through at Stettin [in Poland] for months. After that there was a lot of anxious waiting and rumors of every kind flying around, but finally the happy day came and the old Flying Fortresses came roaring over the town in the midst of a thunder storm and we had our "Victory" march through town to the airfield. The guys went wild – guess it was about the happiest day in our lives.

Things weren't so bad all through. We were in one of the "best" camps in Germany (no rough stuff) and apart from food and the monotony of prison life, we couldn't complain much. In Feb. and

March the Red Cross parcels ceased and on "Jerry" rations, we darned near starved. Some of the guys were almost too weak to go on Roll Call twice a day (so they said) but I never felt that bad – just plain raving hungry, so you'd talk of nothing else and dream of it at night. Guess I lost about 25 pounds or more – anyhow, in April we got a Red Cross parcel per man per week, so things were fine. After we were liberated, they gave us all the 40,000 pcls. in stores (4 per man) and we practically cleaned them up in a little over a week. Talk about eat! I weigh 175 now so we gained back what we lost and are they ever feeding us like kings here at this place – MAN-O-MAN! . . .

I suppose you want to know how this all started . . . on the night of Jan 5, we were breezing along homeward from Hanover, after a "successful" trip, and everything was going fine for about 20 min. after the target, when our operational career was suddenly ended by a dirty "Messerschmitt 210" which sneaked underneath us and gave us a burst in the belly with an upwards firing 20 M.M. Cannon, the burst obligingly missing me by about two feet, killed poor little Ginger Moore who was standing by the skipper, and the "incendiaries" setting the whole interior a mass of flames instantly, also the bombays underneath us. Vince told the crew to "bale out" and I don't mind saying we didn't argue about it. Suddenly turned from W/Op [wireless operator] to paratrooper is rather a queer feeling, especially at night. We all landed OK, four of us were captured inside an hour. Berry got as far as Dortmund and Vince got as far as Munster but got captured after 3 days (dead beat in the middle of winter). We all got together at Stalag Luft a few days after and have been together ever since . . . one of the luckiest crews in Bomber Command and that's no joke! Very few get away like we did and a fellow sees more evidence of it every day around here. Jimmy's navigator just came in today with one foot! Poor Jimmy wasn't even that lucky. Bob Ford is OK and expect to see him roll in any day. Three of his crew are here now. Keep running into remnants of crews who went through O.T.U. [officer training unit] with you that you didn't even know were shot down. It's been a grim war and it's time it was over. I still find it hard to believe.

Yes! I got my commission "AT LONG LAST!" Charlie and George got theirs too. Mine should date back to Nov. 12, so my F/O was due the day I flew back from Germany. (BIG DAY, EH?)

Must quit now. Will write more soon.

All my love . . . I'll be home soon!

George

Back home, the athletic de Long participated in sportsmen's shows in the United States, demonstrating the skills of a woodsman and guide – log-burling, wood-chopping, and canoe-handling. He later owned a hardware and feed store in New Germany, Nova Scotia. He died in 1993.

THE FIGHTING BEST

*In the final days of the war, during the liberation of the Netherlands, the 1st and 2nd Canadian Corps fought alongside one another for the first time. The Princess Patricia's Canadian Light Infantry's second-in-command, **Major Stuart Cobbett**, reported from Deventer, Holland, to the regiment's founder, Hamilton Gault, in England.*

PPCLI

1 Cdn Div

15 Apr 45

Dear "Sir Hammie" – by now I am sure it must be very old news to say that your boys are fighting on the Western Front. (Before going further, please excuse this pencil work – I have not, I assure you, lost the fine pen that you and DB sent me last Christmas, at the moment it is dry & Holland is short of ink!)

There were no moans when we left Italy although the break with Eighth Army, in which we were the veteran Div, was lamentable. As a soldier I'm sure it will interest you to know that the move of 1 Cdn Corps was the longest move in Corps transport of any in military history.

Since reaching here we have seen a good deal of France, Belgium and Holland, and something of Germany. Our fighting has been mostly in Holland and at the moment is known as a 'pursuit role' – needless to say it is somewhat strenuous but our bag of prisoners is absolutely fantastic (For some reason apparent only to those sitting in very high places the fact that 1 Div is involved is still a secret)! 'Slug' [Lieutenant Colonel Reg Clark] is doing his usual top-drawer job; obviously he comes by his military aptitude very honestly! Again our casualties are proportionately, compared with the bosch, light, but I still develop an increasingly intense hatred of bosch guts every time we lose a brave fellow; as in the last war, Canadians have proved themselves (this is an admission from numerous high-ranking British officers) the best fighters; and in the Cdn army no one can touch 1 Div, likewise 2 [Brigade] – and in 2 Bde [Brigade](?) – need I say more? The élan you inspired, 'Sir' Hammie, lives, by george it does; I know how you will depracate remarks of this kind but, 'great balls of fire' 'tis true . . .

From the Regiment every good wish, and from your master Cobbett kindest personal regards

Yours Stuart

LOVE FROM THE BOSS

*After the Canadian contingent landed at Normandy, **Major Richard (The Boss) Medland** of Toronto commanded A Company of the Queen's Own Rifles. He led his men through France and the Netherlands until the following March, when he stepped on a land mine in a Dutch forest and was severely wounded. Recovering in Horley, the English hospital, he wrote Charles C. Martin, a twenty-six-year-old company sergeant major, who had distinguished himself as a leader and combatant. It was the day before Soviet troops began an all-out assault on Berlin.*

2nd Ca. Gen. Hosp.
Horley, Surrey
7 Apr. 45

Dear Charles,

It is so darn hot here today that I can hardly breath[e]. The weather reminds me of those long, hot days when we raced across France in the wake of the great German Army. Only, here are none of the clouds of dust, the stink of dead flesh, or the excitement of a victorious march. Everything is quiet, nature is settling in its Summer locale, as the trees become feathery in their first bashful green. One can find peace and solace in the quiet of the English Spring – but oh Charlie there is so much missing.

In my younger days I often worked out jig-saw puzzles. At one time I was pretty good. Now I find myself in the midst of the biggest puzzle of my life. It is a puzzle of the mind – but not less difficult because of it. There are some pieces missing though Charlie, pieces which are "somewhere in Europe".

It's ludicrous, what my mind has been doing lately. Scheming this way and that, only to know at the outset that all the scheming of an even more fertile brain than mine could not finish the puzzle without the pieces. But this awful idleness – this emptiness of purpose and life is driving me crazy. And for it, I feel humble and disgusted. For how much better, luckier is my life now, than it was. True I was with friends, but as far as security went, there was none. And my only answer is that I would forgo the security and the comfort of this life in England to be with my men – my best friends – for in them lies my purpose in life – my love and it is my firm desire to extend my total energy towards making their lives, happy, useful and full. But what happens, I am lying here – useless to man and beast. My job was left unfinished and I am now incapable of finishing it.

As time goes on C.C., my heart grows heavy. Time in its inexpendable supplies lies heavy on my hands and the continuous thoughts which run through my mind are of nothing but you chaps.

But all this chatter can be of little interest to you, who have so much to do. You who value life more than any because of the very indefinite nature of it; you who love as no one else can in order to get your full measure of it. I have no right to even appear unhappy. But I do, Charlie, I do to you because I know you will understand.

I will never forget that church service we had on 25 Feb. That was just before our push when we lost Punchy Patterson and all the others. And that night when I got the whole company together. A thrill went through me Charlie – I knew – I could feel the mutual love, trust and respect that was the spark of life to us all. And now that my whole being can look back at those days – those faces – I can realize as I never did how good God has been to me. This may sound like the last will and testament of a dying man. It is far from it. Instead it is the documentary expression of one small, unimportant human being, whose eyes have become clear to bravery and devotion which we so tersely call "duty". Wealthy indeed, is the man who can call all those men his friends. I never talked much about these things Charlie, but it may now be an inspiration to those who are left; those who remember me, to know how I have always felt.

It is the sacred duty of every commander to ensure that his orders are given and carried out so as to bring complete and absolute destruction to the forces of evil. But, and I emphasize this, it is also his most sacred duty to give and carry out his orders so as to ensure the greatest comfort and safety of his men, not vice versa.

Enough for now Charlie. I am always thinking of you. Soon I'll be back I hope. My best to all.

Always your

BOSS

Medland didn't know that he was writing just a day after Martin had been shot during a battle in a Dutch village. Martin didn't awaken fully until May 8, as the voice of British prime minister Winston Churchill came over a hospital radio, announcing the end of the war. Dick Medland won the Distinguished Service Order; Charlie Martin, the Distinguished Conduct and Military Medals. Both survived the war.

JOY AND DISASTER

On May 1, 1945, German radio announced that Adolf Hitler was dead, having killed himself in a Berlin bunker. On May 7 the front page of an "Extra" edition of The Vancouver Sun *read, in type two and a half inches tall, "GERMANY SURRENDERS." Under a London dateline, the story began: "It was announced officially today that Germany has surrendered unconditionally to Britain, the United States and Russia." It ended: "And Allied troops died wiping out the last of the cornered beasts. NOW THEY ARE FINISHED. THE WAR IN EUROPE IS OFFICIALLY OVER."* **Amy White**, *head nurse at a Canadian naval hospital in Scotland (see page 259), was in London for the celebrations of* VE *(Victory in Europe) Day.*

May 8/45

VE+I

Dear Mother & Dad –

Imagine Sunny & I spending VE night in London together! It was really Mon. night VE-I but the town was wild . . . Trafalgar Square was crowded & big army trucks drawn up with search lights set, & a movie tone [newsreel] car Then we wandered back to Piccadilly which was packed altho the buses still getting thru. People selling flags & streamers & noise makers. I think they had taken all the gas rattles [wooden rattles that air-raid wardens carried to alert the public to gas attacks] & painted them up to sell. The city celebrated all night but I was worn out & glad to sit in a train. All day long there was a feeling of celebration all over but no announcement [of the war's official end] until the next day . . .

Lots of love.

Amy.

VE Day was celebrated joyously with parades, prayer services, and street parties across Canada. But in Halifax, the revelry exploded into a riot on May 7 and 8. In author Stephen Kimber's words, it was "a two-day Bacchanalian orgy of boozing, looting, window-

*smashing, dancing in the streets, public fornicating and mindless mayhem." A flashpoint was the antipathy between residents and the 25,000 military personnel, mostly sailors, who crowded the city during the war and resented the men who never joined up, and the city folk who gouged them with high prices. Several thousand servicemen, merchant sailors, and civilians trashed downtown Halifax and parts of neighbouring Dartmouth. **Rear Admiral Leonard Murray** of Pictou, Nova Scotia, the leading local naval officer, was commander in chief, Canadian Northwest Atlantic. He'd directed convoy battles from Halifax as the only Canadian to command a theatre of war. A week after the riot, he confided in his friend, Captain R.F.S. Bidwell of HMS Puncher in London.*

15 Lorne Terrace,
Halifax, N.S.
15th May, 1945

Dear Bidwell:

. . . At the present time we are having a minor war with the civil population of Halifax. No doubt Mary will have sent you the details as far as she knows them, but there has been so much misrepresentation and deliberate lying, not only by the newspapers, but by His Worship the Mayor himself, in trying to clear his own yardarm, that it is very difficult for anyone to know, until the inquiry is complete, what the situation actually was.

The main object of the exercises locally is to prove that the damage done to shop windows was done by Service personnel. If it was ever admitted that the local populace did not only an equal amount of damage, but the larger part of the looting, there would be no case upon which to base a claim against the Federal Government for compensation . . .

. . . I had to take a chance in going out on the streets personally in a sound truck as soon as I could persuade the Mayor to declare the celebrations over, and put on a curfew for civilians and Service people alike. I knew perfectly well that if this expedient failed, I should have to go home and write my resignation, but I felt it absolutely necessary to take some action to get the milling crowds off the streets before dark. I knew that if I failed, military forces would be available in a few hours, but in my estimation the time had arrived to take some action. It worked. Never again can I imagine, and certainly never in my past career, has anything ever given me such a lift as the knowledge that the Service personnel recognized my voice, and in spite of inebriation and mass hysteria, reacted to the call of authority.

It has been passed around the world that the Canadian Navy is an undisciplined Service. It is true that between two and three hundred Naval ratings took part in the smash and grab demonstrations in Halifax on VE day, but the immediate reaction to authority as expressed by my voice to the people in the disturbed area and, even more, the immediate reaction to authority of the thousands of Naval ratings who were spending their VE day peaceably amongst their friends, by putting on their hats and coats and returning to barracks, most of them without any knowledge of the reason for the order, amply demonstrates to me that the Canadian Navy is a highly disciplined force.

. . . They were retained in barracks for sixty hours without any trouble in spite of the slanderous rumours and articles written in the newspapers and uttered over the radio. Their personal loyalty to me has been very touching indeed, and my only fear on letting them out into the streets again was that they might start out to avenge the attack.

As you will have heard, Jones has come down to relieve me, and in five minutes time I go over to Stadacona to appear before a Naval inquiry consisting of Brodeur, Reid, and Adrian Hope. Tomorrow the Royal Commission will be in Halifax, and they start sittings immediately.

Be of good cheer, the Navy has a cast-iron case, and when justice has been done, all will be well.

Yours sincerely,
L.W. Murray

As the inquiry showed, Admiral Murray had made some crucial errors by ignoring the riot on the first night, then dismissing its severity, and allowing another nine thousand sailors to join the spree. Although lapses of city officials had also contributed to the riot, he was forced to retire early, a bitter man.

THE OTHER HALIFAX EXPLOSION

On July 18, 1945, two months after the Halifax riot – and nearly three decades after the collision of two ships in its harbour had levelled parts of the city and killed and injured more than ten thousand people (see page 161) – another explosion rocked Halifax. **Mary (Kitty) Geraghty**, *a former executive assistant with the Canadian Wheat Board in Winnipeg, was a thirty-eight-year-old captain's writer (a kind of secretary) in the Women's Royal Canadian Naval Service (the "Wrens" in the following letter). Founded in 1942, the service signed up nearly seven thousand volunteers over the next four years who served in thirty-nine so-called "non-combatant" occupations at home and abroad. Geraghty wrote her mother in Winnipeg the day after the explosion.*

H.M.C.S. Peregrine
Halifax, N.S.
19th July 1945.

My dearest Mother.

I have just gone through the most amazing night and day of my whole life. I mailed you a letter this morning, that I wrote last night, before things really started to happen . . . you must know by now, through the radio and paper, some of the damage done. But this is how things were at "Peregrine." After the first blast, which happened at 6.35 [p.m.], it was rather quiet, but every Sailor on the base had his own version of what it was. Some said it was an ammunition ship and some said right away that it must be the Naval Ammunition Dump over at Bedford [Basin], which is three miles from Peregrine. While I was writing to you, we could hear the rumpling and then there would be a terrific blast. And Mother, you should have been here to see the Sailors make a dash for the side of the road. In a matter of seconds every man would be flat on his face. It did not take them long to tell the Wrens to do the same. The sky would light up just like day and then bang, away would go more ammunition. It finally got so bad that we were ordered to get into the rig-of-the-day and stand by in case we were needed. By this time, the trucks & ambulances were bringing in Patients from Rockhead Hospital, which is very near Bedford Basin. [In fact, the hospital received no casualties.] Around 11 o'clock we were asked to go to bed, that the worst was over, so to bed we went. Except for rumpling, everything was fairly quiet, but all the men were still out side. Then at 12 o'clock, there was the biggest blast we had ever heard, windows and doors were blown in and out. In about two seconds flat we were all out side lying face down on the road. Wrens and Sailors, Officers and Wren Officers. Mother, I really can't find words to tell you how scared I was. I was even too scared to Pray, but I kept saying Jesus, Mary & Joseph over and over. The boys would say what kind of shells were exploding. You could see them shoot all over the sky.

[After being ordered outside again, the Wrens returned to their dormitory to sleep on mattresses on the floor.] At a quarter to four, another magazine went off, and the building, beds and us on the floor were lifted right up, and, then there was that dead silence that comes before an explosion. Before we could get out side, there was another crash and we all fell flat on our faces in the hall, before the next blast we got out side and down on the Parade square. Oh Mother was it ever terrible. We stayed out until 5.30 a.m., all the time shells and ammunition were flying high, but far enough away from us that we did not have to worry about them landing on us. But, by this time the thing was out of control and they were waiting for the main ammunition magazine to go, which would mean that Halifax would be blown right of[f] the map. All ships in the Harbor made for the open Sea, never did they move out so fast, luckily the

Ile-de-france [the liner-turned-troopship] was more or less away from the danger zone. Every window in the down town district are all out again, just like the V-day riots. But this time it was different . . .

After breakfast and cleaning up our dorm, we went to work, only to be sent back right away, because word had just come, that the main magazine would go up any minute. We could still hear the rumpling but it did not seem so bad in daylight. Nothing happened and we went back to work around 10 o'clock. Then this afternoon, the order to "Clear lower decks" came and that always means something big, every one has to go, even all the Officers, but all they wanted was men to go and fight fires that had started. Needless to say, they nearly all wanted to go, this was around 3 o'clock this afternoon. The men have just come back, I can see them through the window and it is now 9 o'clock and everything is under control, for which I can truly say "Thank God." The Mayor of Halifax spoke over the radio and said the people could return to their homes. The main magazine was saved, because by the Grace of God the fire died down. If you have not already heard or read, there is 50,000 depth charges and gallons of Glycerine there, one depth charge could blow up a ship, so you can imagine what 50,000 (fifty thousand) would do . . . To-night I feel as if I have lived a thousand years . . . Keep this letter Mother, will you please. I would like to read it a year from now . . .

Best love, Mother dear and did I ever think of you last night.

XXXXX

XXXX

Kitty.

An ammunition barge had burst into flames, which spread to the magazine dump full of bombs, mines, torpedoes, and depth charges. That night more than half the city's residents were told to leave their homes. The evacuees caused a massive traffic jam, although many stayed put to watch the fireworks. Buildings shook on their foundations and plate-glass windows blew out across the city. Fortunately the munitions were stored in distinct structures that minimized the fire's spread. Naval volunteers fought the blaze for twenty-four hours and earned back some of the reputation they'd lost during the VE *Day riot. Only one death and a few injuries from the explosions were reported. In 1945 Kitty Geraghty left the Wrens, which disbanded the following year. She later became a manager with the Manitoba Medical Service.*

BERLIN UNDONE

After Germany surrendered, the Allies divided the nation into four occupation zones. The new American president, Harry Truman, Winston Churchill, and Joseph Stalin met on August 17 at Potsdam, a Berlin suburb, to begin planning for peace in Europe and a last assault on Japan. In the weeks leading up to the Potsdam Conference, **Norman Gibson** *was in war-devastated Berlin as a member of the No. 3 Canadian Infantry Corps Band, as he recalled in this open letter home.*

9th July 1945.

. . . From Brunswick the convoy traveled on the great Auto-bahn nearly all the way. Many bombs had hit the highway in the past six years but it was kept in good repair by flying squads of workmen. Even in Berlin it is the streets that remain intact and open for traffic although piles of rubble lay on the boulevards and amid the hulks of the city's buildings. The destruction here is beyond description. You look in vain for a house that has not been damaged in some way . . .

Already there is evidence of severe privation here among the people. In spite of sentrys, the people come round the mess and cookhouse for scraps. Some barter cameras, jewellery, and pens etc., for eats and cigarettes. In the face of the "no-fratting" order [from Field Marshall Montgomery] it creates a difficult problem. A ZEISS IKON Camera for 200 cigarettes is a big temptation to a soldier . . .

Its evident that many Berliners have lived in their cellars for many months. Even in this residential district the rubble has been piled around the outside foundations to counter blast. Fear of the Russians kept many indoors for weeks after the fall of the City. The complexions show the result of lack of sunlight, and their faces are drawn with shock and anxiety. Worst of all is the appeal of the children for food. Be it genuine or not, the heart is touched by a child's simplicity. What a complex problem is Europe to-day . . .

Norman Gibson

No. 3 – Can. Infantry Corp. Band

WHOLESALE SLAUGHTER

On August 6, 1945, the United States dropped the atomic bomb on Hiroshima. The three-metre-long device carried the explosive power of twenty thousand tonnes of TNT. It levelled ten square kilometres of the Japanese city, killing 100,000 people immediately and another 100,000 in the aftermath of burns and radiation sickness. **Gerald Bonwick** *wrote to the editor of a Toronto newspaper.*

August 9, 1945

The Editor

The Globe and Mail

The nations of the world stand aghast at President Truman's announcement concerning the atomic bomb attack on Hiroshima, and this is followed by a British announcement that Japan will be served with a new ultimatum: "We will withhold use of the atomic bomb for 48 hours in which time you can surrender. Otherwise you face the prospect of the entire obliteration of the Japanese nation."

In the name of humanity I protest with every fibre of my being against any ultimate aim in war such as is now indicated. We have execrated the German Nazi Party for their deliberate extermination of five million Jews. How can we possibly contemplate the massacre of over seventy million Japanese? What right have we, or any nation, to plan for or to threaten the destruction of a considerable portion of the human race?

This is not war at all. We have lost all sense of proportion in permitting such wholesale slaughter. It is absolutely outside the pale of human privilege for us to destroy 200,000 men, women and children at Hiroshima whatever may have been the crimes or errors of their leaders at Tokyo. Such wholesale indiscriminate destruction is not according to our traditions.

Do our Allied Governments contemplate in very truth the killing of Japan's entire population? I know, from long personal observation, how cruel and deceptive the Japanese can be; I am no pacifist or appeaser, but no misdeeds or enormities of theirs entitle them to be wiped out as a nation. The vast majority of her people are too ignorant to grasp the meaning of our threat; they know far more about earthquakes than about high explosives or the meaning of "absolute surrender," and doubtless they will be informed by their Government that the Hiroshima happenings were simply an unusually severe earthquake. No ultimatum of ours will reach or move the common people of Japan and in any case they have no machinery for making any response to it.

Then what about the Koreans? Included in the 72,000,000 population of Japan that we hear about there are no less than 24,000,000 Koreans – an enslaved people to whom the Allies have promised independence once more at the conclusion of the war – are they to be involved in the general massacre that is promised? In Europe even a few hundred notorious war criminals are to be given formal and exhaustive trials before they can be condemned to death. How can our Allied nations presume to decree destruction to many millions at 48 hours' notice, the vast majority of whom can have no notion of their plight, and, in any case, no means of avoiding their fate?

Slaughter on such a scale as this would be a crime against Heaven and humanity. Surrender must be obtained by some other course than this. The mere threat of such wholesale murder casts a stain upon the character of every nation that uses it.

Gerald Bonwick
Toronto

On the day this letter was published, a second A-bomb was dropped, this one on Nagasaki. It killed about 75,000 people and devastated a third of the city. On September 2 the Japanese signed a formal peace treaty, ending the Second World War.

IT'S OVER

On August 15, 1945, the world celebrated VJ Day – Victory over Japan. **Robert Collins** *was in London, near the end of what he called an ordinary airman's war. A Saskatchewan farm kid, he had learned to be a ground crewman in the RCAF through the British Commonwealth Air Training Plan. He sailed to England in February 1945, as the British and Canadians were battling across the Rhine. He never saw action, and half a year later, on a trip back to his air base from a visit in Ireland, he spotted a newspaper headline: "FIRST ATOMIC BOMB HITS JAPAN."*

Thursday, Aug. 16 1945

Dear Mom, Dad & Hal,

Well, it's all over! So much has happened since I last wrote that I hardly know where to begin. But of course V-day is the big news, that and the atom bombs. It all happened in such a rapid fire fashion that I don't know what to make of it all. I think, though, that we were, as usual, too soft with the Japs. The atom bomb may be inhuman but I guess we wouldn't feel guilty after what the Japs have done. A few more of those bombs & they wouldn't have stalled their reply. I also see by the paper that the British Empire is not accepting any responsibility for using the bomb. I think that is also darn foolish. We've got it now, for better or worse, and we'll never be able to hide it. We can just hope to God there won't be another war in our Time.

But it's over anyway. It'll be a great day for China & all the fellows in the far East. I don't know how it will affect us. The station was about to be cleared out & then the postings were all cancelled. We are now on four days holiday. I'm just back off leave so don't know what to do or where to go. Guess I'll answer my mail & do some washing first . . .

> Lots of love,
> Bob.

Collins served in post-war Germany before coming home to become a prominent Canadian journalist and the author of three memoirs, including an account of his service career, The Long and the Short and the Tall.

YOM KIPPUR IN BELSEN

Dr. Joseph Greenblatt, who was Jewish, (see pages 299 and 322) wrote his fiancée in April that soldiers' main topic of conversation was "the horrible pictures just released of the prison camps such as Buchenwald etc. recently captured by the Allies. Everyone is imbued with the horror that these pictures depict & if ever there was a reason for hate this is it." In late 1945 a Canadian Jewish soldier, **Signalman Abraham Brenner,** *was serving in occupied Germany when he wrote Bill Berger, editor of a Jewish publication in Montreal that solicited servicemen's letters.*

> [October 1945]

. . . There we were, 10 Jewish Canadian soldiers. While attending our New Year Services at a camp in Hannover [*sic*], we had heard that there was a Jewish settlement in Celle, Germany, and decided to visit it during the Yom Kippur Holidays. When the time came, being granted leave from our various units, we met together, and arrived in Celle a day before Yom Kippur.

Our first greeting was the Jewish flag unfurled in front of the synagogue. Being informed that there were many fellow Jews in nearby Belsen, we unanimously agreed to go over there. After travelling about 30 kilometers, we reached the notorious camp that the world will never forget.

Making our way in, we eventually discovered the Jewish part of the camp. Its people gazed at me in astonishment. This was the first time they had ever seen Canadian soldiers, and it took endless explanations before they finally began to understand that we were those fortunates – Jews from America.

The poor souls encircled us, bombarding us with hundreds of questions. Many were the queries about relatives and friends who had come to Canada during the past few decades. What a pleasure it was to bring news of their distant kinsmen, in those rare cases in which we recognized the names.

The day passed and the time came for Kol Nidre [the prayer at the beginning of the evening service] and the ushering in of Yom Kippur. In front of the Altar, a Hungarian Rabbi officiated. He prayed to the Lord in Yiddish to forgive these people their sins. He was saying these prayers before the same people who had seen their own kin murdered, killed and gassed, for the last six years. These pitiful outcasts were overcome with emotion. The sight was a tragedy – men and women wailing in utter desolation, the men beating their breasts and knocking their heads against the walls of the synagogue. Amongst the ten of us, there was not a dry eye nor unbleeding heart, as we realized of how fortunate we were to have our families living in Canada and not in Europe. They, at least, had not been condemned, as so many of these people had been, for being Jews.

Kol Nidre was then sung, but not in the manner that we used to hear it back home. It was heart rending. The Rabbi chanted with such broken emotion and tears in his voice, that we shall never forget the scene that we witnessed. The responses of the congregation rang out so loudly, that at times it almost sounded as if they were being shouted for the whole world of Jewry to hear. When the time came for Kaddish to be said, there was not a member in the congregation who did not recite it for a mother, father, wife, husband or child. It was as if the whole [world] was in mourning.

The day services were similar. Fasting meant nothing to these people, for they had fasted not only on Yom Kippur but many a time whilst they were in the various stalags.

The tragic part of the services for me was that when I recalled former Yom Kippurs, I could remember seeing children there and venerable old Jews. But here, all whom I saw were between the ages of fourteen and forty. The children and the old people had perished completely.

On forthcoming Yom Kippurs that we hope to celebrate some day in Canada, those scenes that we were able to see, of what has been done to a people, just because they were Jews, will always live in our memories.

One of the Ten,
Signalman Abraham Brenner

Canadian troops were among the Allied forces that liberated the Nazi death camps and witnessed the horror of the Final Solution. Hitler had ordered the systematic annihilation of six million Jews, including 1.5 million children, and the destruction of five thousand Jewish communities. The dead represented two thirds of European Jewry and one third of world Jewry. Historian Robert Gellately, in his book Backing Hitler, *reports on his research study of the twenty-four main newspapers and magazines of the day, revealing that most ordinary Germans did know about the roundup and murder of Jews and other minorities. The Montreal Holocaust Memorial Centre, which was given Abraham Brenner's letter by the Berger family, has broadcast a public appeal to locate Brenner or his family in an effort to return the letter.*

THE WAR TOOK ALL

Douglas Hester of Toronto had been with B Company of the Queen's Own Rifles at D-Day, where he found letters, photos, and a prayer book on the body of a German corporal. After the war, he sent the possessions to the dead man's family in Germany. The man's mother, **Frau Johanna** *(whose last name is withheld for reasons of privacy), replied with gratitude in English, translated from the German by a friend.*

[February 24, 1950]

Dear Mr Hester,

We were deeply moved when, yesterday, your letterbox, papers, and photos of our unforgettable son Ernst arrived here. Take many thousand thanks. How are we able to reward you, that you let us have our boy's last belongings. By our office of The Wehrmacht we formally learned that our boy was probably killed on June 6th 1944 near Berniers sur mer, they could not actually tell us. We, my husband and me, are nowadays old people. We lost five children, Ernst was our last, who takes care of our living. We always hoped, that he would saved us and that our Lord let him come home from that terrible war, but we have to leave this hope too. Today we are old and no one takes care of our living, and the war took all that we possessed in particular my husband was terribly moved losing five children. In this letter you find a photo of my son. Formally, when we were informed of his death we made celebrate a mass for him, take this as a souvenir of a German comrade, whom you saw only dead, but whom was in the deep of his heart has never been your foe. I should be heartly grateful to you. When you reply, write me in complete details, was he hard wounded? Had he lost his arms or legs, or how had he been killed? You can write in English or French as I have found someone to translate the letters. You can hardly imagine what it means to us to know how our poor son died. He was our last consolation, our last hope, shortly all that remained of our five children. And now my husband and me thank you heartly once more and beg you to answer us pretty soon and tell us all about our son. Take in advance many hearty thanks for your kindness.

Sincerely

Frau Johanna

Hester wrote back to reassure the parents: "You can be certain your son was brave, killed instantly, and suffered no body damage."

GARDEN OF GRAVES

In the First World War, **Gregory Clark** *fought as a junior lieutenant with the 4th Canadian Mountain Rifles in northern France to capture Vimy Ridge in the most famous of all Canadian battles. He came home to marry Helen Scott Murray and become a popular writer with* The Toronto Star *in the 1920s. Later, until his death in 1977, he was a columnist for* The Star Weekly *and* Weekend Magazine *and a winner of the Stephen Leacock Medal for Humour. During the Second World War, Clark was a war correspondent in Europe – where his eldest son, Murray, was killed in battle.*

London
Sunday Sept. 2-51

Darling –

He sleeps in a garden.

There can be no other name for it. On a high remote and rolling hilltop with six hundred and eighty nine more of his Canadian comrades, amid roses, hydrangea, golden mimosa, dahlias of every color on earth, so buried and embowered with flowers they can hardly be seen from one another, he sleeps in a scene of such utter peace and serenity that I wonder if I can ever tell you how different it is from anything we have ever seen.

I guess I had better start at the beginning and tell you my whole experience. I caught the 9 a.m. train from London, via Folkstone and was in Boulogne at 1 p.m. noon. The sight of Boulogne almost paralyzed me. I have known it since 1916, and saw it last on May 23, 1940. It has been utterly destroyed, all the ancient and simple and noble waterfront, all the fine big hotels along the high plage. Here and there amid the ruins a new stark red brick building juts up like an ugly spike. In the mood I was in, nothing could be more terrible than the sight of this poor ancient French city . . .

I wandered around the town for an hour or two, looking at the wreckage and the poor, shabby, patient small-town French people before I could drum up the guts to go to the square where the buses start. I caught the 4 p.m. bus . . .

Right where I was let out was a small white cabin, and a white picket fence on either side of it, leading up a sloping field of close-clipped green lawn. The lawn would be maybe a hundred or a hundred and fifty yards up to the crest of a slope, and a hundred yards in width. All enclosed in the white fence.

The bus departed. I stood for a while, looking around. When I went through the wicket gate, I could see vivid flowers along the crest of the hill ahead of me. I walked up the wide lawn, no path, no tracks. As I drew nearer to the crest, I could see the flowers now, a tremendous profusion of them, and no crosses visible except one large memorial cross far at the back of the garden. I had found Murray's number in a little book attached to the wall of the cabin below.

Then I saw a figure moving in the garden, a little half-gnome of a man named Georges Darré, the gardener. He reminded me instantly of someone we know, I can't yet find who – maybe a sort of mixture of our gardener and Andrew King, a small, quick, eager, bent little fellow of about 30. He came down to meet me, and instantly, when I spoke the name I wanted, took me through what I now saw were hundreds of small metal crosses, about two feet high, each bearing an inscription of the name, regiment and date of passing.

I looked at Darré and he lifted his cap humbly and simply vanished away. I fell down to my knees and simply let go. I don't know how long it lasted. It was pretty terrible, this little metal cross, these roses, the dahlias yellow, red, white, mimosa, a tangle of the loveliest flowers you ever saw. I kept looking up and around, trying to get some sort of an answer from the sky, the great garden, the little crosses of his young comrades, all of them, each one of them as dear to somebody as he was to us. I looked back over my shoulder at the cliffs of England so near. Then I looked at the ground and said: "Give me an answer!"

And I found myself saying: "Thank you, God, for letting us have him for the years we did. He might never have been born. He might have been taken from us in childhood. Thank God for the years we were blessed by having him . . ."

And, my darling, that IS the answer. I got up and walked up and down among the rows and the great aisles of flowers, looking at the other names, QOR, Reginas, Royal Winnipeg Rifles, all the boys who fell between Boulogne and Calais, and I tried to pretend I was their father or their friend, so that they would not feel slighted. Darré saw me and came, all bent down in eagerness, up the sloping lawn. I gave him some French money and told him that tomorrow (Saturday) was my son's birthday, and that I was returning with flowers. I wondered if he would be good enough to remember Sept 1 and Christmas, from now on, and put something from us around this precious spot.

I walked about ½ mile north on the road to a little village that I did not recognize as St. Inglevert, coming from the south, and there caught the bus. I went to bed at Galman's [a residential hotel] after arranging with Frank Galman to drive me by car in the morning.

Saturday is market day, and the Dalton square in Boulogne is crowded with farmers from miles around, a huge North Toronto market scene, only all French peasants. One section, against the church, is entirely flowers . . .

Then Galman drove me back to St. Inglevert, and Darré, who should have been at another cemetery that day, beyond Calais, was waiting for me. He and Galman helped carry the flowers up the hill. There, in front of Murray's cross was an immense mass of all dahlias, including those white and purple striped ones, a most glorious display. Darré had thought I meant him to look after it starting today. I thanked him, and he told me all those 690 were his comrades, that is how he had felt for the three years since he had been given this garden. A strange, simple, beautiful little guy. He skillfully planted the fuchsias for me, removing his flowers so that these could be in front. He promised me he would take them up before winter keep them in the greenhouse that is hidden at the back, and plant them each year. He told me the names of the different plants immediately adjoining – a tall single rose bush, deep pink, now in full bloom, a dense bush about waist high, name I could not make out, covered with small masses of mauve flowers; in between, a patch of pinks about the size of a chesterfield cushion, not blooming now, but Darré says they are white and pink. Then a number of small rockery-type plants unknown to me, but including sky blue and yellow.

I took the names of his next companions, as well as many of the QOR who were his longest comrades, and then I had Galman and Darré leave me and go back to the car. I had another pretty bad little time, but darling, the end was exactly the same; the same one and only answer came out of that little plot now covered with flowers from all of us, for a remembrance, and it was – Thank God for letting us have him as long as we did.

This fall or early next spring, a ceremony is being held here, a new memorial erected, and the stones, which have already arrived and are stacked along one side of the garden, are to be erected. These stones are of cream marble, and about 3½ feet high and 18 ins. wide. At the top, carved in the marble, a maple leaf. Then the inscription of the rank, name and regiment. Then a cross. And at the bottom, just above the ground, an inscription sent by the family. On Murray's I took, back when you were too ill to be troubled with it, the closing lines from "Stilicho", his own poetical drama, about this wicked earth

"... this bloody crypt of Heaven,
Will find its peace at last.
– JMC."

And there among the flowers, and on that high and infinitely remote and serene hill, it seems fitting and strange that a young poet from thousands of miles away should make his prophecy in such a setting.

I gave Darré some more money and told him we would keep in touch with him. Galman drove me then to Calais, he and I among its ruins, sought out a little café called the Cheval Gris, we ate lunch together, he took me down to catch the Calais boat to Dover; and I was back in London Saturday night at 9pm.

Now, darling, there it is. Maybe I shall never see it again. But I feel in my heart it is so different from anything we could imagine, so apart, so untouchable, so remote and kindly, I would not hesitate some day to bring you and Didsie, and Greg and Doreen and Beth to see it as I have seen it. For you would get the same answer I got from it. Thank God for the years we did have him, for, as I knelt there, remembering for his birthday all the scenes of his life I could (starting first of all with that morning Sept. 1 either 29 or 30 years ago, when you, all dressed, came to the door of the sunroom at the back of 147 Indian Rd., wakened me, smiled down at me, and said: "Well here we go!") and so on through his boyhood and manhood, I could not help but realize that we were blessed indeed to have had him and known him and shared him with nobody but God.

I hope with all my heart this letter does not distress you, but that you may get the same answer I got, and some measure of the peace that fills me now that the journey and this letter are done.

Greg

Murray Clark was one of 41,992 Canadians who died in the Second World War, nearly 4 percent of all enlistees. Estimates of deaths for other nations vary widely, but rough figures are 270,000 British military and 60,000 civilians; 200,000 French military and 350,000 civilians; 3.5 million German military and 1.6 million civilians; and 10 million Russian military and 7 million civilians.

KOREA, 1950–1953

"Mother, sometimes you can't help crying"

Spike Nickson (left) and Gord Croucher of the Royal Canadian Electrical Mechanical Engineers, attached to the Princess Pats regiment, relax on mail day in Korea while a Korean "houseboy" looks on.

By 1950 the Canadian military was back to normal: starving for men, materiel, money, and leadership. The vast army, air force, and navy of middle-class men who had served in the Second World War were on civvie street, building careers and families. In the pre-dawn hours of June 25, when ninety thousand troops of the North Korea People's Army staged a surprise attack on South Korea, Canada was caught flat-footed and floundered as it tried to mount a measured response.

In the previous five years, the actors in the great global drama of the Second World War had recast themselves to perform new roles in Asia. Japan, the beaten giant, was now under the heavy heel of the United States and the occupying army of General Douglas MacArthur. It no longer controlled the largely mountainous penin-sula of Korea, as it had since the turn of the century. The United States, meanwhile, was in the first stage of McCarthyism, the national paranoia over communism.

Joseph Stalin's Soviet Union, which had switched sides from the Axis to the Allies during the war, froze out North America and the major European nations as the Cold War deepened. In the summer of 1945 its troops had swept down from Manchuria to occupy

Korea north of the 38th Parallel, and it had installed the Moscow-trained Kim Il Sung as the strongman premier of nine million in the Democratic Peoples' Republic of Korea. In the south, Japanese forces had surrendered to the United States and the Ivy League–educated Syngman Rhee, who had considered himself president-in-exile, became the unpopular, autocratic leader of 21 million in the Republic of Korea (ROK).

Neighbouring China, under Chiang Kai-shek, had sat on the sidelines through the early 1940s. A communist nation since Mao Zedong won the civil war in 1949, the People's Republic of China was wary of any western incursions near its border and, when challenged, proved eager to invade and pluck spoils from South Korea.

The newly created United Nations (UN) had intended to oversee free elections in a unified Korea, but Stalin barred its representatives from setting foot in the north. The Soviets, certain that President Harry Truman would not call on his American forces to defend South Korea, were fattening up the North Korean military with their tanks and planes, advisers, and, eventually, combat pilots.

The unexpected assault on the south galvanized both the UN, which insisted on an immediate ceasefire – a demand North Korea ignored – and the United States, where Truman called on MacArthur to reinforce South Korea's ragtag army. When the world body asked its member nations to pledge troops to the cause, France, the Netherlands, and Belgium quickly signed on.

Canada, a participant in the UN and the year-old North Atlantic Treaty Organization (NATO), was duty-bound to respond. In practice, however, it was a martial weakling with no significant standing army to offer its allies. And the anti-military administration of its new prime minister, Louis St. Laurent, had no real will to resurrect one. The nation, then with a population of fourteen million, had slightly more than twenty thousand soldiers and seven thousand sailors. The Liberal government, not wanting to leap into the American-led adventure, delayed committing Canada fully to assist the UN effort in Korea.

On June 30, 1950, it finally did assign three Canadian destroyers – HMCS *Cayuga*, *Athabaskan*, and *Sioux* – to serve under UN

Command in Korean waters, and the next month earmarked the RCAF's No. 426 Squadron to do airlifts between Washington state and Tokyo. Prime Minister St. Laurent was being pressured to enter the fray by the UN's secretary general, Trygve Lie, and even by St. Laurent's own peace-loving Canadian external affairs minister, Lester B. Pearson, a strong supporter of the UN, if not the United States. It took well over a month after the North Korean advance for Ottawa to contribute a Canadian Army Special Force of ground troops.

By then the war – or what both Truman and St. Laurent pre-ferred to call a "police action" – was well under way. On June 25, the day the UN Security Council had voted to aid South Korea, the North Korean 4th Division penetrated its southern neighbour's capital, Seoul, killing or capturing nearly half the original 98,000 undisciplined ROK troops. Another division was on its way to the western coastal city of Inchon. The South Koreans and the first American infantry units were in full retreat.

On CBC Radio on August 7, St. Laurent announced the decision to heed the UN's call. The next day Australian-born Brigadier J.M. Rockingham of Vancouver accepted command of the force of almost five thousand. The six-foot-four Rocky, a popular, decorated veteran of the Normandy invasion, was the commanding officer of the Royal Hamilton Light Infantry. He'd become post-war leader of a militia reserve brigade and the civilian manager of a bus company.

Over the next few days, hundreds of rootless men lined up at recruitment centres across Canada. So eager was the military to raise a force that it took almost anyone who showed up. As the official Canadian history of the Korean War notes, "Among the anomalies of this unique method of recruiting, the enlistment of a man with an artificial leg and one who was 72 years old stand out as highlights." Over the next two years, a fifth of the ten thousand enlistees had to be discharged; another 1,500 had deserted.

The first Canadians in action – and the first Canadian sailors to fire on an enemy since 1945 – were aboard *Cayuga* in the Yellow Sea. On August 15, 1950, they were off the southern port of Yosu shelling North Koreans with four-inch guns. A month later *Athabaskan* was among 260 warships assaulting Inchon to support the landing of eighty thousand American Marines, who seized the port and inspired a UN counter-attack that sent South Korean troops north across the 38th Parallel. It seemed as if the police action would soon be over.

But in October, China – fearing American designs on its border – moved in, as surreptitiously as it could, with six armies of 180,000 men. On November 26 they made a massive surprise attack in the region between the North Korean capital of Pyongyang and the Yalu River, which sent the South Korean and American forces fleeing. A day earlier, the first full contingent of Canadian ground troops had sailed from Seattle. Before going into battle, the raw recruits of the 2nd Battalion Princess Patricia's Canadian Light Infantry (PPCLI) were trained on-site in Korea – at the insistence of their leader, Lieutenant Colonel James Stone, a former farmer and forest ranger and a shrewd, admired alumnus of the Second World War's Italian campaign.

The men who'd joined the Canadian armed forces after 1945 – and those who enlisted for Korea – were a different breed from the vets of 1939–45. Defeating Hitler had been a communal act, a patriotic duty that attracted a broad range of social classes of diverse disciplines. Fighting the faceless communists in Korea was a more mercenary decision. Many of the enlistees were restless, their lives unresolved.

As it turned out, they were not well served by their superiors. In *Blood on the Hills: The Canadian Army in the Korean War*, military historian David J. Bercuson writes: "Canada's soldiers went to the peninsula poorly armed and equipped, inadequately trained for the type of war they were about to fight, unprepared for their encounter with Korea and the Koreans, and ready to do battle based on their experiences fighting the Wehrmacht."

They encountered endless hills and rice paddies fertilized with human waste; land mines and napalm; and enemies who attacked while blowing bugles and whistles and beating sticks. It made for a "police action" very different from what any of them could have imagined.

DEATH ON THE RAILS

With no suitable winter training sites in Canada, the new troops were sent to Fort Lewis, Washington. Between November 11 and 21, 1950, 286 officers and 5,773 men travelled there in Canadian National Railways (CNR) passenger cars that had borne immigrants across the prairies at the turn of the century. On the final day of Operation Sawhorse, 338 members of the 2nd Field Regiment Royal Canadian Horse Artillery (RCHA) were aboard a seventeen-car train near Canoe River, British Columbia. Among them was twenty-one-year-old **Lieutenant James Glassco Henderson.** *He wrote his fiancée, a teacher in an Ontario army camp, about what had happened when the troop train met the Transcontinental Flyer, eastbound from Vancouver, on the same track.*

23 November, 1950
Wainwright, Alta.

My Dearest Ruth,

We arrived here yesterday after the train wreck. CNR assured me that you had received a telegram saying that I was OK.

I was sitting in the officer's car (#44) which was at the back of the train at 10:35 on Tue morning. I had just come back from the front of the train where I had been issuing books to the boys. There was a bit of a bump. Not much worse actually than as if the engineer had put the brakes on. I looked across the car and noticed that a window had been broken by the shock. I realized that we must have hit something and so I went to the space in between the cars and looked out. All I could see up by the engine was a huge cloud of steam. I started to go up through the cars but it was so crowded I jumped out and ran alongside the train up to the front. When I got there I got the shock of my life. The two engines were completely smashed beyond recognition. I still find it hard to believe that two huge railway engines could be so completely smashed. The baggage car of our train was completely gone. The first passenger car (#31) had been smashed to the right of the track and #33 was to the left.

#32 was right on top of #33. Just as I got there a man walked out of the wreckage. He was completely covered with blood. Its funny how I can remember him because actually he was not hurt nearly as badly as many others I saw later.

The next half hour is very hard to remember because most of us were so busy trying to get the wounded out of the mess. After it slowed down a bit I saw that there were too many people doing nothing so I took a few men back to the car they had set up as an emergency hospital. There was work for us there and for the next little while the party I had was kept busy setting up a morgue in one of the cars and carrying the dead back to it.

Finally the hospital train arrived and they started to pull us back towards Jasper. We got there in 5 or 6 hours later and two new cars were added to the train. I got what survivors there were from the smashed cars back to them and had them bed down.

I was kept up all night dishing out chocolate bars and cigarettes and making sure people were comfortable and generally supervising the last two cars.

About six in the morning a nurse came back and looked at me and told me to go to bed. When I explained that I did not have one she took me to her compartment (they had saved them for the nurses) and she made me lie down on her bed. I didn't even take my boots off – I just collapsed. She, or somebody, must have put a blanket over me because when a sergeant woke me up about two hours later I had one on.

We got to Edmonton about 8:30 and I had the boys clean the car up. Then they put on a diner. The original diners on the train were being used as a hospital. I had the boys eat and settled them into their places. The Red Cross came on board with candy and cigarettes. We finally left Edmonton and came to Wainwright where we will stay until we can reorganize. Half of the Regiment is in Fort Lewis and we will join them in a few days. The "esprit de corps" is marvelous and we feel much more of a unit than before even though we have lost quite a few.

I will write again soon.

Wednesday Morning
[November 29, 1950]

Just a quick note before we leave here and try, once again, to get to Fort Lewis.

We had a party last night. It was a wild one. Sam Pinkerton and Terry O'Brennan had stayed behind at the scene of the train wreck and were both angry about two issues. They were convinced that one Gunner was still alive in the washroom of the railway car that was standing on its end. They believed they could see blood trickling down the side of the car and reasoned that a dead person does not bleed. Be that as it may no one ever got a chance to find out. Shortly after the Army turned patrolling the wreckage over to railway officials the whole thing caught fire. Apparently a railway man threw a lighted flare in a pool of oil. He said that it would take a week to clear the main line if they did not burn it. Our people had managed to keep it from burning for over 12 hours and were furious, particularly in view of their belief that one man might still be alive in the wreckage.

A lot of anger was expressed last night and there was quite a bit of broken glass lying around when I went in for breakfast . . .

All my love,
Jim

A CNR communications error had sent the troop train on to the same track as the Transcontinental. Twelve RCHA men and four CNR crew died in the crash; four more soldiers died en route to hospital in Edmonton, and another in hospital. Four bodies were never found. Fifty-two artillerymen and six railwaymen were injured. The regiment had more casualties in this accident than it would during a whole year of Korean combat.

DECAPITATION AND SLAUGHTER

On January 1, 1951, Chinese and North Korean armies mounted a New Year's offensive and three days later recaptured Seoul. The

Princess Patricia's Canadian Light Infantry – PPCLI or the Princess Pats – were undergoing tough field training north of the port of Pusan in a valley along the Miryang River. By mid-January the area became a battle zone as the Canadians went after communist guerrilla snipers. At first **Sergeant Alex Sim** *was in an anti-tank platoon with his second-youngest brother, Jim, and a cousin. During the Second World War Alex had lied about his age and – after altering the date on his youngest brother's birth certificate – had joined the Canadian Army at sixteen. Now he was twenty-six, writing home to his wife, Dina, in Calgary.*

Miryang Korea
28 Jan [1951]

Hi Darling,

. . . There's been nothing much happen since the last time I wrote except that the Gook [Korean] Police had a run in with a band of Guerrilla's & killed three of them & cut their heads off, so the next day our Platoon officer went down to the Police [barracks] & brought a head back with him to show the boys & believe me there were some pretty pale looking boys around when they saw it, so then he went & got his picture taken with it & I asked him to give me one to send home . . . Our Platoon is supposed to be going out hunting these Guerrillas that are raiding a small town about 18 miles from here, we're taking our .50 Calibre Machine Guns – Bren Guns & 60 M.M. Mortars to shell the Hills first, then the Lt. and I are going to take the remainder of the Platoon in on foot with Rifles & Bayonets to finish the job of cleaning them out as there's only about 150 of them . . .

[Chongon] 20 Feb [1951]

Well we have really moved into the line now. We moved up on the 17/18 Feb. through a real blizzard, cold, wet, and snowing, slippery roads and some vehicle accidents. We are part of the 27th Commonwealth Brigade which consists of Argyle & Sutherland

Highlanders, Middlesex Regt. Royal Australian Regt. & 2 PPCLI our support units are New Zealand Artillery, Indian Field Ambulance, US Mortar Bn. and US Tanks. Quite a combination aye. Our young soldiers got a real shock yesterday. We came up to a village in the morning and Jim [his brother] had just said we had seen no signs of war yet, as we came into the village we found the bodies of about 65 or 70 dead Americans, it seems they were a Recce [reconnaissance] outfit that all went to sleep in the village and were ambushed during the night. I took a Patrol forward this morning & we captured two Chinese who told us what happened . . .

Sixty-five men of the U.S. 1st Cavalry Division, pursuing Chinese soldiers, hunkered down in trenches in their sleeping bags. The enemy sneaked up on them overnight and bayoneted and burned them to death. The PPCLI's 2nd Battalion was moving with UN troops towards the 38th Parallel over steep, snow-buried hills in bone-chilling weather. In late February the Canadians suffered their first losses: ten dead and more than twenty wounded within a week.

THE BATTLE OF KAPYONG

*By the end of March 1951 the Canadians were advancing into the Kapyong valley south of the 38th Parallel, about forty kilometres northeast of Seoul. More than 200,000 Chinese and North Korean troops were massed to attack – outnumbering the UN troops at least three to one. On April 22, in one of the worst battles of the Korean campaign, the enemy cut off an ROK division. The PPCLI were charged with keeping an escape route open through the valley and preventing any deep infiltration. With a British regiment to their left and Australian and New Zealand regiments to the right, they had to hold Hill 677 as the Australians were forced to retreat. **Sergeant Alex Sim** was there.*

Korea 28 Apr. 51

Hi Darling,

I guess by now you have heard or read about our latest activities. We were out on the 19th for a rest period but everything fell apart on the 23rd as we were rushed back into the line to block a Chinese Advance, they had broken through the R.O.K. Division in the line and there was nothing to stop them, 2PPCLI & 3RAR [Royal Australian Regiment] were rushed up to stop the Chinese. We moved into position at night on 23rd & on the morning of the 24th we discovered we were surrounded, Jock [Holligan, another platoon sergeant] & I discussed this by radio & agreed it looked like it could get interesting. It sure did. We were cut off from 23rd until afternoon of the 26th when the U.S. Tanks finally broke through to relieve us. We are now occupying defensive to re-group & start it all over again. While we were surrounded, Jock & I had a first class seat to watch the Air Drop of Ammo & supplies. I had taken my Platoon up to reenforce Jock after the attack on his position the night before. We sat on the hillside & watched the C119s (Box Cars) do the Air Drop. We thought at first that it was the U.S. Para Troops coming to help but it was only Ammo & supplies a bit of a disappointment. It looks like I'll be busy for awhile now as Defensive Ops. means lots of Patrols & that is my Gang.

All My Love Darling
To You & The Kids
<u>Sonny</u>

Completely surrounded, reduced to firing small arms, but resupplied with an air drop from big-bellied American C-119 Flying Boxcars, the Princess Pats defended the hill over two days and a night of fierce fighting. Sim's platoon was saved by the mortar fire of a platoon commanded by Lieutenant Hub Gray, which destroyed a threatening Chinese machine-gun position. Early on April 25, 1951, the enemy overwhelmed Privates Bruce MacDonald and Maurice Carr of the Princess Pats, who were fighting with Vicker machine guns, and two Korean houseboys armed with U.S. army rifles. **Captain**

*Andrew Foulds later sent a handwritten letter to MacDonald's
mother in Peterborough, Ontario.*

2 Bn PPCLI

CAPO 5002

VAN. B.C.

31 April 51

Dear Mrs MacDonald –

I am writing to you to convey the deep sorrow and regret shared by
my platoon and myself at this time in the loss to us of a first class
soldier and man and to you a precious son.

It is my intention to let you know the sequence of events surrounding the death of your son so that you will know the true picture.

The R.O.K. forces were attacked in strength by the Chinese and
broke in the face of the enemy, leaving a gap in the line. Our Brigade
was rushed in and we were the left forward Bn [battalion]. The
Machine Gun section that Bruce was with as No 2 of one gun was
under command of the left forward company which was situated on
the forward slope of a hill. The Chinese attacked at 0100 hours on
the dark night of 24th [actually 25th] April and this attack was beaten
off. They regrouped and attacked again at 0300 hrs at which time
they overran the position.

Bruce continued to feed ammunition into the gun until both he
and the No 1 were killed by a Chinese grenade. His actions at this
time no doubt saved the lives of many of his comrades who eventually retook the position.

That Mrs MacDonald is the story and although little consolation
for the loss of your son, it will perhaps in the knowledge of how he
died, make you even more proud of our Bruce.

Yours very truly

AFoulds

Captain.

*Ten of the Princess Pats died, and twenty-three were wounded.
"The New Zealand gunners saved our asses firing their twenty-five-*

pounders like damn machine guns," recalls Private Gord Croucher
of Kamloops (see page 374). Together, the troops of the two nations
had bought the Eighth U.S. Army enough time to establish a new
line north of Seoul and save the capital. For their gallant action, the
2nd Battalion PPCLI earned the U.S. Presidential Unit Citation – the
only Canadian regiment ever to receive it.

SEOUL UNDER SIEGE

Meanwhile, UN forces were fighting to establish lines along the 37th
Parallel, and by mid-March they had retaken the South's capital.
On April 11, 1951, the Royal Canadian Regiment, the Royal 22e
Régiment (the Van Doos), the Royal Canadian Engineers, the Royal
Canadian Dragoons, and the Royal Canadian Horse Artillery were
sailing to Korea. That day President Truman fired General MacArthur
over the commander's plan to carry the war into China – and to drop
as many as twenty-six atomic bombs, which might well have ignited
a world war. (He was replaced by the more respected Lieutenant
General Matthew B. Ridgway, nicknamed Old Iron Tits for the
grenades he flaunted on his chest.) Canadian broadcaster **Brian
Meredith**, a major working as a press officer with the British
Broadcasting System during the Second World War, was now senior
information officer with the UN Commission for the Unification and
Rehabilitation of Korea. The day after McArthur's recall, he wrote
his family in Canada.

12 April [1951]

Dearest People,
. . . The prospects are uncertain. The news tonight was of the incredible but I suppose inevitable retirement of MacArthur, the most
colossally indiscreet general history has produced. This increases
uncertainties. The one certainty I want to cleave to is that I shall be
home in mid summer, and in Canada . . .

The launch of the Chinese spring offensive on April 22 unsettled res-
idents of Seoul, as Meredith reported to his wife.

Seoul, 25 April [1951]
Well darling . . . I have landed in Seoul on the eve of what looks like
the third evacuation of the city. In fact 90% of the official evacuation is complete and I am sitting on the floor of the small hotel used
as Civil Assistance Command billets hoping we won't be turfed out
during the night. The morrow may bring better news, for rumor has
it that the Chinese are taking very heavy punishment and, unusually,
are surrendering in some numbers. But at the moment it looks bad;
and the sight of Seoul with refugees once more heading south, and
with yesterday largely spent [in] watching wailing moppets picked
up from the streets being shipped off by truck, doesn't make for
cheerfullness . . .

You would be impressed at the hardihood with which I am surviving the smells and horrors about me; and I assure you they are
many. A hospital being evacuated isn't pretty; nor were the orphans;
and among the orphans I saw were the lot to whom I gave the first
air mailed box of clothing, those I visited on the eve of my last evacuation. They were looking well and happy and are probably best left
where they are. Most of the other children from that institution had
been removed southward. I cannot say that I found any of them
wearing any of the garments that might conceivably been in that box.
They were even dirtier and more ragged than before. But as I say,
they looked well. Most Korean children do. They're the ruggedest
lot I've ever seen in my life . . .

I have entered into another world up here, and I am taking every
care that it shall not be the next one . . .

Much love

B.

COLLEEN THE RED

The remarkable **William Henry (Harry) Pope**, *born in Gistoux, Belgium, was the great-grandson of his namesake, a Father of Confederation, and the son of a Canadian lieutenant general. Harry had served with Canada's Royal 22e Régiment (the Van Doos) during the Second World War. He was captured while trying to rescue two wounded comrades, but escaped to fight behind enemy lines before rejoining his regiment. He was keen to fight with the Van Doos in Korea, and in the spring of 1951 arrived in Seattle to join the regiment at Fort Lewis. One night he noticed an anti–Korean War meeting held by the Socialist Workers Party in his hotel and, on sitting in, noticed an attractive blond party member named Colleen – whom he pursued to a social evening and then to another meeting being addressed by a former secretary to the Russian Revolution leader Leon Trotsky. He got a date with Colleen. But when he admitted his attendance at Marxist meetings, he was posted back to Ottawa as an adjutant of the No. 1 Army Administrative Unit. Desperate to get to Korea, he wrote his commanding officer.*

25 April 1951

Lieutenant Colonel McClelland
Commanding Officer, 1 AAU
Dear Sir:
My Battalion is en route to Korea. From newspaper reports of the battle now going on there, it is obvious that it will have a hard and bloody fight. I feel that being removed from my Battalion ten days before it sails for the Front brings dishonour upon me. I can only be vindicated by serving with my Battalion, and that as soon as possible. I therefore request that I be reposted to the 2nd Battalion, Royal 22e Régiment immediately, if possible before it makes contact with the enemy. If it is felt that my continuing interest in political questions renders me a liability in my present rank, I am willing to serve His Majesty in action in any inferior rank that may be decided upon.

[W.H. Pope]

In a note to the CO, the unit's adjutant general sent the letter back with the remark: "The Americans would find him a liability in any rank." But Pope got to Korea as an adjutant, in spite of Colleen, and eventually became a major with the Van Doos, winning a Military Cross for "enthusiasm, competence and coolness under fire." After the war he became executive assistant to the national Co-operative Commonwealth Federation (CCF) leaders Hazen Argue and Tommy Douglas and taught economics at Toronto's Ryerson Polytechnical Institute (now Ryerson University) for twenty years.

A PHONY WAR

Over the next three months the UN forces drove north and dug in on the 38th Parallel. It was a holding action in a static war with limited attacks to consolidate lines, as the Soviets proposed a truce to the UN and talks began July 10. But late the following month the communists broke off negotiations. **Corporal John Meehan** *of Vancouver had joined the 57th Field Squadron of the Royal Canadian Engineers in New Brunswick and came to British Columbia before heading off to Korea. In Vancouver he'd met Diane Davies, to whom he wrote.*

Korea
May 28th 1951
SS 800122
57th Ind Fld Sqdn R.C.E.

Hi Darling,

. . . Well I suppose that its been announced in the papers back there that we're in action. Well I suppose that's right as the noise is quite bad now. From where I'm sitting I can see the famous 38th Parallel. The Chinks [Chinese troops] haven't stood still for very long lately as we shove them back, and I don't think that it will last much longer. I hope not anyway. It's a kind of phoney war all the way through. Tell you're Dad he wouldn't believe it was a war at all if he could see it. I know I didn't. Its not like the last war at all. But still it goes on and the dirt and filth is still here so its not such a pleasant place to be. But I think this time its going to end and very soon maybe we'll all be back home. As for me I'm heading for Van to keep a date I've got there when I finally get there.

Meehan was back behind the lines when he wrote two months later.

July 30th 1951

. . . We have a great time here finding and clothing the little Korean kids lately. There's lots of them here. They come in with no clothes on at all and go out all dressed up and fed. Once you do that for a kid here and you have a slave for life. I've got about four following me all the time. (Old father Bountiful Meehan they call me) But a kid is a kid in any country so you can't turn them away, although it gets embarassing at times.

It's a beautiful evening here right now. Nothing to bother you but about 20 million flies and bugs which seem to have no place to go except to crawl all over me. What a country for bugs. Think I'll look up a show and go to it when it gets dark. I seen a couple in the last few nights. "Cry Danger" and "Born Yesterday". Did you see any of them? I sure liked the blonde in "Born Yesterday". Its sure a great pastime to be able to go to a show in the evening . . . That's O.K. back here but when you're up front you don't get them.

The Korean War was the first conflict in history to use helicopters to deliver cargo to ground troops, land combat units, and evacuate wounded. But while the Americans used choppers widely (as viewers of television's M*A*S*H recall), Canadians relied on planes, such as the single-engine Auster, for reconnaissance. Meanwhile troop morale was at low ebb: that summer a team of officers from Ottawa reported from Korea that Canadian soldiers were "suffering from a complete disregard of [problems] fundamental to discipline (other than battle discipline), health, welfare and morale all of which contribute to conservation of manpower."

Sept 20 1951

. . . Well a lot has happened since I last wrote to you. I got a chance to fly over chink country the other day in a spotting plane and sure jumped at the chance. I had quite a flip too. We were over enemy country for 1½ hrs. But it was quite dull and nothing much happened. But it was a good change.

Ah yes here's something you will probably read about in the papers or been on the news. The other night one of the boys went on the rampage and shot 3 Koreans. As he was in my section and I was Cpl. of the guard believe me I had some time. Poor fellow is in for a rough time. He was one of the quietest fellows you would care to meet and no one around here suspected him of all people. Well the outcome of the whole thing is I have had to answer [a] million questions as I went out and got him. I sure hated to lose him out of my section . . .

John

Meehan returned from Korea after the war and married Davies; he joined the RCAF and served until retiring in 1968.

BATTLE CRIES

*Traumatic stress disorder was called battle fatigue in the Korean War. **Craftsman Gordon Croucher** was with the Royal Canadian Electrical Mechanical Engineers (RCEME), which kept the vehicles, tanks, and weapons of Canadian and other UN forces in fighting trim. He was attached to the Princess Pats, doing double duty as an infantryman, when he wrote to his mother.*

June 6

Dear Mother

. . . One of our RCEME fellows was taken to the hospital with something called battle fatigue. The way my heads been aching lately, maybe Ill be next . . . gosh do I ever hate this country and the people in it . . . by the way we are just North of Seoul now near the 38 parallel and our boys are over the 38th . . .

[September 6, 1951]
Imjin River
Korea
"F" ech PPCLI

George Myers is going home I guess he's not in the line now. The doctors say mentily unstable in other words he's too nervouse. I guess he's got bad nerves so they will probably send him home . . .

[September 28, 1951]

I hope my letters have been reaching you alright. I write as often as possible at least one a week.

Im just feelling homesick and blue right now. homesick for civilization and Canada.

Ive seen a lot here enough to make a person different. Ive seen human suffering at its peak. I hate it. This war is a war against common people and its not nice too see starving people on the roads and not being able to help.

A Korean farmer wants to know why his wife and kids were killed can you tell him,? will he understand? I guess the answer is no! he can't read or write, he don't know politics, he just knows feeling and emotion. Its heartbreaking his home destroyed. His land a battlefield no place too turn for food or shelter he's one in millions.

Mother sometimes you can't help crying and Ive seen tough fighter soldiers do it.

You get a different outlook on life here and war. My God but these people suffer.

I want to get home. just to get away from this. before I break down. A person can stand so much and then they call it nervous breakdowns or here they call it battle fatigue. it starts by being jumpy and headaches, which I got both, a continuous headache and Im jumpy.

So's a lot of other guys. No wonder they send a person home after so long here.

I should be getting to bed, Im very tired

So

Lots of Love
Gordon

Canadian military historian Bill McAndrew has pointed out that field psychiatrists in the Korean War had to relearn techniques first identified in the Great War to deal with battle fatigue. They gave the affected soldiers "rest and reassurance; returned those who were simply exhausted to their units as quickly as possible; sent those unable to return to labouring companies where they performed useful non-combat work; and evacuated the worst cases for more extensive treatment." Gord Croucher made it through the Korean War and became a well-known photographer for The Vancouver Sun *and* The Vancouver Province.

SHOOT THEM ALL

Alex Sim (see page 365) had been feeling some of the same pressures arising from the futility of the war and the plight of the Korean civilians, as he reported to his wife.

Imjin River
Korea
7 June 51

Hi Darling;

. . . there's nothing to be Happy about over here except that I'm a member of the Cdn. Army, which makes me proud but as for being Happy, you can't do it in this country, all we ever see are Refugees, Women & Kids half dead from Starvation – go into a Village & find Dead civilians everywhere some Shot or Killed by Shellfire others Burned in Napalm or killed by Land Mines, there's really not much to be happy about over here, it's not at all like Europe was – these People are like Dumb Animals they don't realize a lot of them that guns are used to Kill People – they don't understand that if they don't leave their Houses in our Area of Defence that we will shoot them & Destroy the village & we have to do it as the Chinese get into these villages & the only way to get them out is to Kill them & you can't tell who is enemy & who isn't so we shoot at them all, now do you understand this war, I don't suppose you do because I don't understand it myself, but I do know we'll win how long it's going to take I don't know . . .

> All My Love Darling
> To You & the Kids
> Love.
> <u>Sonny</u>

Sim left Korea in one piece to return to Canada in early August 1951. His brother and cousin also survived the war.

STINKING OLD HILLS

*Although peace talks resumed in late October 1951, the Canadian forces faced a series of Chinese assaults in November – culminating in heavy bombardment of an American-occupied hill on November 22, which spread to a position held by the Royal 22e Régiment. The enemy took Hill 355 from the beleaguered regiment and over the next two nights command of the rocky height passed back and forth, exposing the Van Doos to further attack. After four days and nights of shelling, the Americans finally won it and the Van Doos had held their ground. UN and communist forces soon agreed on a ceasefire line and even exchanged prisoner-of-war lists in mid-December. But armistice was still a distant dream. **Private Roy Fischbach** of the Princess Pats sent a Christmas letter to his sister's girlfriend in Alberta.*

[December 1951]

Dear Blanche,

. . . Here's a little poem I made up one nite after duty, you can sing
it to the tune of "So Long It's Been Good to Know You". All the
boys in the Unit seem to think it rather appropriate. Hope you'll like
it as well, Here goes . . .

> "Canadian Calypso"
> Come all you good people & listen to me
> I'll tell you a tale of the war in "Koree".
> Where the bullets are flying & comforts are few
> And soldiers are dying for people like you.
>
> Chorus, So Long it's Been Good to Know You . . .
> 2. Now all you civilians won't you listen here
> We've fought in this country for over a year
> With nothing accomplished & even less gained
> In these stinking old hills too long I've remained
> Ch
> [3.] This war is a farce all us soldiers agree
> We'd all like to leave this place called "Koree,"
> So pack up the peace-talks & call off the war
> And send us all back to our own native shore
> Ch
> [4.] Now here is the end of my sad tale of woe
> I'm going on leave to old Tokyo
> I'll get me a woman buy ten kegs of beer
> Then fight the Chinese for as long as I'm here.

Composed Dec 11th, 51

R.A.F.

Fischbach survived the war.

TAKING A CHANCE

HMCS Nootka *and* Cayuga *were among eight Canadian tribal-class escort destroyers (named for native tribes) deployed by the* UN. *In early 1951 they came under fire at Inchon during shelling that flattened the port. Not long after,* Cayuga *became notorious for having as her ship's doctor an American con artist named Ferdinand Waldo Demara Jr., posing as Canadian Lieutenant Surgeon Joseph C. Cyr. After he performed courageously under shellfire in 1951, his shipmates told the press about him. He was unmasked on the ship later that year after successfully treating a captain's infected tooth, patching up three wounded South Korean guerrilla fighters, and even amputating a foot.* **Lieutenant Peter Chance** *of Ottawa, a navigator who had befriended him, was among the crew members taken in by the imposture, as he told his wife in Victoria.*

Nov. 6. 1951

Good morning my darling

. . . Every paper I pick up now has a little piece on Joe Cyr. Well we still dont know for sure who he is but were quite positive its not Joe Cyr and altho likely but not for sure he is probably Cecil B Harmann. I suppose he is a little off his rocker somewhere but we all liked him in a messmate way and thought him capable as can be as a Doc. But what a forger he turned out to be and a J.P., a lay Brother "father John". The whole affair became quite fantastic as the little bits of the Jigsaw fitted together from articles of gear found in his cabin. You see after he was confronted with the news by message from HQ that he was an imposter, Cappy [Captain James Plomer] saw him and showed him the Signal. Joe apparently broke down in the interview and by the show of documents Cappy felt nearly convinced that all was well. Then Doc decided to commit suicide we think by an overdose of phenol barbatol. [HMS] Ceylon's Doc looking at him saw he was drugged but still alive and they fixed him up there. In the meantime Don & Willie were detailed by Cappy to raid Joe's cabin for evidence and they really came across stuff that would shake anyone. Forged documents of all kinds – a state seal U.S., clerical dress, and a lot of other things that aroused suspicion to say the very least. The proof was here. But not one private letter, bill, receipt or anything, not a photograph of anybody – and he spoke of marriage to Margie Ball a Nurse in Stad [the Royal Canadian Naval Hospital at HMCS *Stadacona* in Halifax] not a thing. So anyhow he's gone and we all feel sorry for him really. He is awaiting return to Canada . . . So all in all were having our little domestic problems as well as those of more grandiose nature . . .

Haeju

Feb. 24. (52)

Darling Pegs.

. . . I see where Joe Cyr was picked up in trying to enter a morticians college under an assumed name in Chicago. I suppose that type will never learn until he's behind bars – if then . . .

Your

Peter

Demara went on to further masquerades, and Tony Curtis portrayed him in a Hollywood movie, The Great Impostor. *Peter Chance later had numerous staff positions on shore, including at naval headquarters in Ottawa; he retired as a commander in 1970, and served as Osgoode Hall Law School's first executive director in Toronto before returning to the West Coast.*

DESTROYERS AND SAMPANS

By 1952 the war at sea in the Korean theatre was mostly monotonous patrolling and the occasional bombardment. But HMCS Nootka had some intriguing encounters under **Commander Richard M. Steele,** *who in the last war had sailed on Russia's dangerous Murmansk Run and in the D-Day invasion. He wrote a personal* *letter to Canada's director of naval information about his experiences in the Yellow Sea.*

Oct.7/52

Cdr Wm. Stange,
Director of Naval Information.
. . . We came back north to the Carrier Force for a patrol and then went in Command of the Task Unit defending the Islands in the [Haeju] Gulf. The enemy who had been inactive in this area for some time suddenly blossomed forth in very aggressive style . . .

The Cruisers Newcastle and Belfast joined and very considerately designated that I retain Tactical Command which gave me a great deal of priceless experience and, when it was through, considerable confidence.

With the Naval Gunfire, the guerrillas and the air weapons we completely defeated the enemy in his drive and he has not molested our forces in that area since. There were casualties nearly every day but none of them Canadian.

In accomplishing our end, Nootka was taken under fire on seven occasions but with success resulting on our side on each occasion . . .

We have just completed a full inshore patrol in the Chinampo Estuary and have again run into some considerable excitement and some fantastic good fortune as is usual with us.

Slightly more than a week ago we detected what we considered an outsider among some friendly clandestine junk movements one night. We did not like the pattern of his movement and we attempted to intercept him but he gained shelter behind the two fathom line before we could reach him. Observing it was a strongly defended point on the mainland, I decided against sending my motor cutters after him, for having used them extensively in a number of dangerous missions, I felt their luck had been rather heavily traded on.

We reported to the C.T.U. [commander task unit] that we considered the Channel may have been mined and asked that an immediate check sweep be carried out the next night. The sweepers having just completed that channel that day and departed the area we realized how unpopular we would be. The sweepers returned the next night and did a very thorough search of the area we asked. They were not gone an hour before we detected a contact which commenced tracing a pattern similar to the night before [a twenty-five-foot sampan propelled by oarsmen, which had been laying magnetic mines] . . . We moved close inshore to the south of him and ran up in shallow water at twenty knots and succeeded in cutting him off. We closed him to fifty yards talking to him quietly in Korean; explaining that all our big guns were trained on him and loaded. If he did exactly as we told him we would not shoot but if he disobeyed any instruction we would blow him to pieces.

We then told him to alter away from the coast and keep moving slowly out to sea. This he did. We asked who he was and what he was doing but there was no reply. At this point we saw what we thought were underwater swimmers with large black objects leaving the junk and heading toward us but still wanting them alive we did not open fire. We went astern on our engines to get a good strong wash running up each side of the ship and then backed slowly away until we found we could pick up the junk and the objects on our Radar. We opened the range a little and put several 40 m.m. shells in the junk so she would fill with water and be unmanageable for the enemy but still leave her intact for our inspection. We could see the objects in the water remaining in fairly static positions within a cable of each other.

We sent away the #1 landing and boarding party and just when they gained the position of the contacts a great deal of firing broke out and communications with the boat went dead.

We moved back in closer to them and they returned to report they closed the first object (which we considered might be floating mines) and put a very weak light on it to find a North Korean Naval Officer just commencing to open fire on them with a machine gun.

They shot him before he had inflicted any casualties. He was floating in a big rubber ring. These were the black objects we had seen coming over the stern of the junk.

Rather than send my boats back in among the remaining three groups which had a considerable advantage in the dark, I informed the C.T.U. that I intended to wait till daylight and go in and pick them up with Nootka.

In the interim we sent the boat to take the junk which it did and towed it slowly away to seaward, while we held the contacts on Sperry Radar. As soon as it was daylight we ran in and picked up five prisoners who dropped their machine guns over the side and were very mild. We asked the first who he was. He replied, "Communist". The two officers resisted being taken on board and tried to delay us, evidently, with the hope the shore batteries would take us to task for we were in to about 3000 yards, however they did not. Finally one of them tried to drown himself but our men put a line on him and hoisted him in. We managed to get one to talk later that morning and before the day was out we learned a great deal of very valuable intelligence. He admitted they had mined the area with new type mines, told us where they were laid, the details of the period delay mechanisms, where the mines came from, that they were Soviet Ground Mines of aluminum construction with nearly a ton of explosive. He told also that they were delivered from Chineju one at a time by night in a large truck.

He told us the exact location of another field he had laid and explained that this effort in which we had captured him, was specifically aimed at getting us not just the ships passing up the channel. He told us the total number of mines that he knew of, and where they were stowed.

This was very gratifying and fully repaid the worry and strain of refraining from putting a squid bomb into them the night before; instead waiting for three hours close in and then moving in so close in daylight to get them. This incidentally is the third time we have ourselves captured enemy prisoners without any assistance from other sources. On two other occasions we have taken prisoners in joint efforts. The prisoners were all armed with a generous supply of hand grenades and each with a machine gun. In the junk there was a reserve box of grenades.

An interesting moment in the evening's effort was the first time the junk was taken in tow in the dark. Previous experience has proven that it is unwise to go alongside them in the dark for one of the ships working with us one night had three prisoners standing up in their junk with their hands in the air over their head in surrender. The boat pulled alongside and the North Koreans who had hand grenades with the pins pulled out clutched in their hands just flipped them in the boat and killed five of the crew.

Our boat therefore pulled up some distance away in the dark and tossed a grapnel into the junk then started to tow it towards Nootka. The grapnel came away and as the boats crew overhauled it to toss back in, they pulled the grapnel out of the water and found two Russian Hand Grenades on the prongs. These were dropped back in the water and shaken off; then the process was repeated . . .

We have done quite a bit of shooting at the enemy, have been under fire more often than anyone else . . . fired our torpedoes regularly, had quite a few qualify educationally, so we are getting to be quite a proud ship . . .

[Commander R.M. Steele]

Steele earned a Distinguished Service Cross for his command of Nootka from October 1951 to January 1953. At the end of 1952 the destroyer returned to Halifax via the Mediterranean, becoming only the second Royal Canadian Navy ship to circumnavigate the globe.

THE BLEACHING BONES

Hill battles continued into the so-called Twilight War, most notably the heroic October 1952 defence of Kowang-san mountain at Hill 355 by a hundred Royal Canadian Regiment troops facing about 1,500 Chinese. In November, Dwight D. Eisenhower – the legendary general of the Second World War – was elected U.S. president and, prompted by General Douglas MacArthur, again raised the spectre of nuclear war. The following spring Joseph Stalin, the architect of the Soviets' Korean involvement, died. The two events combined to encourage more serious truce negotiations. By early May the combatants exchanged ill and wounded prisoners of war. **Lance Corporal Andrew Brodsky** *of Spryfield, Nova Scotia, had been in Korea with the 56th Canadian Transport Company since autumn 1952, when the 3rd Battalions of the Canadian infantry regiments arrived. He wrote his mother in London, Ontario, from behind the front lines.*

May 4/53

Dear Mum,

. . . Yesterday I was in Seoul on detail and the day before yesterday I went with my section to Inchon with the troops on rotation and rest leave commonly known as R and R. There is a nice rest centre at Inchon where the men just loaf around. They let Inchon leave every two months about. It is right on the sea coast of Korea and also near the seaport of Inchon itself which is the base of the South Korean shipping industry.

In Seoul there are signs put up all over the city due to the past and present peace talks at Pan Mun Jon between N.A.T.O. and the communists. The signs read as follows: "Advance Young Men To The North", "Pick Up Your Arms Young Men And Advance To The North", "No U.N. Settlement Without A Unified Korea", "Give Us Unification Or Death". These signs are written in Korean and English. Also there have been big parades in Seoul, demonstrations calling for a continuation of the war and advancing to the Manchurian border. The last few days all U.N. troops were warned off the streets during these parades due to possible riots or acts of violence, due to the fact that some Koreans do not like the U.N., as they think that they are not acting in the interest of the Republic of Korea. Everywhere we go outside our own platoon area we have to go armed with live ammunition in the city of Seoul. You don't even go shopping without a rifle, pistol, or sten gun. If caught by the M.P.'s of any of the N.A.T.O. forces without these arms, or if one is found to be without ammunition, or the weapon one carries is not in proper working order, we are liable to arrest and prosecution (military), which in this country is very severe – either a heavy fine or detention, which, I am told, is the worst yet operated by an army of the British Commonwealth in the last half century, so it pays to behave and stay out of trouble . . .

I am now in charge of a transport section all to myself. I have under me one L/Cpl., six privates, and one driver mechanic, and six two and one half ton six-wheel vehicles . . . [We] take them in and out of the front line. We see the tracer bullets and hear the outgoing and incoming shells landing. Occasionally Intelligence gives the word to double the guard due to the possibility of infiltrating patrols coming out of the hills and attacking our rear positions – one of which I am now working out of.

Sometimes one of my friends and I take a walk up the hills in the surrounding country for target practice with our army rifles. On some of these excursions we often come upon old Korean, Chinese, American, and Commonwealth positions. We view the old trenches and bleaching bones and rusted bullets, rotting clothing, and old equipment of soldiers who fought and died never to return for whichever cause they believed in – some forced to fight, some for money, some for glory, some for their ideals – whether in vain or not no one yet knows; no doubt time and future history will tell the finis of this piece of military history written in blood, destruction and poverty, eventually.

Seoul is building up, and the battle-scarred ruins of a once pros-perous city which boasts of some once very fine pieces of Japanese and North American architecture is again assuming the appearance of a busy city . . .

Love,

Andy

Finally, on July 27, 1953, the three-year war ended. General Nam Il of the Korean-Chinese delegation and Major General William Harrison of United Nations Command signed an armistice agree-ment at Panmunjom, Korea. It created a military demarcation line that bisects the village just south of the 38th Parallel. That autumn the two sides began exchanging prisoners. Although most Canadians

*had left by the following spring, five hundred remained until as late
as 1955; the last Canadian soldier came home in mid-1957.*

HUBBUB AND HOT BATHS

Captain Kenneth Cameron *of Ottawa was a latecomer to Korea as
a master warrant officer with the 23rd Workshop of the Royal
Canadian Electrical Mechanical Engineers. He later served with
the army in Canada and in Germany, attached to Canadian NATO
headquarters.*

Chogam Mi

Korea

1 Feb 54

Dear Mom and All

Just a few lines to let you know that I am well and reasonably happy
now that I can say I'll be home next month. It has been a long haul
but it is almost over.

There has been little of interest this past week to write about
since the POW exchange came off without any trouble. We were on
the alert and ready to move but fast but fortunately our fears were
baseless.

I suppose the Reds could still make trouble which I hope they
won't, but if they do, I hope we will be on our way home. I've had
my fill of this country but I must admit I would like to come back to
Japan some time. It is a wonderful country and the people are grand
if you can forget how treacherous they were at one time . . .

For the past two days the American station in Seoul has had a
marathon program of popularity records in aid of the March of
Dimes and they have been running a contest with all the units in
their listening radius.

At least once every fifteen minutes they play "The Dear John
Letter" record which, if you haven't heard it before is one the soldiers want most not to hear . . .

Tonight as I write they are playing all of Spike Jones records and the racket combined with the machine guns of the troops training near us is something to hear. As a rule the evenings are so still and quiet that the stillness is nerve wracking but I'm getting used to the noise again and I'll be ready for the hubbub of Canadian cities again . . .

. . . Oh! How nice it will be to have a nice hot tub bath again . . .

Write soon and for now Sayonara.

Your Loving Son

and

Brother

Ken

In the police action that became a war, there were 843,500 South Korean casualties, half of them fatal. North Korea had an estimated 520,000 dead and wounded, and China had 900,000. The United States, which sent 1,319,00 troops, had 54,246 fatalities and 103,284 wounded. Canada sent 26,791 troops to Korea, of whom 516 died and 1,255 were wounded. Canadian survivors came home to a nation that didn't want to hear about Korea, although Prime Minister St. Laurent did receive the 1st Battalion of the Royal Canadian Regiment after it paraded through Ottawa. Not until 1992 did the government agree to give Korean vets the Canadian Volunteer Service Medal. In 2003, as the world marked the fiftieth anniversary of the armistice, the Korean peninsula was still split, North Korea had become a nuclear threat – and President George W. Bush declared it part of an "Axis of Evil" that included Iran and Iraq.

PEACEKEEPING, 1954–

"Hatred is deep, and everyone has a gun"

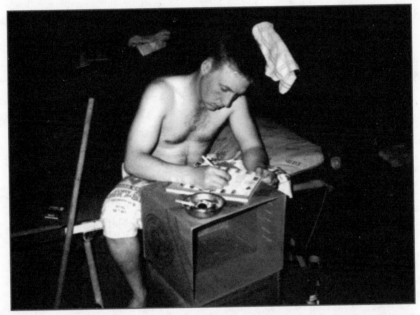

*Employing a cardboard box as a table in Kuwait during the early 1990s,
Corporal Mark Isfeld, a member of Canada's 1st Combat Engineer Regiment,
writes his parents in Courtenay, British Columbia.*

It was Lester Pearson who, as external affairs minister, proposed during the Suez Crisis of 1956 that the United Nations (UN) mount an emergency force to supervise a ceasefire between Israel and Egypt. (The next year he was awarded the Nobel Peace Prize, and six years later he became prime minister.) Major General Tommy Burns, who'd been eased out of Canadian command during the Second World War in Italy, headed the world's first true peacekeeping mission. And Canada was among the ten nations that contributed to that UN Emergency Force of nearly six thousand lightly armed troops. Since then Canadians have been involved in almost all such UN peacekeeping ventures – more than forty of them – ranging from a thirty-year stay in Cyprus to a six-month tour of duty in Afghanistan.

Yet the reality is that Canadian motives for keeping the peace in other countries have been mixed and mostly self-serving. Canada has not been the neutral country of national mythology. As a "middle power," it played its largest post-1945 role by staunchly supporting the western alliance during the Cold War. When those hostilities ended about 1990, the alliance participated in the Middle East and the Balkans to shield itself from crises that could affect its economic and political interests.

Generally, Canada's peacekeepers have been a great credit to their country. They have acted as unarmed military observers and as armed troops, operating mostly under the banners of the UN and the Canadian-inspired North Atlantic Treaty Organization (NATO). They've disarmed combatants, protected civilians, cleared land mines, repatriated refugees, supervised free elections, guarded humanitarian shipments, and served as a Rapid Response Force during natural disasters. More than a hundred have died on the job, and hundreds have been wounded while serving with the UN forces' Blue Berets. Some of the early peacekeepers faced the mind-rattling shock of new cultures. Others serving in recent years as soldiers came home with post-traumatic stress syndrome.

With the Cold War's thaw, the world mounted two dozen new peacekeeping operations from 1991 to 1996 – six more than during the previous four decades. At one point nearly eighty thousand UN peacekeepers were serving around the globe, Canadians prominent among them. In the past they usually maintained the peace between individual states, although in the early 1960s Canada participated in a major mission in Africa that encountered heavy fighting in trying to bring the breakaway province of Katanga back into the Congo. During the 1990s, however, UN forces began to monitor more internal conflicts, like the one that split the former Yugoslavia. While NATO oversaw a military intervention in the war-ravaged province of Kosovo, the peacekeepers were mandated by the United Nations in 1999 to establish a UN-led interim civilian administration.

Canada has also been part of four major non-UN missions: the International Commission for Supervision and Control in Vietnam (1954–73), the Commonwealth Observer Team for Nigeria (1968–70), the International Commission for Control and Supervision in Vietnam (1973–74), and the Commonwealth Monitoring Force for Rhodesia/Zimbabwe (1979–80). The Canadian contingent in Bosnia-Herzegovina – about half of Canada's more than 2,400 peacekeepers deployed in early 2003 – fell under the NATO mandate.

Men and women serving Canada overseas put themselves in harm's way to help make the world more peaceful – whatever their country's motivations in sending them.

SETTING THE STAGE

After the Second World War, the victorious nations occupied Germany, dividing it into four zones. Then, after the Korean War, Canada honoured its obligation to NATO by posting 5,600 infantry in north-western Germany to meet a potential Soviet attack. Their presence there was a prelude to the true peacekeeping task that other Canadian troops would assume decades later as factional fighting rocked Europe (see page 403). In 1954 Captain John Alexis Rossiter, a battle-tested veteran from Bonavista Bay, Newfoundland, was with the 2nd Battalion, Royal Canadian Regiment. He, his wife, and four young children lived temporarily in an old inn run by the Wiemers, whose son Willi had been an officer with the Wehrmacht. Freed after years in Soviet prison camps, Willi had walked west to Germany and had just arrived home when **Nikki Rossiter** *wrote her in-laws in Halifax.*

[Nov. 16/54]

Dear Mom and Dad,

. . . Then came November the sixth! That really should be entirely in capitals. For it was a day to remember. Alex [Nikki's husband] and I had planned dinner as usual in our living room and then on to a mess party with the R 22nd R [Royal 22e Régiment, the Van Doos] . . . The wine for dinner was Herr Wiemer's best – Bordeaux, since anything French is Germany's ultimate and there was champagne cooling for after. We had steaks sometime during the meal but the entrees and hors d'oeuvres almost made one lose track of the main course . . . So there we sat in Hotel Wiemer in all our formal splendour with a five piece orchestra to entertain the six of us. Suddenly we heard creaks and giggles and unslippered feet, and from all the bedrooms crept little people . . . Between kinder and music we were quite entertained until our soldier-chauffeur arrived to take us off to the party. It was a nice party, we had a good time, and we came home about two. Karen and Ryck were in bed, but Willi, Marge and Ed were waiting up –

We made a loving cup in the ice-pail and passed it round until Alex and I decided it was time for bed and took off.

About three-fifteen we came to with a thud, screams, shouts, bangs and scuffling. Doors flew open and downstairs raced Alex and me closely followed by the other Canadian adults. Willi, who for four years was a prisoner in Russia had got quietly plastered and now not so quietly was attempting matricide, patricide, fratricide and just plain murder. He was really violent – pulling doors off their hinges, smashing furniture and glass while his parents, brother and various guests screeched, screamed, shouted and wrung their hands and wept. Alex took over – Ed and I put the Wiemers, Ma, Pa and brother, to bed, sent the maids to their rooms and reassured the guests. Then Alex sent me up to bed and he and Ed poured a great deal of good Canadian rye down Willi's throat. He took it not unwillingly and about five a.m. Alex finally got Willi to bed.

He was a sad, sorry slob next morning and in the awful throes of alcoholic remorse. It was the first time he had got drunk since 1944 and I hope the last. But the damage was repaired, apologies given and accepted and we're all back to normal.

But no birthday I feel will ever be the same again and I shall never use my ice-pail without remembering November 6–7/1954 . . .

Love,
Nikki

INDOCHINA WITHOUT CHARM

Duncan Robertson of Allan, Saskatchewan, served in the Second World War and, after getting a degree in English and history, rejoined the army. He was with the 27th Canadian Infantry Brigade as part of the NATO forces in Germany when, in 1955 and 1956, he was in Vietnam as a member of the International Commission for Supervision and Control, which included delegations from Canada, India, and Poland. France had colonized Vietnam, Laos, and Cambodia in the 19th century, and not until 1954, after severe battles in Vietnam, did it relinquish control. A captain with the Royal Canadian Ordnance Corps, Robertson was among several hundred Canadian observers on the non-UN commission that supervised the ceasefires, withdrawal of French troops, and movement of refugees.

3 Apr. 55

Dear Family:

I have just seen (I'm sitting on a balcony affair with the moon shining) the most frightful meal. 3 large snakes, that the Vietnamese guards bought in the market, Large (about 3 ft. long and 2" in radius) and squirming. Everyone assures me they are "tres bon", but I'm not so sure! They do not understand the fertile Celtic imagination! . . .

30 April 55

. . . Came back to Tourane yesterday. A great relief to be rid of the Polish Delegation for a while. I'm afraid that we in the Empire have been too fortunate. This Communism is the most horrible thing I have ever seen. You cannot trust anyone – all statements are false – armed guards are all over the place – I must admit – I have never been interested in current affairs as such and the way they are usually presented leaves the average individual cold – BUT – this business is very serious, dangerous and treacherous . . .

Dong Hoi

Feb. 1 56

. . . This place is quite frightful – on Sunday night the damned fools put on a concert – 1½ hours of dances and songs. Horrible. Apparently some ass of a Canadian complained that there was not enough entertainment! So this is the result. I sulked my way through it and disagreed with the major who is inclined to believe that these people are trying! Oh well – I never will win the Lester B. Pearson prize for diplomacy. I suppose they'll have a film this Sunday. Some nice bit of propaganda and everyone will applaud . . .

4 Feb. 56

. . . The natives are on the March again. At 5 A.M. they were paddling around the road outside our villa (a somewhat grand name for an extremely sad building) all carrying flags and shouting slogans to the effect that peace and Uncle Ho's ideas might live for 1000 years . . .

Still Saturday

. . . Must give more details of the parade. We were informed that the leaders of the thing wished to see the team and talk to us . . . the President of the Women's Organizations, the head of the Catholic League, a Buddist [sic] priest, the head of the Young Peoples Organization, the head of the Student Society (a nasty looking case he was too) the President of the Business Womens Society and last but by no means least the President of the Intelligentia (later interpreted as the Intellectuals). They rambled on and on, all made speeches which were all about wicked Americans Imperialists and Diem's [South Vietnamese] Government which apparently spends all its time raping, murdering pregnant women, closing schools and just generally being miserable. There is no freedom of religion in the South apparently. I was at a loss to get this point as 90% of the churches in the North are closed and I for one cannot so much as get close to a priest (in case I start plotting I suppose!) yet the Churches are full in the South! Such a pity that I am so blind I suppose! . . .

Yours affec.

Duncan

"For the first time in my life I was a witness to active Communism and was also in a position to observe some of the persecutions of the

Church," Robertson later recalled. "This undoubtedly had some influence on my subsequent decision to leave the Army and study for the priesthood, which I did in 1957." After serving as a priest for eight years, he became an academic librarian. In 1994 he received papal dispensation from his priestly obligations and later married.

PAKISTANI FOLLIES

India and Pakistan became separate dominions, independent of Britain, in 1947. Under a partition scheme, the state of Kashmir was free to join either nation; its accession to India triggered a dispute between the two countries. In early 1971 **Major John Liss** *of the Royal Canadian Army Service Corps – a University of Alberta graduate who'd served overseas with the UN and NATO – arrived with the United Nations Military Observer Group in India and Pakistan (UNMOGIP); by year's end, full-scale war broke out. He wrote to his wife in Ottawa.*

19 Oct 71

Dear Marianne

. . . Yesterday I was ordered to proceed from Pindi to Srin to see the General to explain some things which we had seen on our last trip. It is very hard to pass information over the radio and anyway most of it was classified and since both sides listen to our radio, it was not possible to send it that way anyway . . . the things we saw are causing quite a bit of concern and tension and they are quite important just now even tho they seem on the surface to be very minor in nature . . .

. . . I was supposed to go to the Indian side but Rawalakot [at a height of 1,820 metres in a saucer-shaped valley] is on the Pak side. It is the toughest station on the mission just now as there is a lot of activity and besides that it is a mountainous area with few roads. In addition the accommodation is not too good. Anyway, you can rest assured that a couple of young fellows there are going to be doing the hard climbing. I'm going to do the easy ones . . .

28 Oct 71

. . . I arrived in Rawalakot last night at 6 30 PM. This is a very busy station with an awful lot of work to do. Unfortunately, the fellow who I am replacing as OIC, a Canadian LCol, has decided to go on a drunk and he has not really been too much help today so the handover has not been as I would have liked it. I'll be glad to see the last of him tomorrow at 8 AM . . .

27 Nov 71

. . . This morning I went down to the local hospital to get my cholera shot. This one is obviously working as my arm is sore as can be and I have a bit of fever. The doctor who gave me the shot was the same one who gave me the last shot in Bhimber. It never ceases to amaze me how people come out of one of those places alive. The hospital is so filthy that it defies description and the staff fit right along into the scene. I took my own sterile disposable needle down, but while the Dr was giving me the needle, a fellow came in and poured coal onto the fire and the place was thick with dust and smoke. The windows were grimy and obviously the floors were impossible to keep clean. Yet the whole time there was a steady stream of people, both civilian and military, going in and out.

The situation here remains calm and quiet although out in the east it seems to be getting quite hot. I still don't know who or what to believe as obviously someone is lying. Perhaps both sides . . .

. . . Today I had to make up our plan of work for next week and it took a moment or two to realize that we will be in December in a few days and that Christmas is almost upon us. I guess I'll have Christmas out of a can . . .

Love John

Liss left for home in January 1972. In July, India and Pakistan signed an agreement defining a Line of Control in Kashmir – running from the Punjab plain to the Karakoram peaks – that was almost the same as the ceasefire line established by a 1949 agreement. India argued

that the mandate of UNMOGIP had lapsed because it referred specif-
ically to the ceasefire line under that earlier agreement and didn't
extend to the line established in December 1971. Pakistan disagreed.
The UN secretary general argued that UNMOGIP could be terminated
only by a decision of the Security Council, so the Military Observer
Group remained.

KASHMIR LIFE AND DEATH

Six years later the India–Pakistan dispute was still going strong.
***Major Stephen Brodsky** (brother of Andrew Brodsky, a lance corpo-*
ral in Korea; see page 385) was a Canadian observer among the forty
or so army officers representing about ten countries in UNMOGIP.
At age forty-five, he had served with the Canadian Guards Regiment,
the Royal Canadian Regiment, and the Princess Patricia's Canadian
Light Infantry. His job was to report ceasefire violations and inspect
the front lines for evidence of buildups in troops or weapons and
any changes in defensive positions. He wrote to his wife in Victoria,
British Columbia.

13 Apr 78

Hello my Kit,
This afternoon we returned from a hard four-day field task. It was
satisfying to do an honest job, and so did the other two, Roger and
Tor. We're all three in quite good condition, and so when I say we all
have aching muscles, you can know that we did a job hardly known
to be done by most members of the Mission, although all sorts of
them lie to claim that they have . . .
   . . . I go by jeep for about an hour and a half to a village that is
the farthest point I can get by vehicle. I'm met by two guides, a lance
naik [corporal] and a sepoy [private] from the company area I'm
checking. I've taken my rucksack in preparation for an overnight
stay at the [company] HQ in the hills, because the CO has told me
the task will take me two days, and is extremely tough going. The

guides don't want me to take my pack. There's a sleeping bag at the company position for me, and the route is too steep and tough for carrying loads if avoidable. I strap a jacket liner and water bottle to my belt, and we set off. It's a beautiful day – blue sky, warm, with snowy peaks above us. Our first leg is over rocks along a swiftly flowing nullah [rivulet], and soon there is a floor of needles. The route so far is a beguilingly gentle uphill clamber. We arrive at the remains of a house evidently built by the British, a sort of summer cottage. There are bunkers nearby, housing a couple of under strength infantry rifle sections, and there's a switchboard operator in an out building, with an exchange into which a lot of wires lead. My first new information. We stay here for chai after one hour on the march. I drink sweet milky chai from a sticky glass. We call a stop of this sort a "chai ambush." I catch my sepoy guide sneaking a chew of green hashish from his little tin. I gesture to him that I see nothing. Out of curiosity, I check out their rifles lying on the grass. Clean and well maintained, but no ammo! On our way again. The route becomes steeper. My heart begins to race. We follow goat tracks, zig-zagging upwards on an almost vertical slope. My guides have only their rifles, and I have only my stick and belt. I'm surprised; I'm keeping up well, and one of the guides is panting. Soon we are slip-ping and sliding. The tracks have become rivulets of melted snow water. And now we're sinking into slushy snow in patches on the trail. By early afternoon we arrive at the first and lowest platoon of the company . . . The platoon obviously is badly under strength, and I've been given lies to make it appear otherwise. We start out uphill again for about another hour, going strong, chest like a regularly pumping bellows. The air is thinner, and I can tell the difference. More snow, a bit crisper, and the air is cooler. Now at mid afternoon we arrive at the [company] HQ . . .

. . . We bound down the hill. Somehow, I have tremendous energy. My guides are slipping, sliding, and falling. The sepoy keeps falling behind. I glory in a sense of well-being. We reach the nullah in the valley. The lance naik has had to warn me about running precipi-tously straight down the mountain, rather than following the zig-zag goat path. "Dangerous area," he says. There are unmarked mined areas. The evening before, we had heard an explosion, and all three of us automatically checked the time, and started counting seconds from shot to burst. What if it had been a cease fire violation? It wasn't. The CO told us later that four children had picked up an old Indian AP [anti-personnel] mine left from the last engagement. Two of the children died instantly, one lost his hands and a girl lost her face. I stick to the goat path . . . Night is falling rapidly, and before long we're driving in headlight-pierced blackness, sheer drops on our left, stopping and backing manoeuvering gingerly to get past bedford trucks and busses, the civilian transport that rolls at night. It's terrifying enough in daylight. Now it's horrific, and my knuckles must be white on the "chicken bar".

We arrive safely. I burst into Roger's quarters – sweat-begrimed, dust caked, and jubilant . . . Javaid (CO) comments that I must be tired, and trying to look fresh. I simply smile and say, "Oh should I be tired?" . . .

I love you

Steve

The last Canadian was pulled out of UNMOGIP in the following year, 1979. Brodsky returned home to teach at the Canadian Forces Officer Candidate School and Staff School in Chilliwack, British Columbia, and at Royal Roads Military College in Victoria, and to write. A quarter-century later, the India–Pakistan dispute was threatening to explode into war between the two nuclear-armed nations. In 2003 there were no Canadians among the forty-four military observers and twenty-four international civilian personnel from nine nations currently in the military observer group.

TAKING CARE OF KUWAIT

When Iraqi troops attacked Kuwait on August 2, 1990, the United States launched Operation Desert Storm to expel the invaders from the Persian Gulf state. Canada proposed and then joined a United Nations coalition of more than thirty countries to support the Americans. An expeditionary force of about four thousand Canadian personnel performed a minor role in the Persian Gulf War. After the Iraqis capitulated in April 1991, Canada contributed as a peace-keeper with the UN Iraqi–Kuwait Observer Mission, which offered humanitarian aid to displaced Kurdish refugees and served on weapons-inspection teams. Canada's 1st Combat Engineer Regiment cleared the demilitarized zone between Iraq and Kuwait of thousands of land mines the Iraqis had left behind. **Corporal Mark Isfeld,** *a twenty-eight-year-old Nova Scotian, was one of about fifty Canadian engineers in the zone. He wrote to his parents in Courtenay, British Columbia.*

April 30, 91

Hello Again.

. . . again a day to remember we went to Ummqasar [a small Iraqi town] to the hovercraft site. On the way there, we drove through the killing field, and it stunk of death a most terrible stench as you can imagine. The destruction was awesome close up. Tanks APCs [armoured personnel carriers] cars trucks full of holes, piled up, burned, upside down unreal!! Wait till you develop the pictures! The battle field and destruction went from Kuwait City right to Iraq. I also got to see the burning oil fields even closer than before, it really makes you sick to see it. I counted 68 wells in one and 52 in another and those are just what you can see on the outside cause of the smoke!

We drove through one of the refugee camps and it was terrible. But all the little kids came running and waved. All the people seemed real happy to see us. The little kids run top speed in bare feet! over glass and rocks and metal! They wave and laugh hysterically, its a good feeling, and like being in a parade that is miles and miles long. The kids in Iraq I felt more sorry for cause they are not in a good way, living in decrepit buildings with garbage everywhere and they are starving. We were throwing our rations to them. It was quite a sight as they would ask us for food point to their mouths or stomach but all smiles. They wanted our water as much as food. There was two little boys who came out that we gave some food to. Very good feeling until he went back to the crowd[;] some other children chased the crap out of him to take it[;] he had bare feet and seemed to have fared very well last glimpse I had. I hope he got home allright, Im sure he was taking it home to share with his family . . .

I saw a little boy being pulled by his brother on a makeshift cart. The little boy had no legs. Also there were kids on crutches all over, and bandaged kids missing feet and arms. It's no wonder, a little boy about 8 years old came up to a guy when we were clearing an area and he was all smiles holding a live grenade! Buddy snatched it from him and told him as best he could not to touch anything.

We found a lot of ordnance I mean a lot and we only cleared a small area!

That's about it for today . . .
Mark

After newspapers reported the dangerous work of the Canadian engineers in Kuwait and Iraq, the men received letters from pen pals, including Ken Johnson, with whom Isfeld began corresponding.

Doha KUWAIT
AUG 1 1991

Dear Ken!

. . . I just came back from leave in Canada last week and I will never take for granted again our beautiful country. I noticed the sweet smelling air the most and I stood out in the rain and walked barefoot in the grass.

But truly we are blessed I feel so sorry for the people here. they are so ignorant, scrat[ch]ing an existance from the dust while their leaders spend all their money on arms.

We just returned today from the northern most O.P. [outpost] in Iraq. It was like traveling on the moon. We were in an area where seven million people died during the Iran-Iraq War. A wasteland,

devestated; evidence of war very accute. Many huge junk yards of
military vehicles and tanks . . .

The day before I went on leave, the American ammo dump beside
us exploded. It gave me a taste of a real life disaster and an idea of
what combat must sound like. There was one or two killed and about
fifty injured. We set up an MIR [medical inspection room] in our
junior ranks mess and helped them out as best we could . . .

Sincerely thanks

Cpl Mark Isfeld

*The ammunition dump that had burned and exploded at Doha,
twenty kilometres north of Kuwait City, seriously wounded nearly
one hundred American soldiers; about four hundred others suffered
lesser injuries. Isfeld and the other Canadian combat engineers,
under Major Fred Kaustinen, gave first aid to the victims. Although
the U.S. commander sent a letter of praise to the engineers, National
Defence headquarters in Ottawa hushed up the incident, apparently
to save the Americans from embarrassment. But in 2001 it was
learned that the dump had held depleted-uranium-tipped shells. The*
Ottawa Citizen *found that ten of the eighteen combat engineers it
could locate had suffered from forms of immunodeficiency-related
illnesses; others had children with "congenital anomalies." Colonel
Scott Cameron, the Canadian Forces' surgeon general, said that
American scientists had found that "exposures were well below the
threshold levels at which health effects occur." A German scientist,
however, said that the men had been exposed to "a cocktail of cancer-
causing substances." In late 1991 Mark Isfeld married an American
mother of two children, and the following year he went to Croatia
as a peacekeeper.*

WELCOME TO SARAJEVO

*By the early 1990s, the federal government was reducing the strength
of the Canadian Forces and pulling most of the nation's troops from*

Europe – while at the same time trying to raise their profile with the public. An opportunity arose with a renewed crisis in the Balkans, which had been in various stages of war for more than six centuries. Now the area's three major ethnic groups – Serbs, Croats, and Bosniacs (Bosnian Muslims), first united under the flag of the Yugoslav kingdom in 1919 – were waging a fierce civil war. In August 1990 Serbian and Croatian police forces clashed; less than a year later Croatia and Slovenia became independent republics. In January 1992 the United Nations sent ten thousand Blue Berets to the former Yugoslavia as a United Nations Protection Force (UNPROFOR) to shield civilians. Canada drew the crucial Sector West zone south of Zagreb, the Croatian capital. The chief of staff of UNPROFOR was **General Lewis MacKenzie** *of Truro, Nova Scotia, a UN negotiator during earlier peace talks in Yugoslavia. Hardy, creative, and seasoned, he had three decades of military experience – including seven peacekeeping missions, from the Gaza Strip to Central America. On April 6, 1992, the European Community granted Bosnia-Herzegovina its independence, although its government had just collapsed. Shooting and looting erupted in the capital, Sarajevo. Anarchy reigned, but a UN force formed and led by MacKenzie had no authority to intervene. He wrote an open letter to friends and colleagues in Canada.*

From Brigadier-General L.W. MacKenzie C.D.

Sarajevo

19 April 1992

Dear _____,

Well, it's springtime in the Balkans, and history is repeating itself as the various ethnic groups (Muslims, Croats and Serbs) seek to exterminate each other; except this time it's by artillery rather than swords.

The deployment of our twelve infantry battalions and two engineer regiments is pretty well on schedule into the United Nations Protected Areas (UNPAs) in Croatia. So far the Canadians (both infantry and engineer battalions), and the French, Russian, Belgian (with a platoon from Luxembourg), Czechoslovakian and Danish battalions are on the ground, and hopefully the Polish, Nepalese,

Argentine, Jordanian, Kenyan and Nigerian battalions will arrive within three weeks.

The UNPAs are relatively quiet, with *only* 100–200 ceasefire violations per day. In my estimation, there is no ceasefire; however, the UN likes to say it is "holding". Both major players, the Croatian Army and the JNA (Yugoslavian Army) have picked up the habit of moving close to UN positions to protect themselves from counter-artillery fire. I have asked them to keep at least a kilometre away – time will tell. Once we have all the battalions in each one of the four sectors, we will assume responsibility for protecting the people in the sectors and will monitor the local authorities and police forces. Sounds simple but execution will be difficult in the extreme for a number of reasons.

Most of the villages in the various sectors are dominated by Serbs, who are currently executing a policy of "ethnic cleansing" – that is to say, evicting the non-Serb occupants at gunpoint and destroying their homes once they leave. If the occupants don't leave, the Serbs destroy the houses and the occupants. The Croats are carrying out similar actions in their area of Sector West, which the Canadians partially occupy.

The other major problem results from the move of the line of confrontation since the [UN special representative Cyrus] Vance ceasefire in December. In a number of sectors, the JNA has moved forward up to twenty kilometres from the boundary of the UNPA since the ceasefire and are protecting the Serb villages in what we affectionately call the "Pink Zones". Our responsibilities are legally confined to the UNPAs and it would take the [UN] Security Council to change them. Obviously the Croatian authorities would object, as that would be an encroachment on their territory. The JNA are equally adamant that they will not withdraw from the "Pink Zones", thereby leaving the Serbs to the wrath of the Croats. We have some ideas on how to manage the situation; however, it will require flexibility on both sides and I don't believe that word even exists in Serbo-Croatian.

While all the above is going on up front in Croatia, we at the HQ find ourselves mired in the problems of Bosnia-Herzegovina (BiH).

For political reasons, we were directed to locate our headquarters in Sarajevo, the capital of BiH. It was a smart political decision but, as we warned them in New York, very unwise from a military point of view. The airport is one of the most unreliable in Europe due to weather patterns and we are some six hours away from our forward troops by road – when the roads are not blocked. Having our own aircraft resources will help; however, they are at least a month away. We have promises of helicopter casualty evacuation from both sides, which eases my concerns a bit.

Bosnia-Herzegovina has slid into anarchy, with the Serbs abandoning the Presidency and setting up a parallel organization in the hills. When they left the Ministry of the Interior, they took the guns (and most of the armoured cars) with them, leaving the city open to thugs and looters. Each side is now flexing its muscles as the European Community tries to work out a "cantonization" plan, which would see ethnic groups concentrated in specific areas of the republic. It will not work; however, the diplomats are still trying. In the meantime, the three sides and the JNA are destroying the republic and its capital. Everything from 152-millimetre artillery, 120-millimetre mortars, anti-tank weapons and heavy machine guns are methodically destroying most of old Sarajevo and a large number of towns and villages throughout the country. MIG-29s are acting as peacekeepers as they do low passes over the troubled areas in an attempt to intimidate everyone.

The capital is quiet during the visits of the Vances and the [European Community's Lord] Carringtons of the world. Everyone gets a good night's sleep and starts afresh on the VIP's departure.

Tragically, there is no solution that I can postulate. Hatred is deep, and everyone has a gun and calls himself a sniper. Hundreds of years of ethnic violence and intolerance are dredged up at each meeting; everyone thinks that theirs is the just cause. From my impartial point of view, there is more than enough blame to go around for all sides, with some left over. We will continue to try and operate from Sarajevo; however, nothing is functioning (including the post, so I will have this mailed from Belgrade or Zagreb) and food and fuel are running short. As a result, numerous humanitarian convoys are regularly hijacked. Naturally, everyone wants us to provide escorts and all we have are staff officers with pistols! In fact, I lie, as we have an outstanding platoon of Swedish military guards who give increased meaning to the term "professonalism". I feel very safe as they escort us in the execution of our duties in some very sensitive parts of town.

As a final point, the work here is by far the most challenging of my career. We have now worked fifty-two days straight and it was all good operational stuff. I am blessed with an outstanding commander, Lieutenant-General Nambiar from India, who is ideally suited to the job. I like to think we make a good team. I have an outstanding personal staff led by a Canadian major, Steve Gagnon, and in spite of the situation, we are enjoying practising our profession. Hopefully, we are doing some good, but only time and CNN will tell.

Warmest personal regards,

Lew

Little more than two months later, MacKenzie's forces were joined by the Royal 22e Régiment, the Van Doos, which over thirty days secured the Sarajevo Airport. While taking artillery fire, they kept the airport open for the daily delivery of three hundred tonnes of humanitarian aid. In 2002 the Van Doos received a new Canadian honour from Governor General Adrienne Clarkson, the Commander-in-Chief Unit Commendation. MacKenzie was awarded the UN Medal of Honour. He left Bosnia on August 1 and, after commanding Canadian army troops in Ontario, retired in March 1993.

SCANDAL IN SOMALIA

In 1992 Canadian peacekeepers were deployed to Somalia in eastern Africa, where at least 300,000 Somalis were dying of starvation. Anarchy ruled as tribal warlords and armed thugs prevented aid from relieving the famine. The first troops of an American-led mission of about 28,500 from UN member nations, trying to stave off disaster, invaded Somalia in the first peace-enforcement mission since the end of the Cold War. Canada's contribution included nine hundred members of the Canadian Airborne Regiment. They were part of Operation Deliverance – but what a few of their men delivered was torture and murder. **Major Barry Armstrong** *of Calgary was a military surgeon with nearly twenty years' service who, on the night of March 4, 1993, examined the body of Ahmed Afrahow Aruush. Aruush had been killed and another Somali wounded while fleeing an Airborne squad that had planted bait – food and water – on the edge of the regiment's desert camp and watched for foragers through night-vision goggles. Dr. Armstrong wrote his wife in Ottawa.*

Service Commando
Op Deliverance Somalia
CFPO-40
Belleville, ONT
KoK 3Ko
13 March [1993]

Hope that You Get this Before Flying!
Dear Jennifer, my Gem:
Sorry that it's been so long without a letter. Partially I was fairly busy, but mostly I've been trying to make sense of it all, before I write you.

On 17 Feb our boss LCol Mathieu, Airborne Regiment Co C.O., laid down "The Law" re: Organisation of the Somalis' political committees. On 18 Feb a demonstration was throwing rocks and the soldiers shot warning shots (one Somali injured by ricochet) and they then fired into the crowd, killing one and injuring another. The two injured Somalis were treated at the C.F. Hospital, and one is still there . . .

While that was going on, I was working downtown at the Belet Uen Hospital. The demonstration moved to the main street outside the hospital and 3 people (Somalis) were injured by rifle fire in the restaurant across the street. A grenade was thrown between 2 passing CF trucks and exploded just outside the operating room, where I was doing a scalp flap operation, at Belet Uen Hospital. I kept operating, treating the injured then we transferred those injured by Canadians to our hospital and kept operating until 0230 A.M.

On the 21 Feb our compound had some "burglar" visitors and many shots were fired at the (? unarmed) Somalis. They fled and were chased through the hut village. One of our vehicles crashed through a hut and ran over a sleeping boy (therefore another patient). We're hardly controlled friendly peacekeepers, are we?

There's a very big racist thing going on here (Canada Good, Somalis bad is the basic Airborne prejudice).

3 March – Recalled in mid morning from Belet Uen hospital. An American Hummvee (= jeep) ran over a mine. We got 5 casualties to treat. The worst arrived first, by helicopter about 2 hrs after the mine accident. Looking back now, I guess he probably died a few minutes before, or at the time the helicopter arrived here. We tried to resuscitate him with full Advanced Trauma Life Support honours, and had to pronounce him dead 35 minutes after arrival. He was an American medical assistant well-known to, and well-liked by many of us (the 9th U.S., 7th coalition fatality).

4 March – Our hero soldiers. Oh how proud the elite Airborne soldiers are! They shot 2 Somalis in the back, because they were trying to climb through our 8 feet thick, 6 feet high barbed wire fence. One was shot in the back with a shotgun from approx. 15–30m. away as he was running (unarmed) away from the camp. The other was shot in the back (he was unarmed) with a rifle. Then he lived a few minutes, and by his wounds, he was executed by 2 or more shots to the head/neck as he lay on the ground, still alive/conscious. These brave Airborne soldiers. We treated the shot gun injury at our hospital.

I made a telephone report to the Headquarters in Mogadishu stating that it appeared to be cold-blooded homicide, phoning at 0230 the next morning. I wrote a description of the rifle fatality and gave it with Polaroid photos of the head/neck wounds, to LCol Mathieu our C.O., and then . . .

Cover-up. Damage control. Don't make waves. Nothing that could affect the political aspirations of our [Conservative Defence] Minister (would be Prime Minister) Kim Campbell.

It makes me wonder if Canada is such a great country after all. It makes me want to resign and picket in front of Ottawa's "Peace-keeping Monument". The Airborne has learned too much from the lawless thugs of Somalia!

Sorry, but that's as calm as I can be, and you probably don't want to wait any longer (for me to calm down) before writing . . .

Love you dearly,

Barry

After examining Aruush's body, Dr. Armstrong cried. That night he was told that officials in Somalia and Ottawa were already doing "damage control." Within two days he formally informed the local Canadian Forces commander, Colonel Serge Labbé, and the Airborne commanding officer, Lieutenant Colonel Carol Mathieu, that he believed the Somali man had been murdered. Both officers, he said, dismissed the allegations. He later wrote to his parents.

13 March 93

Dear Mom & Dad

. . . I'm still quite upset by the shootings last week. We've had a daily problem with 'looters' sneaking through our fences. The fence is now barb and concertina wire 6 feet high and 8 feet thick.

Last week they confronted 2 unarmed Somalis who were trying to crawl under the wire and chased them away (that's O.K.). Then they apparently shot one of them twice in the head/neck, apparently while he was laying on the ground. (Definitely not O.K.) This reminds me of the horrible way the Nazi S.S. dealt with Canadian prisoners of war, gunning them down unarmed/in the back.

I made a written report to my boss Lieutenant Colonel Mathieu who is Commandant here in Belet Uen. I made a telephone report to his boss's H.Q. in Mogadishu (which commands all Canadian troops in Somalia) using the words "abhorrent" and "homicide".

No investigation is underway, let alone punishment. Apparently the Minister of Nat. Defence, Kim Campbell, might be embarrassed by these revelations (I doubt that . . .). I had thought that Watergate and Iran–Contra had shown that covering up official crimes does not work in this era of tele-journalism.

Oh well, if Jim Hawkes [Conservative Parliamentary whip] is running against Kim Campbell, and if she doesn't investigate and settle this war crime, maybe I should let him know. What is your status during the leadership race?

> All the Best from the
>
> HOT
>
> DRY
>
> DUSTY
>
> Horn of Africa
>
> Barry

In mid-April, Armstrong was on leave with his wife in Nairobi, Kenya, when he bumped into members of a military police team that had been investigating the killing of another Somali. Sixteen-year-old Shidane Arone had been tortured and beaten in the camp by Airborne 2 Commando soldiers. Armstrong warned Master Warrant Officer Paul Dowd that he would resign his commission and go to the press if his concerns were not investigated. Military headquarters in Ottawa ordered a hush-hush investigation. Just after Jennifer Armstrong left Nairobi to fly home, her husband slipped this note under the door of Lieutenant Colonel Peter A. Tinsley, a Canadian Forces prosecutor investigating the Arone death.

14 Apr 93, 1600 hrs

LCol Tinsley

Sir, I am the CF Trauma Surgeon employed at Belet Huen, Somalia. I've been on leave x 16 days and have missed your investigation. It may have focused on the (apparent) beating of a civilian 16/17 Mar 93.

Like that death which was "covered up" at first, there was another incident, 4 Mar 93, when two unarmed civilians were shot (by CF soldiers) in the back while running away. One was injured and brought to the Canadian hospital. The second was injured and some minutes(?) later apparently was dispatched by two or more, additional shots to the head, probably while he was lying on the ground, defenceless and unarmed.

I reported this to Canadian Joint Force HQ, Mogadishu, by phone as an apparent set of War Crimes including a homicide. The report was made by phone at 0200 hrs, 5 Mar 93.

A report, with written description of the injured injuries and lethal wounds was given to my superiors, including I/C Medical Platoon, O/C Service Command Commando, and CO Cdn Airborne Regt on 6 Mar 93. Photos of the dead man's wounds were included.

I also had a long discussion, on 6 Mar 93, with CO Airborne Regt, pointing out the escalation of rights violations and wanton violence by CF soldiers. LCol Mathieu did not feel that there was a problem. If he had exerted his leadership soon after 4 Mar, perhaps later events would have been avoidable.

If your investigation has not examined in detail the Incident, 4 Mar, I would seek your assurance that such an investigation is underway. We should not cover-up preventable Canadian War Crimes, but seek to maintain our respected world position as peacekeepers.

Major Barry D Armstrong
O/C Surgical Section

A distraught Jennifer Armstrong, whose father had been in the military for three decades, had told a friend there was more to the Somalia story than the media were reporting. When the friend informed The Toronto Star, *a reporter approached Mrs. Armstrong, who read him portions of her husband's letter about the murder. The resulting articles prompted controversy. Armstrong was sent home to Ottawa, and anonymous callers told reporters he was mentally unstable and professionally incompetent. In October a major was convicted and a captain acquitted in Aruush's death, but no one above those ranks was called to account. A corporal charged in the Arone death tried to commit suicide and was left brain-damaged and unfit to stand trial at court-martial. Early in 1995 CTV News showed a videotape of hazing activities at an Airborne initiation ceremony. Two months later the regiment was disbanded, the first in Canadian history to die in disgrace. The Liberal government appointed a three-man commission of inquiry, which Ottawa disbanded after eighteen months without allowing it to answer key questions about the Somali deaths. In his book* Somalia Cover-Up, *one of the three commissioners, Peter Desbarats, said of Major Armstrong: "It was his persistent revelations, along with the death of Shidane Arone and the television broadcasts of the hazing rituals, that created the public outrage that forced the government to react by disbanding the Airborne regiment and appointing me and my fellow commissioners." He described the doctor as "a thoughtful and conscientious soldier coming to grips with an appalling reality." Armstrong retired from the military in 1997 and in 2003 was the lone surgeon in Dryden, Ontario.*

THE BALKAN MINEFIELD

The festering civil wars in the Balkans continued to explode into unimaginable violence throughout the 1990s. In 1994 **Mark Isfeld** *(see page 401), now a master corporal, was on his second tour in Croatia with Canadian combat engineers attached to the Princess Patricia's Canadian Light Infantry, who were trying to de-mine the country – as he told his parents, Brian and Carol Isfeld.*

Donje Biljane
Croatia (Serb territory)
April 27 94

Sorry for not writing sooner, basically I have been totally uninterested in writing, between being sick and overworked I have not had time. Though my thoughts are always with you.

My section [eight persons] has broken some sort of record for a Canadian FE [field engineer] section for most mines lifted since world war II[:] up till today we have recorded over 270. All these are a mixture of anti-tank and personell. The reason there is so many is due to the fact that we are basically on the front line of a newly formed line of seperation, basically a demilitarized zone. There are continuous shot reps [reports] and shell reps[;] no one has been shot at that Im aware of[,] mostly drunken Serbs or Croats pissing in the wind.

There has been a mine accident which you are already aware of in which an Iltis (jeep) ran over a mine in an area we (Dave's section) had cleared[;] they were right there when it happened . . .

Needless to say we are being very careful, trying not to let complacency set in. Soon we will have all the patrol routes cleared of mines and the adrenaline levels will level out and we can fall into a routine. As for now without a doubt us engineers are the most sought after and respected soldiers on the line not to mention the least envied . . .

I have made some good friends on both sides but one particularly good friend, Filip a Croatian Lt infantry soldier. Together we became friends in a way that is hard to explain[:] he knows I know and no one else can. We cleared a field of six [anti-personnel] mines in waist high grass with trip wires all around. When we had it cleared we shook hands as if the unspoken words were understood. I had to explode, with C-4 [an explosive], two of the mines because they were unsafe to handle. Filip is without a doubt my most reliable ally in this operation[;] he looks at mine records and takes me aside and secretly gives me numbers types and locations. I then work on him to "come lift with us"[.] He is very concerned about my welfare and is constantly looking out for me[,] telling me "Mark in this area you go slow"[.] He is truly in the mood for peace.

I gave him one of [Mom's] dolls for his three year old daughter and a canadian flag[;] he keeps trying to get me to drink Pivo or Vino but I told him Im alergic every time I drink I get drunk . . .

Tomorrow we are taking a break from mine lifting the next day we will empty our storage area of about 90 mines that will be fun, big boom! . . .

All my love I'll write again soon.

M.

The "Izzy dolls" that Isfeld handed out – boy dolls with blue berets and girls with bonnets – were crocheted by Carol Isfeld from scrap wool. "The dolls are a hit, Mom, don't stop making them," he told his mother. She began making another batch.

June 3 [1994]

. . . Greg James is my section commander he's a good guy and we get along real good he is another Newf. Together we made a massive discovery of AMMO and even a .50 cal machine gun in the ZOS [zone of separation]. There was three of us and we thought we had finished finding all the mines and ammo that was cached and left lying around, but we were getting ready to leave and had a Serb sign a piece of paper saying it was OK to take. He seemed too eager to let us have it, so we wandered around a bit more and voila we found a door we hadn't checked and it led to another we opened the door and we near shit[:] PAYDAY! Jackpot! a room the size of your living room packed with everything in cases from Antitank rocket launchers to mortars, 269 6mm mortars, 4000 rnds small arms ammo, 200 rnds 50 cal. incendiary rounds, 5000 Anti Aircraft rounds. the list goes on cases of mines, AT [anti-tank] & AP [anti-personnel] with all the fixins. Plus to top it off a machine gun.

The next thing you know our Serb friend says shit. and fucks off. So we wait, radio for support and lock and load. Within 15 min we had another Eng[ineer] section a Medic truck and scads of infantry OC [on location] with us . . .

Shortly after our serb friend f.ed off he showed back up with the local serb commander who acted surprised to find the cache then moments later asked for his 50 cal back. I'm glad the serbs didn't come back with weapons cause we would have had to take those away too.

Anyway, we were the talk of the town for awhile and the Serbs were pissed off real big. They threatened us and tried to deny access to the ZOS. Some negotiations went on but in the end we keep the cache and they learn the lesson . . .

Anyway that's it for now forgive my messy writing but I'm writing on my lap.

With love
Your son
M.

On June 21, 1994, the thirty-one-year-old Isfeld was removing mines in a Zone of Separation in southern Croatia. He and five others were trying to clear a path to a waterpipe that had been blown up. The armoured personnel carrier he was guiding set off a mine hidden in tall grass, wounding Isfeld and two other engineers. He died in a helicopter en route to a field hospital. His mother continued to make Izzy dolls, and, inspired by newspaper articles and word-of-mouth in the military, thousands of other mothers have since started crocheting them. In 2000 Carol Isfeld was chosen Silver Cross mother for the national Remembrance Day ceremony in Ottawa. She and her husband, Brian – activists in the Canadian-led global campaign to halt the proliferation of land mines – received special awards at a meeting of the 107 countries that signed the Mine Ban Treaty.

CROATIA'S KILLING GROUNDS

In the fall of 1994 **Private Kurt Grant** of Spencerville, Ontario, was in the Krajina region of Croatia on Operation Harmony with the 1st Royal Canadian Regiment. Son of an air force major, he had studied industrial engineering and done project-management consulting before going overseas as a peacekeeper. A master corporal with Ontario's Brockville Rifles militia unit, Grant accepted a reduction in rank and went as a front-line private while the UN troops were still attempting to keep Croats and Serbs apart. At the time, Croatian

Serbs had allied with Serbians and Bosnian Serbs to slaughter the Muslim and Croatian majority in an "ethnic cleansing." Grant wrote to his wife of five years.

4 Oct 94

My Dearest Catherine

I am writing this to you while sitting in a tent, in a town called Donja Bruska. This place has been nicknamed our "one-week leave center," because all we do here is sleep, eat, and when on patrol, drink wine with the locals. The locals love us here, and believe it or not bring the wine right to the gate in pots.

There are two groups of people here, Serbs and Croats. Not a single Moslem to be seen. The three young couples in town are refugees, whom the Serb government have moved here. All the old people are Croatian and have lived here forever.

This is a hard country, everything is made of rock, it's a wonder there is any soil here at all. What soil there is, is augmented heavily with compost, and is red as P.E.I. mud. All the old people get up and drink wine, or aracia (moonshine) right from breakfast till bedtime . . .

I want very much to talk to you, but the phone has been broken for the past week. By the time you get this letter though, I will have talked to you again. Sadly it will be a short call because we're told some PPCLI officer racked up a 100,000 DM phone bill. As a result we're told only 20% of the phone budget is left. This will result in us having only a five-minute call once a week until things change . . .

27 Oct. [1994]

. . . I'm in Donja Bruska right now, and there are four Serb families who have been moved here. All are in their 20's and 30's. All have one or two children of preschool age. To be perfectly honest with you, I don't trust them. I like them, but I don't trust them. The old here are just that, old. Most are past retirement age and are still out in the fields working. They walk everywhere they go – there are no cars. That's not true, there are cars, just no gas. Besides, this is the equivalent of the back woods. Things take longer to get out here.

There are no middle-aged people here, there's just the young, the old, and abandoned houses.

Just up the road from us is the gate for camp Alpha. The Serbs are supposed to be training about 1000 new 18-year-old recruits. Whenever we approach their front gate, you can see whoever is on duty getting nervous. They're under direct orders not to talk to us. Even so, some will talk for a little bit in better English than my SerboCroat. If someone in the camp decided they wanted to overrun this place, we'd be toast. But that will never happen so please don't worry . . .

I've been keeping my diary with details of what's been going on and I intend to bring it to England for you to read. These are some of the highlights from the first two weeks on the ground:
– our foot patrol in Rodaljice takes us past a house where 29 Croats were decapitated.
– there's a church 100 m from our camp in Rodaljice. The roof is blown off and someone defecated on the altar – twice. The grave-yard is a mess, graves opened, headstones broken, bones scattered, that sort of thing.
– we drove past a school in the town of Ziminic on one of our patrols, where children and teachers were lined up against a wall and shot. The bullet holes and blood stains are still in evidence.
– there is a graveyard where the Serbs went in and dug up the graves, and scattered the bones.

Each day as we drive though the countryside, the evidence of ethnic cleansing is evident. Entire villages are destroyed. Other places (like Rodaljice) half the village is empty and ransacked, and the other half seems normal. It makes you want to shake your head.
But on to cheerier subjects. Most of our time here in Bruska is spent playing game boy, watching movies, playing trivial pursuit, or writing letters. There's a six-hour radio watch, between 2400–0600, that we split into two hour blocks that everyone takes turns doing. During

the day, we send out three two man patrols. It's pretty much on a volunteer basis, but everyone does it. The truth is, we're bored to tears out here . . .

8 Nov. [1994]

. . . Undoubtedly you've heard and been told about the fighting that's going on in Bosnia. Fear not my sweet, for I am quite safe. The fighting is in another country, and may as well be on the other side of the world for all the effect it has on us. We sit around at night and watch CNN to get the latest updates, then try to marry that up with what's coming down in orders. But like mushrooms we rarely get a glimpse of the big picture.

You asked me once where I lived. The truth is, I live in what's called an Iso trailer. This is just a fancy name for a sea container with windows and a door. There are four of us in our trailer, so things are a little crammed. We have two sets of bunk beds, a double locker, 12 barrack boxes, a rifle rack, four duffel bags and four rucksacks packed into an area the size of . . . well . . . a sea container. With all the kit packed inside, we all sleep on the ground outside the door. Just kidding, we really sleep on top of the trailer.

The routine around here is pretty straightforward. One week at Bruska, one week camp security in Rodaljice, and one week patrolling. This is our week for patrolling, but because we aren't going to start patrolling until Thursday, we've taken over the 0600–1200 at the gate at Rodaljice. This is the second time this week I've pulled duty and frankly I don't mind. It forces me to get up early, and it gives me lots of time to write to people. In all honesty, I've written more letters in the past thirty days than I've written in the past thirty years. I think I've found a new hobby . . .

Six weeks before Grant left for Croatia, his wife had been diagnosed with multiple sclerosis.

14 Nov. [1994]

. . . Last we spoke (Thursday, I believe) you had just come from a visit to the doctor. It pains me to think that I will be unable to nurse you back to health should it be required. It has become one of my more pleasant duties as husband and guardian of our humble kingdom, and while I do not look forward to its occurrence (for it means discomfort to you) it is a duty from which I do not shrink . . .

As I told you on the phone, I am in Donja Bruska. Almost from the moment we arrived we have been in a heightened state of alert. Code orange it's called. It's most inconvenient, as we have broken into three groups and are on rotating eight hour shifts, which of course affects our eating and sleeping habits. The reason no doubt, you are already aware of. Bosnia is in the midst of a war in what's called the Bihac pocket. It appears the Krajina Serbs have been shelling the Bosnian government troops from their side of the border. This is a no no as the Krajina is considered a UN protectorate. The Croats have said they will launch a counterstrike in support of the Bosnian Croats (confused yet?). In order for the Croats to get there from here, the Croatians have to go through our (battalion's) positions. They also said they wouldn't mind taking pot shots at anyone in their way (that would be us). Be assured in the knowledge that I am quite safe. While we have orders to stop any heavy equipment moving in our area, our platoon tasking is only to observe, and continue to protect our two villages . . .

I would tell you more, but I'm limiting the details so that it doesn't worry you needlessly (not that there's much to worry about anyway). It is one of the reasons I am keeping a diary . . . I love you my sweet, never forget that. It won't be long now until we will be together again.

Your loving husband.

Kurt

In his diary for Christmas Day, Grant talked of a visit he and a friend made to a cemetery near his camp. They were shocked at "the destruction wrought by a vengeful people": Serbs had destroyed the chapel with explosives, opened graves, and scattered human remains. Standing amid the destruction, he was reminded of lines from a poem by William Blake: "O for a voice like thunder, and a tongue/ To drown the throat of war! – When the senses/ Are shaken, and the soul is driven to madness,/ Who can stand?" During his tour in Croatia, Grant was attacked by an anti-tank rocket launcher and rifle grenades and shot at several times. He returned in April 1995 to Ontario, where he became a consultant in the defence industry and a reservist with the Brockville Rifles.

Hundreds of thousands of Serbs and Croats died during the civil strife. In early 2003, Bosnian Serb president Biljana Plavsic pleaded guilty to war crimes against humanity and a United Nations war crimes tribunal sentenced her to eleven years in prison. In March 2003, snipers assassinated the reformist prime minister of Serbia and Montenegro, Zoran Djindjic. At this writing, the trial of former Yugoslav president Slobodan Milosevic, on charges of genocide and war crimes during the Balkan wars, continued.

AFGHANISTAN, 2002

"We are safe and will be"

Sergeant Debra Keegan, a postal clerk with the Princess Pats, hauls
Canada Post mailbags out of their cases at Waters Bivouac, the Canadian
camp in Afghanistan during Operation Apollo in 2002.

In the wake of September 11, 2001, Canadian troops were called upon to support an American-led invasion of Afghanistan. Invoking an agreement that any attack on a nation in the North Atlantic Treaty Organization is effectively an attack on all NATO nations, Canada said it was acting in self-defence. Major Sean Hackett of the Princess Patricia's Canadian Light Infantry, who served as an officer in Bosnia as well as in Afghanistan, says: "All missions to the former Yugoslavia over the past ten years, be it Croatia or Bosnia, could be considered peacekeeping. The Afghanistan mission in no way, shape, or form fits this mold. We were authorized and fully intended to carry out combat operations against al-Qaeda or residual Taliban elements. We were not peacekeepers."

As Foreign Minister John Manley said in early 2002, "If you want to play a role in the world, there's a cost to doing that." The cost in the case of Operation Apollo was six Canadian navy ships (nearly one third of the fleet), six transport and surveillance aircraft, and more than two thousand troops, including a special Joint Task Forces 2 commando unit trained to counter domestic terrorism. It was the largest force of any kind Canada had sent abroad in half a century.

Another price Canadians paid was the deaths of four Princess Patricia's paratroopers and the wounding of eight others. In April 2002, U.S. warplanes accidentally bombed them during a live-fire training exercise near Kandahar. Amid the shock and grief, the media described these casualties as the first suffered by Canadian forces in "offensive combat operations" since Korea. One distinguished military veteran took exception to that categorization. Major General Lewis MacKenzie, who'd commanded United Nations (UN) troops during the Bosnian civil war a decade earlier (see page 404), wondered, "Who came up with this ridiculous category? Are we to await the first casualties in 'defensive combat operations'? Is there to be a sub-category for victims of friendly fire? Give me a break. Let the record show that these fine young men were killed while serving their country and let the same record show that there have been twenty-three others laid to rest as a result of enemy action and accidents in the former Yugoslavia."

MacKenzie made the point that Canada is not just a peacekeeping nation: "The primary role of our military is to train for war." That's one side of a debate about our armed forces. The other has been argued by the Conference of Defence Associations (CDA) – with 600,000 members, it's the country's largest military lobby group – which maintains that the Canadian Armed Forces are ineffective both as a standing army and as a peacekeeping force. In a blueprint for this century, the organization urged the federal government to support the forces in a role more suited to what it called Canada's human-security focus: "that of creating a highly efficient armed force that is primarily focused on the task of peacekeeping, with a limited war-fighting cadre of regulars and reserves."

The debate became all the more relevant as the government announced that, in August 2003, 1,800 more Canadians would be deployed to Afghanistan to join an international peacekeeping force.

The year before, the first of our troops in Afghanistan were writing letters home on paper and by e-mail. Here are the voices of two of the four men who died in the "friendly fire" bombing, two of the eight who were wounded, and two of their commanders.

DON'T THINK ME WEAK

*The first contingent of Canada's Afghanistan-bound troops – 750
members of the Princess Patricia's Canadian Light Infantry (PPCLI)
and the Lord Strathcona's Horse light-armoured regiment – said
goodbye to their families in Edmonton on January 31, 2002. This
was Alpha Company, the elite paratroopers of the 3rd Battalion of
the Princess Patricia's Battle Group. They would serve alongside soldiers of the U.S. 101st Airborne at the junk-strewn remnant of an
international airport at Kandahar (or Qandahar), Afghanistan's
second-largest city, which had been a pivotal centre for the Taliban
controlling the country. The Canadians' desert base, fronting on low
hills, was about forty kilometres west. Alpha Company's key job
was security patrols, watching for al-Qaeda forces – Osama bin
Laden's militant Islamic terrorists – whose former training camp was
about ten kilometres south of Kandahar. **Corporal Curtis Hollister**,
a twenty-eight-year-old from Cupar, Saskatchewan, had served two
tours in Bosnia as a PPCLI peacekeeper and was now in Afghanistan,
leaving his girlfriend and family behind.*

[2002]

Dear Mom & Dad, Shannon & McKenzie,
Today is the 26th of February, my 16th day in Afghanistan, we are
doing perimeter security around the airport.

I'm looking forward to getting out of the base and into the countryside which is very arid and rugged, but in the last week it rained
and pretty good too, it's the most rain they've had in 6 years.

I live in a small tent with one other person and space is very
cramped as [we] live within sandbag walls which help to protect
from mortar & rocket attack.

I got to watch the gold medal Canada–US Olympic hockey game,
it started at 12 midnight here, and it was great for Canada to win as
it shut up all those mouthy US soldiers.

We eat ration packs everyday, and what they call a fresh breakfast, but all it is is large sealed tray, one with sausages, another with eggs, and one with grits and I hate [them] with a passion.

We get some fresh fruit ever[y]day, so that's a big boost to morale.

In our platoon with all our duties we're lucky to get 4 hours sleep a day, and you get in different periods . . . 2 hours, 45 mins etc. to equal 4 hours. There is nothing to do here but work eat & sleep, and maybe write a letter while on shift.

The most striking thing about this place other than the climate is the continual smell of burning human waste, because we have no way of disposing of the waste. The penalty for theft among the soldiers is that you have [to] burn the POW's waste.

They have a shower here in camp, but usually it's cram[m]ed full of WOG's [worn-out grunts – rear-echelon personnel] so I've only had one shower since I've been here, but I bird bath every day. It's very dirty here, sand gets into everything and it's impossible to stay clean. I won't wear my contacts, and it's just my glasses while I'm here. On that I don't know when we're getting out of here to come home, but they said no shorter than 4 months. I'll try and let you know what happens with my redeployment date, but it seems nobody can confirm anything, as I write this our canadian mail service is still not working . . . but I did receive my pay statement, big hairy deal.

If you could, would you send me a care package? I'd like some wet ones as they work really well on the private area's, some junk food like cheezies, spitz, and maybe a container of flavoured coffee like French vanilla, Irish creme. Just one because I don't have a lot of room to store things.

I hope you are all doing well out there in Cupar. I'll try to phone you more often, but right [now] we're limited to 40 minutes a month and guess who I spend that on, she just won't let me hang up . . .

They've put us on methoquine an anti-malarial drug which has psychological side effects on some people; but hasn't effected me at all . . .

You may think this is weird but I've started reading the bible over here and find comfort in its passages, don't think of me as weak

for reading it, but it helps me out while I'm over here . . . Hope to
see you soon!!

Love

Curtis

THE THREAT IS THERE

*Major Sean Hackett, a graduate in military and strategic studies from
Victoria's Royal Roads Military College, had joined the Princess Pats
as a second lieutenant in 1991. He spent a year with a commando
unit of the Canadian Airborne Regiment before it was disbanded after
the Somalia scandal, then served with the 3rd PPCLI Battalion Group
in Croatia for six months in 1992–93. After becoming a major in
2000 with the Canadian Mechanized Brigade Group, he rejoined the
PPCLI as officer commanding the Alpha Company paratroopers. In
Afghanistan, the thirty-seven-year-old wrote frequently to his parents
in Brighton, Ontario, and his wife, Iana, in Edmonton.*

Forces Air Letter

3 Mar 02 (One month in Theatre)

Dear Mum and Dad

. . . Life is busy. Attending and giving orders groups, touring the
defensive line and keeping up with defensive improvements, planning, checking on the troops – never enough time to do it all. I find
it hard to keep up with writing, and have been far less diligent about
keeping a detailed journal. Time seems a precious commodity and I
usually defer to the need for sleep whenever possible. I average 4–5
hrs per day – hard to sustain over the long haul. I live in an old
utility room/bathroom with no fixtures and plastic (now) over the
window; makes for an interesting night when the wind sweeps in as.
it is prone to do occasionally – bringing the dust and sand. The
incessant noise from aircraft (or anything else for that matter) has
become monotonous/routine. I'm often too tired at any rate. What

else? No running water; I shit into a 45 gallon drum in an open air privy, and these are burnt when full! – adding to the dusty desert aroma! Cold/cool at night, getting warmer (by day) as each day comes. Hard rations – much preferred over the morning hot 'meal' that gets pushed out to the line. I swerve on that, less the fresh fruit, as I consider it mostly inedible! I keep clean though, despite the grit, liberally using baby wipes and hand sanitizer whenever possible. Though there are support personnel in the rear with more access to amenities (go figure – as with any army since the [ancient Greek] Hoplites!) guys on the line resign themselves to bird baths or expedient showers. I had my second shower since arriving here on 3 Feb, only 48 hrs ago! Simple pleasures.

This tour is shaping up to be quite an experience – a complete eye-opener. Such a moonscape and hard to believe I'm in this part of the world. Bizarre. I'm not sure how I feel about the threat – it's definitely there; an unpredictability, more pronounced than in Croatia 10 years ago; perhaps due to the nature of why we came in the first place. An important mission for Canadians to understand the need to be here. We are doing well and bring a lot to the Coalition. I hope everyone is well, and if and when an internet outlet materializes, communication might be easier. Until then, it's the old way.

Love to you both, take care, and love to the clan, your son,

Sean.

DON'T WORRY

Private Richard Green, who'd been a peacekeeper in Bosnia, wrote from Afghanistan to his beloved paternal grandmother, Joyce Clooney of Bridgewater, Nova Scotia; as an infant he had lived with her for a few months. When he was in Bosnia, she'd sent him canned clams and Kraft Dinner. Of his time in Afghanistan, he'd reassured her that there was nothing to fret about. "To us, Ricky, you're a little boy," she replied.

9 MAR 02

Dear Nan, how are you? Not too worried I hope. Things are O.K. over here so you don't have to worry. Never believe anything you hear on the news either. We've been hearing some of the stuff the media has been saying and none of it is even close to the truth. I guess nobody would be interested if it didn't seem exciting but the truth is that it is pretty boring . . . However there's still no word on when we're getting out of here. My personal opinion is June but doesn't really stand for much. Well I've got to go for now. I miss you and hope to see you soon.

Love Always

Rick

BOREDOM AND FEAR

Sergeant Marc Leger of Lancaster, Ontario, was nineteen when he signed up with the PPCLI in 1993. Seven years later, while peace-keeping in Bosnia, he became concerned about the plight of Serbian refugees in the Livno Valley, who were being ignored by international aid agencies. He held a town-hall meeting and convinced the people to appoint a mayor; after he refused the job, they declared him the honorary King Marco. Eventually, with the assistance of his commanding officer and the Canadian ambassador, he helped them restore their homes and their hope. In this letter to his wife's grandmother, Phyllis McDonald of Cornwall, Ontario, he expressed his concern about the people of Afghanistan.

11 MAR 02

Dear Nan

. . . Thing's here are kind of boring so far, at first I found [it] strange living 200m from the runway of a airport however you get adjusted to noise quickly.

I've had the opportunity to leave the camp a couple of times so far. It's incredible to see this degree of poverty. They honestly live in mud & brick homes. We are always amazed at what we see, a good example of this is when we drive on this one road we must drive around a grave that is on the road & their is no mistaking their grave sights because the body is always facing east & they dont bary them, they just place rock over the body & if there lucky they get a large rock for a head stone . . .

Now I want to thank [you] for all you have done for me over they years and especialy with all that has happen in the last couple of month. It's great knowing that I have some[one] to help me take care of the most special person in my life, Marley . . .

Love,
Marc

The six-foot-four, Hollywood-handsome Leger and the tall, red-headed Marley Mcintyre had fallen in love when they met in 1991 at a football party in Cornwall. They were married four years later. A month before Marc left for Afghanistan, Marley miscarried their first child at fourteen weeks.

11 MAR 02

Dear Marley
. . . I l♥ve you very much and I'm always thinking of you. I just want you to know that you are my everything. The other night I had a dream that I had you in my arms & we were both lieing around on our bed with the dog of course and it was a great fealing knowing that I have such a good life with you . . .

12 MAR 02

. . . The other day Travis & I spent the hole day burning shit, we even took a few photos of the event. We had the flames so hot & high that we melted the out house door as well as the communication wire for the camp. I'm expecting them to tell us that we no longer have to do this duty becaus it cost them to much when we do it . . .

[Undated, 2002]

. . . After talking with several groups & organizations I found out that their are a hand full of people who are scared to be here. This I can't understand we have the world largest & best military power [the United States] & still they don't feel safe. Why do thease people join the army I will never know . . .

Love allways

Marc

PLAYING DETECTIVE

Before **Corporal Shane Brennan,** *a twenty-eight-year-old para-trooper, left for Afghanistan, his mother in Collingwood, Ontario, Debbie Brossoit, had warned him about going to war. A few days before he wrote this letter, he'd told a Canadian Press reporter: "We've been living in a hole for the last month. Even a ride outside the camp was a big thing – like Dad's taking you to Dairy Queen or something."*

March 13 [2002]

Dear Mom,

. . . We are living in two-man trenches by day and by night the same. We sleep in two-man tents, which is almost like camping out in Black Ash [a campground near Collingwood]. We arrived here on the 12th of February and should be on the front line until the 30th of March. That's a long time to live in a trench looking out into a few trees, razor wire and loads of dirt. The dust here is crazy. We have had two dust storms and I think I have inhaled enough dust to last three lifetimes.

The sun out here is hot . . . my tan is looking good already. You'll have to excuse the writing – I am writing on a flimsy pad in my trench with my buddy watching outside. Things here as far as the war goes are mostly quiet. We are safe and will be. We have all the technology to see in the darkness. I even use a thermal system that detects heat sources day and night. I see lots of wild bugs and other weird animals.

So far, my unit and I are doing what is called detective operations, which means we are all on the outside of the camp/airfield as the first line of defence. This week, I will be leaving camp for six days to observe a certain area for terrorist activity, working alongside the local Afghani army. It should be a good time . . .

Love always,
Shane

After writing this letter, Brennan was sent to an observation post about a half-hour from the Kandahar airfield: a mud-walled compound in the desert manned by friendly, elderly Afghani soldiers bearing AK-40 assault rifles. He said later, "It was just remarkable to go in and sit on their mats and have a shoeless dinner with them, playing Pakistani cassette tapes in a hut lighted with Canadian Coleman lanterns."

HARPOONING

*Corporal Shane Brennan and **Major Sean Hackett** were among five hundred Canadian and one hundred American troops involved in Operation Harpoon, a ground assault targeting caves and other positions of Taliban and al-Qaeda fighters who were believed to be holding out on Whale Ridge in eastern Afghanistan. Hackett wrote to his wife from an air base near Kabul.*

20 Mar 02
[Bagram]

My Dearest Babe,

. . . We're still waiting for airlift from Bagram to Qandahar after finishing up our involvement in the latest op – Op HARPOON, part of the tail end of Op ANACONDA that started 2 March.

I remember it being somewhat of a hard concept to grasp . . . with us flying into what we understood to be a combat zone, while you were returning from your Italy trip. A blackout was put in effect prior to the operation for reasons of OPSEC [operations security], but I couldn't help but think what it would have been like for you if anything had happened.

Our Chinook helicopter took off at about 0530 on 13 March (1030 PM 12 March your time) for the 1 hr 15 min flight to the Shah-I-Kot Valley and 5 arduous days. Despite the uncertainty (and lack of Taliban/Al Qaida) it proved to be an excellent shakeout for the Company – moving through some demanding mountain terrain. Many lessons learned. All back safe and sound on the 17th. We were treated to some pretty amazing Chinook Helicopter flying to get us in and out – and at one point from the base of the mountain back to the top . . .

21 Mar 02
(Qandahar)

. . . well certainly a loose interpretation of home, but home for now. Probably the most content and comfortable I've been to date. We finally arrived in Qandahar approx 1230(Z). By 1430 I was happily set up in my own 4-man tent with all my kit from the trip (no thanks to the knobs who never covered our kit pallets during the rain!).

Santa Claus would have had stiff competition from the piles of packages awaiting all the soldiers in the company. Attention soon shifted from the set up work to breaking in to the goodies!

. . . You're no doubt thirsting for news but I can't tell you much you don't already know. We'd been on the defense in Qandahar from 13 Feb until 9 Mar. then found ourselves off to Bagram (50 km North of Kabul) to launch offensive operations in Paktia Province near the Pakistan border (area between Gardez and Kwost) All that is now done; we've left dirty, smelly Bagram and are back, to do what other than live-fire training – who knows? We no longer need to burn our shit as they use Port-a-Potties that get cleaned out. A seat, rather than a hole in a piece of plywood! Luxury! . . .

29 Mar 02

. . . I'll try and take a picture soon as that disposable camera is almost done. I got a little snap-happy today as I went on a 90 min BlackHawk helicopter recce [reconnaissance] well south into the desert from Kandahar. It was to look at a potential live fire trg [training] site – basically a mountain shooting up in the middle of nowhere! The changes in desert topography were amazing and left me feeling in a very alien world. The landscape changed from super flat, white, hard pack desert to wadis supporting local life, Bedouin nomad dwellings, camels, goats – before a sudden change to endless, desolate orange sand dunes. Fascinating, and a completely new and different perspective. Needless to say, not many shots left. Awesome flight with the door open and so close to space. Hopefully, the pictures won't be too bleached out through overexposure. We are moving into a cycle of ongoing readiness training and waiting for a mission. I can say that I've yet to face fire or potentially even come close – no doubt a good thing – but, my initial impressions of going into a combat zone were captured in a hand-draulic letter you should get eventually. So no, there doesn't appear to be too much danger at the moment . . .

Your loving husband,
Sean

BE CAREFUL

Private Rick Green wrote regularly to his fiancée in Edmonton, Miranda Boutilier; they'd been friends since their childhood in Nova Scotia.

3 APR 02

Hey Sweetie!
It's April! Another month has passed. It's very hot over here. It's "slaps you in the face hot" and it's not even summer yet. That's no good at all. I burned my thumb last week. I forgot to tell you. I burned it on

the barrell of my C-9 machine gun. The blister was bigger than my thumb nail. It's a second degree burn. It'll take a couple of weeks to heal. It looks "yucky." I used a Miranda word. I miss you Princess. How are things going in Edmonton? No problems I hope . . .

I worry about you all the time. Is there anything you need me to try and do for you? I don't know what I can do but I'll try. I love you princess. I miss you so much. Be careful, have fun and don't forget about me.

CALM BEFORE THE STORM

*As some of his men went on leave before preparing for a major live-fire training exercise in the desert, **Major Sean Hackett** e-mailed his wife about the visits of Canada's defence minister, Art Eggleton.*

5 Apr 02

. . . Hopefully you saw some coverage of the Minister's visit. The weather really crapped out. Extremely funny, and we all had a good laugh. At least until an hour or two after the parade – then things weren't so funny, with severe winds over 50–60 knots. Some tents collapsed in the wind and rain, with shit blowing all over the place. An outrageous storm. Only place I've ever been where blowing sand and rain translates into 'mud' rain! That was yesterday. Today was a long hot one on a live fire range where we used every weapon system in the inventory – it was pretty awesome. Tomorrow, more of the same. 48 hrs of fun and then onto other things. First troops leave for the one and only 96 hr pass soon.

6 Apr 02

. . . I'm just waiting for it to get really unpleasant, perhaps with some creepy-crawlies. You should see the size of the beetles out here. Your classic black, hardback, industrious dung beetle with the big front mandibles (help me out here on the entomology). One of the tps [troops] was quite amused by the way they swarmed his you-know-what, breaking it down and rolling it all away. Maybe it's not as filthy around here as we think!

7 Apr 02

... At 1030 I went off to play a soccer game against the local Afghans. The BG [battalion group] scraped together 12–14 guys, but I think the ringers will start coming out of the woodwork. Last wk they beat us 3–0 (I wasn't there last time), but today it was only 2–0. I think they're starting to smell some competition. You could tell because they got a lucky lob goal using the setting sun, and the score stayed 1–0 well into the 2nd half ... I'm not so young anymore, and certainly not game fit. The field was hard pack desert/adobe dirt. Believe me, not a lot of slide tackling happening. Pretty hard to stop, but at least I wore my Hi-Techs for traction ...

LOVE ALWAYS

Private Rick Green didn't tell Miranda in this letter that he'd bought an engagement ring with three diamonds while on leave in Dubai, United Arab Emirates.

17 Apr 02

Hi Sweetie, how are you? I'm OK. I got your parcel today. It's been here for about 2 weeks. Somehow 2 pallets of mail were lost. It was just found last night. I'm listening to your song right now. Thank-you for everything. We have to go to a place called Khost for 3 weeks. We leave tomorrow or the next day. We should have phones so I should be able to call you. I'll try to call you before we leave ... I don't have anything else to say for now honey. I really miss you. I love you so much Miranda.

Love Always
Rick

Within hours of writing this letter, Green joined seventy-nine others in Alpha Company for their routine live-fire training exercise at Tarnak Farms at the foot of a craggy mountain range, where Osama bin Laden's al-Qaeda followers had once trained. A few hours later, as the PPCLI were firing their machine guns and rocket launchers into the desert night, two majors in the U.S. Air National Guard, flying F-16 jet fighters overhead, apparently believed they were under attack. One of them dropped a five-hundred-pound, laser-guided bomb on the firing range below, killing Rick Green, Marc Leger, twenty-six-year-old Private Nathan Smith, and twenty-five-year-old Corporal Ainsworth Dyer. Shane Brennan and Curtis Hollister were wounded by shrapnel, as were Private Norman Link, Sergeant Lorne Ford, Master Corporal Stanley Clark, and Corporals Brian Decaire, Réné Paquette, and Brett Perry.

CONTINUE YOU MUST

Lieutenant General Mike Jeffery, a soldier since 1964, commanded the Canadian contingent on a United Nations force that successfully oversaw the first free election in an independent Namibia in 1989. After serving in several senior staff positions at National Defence Headquarters in Ottawa, he was appointed in 2000 as chief of the land staff (CLS), responsible for the operational readiness of the army, including matters of morale. He wrote the Canadian Armed Forces' formal response to the Kandahar tragedy.

LETTER FROM CLS TO 3 PPCLI (KANDAHAR)

19 April 2002

1. Let me begin by expressing my deepest condolences to the families, friends and comrades of the soldiers killed in Afghanistan. Our thoughts and our prayers are with you today. Every member of the Canadian Army shares in your sadness. You have lost husbands, sons, and friends and we have lost four of our own. They were a

part of your family and they were a part of our family. We will miss them all.

2. As senseless as this tragic incident may seem, these men did not give their lives for naught. They died fighting for what they believed in. They died serving their country. They gave their lives in the midst of a struggle to restore peace and security to our world. For this we owe these fine soldiers, and their families, a great debt of gratitude.

3. Our thoughts are also with the families of the eight soldiers who were injured in Afghanistan. We are hoping and praying for the best. I have been assured that they are being given the highest standards of medical care. We hope to see all of them recover in the near future.

4. This has been a tremendous blow to the Canadian men and women serving in Kandahar, and to all members of the Princess Patricia's Canadian Light Infantry. To those in theater: take some time to grieve for your comrades. Look to each other for strength in this difficult time. Give voice to what you are feeling, and reach out to those around you. Together you have built a close-knit team. Together you have endured harsh conditions and dangerous circumstances. By relying on each other you will find the strength to persevere.

5. It won't be easy to continue with your mission, but continue you must. You are all professionals, and the difficult job that you have been given is not yet complete. I have no doubt that you will continue performing at an outstanding level and see this task through to the end.

6. There is a great sense of shock and grief being expressed here in Canada. Below the surface of this sorrow is something else – a profound sense of pride. Our nation is proud of you and proud of what you are doing. Canadians have known all along that you have a tough job to do and today they have a real sense of the sacrifices being made.

7. Our thoughts are with you all. Godspeed.

M.K. Jeffery
Lieutenant-General
Chief of the Land Staff

A friend in Alpha Company found the ring Rick Green had bought his fiancée and brought it home with Green's body. "I'll never take it off," Miranda Boutilier said. Marley Leger read a final letter to her husband, Marc, at his funeral service, in which she wrote: "I can't wait until we meet again. And until then, I'll hold you close to my heart and I promise to live my life as fully and completely as you did and I promise to keep your memory alive." She oversees the Marc Leger Memorial Fund, which in a year had raised more than $30,000 from Canadians to rebuild a community hall in the Livno Valley of Bosnia, where "King Marco" remained a living presence. Shane Brennan and Curtis Hollister recovered from their physical wounds, although Hollister has suffered from post-traumatic stress syndrome. One of the American pilots received a reprimand and retired from the U.S. Air Force, while the other demanded a court-martial in an effort to clear his name.

PEGASUS RISING

*The day after the friendly fire disaster, **Major Sean Hackett** sent his wife this e-mail. "At that point," he said later, "we were still dealing with the loss, and as the company commander my outward disposition would no doubt be one of repressed emotion (projecting strength) and stoicism."*

19 Apr 02

. . . We are now focused on sending our four home and that will occur later this evening. I'm fine and very occupied ensuring those things I can influence are done correctly, at the same time providing guidance for getting on with the mission. ·

. . . I hope you're doing well and it warmed my heart to hear of those concerned friends who had called you to see how things were. It's times like these when I think one sees the true face of many . . . particularly at a workplace like the one you currently endure. I'm glad to hear some are concerned about what their soldiers are going through so far from home on their behalf. But if you told them there was a war on, some would give you an incomprehensible and perplexed stare, as if to say, "What war?"

. . . Earlier this evening we conducted a moving ceremony and loaded the remains of the four who died onto a C17 transport plane – for Germany and then home. It was hard to stare into such a large plane while paying respects. Then again there are many images seared into my memory from that night, and to a lesser extent, in the hours following. We have heard there will be a memorial service in Edmonton on the 28th (and that a 20 Apr Family Day will still go ahead). Now, our attention here must focus on the progress of those on the mend.

The major is the youngest son of David Hackett, who served with the British Royal Navy in the Second World War and in its submarine service in the Korean War. His father is an amateur poet who knows the significance of the winged horse of Greek mythology, Pegasus, ridden by the first airborne warrior, Bellerophon, which the 1st Canadian Battalion adopted as an insignia. Sean Hackett addressed this e-mail to his brother Jon and sent copies to other family members, including his wife.

21 Apr 02

. . . My attention span isn't too sound either. I'm afraid I'll not be able to do your newsy report justice by writing at length. It's late and I'll already be hitting the 4 hr sleep mark before getting up for PT Mon AM. Am also in the process of calling Mum/Dad. I don't think I've called them since I got here (1 Feb). Poor form. But with all the email banter transitting back and forth, mail is becoming superfluous – less packages, or pictures. Though digital is good – I think that will be the way to go. No doubt you catch the news, I'll try to send you some attached articles. One was filed today as some of us sat down to recount some details of that night. There's also a good editorial from the Natl Post that puts "friendly fire" in perspective – seeking to counter the negative and completely counter-productive

America bashing which some Canadians just can't seem to get over. Very disheartening, when armchair anger is voiced with no concept of what things are like over here on the ground. I can assure you, American air coverage is a pretty important security blanket for us, regardless of the horrible error in judgement of one individual . . . then again, we could all make errors in judgement that cost lives – the nature of the profession. I could not have asked for a better company of men to have endured our trial by fire the other night. The response was incredible.

. . . but, in short, I've seen some things . . .

. . . Dad has written Haiku no. 88, inspired by the incident and the A C[ompany] reaction. I'm sure he can send it to you but it goes like this:

> Pegasus rising
> from the death and destruction
> reaching for the sun.

ACKNOWLEDGMENTS

We are deeply indebted to numerous people across Canada who helped us compile a century's worth of correspondence for *The Book of War Letters*.

Our gratitude must first go to the original letter writers – or their immediate or extended families – who allowed us to expose these often emotional and revealing private communications to the public eye. Their names appear in the list of permissions that follows.

We couldn't have created this book without the contributions of archivists across the country. Prominent among them is Tim Dubé, the military archivist with the National Archives of Canada, whose vast knowledge of his specialty led us to so many significant letters. His colleagues at the Archives played their usual helpful roles in making our research task in Ottawa pleasant and productive. So too did the Canadian War Museum's Jane Naisbitt, head of the Library and Archives, and collections manager Carol Reid, who along with their staff – including Maggie Armour-Doucette and Denis Fletcher – were so accommodating during a hectic period at the museum. Isabel Campbell at the Department of National Defence was welcoming and supportive. In Calgary we received great help, again, from Doug Cass and his wonderfully obliging staff at the Glenbow Museum, and from

Jan Roseneder at the Museum of the Regiments and Barry Agnew and Mike Henry (Seaforth Highlanders), Al Judson (King's Own Calgary Regiment), Corporal Regan MacLeod (PPCLI), and Corporal Lee J. Ramsden (Lord Strathcona's Horse). Other archivists who contributed their expertise to this book include Carole Burke and her colleagues at the Montreal Holocaust Memorial Centre; Twila Buttimer of the Provincial Archives of New Brunswick; Norm Holden of the Naval Museum of Alberta; Mark Vajcner and Elizabeth Seitz at the University of Regina; Bernadine Dodge at the Trent University Archives; and Paul Banfield, Jeremy Heil, and Heather Home of the Queen's University Archives. We'd like specially to mention Catherine Seton, who, though not an archivist, not only alerted us to the Queen's University fonds of family friends Eric and Elizabeth Harrison but also made an out-of-town trip to search them for us.

Members of various veterans' organizations who publicized our quest for letters include: Don Ethell, national president of the Canadian Association of Veterans in United Nations Peacekeeping; Gord Croucher, Edward Hansen, Jim Milton, Roly Soper, and Don Urquhart (among others) of the Korea Veterans Association of Canada; Duncan Mathieson of the Naval Officers' Association of Canada; and Don Parr-Pearson and many others of the Seaforth Highlanders. Among those individuals who offered us their military expertise and contacts are Stephen Brodsky and Sean Hackett. Dr. Barry Armstrong, Brian and Carol Isfeld, and Bill Whalen worked hard to provide us with originals of personal and family correspondence.

Once more, people in the media were responsive to our appeal to the public for letters from their private archives. Among those assisting us were Judy Brandow (*goodtimes* magazine), Chris Dafoe (*Winnipeg Free Press*), Annalee Greenberg (*The Beaver*), Christine Langlois and Catherine Gray (*Canadian Living*), and Rebecca Wigod (*Vancouver Sun*). Ron Corbett at the *Ottawa Citizen* was helpful with a key contact.

We would be remiss not to acknowledge the huge debt we owe to Canada's military and popular historians who ploughed the field so deeply before us and on whose work we relied to place the letters in context. An incomplete list includes: Ted Barris, David Bercuson, Pierre Berton, John R. Bishop, Peter Chance, Norm Christie, Terry Copp, Daniel G. Dancocks, Serge Durflinger, John A. English, Fred Gaffen, John Gardam, Jack Granatstein, Brereton Greenhous, Michel Lavigne, Bill McAndrew, Sean M. Maloney, John Melady, Desmond Morton, Les Peate, C.P. Stacey. Of course, we remain responsible for any errors or misinterpretations of fact.

Finally, our special thanks go to friends and colleagues who assisted us in our work. Penny Williams and Babette and Paul Deggan translated several of the letters from French with flair, and fellow islanders Barbara Bingham and Nadyne Hindle typed many into computer files, valiantly deciphering often cryptic handwriting. Another Bowen Islander, Rebecca Salmon, with the kind assistance of Dan Heringa, took great pains to photograph salvaged war letters. Frank Ianni was again an indulgent host during our stay in Ottawa. Fred Jazvac and Terry Morgan drank a beer and sought letters at the Legion in Southhampton on our behalf.

At the following archives, museums, and libraries we obtained letters in the fonds or collections indicated or found letters from the people named:

The Canadian Letters and Images Project, Malaspina College: Robert S. Robinson collection; George Adkins collection; Dutton Advance Collection;

Canadian War Museum (Lawrence Buchan, W. Gerald Cosbie, Terry Fairbairn, Norman Gibson, Joseph Greenblatt, Jack P. Griss, Charles Cecil Hendershot, Warren Francis Hendershot, John Henry Kaye, John McManus, John Osborn, William Otter, Claude Snider, Edwin Worden, Elaine Wright);

Department of Heritage and History, Department of National Defence (W.A. Bishop, Charles Bradley, Harry Crerar, R.H. Dunn, Bernard Montgomery, Leonard Murray, Guy Simonds, Richard M. Steele, George Tidy);

Glenbow Museum: Noel Adair Farrow fonds, Duncan and Archie Campbell fonds, Ian Fowler fonds, Lorne and Betty Goat fonds,

Mike Mountain Horse (newspaper files), Lord Strathcona's Horse (Royal Canadian) fonds (Sam Steele), Angelina and Antonio Rebaudengo fonds;

Museum of the Regiments (Agar Adamson, Stuart Cobbett, Gordon Flowerdew, Grant Philip, Herbert Samson, Alexander Thomas Thomson, Douglas Cameron Thomson);

National Archives of Canada: Agar Adamson fonds, Letter from Captain William Bate, Mary I. Buch fonds, Gregory Clark fonds, Arthur William Currie fonds, William Doskoch fonds, William M.R. Griffin and Peter R. Griffin fonds, Sophie Hoerner fonds, Lambart family fonds, Frederick J. Lee fonds, John McCrae fonds, William Lidstone McKnight fonds, J. Frederick Ramsay fonds, Percy Robert Rooke fonds, Ernest William Sansom fonds, Wilfred I. Smith fonds, Sprague family fonds, Richard Ernest William Turner fonds, Georges P. Vanier fonds, Frederick Horsman Varley fonds, M. Amy White fonds, Claude Vivian Williams fonds, Department of National Defence fonds (Directorate of Internment Operations);

New Brunswick Provincial Archives: Albert M. Belding fonds;

Queen's University Archives: Bert and Don MacKenzie fonds;

Trent University Archives: Fowlds Family and Business Records;

University of Regina Archives (Gladys Arnold).

We are grateful to the hundreds of people who submitted letters, and we regret not being able to list all who did so. The following people sent us letters or gave us permission to use letters written by those whose names are in boldface type: John R. Allan (**William Ross**); Frances E. Ballantyne (**Chattan Stephens**); Donna Bath (**Edward Bath**); Robert Blondin (**Paul Baillargeon, Henri** of Royal 22e Régiment); Helen Boody (**Claude Williams**); Miranda Boutilier (**Richard Green**); David Bree (**Stanley Rippingale**); Glenn Roy Browne (**Charles W. Gordon**); Marie Blanche Bruner (**Roy Fischbach**); Barbara Christie (**John Ross, Rowland E. Brinckman**); Joyce Clooney (**Richard Green**); Mary Jane Cowan (**Donald McCullough**); Mary

Gillis (**Edis A. Flewwelling**, with his permission); John Gardam (**Harry Pope**); Brian Goodyer (**Robert Goodyer**); Gregory Clark (**Gregory Clark Sr.**); Doug Hester (**Frau Johanna**); Meggan Hutton (**Naomi Turner**); Brian and Carol Isfeld (**Mark Isfeld**); Jean Busse (**David Brenton**); Maureen Johnson (**Maurice Park**); Pat Johnston (**Mary Geraghty**); Hope T. Kerr (**Homer Thompson**); Nelson Lachance (**Stephen Dalton**); Michel Lavigne (**Jean-Paul Sabourin**); Marley Leger (**Marc Leger**); Les Grant (**Danny** and **Ann Jensen**); Mary Lindgren (**George Adkins**); Veronica Lord (**Leo Keating**); Fred Macdonald (**Andrew Foulds**, with his permission); Don MacFie (**Ken Canning**); Helen Mackay (**Barlow Whiteside**); Jean Mackenzie and Wayne Ralph (**W.G. Barker**); Donald MacKenzie (**Frederick Donald MacKenzie**); John MacLeod (**William Livingstone**); Judith Mader (**George de Long**); Denny May (**Wop May**); Katherine McIntyre (**J.C. McRuer**); Diane E. Meehan (**John Meehan**); Gerry Moen (**Leonard Chase**); Georgina Moxam and family (**George D'All**); Brian Munro (**J. Calder Munro**); Nancy Ludkin (**Ernest Ludkin**); Shirley Nygren (**Orville Fleming**); Shirley Rowat O'Connor (**William Rowat**); Bar Parker and Adela Smith (**Robert Duncan**); Jack Porter (**William A. MacDonald**); Keith Rodgers (**Chester Rodgers**); Dr. C.E. Robinson (**Charles Baker**, with his permission); Ronald Sargent (**Edward Sargent**); Lorine McGinnis Schulze (**Patricia Tuckett**); H.L. Scott (**Harry Scott**); Catherine Seton (**Eric Harrison**); Margaret Simpson (**Grant Philip**); Georgette Smith (**George Lawton**); Edwin Sprague (**Charles Sprague**); Jim Steel (**Gordon Patrick**); Kathleen Stokes (**Robert Rooke**); Steven and Don Stothers (**J. Cannon Stothers**); R.H. Thomson (**Arthur Stratford, Jack Stratford**); Norma Varley (**Frederick Varley**); Phil Vogler and the *Berwick Register* (**W.H. Snyder, W.T.M. MacKinnon, David Borden**); Bill Whalen (**Jim Whalen**); Stephen Workman (**Mabel Ross**); Bill Worton (**Alan Girling**).

The following gave us permission to use their own letters: **Barry Armstrong, Shane Brennan, Andrew Brodsky, Stephen Brodsky, Ed Brunanski, Mary Buch, Kenneth Cameron, Cliff Chadderton, Peter Chance, Robert Collins, Lois MacDonald Cooper, Gordon Croucher,**

Kurt Grant, Bob Hackett, Sean Hackett, James Henderson, John Liss, Lewis MacKenzie, Gillean MacKinnon, Richard Medland, Tom Quinn, Duncan Robertson, Kathleen Robson Roe, Jack Rose, Alexander Ross, Alex Sim, and Robert Tweedie.

PHOTO CREDITS:

Page 1, Glenn R. Browne; page 11, John Henry Kaye fonds, AN19830041-259, © Canadian War Museum; page 67, Canadian soldier writing a letter, France, July 1916, CWM19920044-504, © Canadian War Museum; page 203, National Archives (PA 132881); page 357, Gordon Croucher; page 389, Brian and Carol Isfeld; page 423, Department of National Defence; back jacket and editors' photos, Rebecca Salmon.

BIBLIOGRAPHY

Adamson, Agar, *Letters of Agar Adamson, 1914–1919* (Nepean, ON: CEF Books, 1997).

Adamson, Anthony, *Wasps in the Attic* (Toronto: Self-published, 1987).

Barris, Ted, *Deadlock in Korea: Canadians at War, 1950–1953* (Toronto: Macmillan Canada, 1999).

Bercuson, David J., *Maple Leaf Against the Axis: Canada's Second World War* (Don Mills, ON: Stoddart, 1994).

———, *Blood on the Hills: The Canadian Army in the Korean War* (Toronto: University of Toronto Press, 1999).

Berton, Pierre, *Marching As to War: Canada's Turbulent Years 1899–1953* (Toronto: Anchor Canada/Random House, 2001).

———, *Vimy* (Toronto: McClelland & Stewart, 1986).

Bishop, John R., with G.W. Stephen Brodsky, *The King's Bishop* (Cobble Hill, BC: Mossy Knoll Enterprises, 2001).

Blondin, Robert, and Gilles LaMontagne, eds., *Chers nous autres: un siècle de correspondance québécoise* (Montréal: VLB Éditeur, 1978).

Broadfoot, Barry, *Six War Years* (Toronto: Doubleday Canada, 1974).

Brown, Stanley McKeown, *With the Royal Canadians* (Toronto: Publishers' Syndicate, 1900).

Buch, Mary Hawkins, with Carolyn Gossage, *Props on Her Sleeve: The Wartime Letters of a Canadian Airwoman* (Toronto: Dundurn Press, 1997).

Chance, Peter Godwin, *Before It's Too Late: A Sailor's Life* (Sidney, BC: Self-published, 2001).

Christie, N.M., *For King and Empire: Canadians in the Second Battle of Ypres, April 22 to 26, 1915* (Winnipeg: Bunker to Bunker Books, 1996).

———, *For King and Empire: The Canadians at Mount Sorrel* (Ottawa: CEF Books, 2000).

———, *For King and Empire: The Canadians at Vimy, April 1917* (Ottawa: CEF Books, 2002 rev.).

———, *For King and Empire: The Canadians at Passchendaele, October to November 1917* (Winnipeg: Bunker to Bunker Books, 1996).

———, *For King and Empire: The Canadians at Amiens, August 8th to 16th, 1918* (Ottawa: CEF Books, 1999).

———, *For King and Empire: The Canadians at Arras and the Drocourt–Queant Line, August–September 1918* (Nepean, ON: CEF Books, 1997).

———, *For King and Empire: The Canadians at Cambrai and the Canal du Nord, September-October 1918* (Nepean, ON: CEF Books, 1997).

———, *Futility and Sacrifice: The Canadians on the Somme* (Nepean, ON: CEF Books, 1998).

Clarke, Peter, *Hope and Glory: Britain 1900–1990* (London: Penguin Press, 1996).

Collins, Robert, *The Long and the Short and the Tall: An Ordinary Airman's War* (Saskatoon: Western Producer Prairie Books, 1986).

Cooper, Lois MacDonald, *Wartime Letters Home* (North Bay, ON: Lois Macdonald Cooper, nd).

Copp, J.T., *Battle Exhaustion: Soldiers and Psychiatrists in the Canadian Army, 1939–1945* (Montréal: McGill-Queen's University Press, 1990).

Creighton, Donald, *Canada's First Century* (Toronto: Macmillan Canada, 1970).

Dancocks, Daniel G., *Legacy of Valour: The Canadians at Passchendaele* (Edmonton: Hurtig, 1986).

Desbarats, Peter, *Somalia Cover-Up: A Commissioner's Journal* (Toronto: McClelland & Stewart, 1997).

Egener, Norah and Fred, *A Time Apart: Letters of Love and War* (Owen Sound, ON: Ginger Press, 1995).

Foster, Charles Lyons, *Letters from the Front: Being a Record of the Part Played by Officers of the Bank in the Great War 1914–1919* (Toronto: Canadian Bank of Commerce, 1920).

Fussell, Paul, *The Great War and Modern Memory* (New York: Oxford University Press, 1975).

————, *Wartime: Understanding and Behavior in the Second World War* (New York and Oxford: Oxford University Press, 1989).

Gaffen, Fred, *Forgotten Soldiers* (Penticton, BC: Theytus Books, 1985).

Gardam, John, *Korea Volunteer: An Oral History from Those Who Were There* (Burnstown, ON: General Store Publishing House, 1994).

Granatstein, J.L., *Canada's Army: Waging War and Keeping the Peace* (Toronto: University of Toronto Press, 2002).

————, and Desmond Morton, *Bloody Victory: Canadians and the D-Day Campaign 1944* (Toronto: Lester & Orpen Dennys, 1984).

Grant, Kurt, *All Tigers, No Donkeys: The Diary of a Citizen Soldier* (St. Catharines, ON: Vanwell, 2003).

Greenhous, Brereton, *The Making of Billy Bishop: The First World War Exploits of Billy Bishop, VC* (Toronto: Dundurn Press, 2002).

Groom, Winston, *A Storm in Flanders, The Ypres Salient, 1914–1918: Tragedy and Triumph on the Western Front* (New York: Atlantic Monthly Press, 2002).

Kitagawa, Muriel, *This Is My Own: Letters to Wes and Other Writings* (Vancouver: Talonbooks, 1985).

Kimber, Stephen, *Sailors, Slackers and Blind Pigs* (Toronto: Doubleday Canada, 2002).

Lavine, Michel, with James F. Edwards, *Kittyhawks Over the Sands: The Canadians and the RCAF Americans* (Victoriaville, QC: Lavigne Aviation Publications, 2002).

Levine, Alan J., *The Strategic Bombing of Germany, 1940–1945* (Westport, CT: Praeger, 1992).

Livesey, Anthony, ed., *Are We at War? Letters to The Times 1939–1945* (London: Times Books, 1989).

MacKenzie, Major General Lewis, *Peacekeeper: The Road to Sarajevo* (Vancouver & Toronto: Douglas & McIntyre, 1993).

Maloney, Sean M., *Canada and UN Peacekeeping: Cold War by Other Means, 1945–1970* (St. Catharines, ON: Vanwell, 2002).

Martin, Charles Cromwell, with Roy Whitsed, *Battle Diary: From D-Day and Normandy to the Zuider Zee and VE* (Toronto: Dundurn Press, 1994).

Melady, John, *Korea: The Forgotten War* (Toronto: Macmillan Canada, 1983).

————, *Escape from Canada: The Untold Story of German POWs in Canada 1939–1945* (Macmillan Canada, 1981).

Metson, Graham, *An East Coast Port . . . : Halifax at War 1939–1945* (Toronto: McGraw-Hill Ryerson, 1981).

Morrison, E.W.B., *With the Guns in South Africa* (Hamilton: Spectator Printing, 1901).

Neilands, Robin, *The Bomber War: The Allied Air Offensive Against Nazi Germany* (Woodstock & New York: The Overlook Press, 2001).

Nicholson, Col. G.W.L., *Canadian Expeditionary Force 1914–1919* (Ottawa: Queen's Printer, 1964).

Page, Robert, *The Boer War and Canadian Imperialism* (Ottawa: Canadian Historical Association, Historical Booklet No. 44, 1987).

Raddall, Thomas H., *Halifax: Warden of the North* (Garden City, NY: Doubleday, 1965).

Roe, Kathleen Robson, *War Letters from the C.W.A.C.* (Toronto: Kakabeka, 1975).

Ross, Alexander M., *Slow March to a Regiment* (St. Catharines, ON: Vanwell, 1992).

Sage, W.D.M., *Battlefield Nurse: Letters and Memories of a Canadian Army Overseas Nursing Sister in World War II* (Vancouver: Sage Family, 1994).

Shephard, Ben, *A War of Nerves: Soldiers and Psychiatrists 1914–1994* (London: Pimlico/Random House, 2002).

Stacey, C.P., and General Staff, Canada Department of National Defence, *Official History of the Canadian Army in the Second World War* (Ottawa: Queen's Printer, 1955–1960).

Taylor, Scott, and Brian Nolan, *Tested Mettle: Canada's Peacekeepers at War* (Ottawa: Esprit de Corps Books, 1998).

Wood, Lieutenant Colonel Herbert Fairlie, *Strange Battleground: Official History of the Canadian Army in Korea* (Ottawa: Queen's Printer, 1966).

Woodcock, George, *A Social History of Canada* (Toronto: Viking, 1988).

INDEX OF LETTER WRITERS